THE RISE OF THE MODERN ART MARKET IN LONDON, 1850–1939

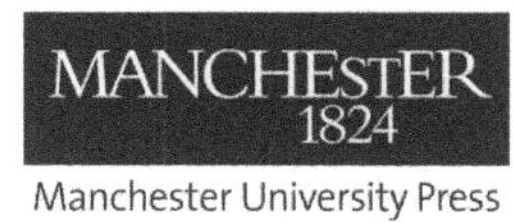

MANCHESTER
1824

Manchester University Press

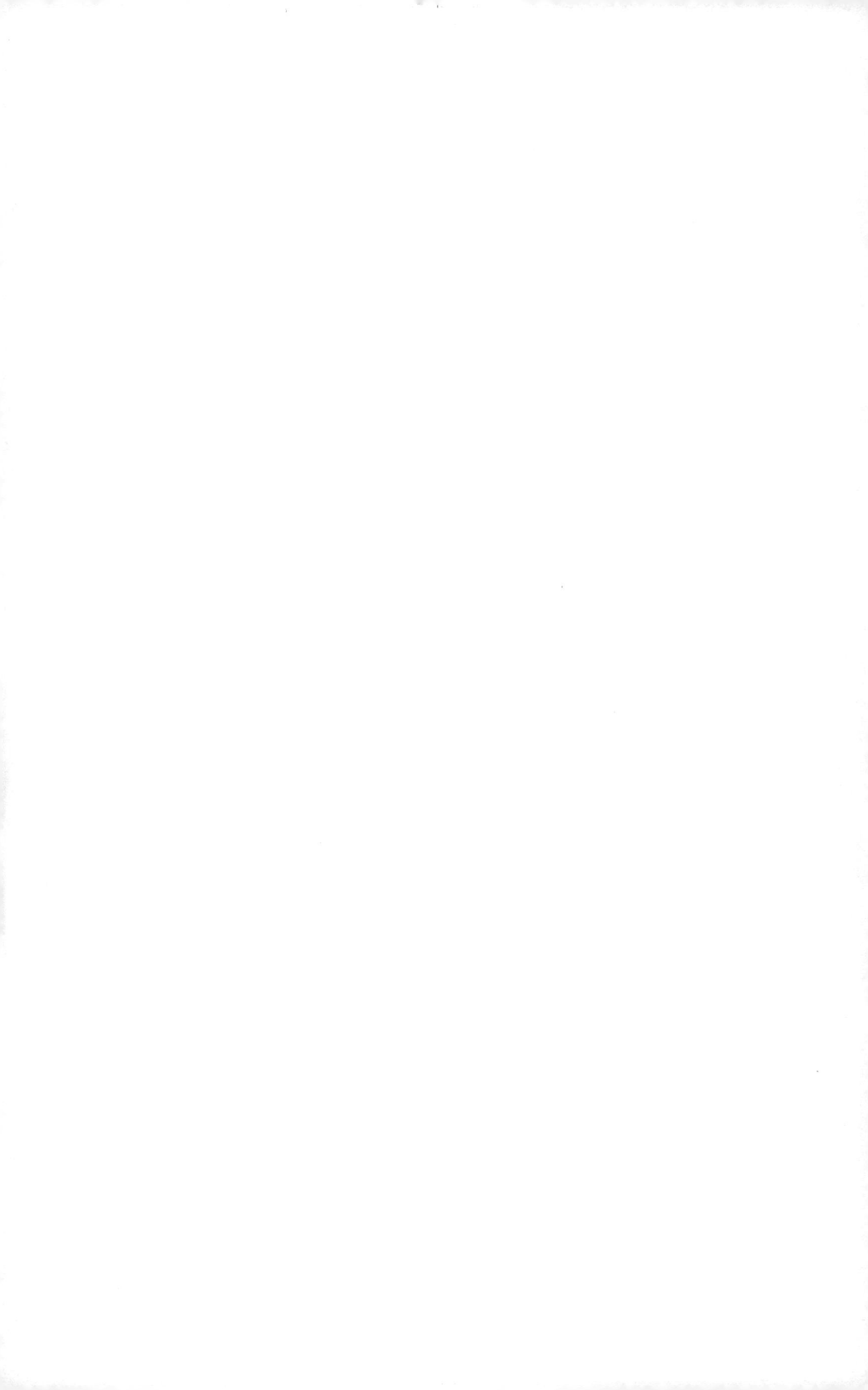

The rise of the modern art market in London, 1850–1939

Edited by Pamela Fletcher and Anne Helmreich

Manchester University Press

Manchester and New York

distributed in the United States exclusively by Palgrave Macmillan

Copyright © Manchester University Press 2011

While copyright in the volume as a whole is vested in Manchester University Press, copyright in individual chapters belongs to their respective authors, and no chapter may be reproduced wholly or in part without the express permission in writing of both author and publisher.

Published by Manchester University Press
Oxford Road, Manchester M13 9NR, UK
and Room 400, 175 Fifth Avenue, New York, NY 10010, USA
www.manchesteruniversitypress.co.uk

Distributed in the United States exclusively by
Palgrave Macmillan, 175 Fifth Avenue,
New York, NY 10010, USA

Distributed in Canada exclusively by
UBC Press, University of British Columbia, 2029 West Mall,
Vancouver, BC, Canada V6T 1Z2

British Library Cataloguing-in-Publication Data is available

Library of Congress Cataloging-in-Publication Data is available

ISBN 978 0 7190 8461 4 paperback

First published by Manchester University Press in hardback 2011

This paperback edition first published 2013

The publisher has no responsibility for the persistence or accuracy of URLs for any external or third-party internet websites referred to in this book, and does not guarantee that any content on such websites is, or will remain, accurate or appropriate.

Printed by Lightning Source

Contents

Figures

Contributors

Julie Codell (Ph.D., Indiana University) is Professor of Art History at Arizona State University and Affiliate Faculty in English, Asian Studies, Film and Media Studies, and Gender and Women's Studies. Her articles on Victorian culture and India under the Raj have appeared in many scholarly journals in art history, English, history and film. She wrote *The Victorian Artist* (2003) and edited *The Art of Transculturation* (2012), *Photography and the Delhi Coronation Durbars* (2011), *The Political Economy of Art* (2008), *Genre, Gender, Race, and World Cinema* (2007), *Imperial Co-Histories* (2003), and special issues of *Victorian Periodicals Review* on the nineteenth-century press in India (2004) and Victorian art and the press (1991). She co-edited (with L. Brake) *Encounters in the Victorian Press* (2004) and (with D.S. Macleod) *Orientalism Transposed* (1998), now translated into Japanese (2011).

Patricia de Montfort (Ph.D., St. Andrews) is Lecturer in History of Art at the University of Glasgow, Scotland. Her research focuses on the published writings and theories of James McNeill Whistler (1834–1903); Whistler's press and literary connections, especially with Ruskin and Wilde; the art press, including relationships between artists, dealers, critics and editors; exhibition culture and the practices and processes of the London art market 1850–1914; and nineteenth-century women artists, especially the work of Louise Jopling (1843–1933). Her current projects include a bio-cultural study of Louise Jopling and a documentary project on exhibition culture in Britain (www.exhibitionculture.arts.gla.ac.uk/).

Pamela Fletcher (Ph.D., Columbia University) is Associate Professor of Art History at Bowdoin College, Brunswick, Maine. Author of *Narrating Modernity: The British Problem Picture, 1895–1914* (2003), she has also published several essays on the nineteenth-century London art market. She is currently at work on a history of the Victorian painting of modern life, portions of which have appeared in the *Oxford Art Journal* and *Victorian Studies*.

Pamela Gerrish Nunn (Ph.D., University College London) is an independent scholar and curator, specializing in the histories of women artists. She has published widely in this field since 1978. Her most recent book, *From Victorian to Modern: Tradition and Innovation in the work of Vanessa Bell, Gwen John, and Laura Knight*, accompanied an exhibition of the same name at the Djanogly Art Gallery (Nottingham, UK) in 2006. She is currently preparing an exhibition of the work of Eleanor Fortescue Brickdale for summer 2012.

Anne Helmreich (Ph.D., Northwestern University) is Associate Professor of Art History, Case Western Reserve University, Cleveland, Ohio and The Getty, Los Angeles, California. Her book *The English Garden and National Identity, The Competing Styles of Garden Design, 1870–1914* (2002) won the Historians of British Art Prize for Best Book on Post-1800 topic. Her work has also addressed issues of gender and women artists as well as representations of nature and landscape.

Ysanne Holt (Ph.D., University of Northumbria) is Reader in Art History at the University of Northumbria. Her book *British Artists and the Modernist Landscape* (2003) reflects her concern with the historical development of ruralist cultures and relationships between landscape representation, cultural memory, and national identity. She is currently engaged in *English Art and Visual Culture in the 1920s*, a monograph that addresses, among other things, critical discourse; dealing and collecting; and the practices of certain training institutions, galleries, and exhibiting societies.

Alexandra MacGilp (Ph.D., University of Reading/Tate Britain) recently completed her thesis on *The London Art World and the Formation of a National Collection of Modern British and Foreign Works at Tate 1926–1946*, as an Arts & Humanities Research Council collaborative doctoral award holder. She is based in London, writes on modern and contemporary art, and curates exhibitions.

Morna O'Neill (Ph.D., Yale University) is Assistant Professor of Art History in the Art Department at Wake Forest University, Winston-Salem, North Carolina. She is a specialist in late nineteenth-century European art, in particular the conjunction of art, design, and politics. She is the author of the exhibition catalogue *'Art and Labour's Cause is One': Walter Crane and Manchester, 1880–1915* (Whitworth Art Gallery, University of Manchester, 2008) and a monograph on Walter Crane from Yale University Press (2010).

Brenda Rix (MA, University of Toronto) is Assistant Curator of prints and drawings at the Art Gallery of Ontario. She has curated numerous exhibitions for the AGO in the area of prints and drawings dating from the eighteenth to the twentieth centuries, and published several exhibition catalogues, including *Our Old Friend Rolly: Watercolours, Prints and Book Illustrations by Thomas Rowlandson* and

Pictures for the Parlour: The English Reproductive Print from 1775 to 1900. Recently, she assisted with the coordination of the exhibition *Holman Hunt and the Pre-Raphaelite Vision* and contributed the essay, 'Prints: Spreading the Word', to the exhibition catalogue.

Anna Gruetzner Robins (Ph.D., Courtauld Institute of Art) is Professor in the History of Art at the University of Reading. She has published widely on aspects of late nineteenth- and early twentieth-century French and British art. Most recently she published *A Fragile Modernism: Whistler and his Impressionist Followers* (Yale University Press for the Paul Mellon Centre for Studies in British Art, 2007). She co-curated the Tate exhibition, *Degas, Sickert and Toulouse Lautrec: London and Paris, 1870–1910*, with Richard Thomson in 2005. She is a specialist in Walter Sickert and her collection of his complete art criticism (Oxford University Press) appeared in 2000. She was a contributor to the volume *Art Made Modern: Roger Fry's Vision of Art* (1999), among numerous other publications.

Andrew Stephenson (Ph.D., University of Edinburgh) teaches Visual Theories at the University of East London. He has published articles on British art and design of the late nineteenth and twentieth centuries; most recently '"Telling Decoratively"': Ben Nicholson's *white reliefs* and debates around abstraction and modernism in the home in the late 1920s and 30s', in *Visual Culture in Britain* (2008) and 'Palimpsestic promenades: memorial sculpture and the urban consumption of space in post-1918 London' in Julie Codell's *The Political Economy of Art* (2008). He is currently working on a study of British modernism 1920–40 and *Patrilenes: Masculine Self-fashioning and Artistic Performance in Britain 1850–1910*.

Malcolm Warner (Ph.D., Courtauld Institute of Art) is Deputy Director, Kimbell Art Museum, Fort Worth, Texas. He is a specialist in Victorian art and the leading authority on John Everett Millais. His publications have ranged widely over European art, with an emphasis on British art, from the eighteenth century to the twentieth. He curated *The Victorians: British Painting in the Reign of Queen Victoria, 1837–1901* at the National Gallery of Art, Washington (1997); *This Other Eden: Paintings from the Yale Center for British Art* (1998); *Millais: Portraits* at the National Portrait Gallery, London (1999); *James Tissot: Victorian Life/Modern Love* at the Yale Center for British Art and other venues (1999); *Great British Paintings from American Collections: Holbein to Hockney* at the Yale Center for British Art (New Haven) and the Huntington Library, Art Collections, and Botanical Gardens (San Marino, California) (2001–2); *Stubbs and the Horse* at the Kimbell Art Museum, the Walters Art Museum, Baltimore, and the National Gallery, London (2004–5); and the award-winning *The Mirror and the Mask: Portraiture in the Age of Picasso* at the Museo Thyssen-Bornemisza in Madrid and the Kimbell Art Museum (2007).

Mark Westgarth (Ph.D., University of Southampton) is Lecturer in Museum Studies at the University of Leeds, and formerly was lecturer in Museum and Heritage Studies, and Programme Leader for the MA Arts and Museum Management in the School of Art and Design at the University of Salford. He is author of *A Biographical Dictionary of Nineteenth Century Antique and Curiosity Dealers, Regional Furniture* (2009) and *The Emergence of the Antique and Curiosity Dealer 1815–c.1850: The Commodification of Historical Objects* (forthcoming, 2011).

Acknowledgements

This book owes its existence to a series of conversations, hosted by generous institutions and enriched by the participation of many scholars. In 2005, we began talking to Anna Gruetzner Robins and Patricia de Montfort about our complementary research projects on the art market, and about how we might work together to address the full breadth and complexity of market practices and behaviour. In February 2007, Victoria Walsh and Anna Gruetzner Robins gathered together 'academics, dealers, critics, curators, and artists' at Tate Britain to answer the questions: 'London is a leading world market for contemporary art, but how has this come about? What role have dealers played? What is the relationship between money and art? How can we study the art market and what can it tell us both of the past and of the present status of art?'[1] We are especially grateful to the late David Robins, who prepared a wonderful meal for the participants in that conference, which sustained and nourished our intellectual congress. The conversation continued later that same month at the annual meeting of the College Art Association in New York in a session on 'A Nation of Shopkeepers: Innovation and the Art Market in Great Britain', led by Pamela Fletcher. We wish to thank Michael North for his encouragement at this crucial juncture of the project. The discussion returned to Tate Britain in 2008 on the occasion of the Association of Art Historians annual meeting and the strand 'Circuits of Exchange and Valuation: The London Art Market in an International Network, 1850–1950' chaired by Anne Helmreich.

In 2008, we had the good fortune to be awarded Getty Research Institute Library Grants and chose to take them simultaneously so that we could continue the dialogue in the archives. As we discussed our projects over coffees and dinners we became increasingly aware of the need to publish the good work we had heard at these various symposia. While at the Getty, our researches were amply supported by the staff there and we wish to thank in particular Sally McKay and Christian Huemer. As the essays gathered here make clear, our authors conducted their investigations across a wide range of archives, libraries, and museums and we thank these institutions for their support of this publication.

We were delighted that Manchester University Press was eager to publish this volume, and we extend our thanks to the staff for their assistance and encouragement. At Case Western Reserve University, graduate students Rachael DiFranscio and Christine Radigan helped to shepherd the project to the publication stage; at Bowdoin, David Israel, Karen Fossum, and Elizabeth Palmer gave invaluable assistance. This project would not be possible without the gracious willingness of our authors to share their research with the field and we thank them most deeply. And, finally, we thank our friends and family who supported us during the travel, research, and writing that led up to this book, including William and Joyce Fletcher; David, Benjamin, and Abraham Israel; Maria Ruvoldt; Catherine Scallen; and Christian Wulffen.

Note

1 www.tate.org.uk/britain/eventseducation/symposia/7903.htm.   Accessed   10 August 2010.

Introduction
The state of the field

Pamela Fletcher and Anne Helmreich

This book argues for the central importance of London as the site for the development of the modern retail market in fine art. It was in London that the structures and mechanisms that have come to characterize the commercial art system, including the paradigms of the commercial art gallery, the professional dealer, the exhibition cycle and its accompanying publicity, and a global network for the circulation and exchange of goods, first emerged and developed into their recognizably modern forms. This new commercial system involved a transformation of the experience of viewing art; of the relationships between artists, dealers, art objects, and audiences; and of the very definition of aesthetic value itself. Its history is thus a vital – and too long neglected – part of the history of modern art.

London was a crucial point of intersection in the networks of circulation and exchange making up the international, cosmopolitan art market. This book begins in the 1850s, when the London market became a pronounced presence on the world stage; tracks the consolidation of the gallery system in the late nineteenth and early twentieth centuries, when the London market was the strongest in the world; and concludes with the inter-war period when changing economic and political dynamics reconfigured the London art market. Taken together, the essays in this book map out the larger patterns of these structures and practices; individually they offer nuanced readings of the complex interactions between them, and the ways individual actors negotiated these new cultural forms.

Such a study is demanded not only by the complexities of the market today, which require a fuller understanding of their historic roots, but also by the practice of art history itself. With the rise of social art history in recent decades, the field has focused increasing attention on contextualization and such social-historical issues as class, race, ethnicity, and gender. Left relatively unexamined are economic factors, including the processes through which value is assigned to art in both the primary and secondary markets – that is, which artists and art works emerge as significant and worthy of acquisition, study, and preservation. This omission is particularly striking with respect to the modern era given the saturating presence of capitalism and the commodity markets, a history to which modern art is often seen as setting itself in opposition. A history of the institutions and practices of the art market relocates modern art within its commercial contexts, and allows for a more historically grounded discussion of the tensions between art and commerce, one which sees the opposition as a variable and intentional product of human action and reaction, rather than an unfortunate but inescapable condition of modern life.

London, 1850–1939: the social-historical context

The significance of London as a locus for many of the processes that have shaped Western society today has long been recognized. London, in the period under discussion, was a major centre for global commodity exchange, facilitated by a highly developed infrastructure of finance, law, transportation, and communication. As the capital city of a global empire, London possessed distinctions of scale and volume that offered it competitive advantage over other leading metropolitan centres. Michael Ball and David Sunderland, in seeking to explain London's exploding growth over the period 1880–1914, point to the 'conspicuous consumption of the wealthy, the world-wide tentacles of the City and Empire, and a terrible exploitation of a mass of poor people'.[1] These factors also allowed for an art market built on the mercantile networks of City and Empire and fuelled by a wealthy patronage class whose desire to possess art works was part of a larger culture of display.

The general economic expansion of Great Britain over the course of the nineteenth and early twentieth centuries brought about the growth of the middle classes and stimulated their ability to own luxury goods. This amplification of the middle class was accompanied by an increased stratification within its ranks. The upper tiers of the middle classes were occupied by the plutocrats, wealthy capitalists who often emulated the landed aristocracy in the acquisition of country house estates and London town houses,[2] followed by the professional classes, who stimulated the craze for small country houses and urban villas. While the plutocrats initially exerted more influence on the art market because of their greater and, indeed, unprecedented wealth, the professional classes arguably came to outpace them through sheer volume, given 'the massive expansion in size and influence which was to carry it to domination in the twentieth century'.[3] The middle strata of the middle class also expanded over this period with increased business opportunities and the growth of government, among other factors. They were distinguishable from the working classes by annual income, housing choices, and lifestyle, which included the ownership of art, whether original works or reproductions, which the art market supplied in unprecedented numbers.

This growth in demand was matched by growth in supply, as London, particularly its West End, became an important site of conspicuous consumption. Shopping, as Erika Rappaport describes, was crucial for the formation of public life in London as well as class and gender identity.[4] In particular, she explains, 'stores presented themselves as safe, pleasurable, and emancipating places for women', a phenomenon that helped to expand the nature of the art buying public as the art world was contiguous with the main shopping district of the West End located along Bond Street and Regent Street.[5] The retail trade, as Rappaport's narrative makes clear, was a minefield of moral complexities. This held true for the art market as well, as Pamela Fletcher has shown in her study of major mid-nineteenth century art purveyor Ernest Gambart, who sought to remove the supposed taint of commercialization from his institution, the French Gallery, and as Andrew Stephenson suggests in his account of the increased presence of single women in the inter-war art market found in this volume.[6] The entry of department stores into the retail landscape helped further to democratize the selling of art as they insisted upon art as a necessary and appropriate component of interior design.[7]

Department stores also capitalized on the already highly developed culture of display in Great Britain. Claire Walsh, in her history of department store displays, traces their roots to the eighteenth century when shops shifted from sites of craft and production to places tasked with selling. This led to the use of 'expensive interior fittings', such as mirrors, glass, and architectural detailing, as well as the increased designation of separate spaces for viewing or browsing and those dedicated to the actual sale.[8] Retail outlets for art, namely art galleries, were arguably among the most lavish mercantile settings in the nineteenth and twentieth centuries in keeping with their ambition to appeal to the wealthy classes. As Anne Helmreich's essay in this volume indicates, the financial outlay for interior decoration extended to the staffing of the galleries, which became increasingly professionalized over the period under study.

Conspicuous consumption relied heavily on the increased circulation of money and the expansion of personal wealth that took place between the mid-nineteenth century and the collapse of the financial markets in 1929. In 1903, as Youssef Cassis reminds us, the chairman of the Union Bank of London, Frank Schuster, declared 'We are, it is admitted, the financial centre of the world.'[9] Cassis explains that the 'city's financial predominance was assured by a combination of financial institutions', including banks, which 'held a leading position in all the markets', insurance companies, and finance companies.[10] It was the home of the stock exchange, among other markets, as well as multi-national corporations and important trading and transportation concerns, including railway and shipping lines.

London not only dominated Britain's domestic economy, it was, as historian Ranald C. Michie persuasively argues, 'a global financial centre', as it 'provided financial services to the world economy', which required technologies of communication, 'organized markets, the business units and … trained and experienced personnel'.[11] London's capacity was built through its role as 'the world's largest exporter and importer',[12] which caused it to outstrip Paris, its closest competitor for the position of leading financial centre. London's financial importance was increasingly threatened in the inter-war period, particularly because of its withdrawal from the gold standard in 1931, the contraction of the international economy following the collapse of the American stock market in 1929, and Germany's out-of-control inflation which led to a hold on war reparations.[13] Nonetheless, as Michie demonstrates, 'even on the eve of the Second World War … the City of London was a much more important global financial centre than New York', a position that would dramatically change after the war.[14]

This general trajectory of increased wealth and capacity until the inter-war period, however, should not mask the volatility of the British economy. While the Great Exhibition of 1851 was heralded as an apogee of British industrial growth and symbolically signalled what has been called the 'mid-Victorian boom', 'the first world-wide commercial crisis' took place shortly thereafter in 1857, triggered by the failure of the Ohio Life Insurance and Trust company.[15] The years 1862 and 1868 also saw recession, and in the mid-1870s the British economy perceptibly sagged to the degree that historians formerly referred to the period of 1873 to 1896 as the Long Depression to describe the general fall of prices over this period. This moniker does not do justice to the continued growth of the economy and expansion of trade, albeit punctuated by panics, which correspondingly affected the art market. The turn of the century was a boom period, despite the declining fortunes of the landed classes and increased competition from the United States and Germany. Britain's Empire as well as its role as an international creditor nation helped it weather this competitive threat but the Great War severely undermined the British economy. Even before the Wall Street Crash of 1929, the British economy appeared increasingly fragile as in the case of the call for a General Strike in 1926. Britain began to retreat from its position of Free Trade under the burden of the Slump (as the Great Depression of the 1930s was called in Great Britain).

This history of overall growth interspersed by dramatic rises and falls fuelled a culture of speculation in which art was caught up. Art was not just a desirable commodity, but also a potential investment. The cultural impact of such fiscal mechanisms as investment or credit has been only relatively recently recognized, largely in the field of literary studies. Nancy Henry and Cannon Schmitt, for example, offer a valuable overview in which they perceptively point out that 'changes in Victorian financial markets and investment practices reflected and influenced broader social change' and in response the Victorians developed new modes of writing and bodies of knowledge.[16] Such transformation also marked the art world, in ways that the essays in this collection explore.

London's modern art market: an overview

The sheer number of art objects created, exhibited, bought, and sold in nineteenth- and early twentieth-century London was extraordinary. In 1864, the *Art Journal* calculated that £400,000 had been spent on works of art that season: £100,000 at exhibitions and £300,000 at auction.[17] By 1911, *The Year's Art* reported over £1,300,000 in arts sales at Christie's alone.[18] Dealers, too, had enormous investments and profits. In the 1860s, art dealer Gambart had £100,000 in capital, while his rival Louis Flatou had £60,000 and Agnew's had £61,000.[19] Exhibitions at both dealers' galleries and exhibition societies routinely reported sales figures of thousands of pounds; Gambart's Winter Exhibition in 1855 resulted in £6,000 of sales from an exhibition of 427 paintings and watercolours; the Society of British Artists recorded the same amount in sales from an exhibition of 840 works (200 of which sold) in 1856.[20] To put these numbers in context, a magazine article in 1868 estimated that 8–10,000 new paintings were exhibited in London each year, and speculated that three times as many were created but rejected for exhibition.[21]

The number and variety of venues for the exhibition and sale of works of art were equally impressive, and London was known across Europe as an entrepreneurial hub for art sales.[22] Auction houses, artists' exhibition societies, dealers and galleries, individual artists, and a mind-boggling array of innovative schemes for promoting art created a complex, interlocking marketplace. Here, we focus on the crucible years of the middle and late nineteenth century and aim to provide a general overview of this unwieldy and constantly mutating system by identifying some of the key players and their financial practices, which shaped the system within which our contributors' case studies took place.

The Royal Academy of Arts

The Royal Academy of Arts held a central – if conflicted – place in the art market. While it was not technically a public institution, it assumed the cultural role of representing and fostering a national school of British art. As an article in *The Times* in 1886 insisted:

> The Academy lives and always has lived, on the footing of a public
> department, and not of a club. Its presumed recognition by the State
> gives it, its members, and their works a dignity and market worth beside
> which the value of their Burlington House lodgings is inconsiderable. All
> Academicians are really aware of their dependence on the public belief that
> their Academy is a public and not a private institution.[23]

The annual summer exhibition of contemporary art was reviewed in almost every periodical and was commonly seen as a barometer of the state of contemporary British art. It became a cliché to begin a review with the question 'Is it a good Academy?' and then to use the display as an opportunity to measure the health of the national school.

At the same time, however, the Academy was widely perceived as a 'great mart' from the time of its first exhibition in 1769 well into the twentieth century and routinely criticized for its commercial interests.[24] The Academy had been granted a charter by King George III, and received indirect state support by being granted use of government-owned buildings at nominal rents. Unlike the French Academy, however, it was not directly funded by the state. The proceeds from the annual summer exhibition were the primary financial support for the institution, and in many years excess profits were invested, creating endowments that provided a measure of financial stability. This system meant that the Academy existed in a grey area between public and private, expected to serve a national civic purpose, but reliant on annual profits for its continued existence.[25]

The ambiguity inherent in this status extended to the ways works of art were sold. The Academy did not directly broker sales of the works in the summer exhibition. Artists could send the 'prices of works to be disposed of' to the Secretary, and visitors were advised in the catalogue that 'persons desiring to know the price of pictures, or other works of art, are requested to apply to the price clerk'.[26] The catalogue also included an index of exhibiting artists and their addresses so that interested purchasers could contact artists directly, rather than the Academy accepting deposits on the spot as other venues did. Commerce was hardly invisible, however. In the mid-1860s, in response to a complaint from the Art Union that the prize winners could not tell which works were available for purchase, the Academy proposed a system of affixing a red star to the frame to identify those works that had already been sold or were otherwise unavailable for purchase.[27] Despite its ongoing need for funds, however, the Academy did not take a commission on the substantial sales that the exhibition generated.[28] The idea of charging a commission or a fee for exhibition was broached as a way to increase revenues for much of the twentieth century, but was regularly rejected. Not until 1977 was a commission (15 per cent) imposed.[29]

Other artists' exhibition societies
Often in competition with the Academy, other groups of artists banded together throughout the nineteenth and early twentieth centuries to exhibit and sell their work. These exhibition societies ranged from large generalist institutions, such as the Society of British Artists (founded 1823), to media-specific organizations such as the two watercolour societies (founded in 1804 and 1832) and the Society of Engravers (founded 1802). As Julie Codell has argued, the increasing professionalization of the role of the artist and the factionalization of the modern art market meant that the numbers of such associations grew exponentially over the course of the nineteenth century.[30] While their institutional practices – such as annual exhibitions and private views – often mimicked those of the Academy, many of these organizations distinguished themselves from that institution by their open membership policy and by their more explicit interest in facilitating sales.[31] Commercial aims were often included in societies' statements of purpose, and many organizations also took concrete and visible steps to encourage buyers. The Society of British Artists published prices in their exhibition catalogues, while the Society of Painters in Water Colours kept a price book in the gallery and employed a clerk to take buyers' deposits and record their names.[32]

The practice of charging a commission on works sold was fairly common, and was sometimes supplemented by charging a fee for exhibition. The Society of British Artists charged 10 per cent from at least the 1860s to the 1880s, with the commission rising to 15 per cent by the 1890s.[33] As printed in the 1860 exhibition catalogue, the rules emphasize the fact that this commission is the only cost incurred, reminding exhibitors '*no other charge will be made* IN RESPECT OF ANY WORKS SENT FOR EXHIBITION. This commission will be charged on the FIRST price sent with any Work of Art.'[34] The Society of Lady Artists charged a 10 per cent commission as well, but had a lower rate of 5 per cent for members. They also charged a fee per picture to all exhibitors, with a higher rate for non-professional artists. This fee would be refunded if the picture was rejected from the exhibition, but not if the picture remained unsold, ensuring that the organization would make some profit even if sales were unsuccessful.[35] Provincial annual exhibitions, such as those in Liverpool and Manchester, also charged a commission of 5 per cent.[36]

Alternative venues
Throughout the period, artists, dealers, and other art world figures devised innovative ways to show and sell work. There are far more examples of such creativity than this introduction can hope to discuss, and we offer here only a few examples that suggest the range of possibilities.

While group shows were a consistent feature of the exhibiting landscape, individual artists also organized exhibitions of their own work in order to gain more visibility and autonomy. This practice had its roots in eighteenth-century attempts by John Singleton Copley and Benjamin West to display particularly large or important paintings in private exhibitions, bypassing institutional venues to show their work directly to the public. This practice continued into the nineteenth century; French painter Théodore Géricault, for example, reaped the fiscal benefits of Britain's liberal exhibiting environment when he showed his painting *The Raft of the Medusa* at the Egyptian Hall in Piccadilly in 1820.

Artists also used their studios as sales rooms. In 1884, the Pre-Raphaelite John Brett, disgruntled by both the Academy and the commercial gallery system, showed his works at his studio every Friday in November and December. He explained to critic F.G. Stephens that he felt that 'the flourishing middleman in London … is no good either to the profession or the public'. He continued, 'I have always been independent of him, so this is no new departure on my part, but one more attempt to give the public a fair field in case they wish to go on their own judgement.' Recognizing the power of the press, he added, 'if you think it worth mentioning in your gossip column it may be of use both to me and them'.[37] In the early twentieth century, exhibitions like those of the Fitzroy Group – whereby Walter Sickert invited colleagues to exhibit in his studio, which he weekly opened to the public – continued this practice of seeking autonomy in the marketplace. Sickert's rationale can be applied to other twentieth-century avant-garde artistic groupings: 'I do it for two reasons. Because it is more interesting to people to see the work of 7 to 9 people than one and because I want to keep up an incessant proselytizing agency to accustom people to mine and other painters' work of a modern character.'[38] Nonetheless, it should be remembered that Sickert's circle, as well as John Brett, also worked closely with commercial art galleries, reflecting the plurality of opportunities for marketing their work available to British artists in the period under study.

At the other end of the spectrum from the studio were large, privately operated exhibition venues, such as the Crystal Palace Picture Gallery and the Dudley Gallery. After the Great Exhibition of 1851, the Crystal Palace was recreated in Sydenham, where it became an entertainment complex run by a private company.[39] In 1856, the directors decided to include a picture gallery among the attractions and hired Charles Wentworth Wass as the supervisor. The exhibition of contemporary art included both British and foreign work, and in the 1860s there were an average of 1,200 works on view at any given time.[40] This was a permanent, constantly changing exhibition. As the *Art Journal* noted in 1862: 'The plan adopted there of having the price of each work distinctly marked upon it saves trouble to all parties … Moreover, the gallery is constantly receiving novelties; for, when a painting is purchased, it is removed immediately, or within a very short time, and its place supplied by another.'[41] As this item suggests, sales seem to have been fairly brisk and a few months later the *Art Journal* reported annual sales of £4,000, a figure that increased to £7,000 by 1864.[42] We have been unable to find any information about the fee or commission structure in these early years, but by 1883 the Picture Gallery was charging a fairly standard 10 per cent.[43] The gallery closed around 1900.

Towards the end of the nineteenth century, department stores and home furnishings stores also began regularly exhibiting pictures. Howell & James held annual exhibitions of paintings on china and tapestry paintings in the 1870s and 1880s. While contributors to these exhibitions were identified as 'lady amateurs and artists' – a sharp contrast to some exhibition societies' insistence on professional status – the conventions of the exhibitions, including catalogues, prizes, and press reviews, were the same as those of other gallery venues.[44] As department stores became increasingly significant sites for the luxury retail trade, their activities in the art market grew. Selfridges had a picture gallery on its third floor, and advertised that in 'our "Academy" … every picture is for sale, and has the price distinctly marked', bringing the sale of art in line with other goods.[45] Waring & Gillow's gallery hosted exhibitions of contemporary watercolours and sculpture, Old Masters, and medals in the early twentieth century, while the Mansard Gallery at Heals was home to avant-garde exhibitions of the Friday Group and the London Group.[46]

Auction houses

By the period under study here, Christie, Manson and Woods had garnered a reputation as the leading handler for art sales, followed by Fosters and Phillips. Sotheby's was initially best known for books, prints, medals, and coins but came to rival Christie, Manson and Woods in the inter-war period. These houses were located in the heart of the art market in London's West End; Christie, Manson and Woods was located on King Street, Saint James's; Fosters was situated on Pall Mall; Phillips was housed in New Bond Street; and Sotheby's located to New Bond Street in 1917. Auction houses were patronized not only by the elites, virtuoso collectors, and the 'middling sort' who had helped to make the auction trade into a 'London institution' in the seventeenth century, but also by dealers.[47]

This latter point underscores the permeability of different sectors of the market. Although the art market is traditionally divided into primary and secondary (re-sale), this division does not cleanly apply in the London context. Many dealers both sold works by living artists that had never been seen previously on the market and resold a range of goods from the Old Masters to contemporary art, while already by the second half of the nineteenth century the auction trade was handling the work of living artists.

Auction sales were routinely reported in the art press. The *Art Journal* published substantial notes on major sales, including purchasers' names and prices paid. *The Year's Art* also published an annual overview of the sales, and information on the relevant commission structures, which were 7½ per cent on pictures, plate, porcelain, furniture, sculpture, and modern drawings, and 10 per cent on engravings, books, sketches, and old drawings in the 1880s, with the latter figure increasing to 12½ per cent by 1911.[48]

Dealers and galleries

Art dealers had long operated in London's art market, primarily in the secondary trade. In the opening decades of the nineteenth century, as Mark Westgarth's essay demonstrates, the secondary market for paintings and sculpture was an integral part of the evolving antique and curiosity trade, centred on Wardour Street. In the mid-nineteenth century, there were several interconnected changes in how dealers operated. One major new innovation was the opening of private fine art galleries, permanent spaces dedicated to exhibition and sale of fine art. The first private galleries emerged in the 1850s and 1860s, and by the 1880s they had become central to the art market. As these new spaces became increasingly common, the centre of gravity of the picture trade also shifted, as galleries clustered in the West End, locating the viewing and purchasing of fine art firmly within London's luxury shopping district and creating a new kind of exhibition culture. In the first decades of the twentieth century some galleries moved to deliberately 'outsider' spaces, such as the Chenil Gallery in the bohemian district of Chelsea.[49]

In the inter-war period, commercial galleries became important sites for the introduction of avant-garde artistic groups, such as Unit One (Mayor Gallery) or the Surrealists (New Burlington Galleries). By the late 1930s, the impending impact of the war began to be felt on the art market, especially after the fall of Barcelona in January 1939, which reinforced the need among artists and dealers to prepare for war. By 1939, 70 per cent of artists reported no income or employment, art schools were closing, and many dealers relocated or closed up shop completely, largely bringing an end to the art market as it had developed over the preceding century.

Print sellers

Print selling was intimately related to the painting market. Many fine art dealers – including Gambart, Thomas Agnew, and Thomas McLean – began their careers as print sellers, commissioning and exhibiting paintings in order to generate publicity and subscriptions for the reproductive engravings. Print selling thus shaped both the financial and aesthetic landscape of art dealing, as dealers were willing to pay vast sums for works they judged would capture the popular taste. Yet, by 1912, reproductive engravings had become significantly less popular, as evidenced by the demise of the *Art Journal*, which had done so much to promote the genre.[50]

The creation of the print market relied on not only a knowledgeable, skilled class of printmakers and print publishers but also a legal framework. Britain's first copyright Act, the 1710 Statute of Anne, protected only books. In 1735, the Engraver's Copyright Act, championed by William Hogarth, protected the engraved image, with exclusive rights granted for fourteen years to those who either invented or designed engravings. The Fine Art Copyright Act of 1862 amended the existing law to include the fine arts; it also specified that the artist could retain copyright through written agreement and established a registry system among other provisions. Artists complained of the burden placed on them to secure copyright, and dealers such as Gambart, who issued a pamphlet entitled *On Piracy and Artistic Copyright*, feared that the bill did not prevent fraudulent copies of publishers' engravings. Foreign print sellers, such as Goupil, were also frustrated since the law applied only to those works whose copyright had been secured in Britain. Copyright was further expanded in 1886 when Britain became a signatory to the Berne Convention, which established a system for the international recognition of copyright and also stated that copyright was inherent to the artist or author.

The art market in action

All of this was a symbiotic system, which individual artists, dealers, and consumers engaged strategically. William Powell Frith's early career offers an example of how a savvy artist could work the system. He broke into the exhibition system with entries at the Society of British Artists and the British Institution, while supporting himself by painting portraits in Lincolnshire.[51] In 1840 he had his first picture accepted by the Academy, an achievement that led to 'joy among the Frith family ... and oysters for supper'.[52] After steadily exhibiting at the Academy and being made an ARA in 1845 and an RA in 1852, he experimented with an innovative subject in his modern-life painting of *Life at the Seaside* in 1854. Following the enormous popular success of this picture and his next large modern-life scene, *Derby Day* (RA 1858), he was willing to risk the Academy's displeasure by exhibiting his next major work with the dealer Louis Flatou. The dealer's original commission for *The Railway Station* (1862) stipulated Frith would be paid £4,500 for the painting, sketches, and engraving rights, and gave Frith the right to exhibit the picture at the Academy first. The artist later gave up this right for an additional £750, a sum that allows us to put some kind of financial value on the prestige of the Academy's imprimatur.[53] Flatou was willing to put up the money because he was confident he could still earn a substantial profit on the door receipts and sales of the reproductive engraving; a confidence justified when a reported 80,000 people flocked to see the painting during its six months on view in London.[54]

Dealers, too, operated through many sectors of the market. They bought pictures from artists directly, from collectors, and at auction. Most owned a stock of pictures outright, and could have tremendous amounts of capital tied up in art, which they would sell at auction at moments of financial pressure. In addition to this inventory, dealers also organized special exhibitions, and the finances of these shows operated on a different model. In such cases, dealers do not generally seem to have owned the exhibited work, but rather took a commission on sales, as well as the profits from admission fees. As the following essays demonstrate, these financial arrangements were as variable as the dealers and artists who entered into them.

The state of the archive

One of the major challenges of studying the art market is the scattered – and sometimes obscure – nature of the available data. Sources range from trade and Post Office directories, which are useful sources for tracing the location of firms and geographical concentrations of businesses, to exhibition reviews and catalogues of specific shows. In this section of the introduction, we provide an overview of some of the available archival sources and the kinds of questions the data they provide can answer.

Dealers' stock books and inventories
Dealers have historically been wary of revealing the prices paid and received for works of art. As Gambart pointed out to Dante Gabriel Rossetti in 1865, 'let me draw to your attention that there is an end to the possibility of business if the producer of any article sold by a middleman publishes the price he obtains'.[55] Many of the commercial galleries operating in the nineteenth century are still in business, and their stock books remain company property. Some records have, however, made their way into the public domain, including the Goupil stock books (15 volumes, 1846–1919) at the Getty Research Institute; the Arthur Tooth & Sons stock books and inventories (London: 1871–1941, 1957; New York branch: 1920–29) at the Getty; microfilm copies of Agnew's London stock books (c.1852–1938) at the Getty and at the National Art Library; and the Duveen archives held by the Metropolitan Museum of Art, Getty Research Institute, and Archives of American Art.[56]

These records hold tremendously valuable information about the art market, but they offer multiple challenges for art-historical interpretation. At the most basic level, the information can be difficult to decipher. Reading the ledgers requires some knowledge of accounting practices, which varied widely from firm to firm. The books often enter the data in some form of code as was the case with the Goupil firm. And in some cases (e.g. Agnew's) the information about prices has been redacted from publicly available books. But interpreting the data is the more serious challenge. The sheer volume of information included requires that such sources be incorporated into databases, so that individual objects and kinds of objects can be followed across time and space, through the hands of multiple owners in exchange for fluctuating prices, often in differing currencies. In art history, such rich information has traditionally been considered within the realms of provenance and the history of collecting, but, as the essays here suggest, this archive would also help reconstruct a fuller materialist account of art and the networks that sustained the market.

The various accounting practices also mean that different sets of dealers' books suggest very different kinds of questions. Working together in the Getty Research Library, we were able to compare directly the books kept by Tooth & Sons and Goupil, and the experience suggested both the promise and limitations of this kind of data. The Arthur Tooth & Sons books are annual volumes; each begins with a list of the carried over stock from the previous year, and then newly acquired inventory was added as it is purchased. This means that the inventory number assigned to any given picture changes year to year, as its place in the listing shifts. This system allows for a very clear sense of what proportion of the stock is being held long term, and how much is turned over quickly. (For example, in the 1880s, the firm handled approximately 1,000 paintings a year, carrying over about 300–350 works each year. In 1882, they began the year with 375 paintings for which they had paid £12,742. Over the course of the year, they purchased 636 additional paintings for a total cost of £58,296.) But this system also makes it much harder to trace the history of a particular object over time, as an unsold object needs to be tracked through each year's book until it is sold. Each listing includes entries for an inventory number, date purchased, subject, artist, size, the seller, the price paid, the price sold for, the sale date, and purchaser (although the sale price is sometimes written in code). Goupil, by contrast, maintained a running list of inventory, making it far more difficult to establish a sound picture of the firm's performance annually. But, it is far easier to track an individual work of art from the moment it entered the firm's inventory. Each listing typically includes artist, title, size, date the item entered the firm, the date the item left the firm, a coded purchase price and price realized, name of patron, and by the late nineteenth century, as Helmreich reasons here, the locations where the work of art was displayed. The stock books reveal, among other topics, with which artists the firm had contractual relationships, the patronage of the firm, the geographic flow of goods, and patterns of price and taste.

Exhibition catalogues

Exhibition catalogues, from exhibition societies and private dealers, offer details of works exhibited and, on occasion, the prices of these works. As Fletcher's essay in this volume explains, there was an enormous variety in the extent and kind of detail included in these catalogues. At a minimum, they generally feature the gallery's name and address, the names of its managers or committee members, the dates of the exhibition, and a numbered list of works exhibited. More detailed catalogues might also include short essays, quotations from the press, and details about the aims and practices of the exhibiting institution. The National Art Library, the British Library, and the archives of Tate Britain have extensive collections of exhibition catalogues.

Auction records

The auction trade can be reconstructed via the records of each auction house as well as the numerous auction catalogues, but also by a variety of published sources, including the *Art Journal* and *The Year's Art*, which published the results of sales, as well as Algernon Graves's *Art Sales* (1908) and George Redford's *Art Sales: A History of Sales of Pictures and Other Works of Art* (1888). Much more work is needed on the auction trade and, in particular, the auction catalogue as it reveals changing structures and types of knowledge in art history and the professional identity and expertise of the auctioneer.

Periodicals and The Year's Art

Specialized art periodicals included significant amounts of data about the art market, including advertisements for special exhibitions, exhibition reviews, data on auction sales and newsworthy commissions, and general fine art gossip. As Codell's and Holt's essays demonstrate, these periodicals aimed at the art world saw commerce as an important and accepted part of the cultural field, and covered commercial as well as aesthetic events in their pages. Generalist newspapers and periodicals also included substantial coverage of the arts, primarily in the form of exhibition reviews.

One of the most useful widely available resources for the study of the art market in this period is a publication entitled *The Year's Art*. Published from 1880 to 1947, the annual volume offered 'A concise epitome of all matters relating to the arts of painting, sculpture, and architecture, which have occurred during the year'. As Patricia de Montfort has pointed out, the volumes were aimed at the professional artist, as they contained an artist's calendar with reminders of exhibition submission deadlines and openings, advertisements for picture shipping firms, and contact and general information for exhibition societies and other artistic organizations in the United Kingdom, Canada, Australia, New

Zealand, South Africa, and the United States.[57] Each volume also included fairly comprehensive lists of exhibitions mounted by private galleries in London, a list of fine art dealers in the United Kingdom, and a directory of artists and art workers.

The state of the field

The study of the art market is truly interdisciplinary, situated between art history, history, literary studies, economics, and material studies. As art critic Sheridan Ford's period study *Art: A Commodity* (1888) reveals, art was firmly regarded as a commodity by the mid-nineteenth century and a system of middlemen, picture shows, and art critics, among other factors, was well entrenched. Yet, as the essays gathered here make clear, this process of commodification was not without resistance and tension. The fiscal exchange value of the work of art, moreover, did not lessen its ability to signify in other ways. Pamela Gerrish Nunn, for example, demonstrates how art could also connote notions of both gender and state identity. Indeed, the authors, working in the wake of Arjun Appadurai's *The Social Life of Things: Commodities in Cultural Perspective*, recognize the ways in which art, as commodity, was interwoven into the larger social, political, and economic fabric of Britain and its Empire.

This volume demonstrates the rich potential for the application of models and theories of consumption to art history and, in particular, the study of the art market. Within the larger field of historical consumption studies, this volume adds to the body of knowledge concerning the long-term implications of the consumer revolution, and, in particular, the expansion of a luxury goods market that began in eighteenth-century Britain.[58] As John Brewer and Frank Trentmann note, the field needs analyses that:

> trace consumption along axes of time as well as space, identifying points of convergence, divergence and rupture. An effective analysis has to take into account the position of different actors and institutions along these axes, examining the power relations and the different discourses and values that give meaning to consumers' actions and the goods and services they consume.[59]

In the essays gathered here, actors examined include artists, critics, and dealers, and institutions include the museum and the commercial art gallery, still among the most important forces constituting the art market today. The emphasis in this collection is on those who created the supply and infrastructure of the market; the 'genealogy of the consumer', to borrow Trentmann's phrase, is touched upon but nonetheless awaits a full-scale study that builds upon the pioneering work of

Dianne Sachko Macleod.[60] In establishing the infrastructure of the London art market over the period of 1850 to 1939, this volume also attends to cultural geography and, in particular, to the development of a new retail geography for art in London that reflects the larger shifts taking place in capitalist production and consumption as these spheres became increasingly distinct, often in coordination with an increase in scale and volume.[61]

Within art history, the art market has been most closely examined in the early modern period, particularly the Netherlands in the seventeenth and eighteenth centuries when the rise of capitalism and Protestantism as well as the diminishing power of the monarchy gave birth to a middle class who could afford and desired fine art objects.[62] Neil De Marchi and Hans J. Van Miegroet provide an extremely useful overview of this literature, considered in the context of methodological approaches, in their introduction to their recent volume *Mapping Markets for Paintings in Europe, 1450–1750*. Their study was a partial model for what we hope to achieve here in that they 'wished to create mappings of local markets, using mapping in the sense of pinpointing what happened, where and when, and adding detail that might explain why' in terms of the emergence of the art market in early modern Europe.[63] Recognizing the specificity of conditions for the 'commissioning, valuation and exchange' is also the strength of the collection *Auctions, Agents and Dealers: The Mechanisms of the Art Market 1660–1830*, edited by Jeremy Warren and Adriana Turpin.[64]

The literature on the genealogy of the London art market is far scantier. Historian David Ormrod, in the collection *Art Markets in Europe, 1400–1800*, co-edited with economic historian Michael North, provides an overview of its origins in the period of 1660–1730. He acknowledges, as we do again here, more than ten years later, that 'economic historians have almost wholly neglected the British art market' unlike the situation for the study of the art market in the early modern Netherlands. He draws a picture of an expanding market, but one without a single centre or hierarchies; instead, 'auctioneers, professional and amateur dealers, immigrant and native-born artists each competed to satisfy a series of distinct demands'.[65]

Ormrod's quantitative analysis offers one form of insight into eighteenth-century Britain, which, as the birthplace of consumerism, has received a great deal of recent scholarly attention.[66] David Solkin has done much work to lay bare the discourses of commerce that shaped art production and reception in this period. His *Painting for Money* offers 'an account of how a visual culture came to be shaped by and for the purposes of commerce'.[67] This is given vivid specificity in Solkin's account of the Royal Academy exhibitions of 1780–1836 in which 'the pretensions of artists to disinterested liberality came into open conflict time and again with the fiercely competitive nature of their trade'.[68] Solkin's emphasis on the role played by art and its discourses in the construction of a newly expansive public sphere is also a major theme of the collection of essays that make up *Towards a Modern Art World*, edited by Brian Allen, which explores the 'institutional and commercial mechanisms of the modern art world' through individual case studies.[69] For a focus on agents, one can turn to individual studies, such as those on dealers William Buchanan and Arthur Pond.[70] Collectively, these studies revise and update Iain Pears's groundbreaking study *The Discovery of Painting: The Growth of Interest in the Arts in England, 1680–1768*, which remains significant in its attention to categories of knowledge and infrastructure still under investigation, including taste, patronage, collectors, and connoisseurs.

With respect to the study of the art market in the nineteenth and early twentieth centuries, studies have concentrated on France and the exhibition strategies of avant-garde artists.[71] This paradigm of Paris as the centre of the modern art world – a paradigm based on the canonical privileging of French painting of the period – has obscured the importance of London as a crucial node in the development of an international art market. Robert Jensen, however, offers a more international approach in his study *Marketing Modernism in Fin-de-Siècle Europe*. He establishes a typology for both artists and dealers who worked to establish the pre-eminence of modern art and attends to the rhetoric and ideologies that shaped the strategic manoeuvres of these agents. Jensen's emphasis on 'symbolic systems'[72] that bind together the activities of artists and dealers working in such locales as London, Paris, Berlin, and Vienna should be balanced by studies that examine the workings of each of these individual markets which, while in a dynamic exchange with other international centres, as Helmreich's essay reveals, were nonetheless shaped by specific local conditions.

To date, much of the scholarly work on the British art market of the nineteenth and twentieth centuries has focused largely on three fields: individual institutions;[73] patterns of collecting and patrons;[74] and the exhibitionary complex, the larger signifying system of the commercial art market but also of the supposedly disinterested realm of artists' societies and museums.[75]

These case studies of institutions, patrons, and exhibitions are balanced by descriptive overviews that reveal the complex richness of the London-based art world, including *Palaces of Art: Art Galleries in Britain, 1790–1990* by Giles Waterfield and *Creative Quarters: The Art World in London 1700–2000*, by Kit Wedd with Lucy Peltz and Cathy Ross. Several scholars have also attempted analytical overviews of this period, beginning with Gerald Reitlinger in *The Economics of Taste: The Rise and Fall of Picture Prices, 1760–1960*. However, as Guido Guerzoni has established, Reitlinger's study, which was based on auction sales reports, is distorted because of incompleteness and over-reliance on select Christie's sales.[76] Guerzoni proceeded to produce his own study of the British painting market

1789–1914 which usefully examines the roles played by supply (artists, art dealers, auctioneers, promotion), demand (collectors, museums, dealers), the structure of the market (imports, exports, production of living artists, auction sales, prices, transaction flows and dynamics, and theories on the return on investment), and variables that affected the British market (economic, political, social, legal, cultural factors).[77] Such quantitative analysis makes clear the complexity of the market and the need to adjudicate various factors before drawing any conclusions. Thomas Bayer, in his dissertation 'Money as Muse: The Origin and Development of the Modern Art Market in Victorian England. A Process of Commodification', also countered Reitlinger's conclusions by building his description of the boom market in Victorian painting on a database of over forty thousand auction sales that he authored.

There has also been significant work on aspects of print culture that relate to the art market. The print trade was intimately related to the market for paintings in that reproductive engravings emulated their source paintings.[78] Yet, as Martha Tedeschi's work makes clear, the print trade was arguably a sufficiently developed market in its own right. Tedeschi's recent article, '"Where the Picture Cannot Go, the Engravings Penetrate": Prints and the Victorian Art Market', argues that prints helped to galvanize the growing middle classes into 'an engaged, art-collecting public'.[79] Her dissertation offers an even broader consideration of the print market by addressing the reproductive print market, changes to this market created by the intervention of photography, the rise of original printmaking as a response to the glut of mass-produced imagery, and the role of the art press in connecting consumers to the print trade.[80]

Tedeschi's attention to the role of the art press is symptomatic of the greater recognition scholars have recently accredited art critics and editors as agents in the market. Helene Roberts's important early essay, 'Exhibition and Review: The Periodical Press and the Victorian Art Exhibition System' laid the groundwork for subsequent analyses by such scholars as Laurel Brake, Meaghan Clarke, Julie Codell, Pamela Fletcher, Kate Flint, Patricia de Montfort, Elizabeth Prettejohn, and Hartley S. Spatt.[81]

Overview of the book

Building on and revising this body of literature, this volume aims to demonstrate the interconnectivity of such figures as artist, dealer, critic, and curator, and to conceptualize the art market as a dynamic, relational system. The contributors, by and large, use the methodological approaches of art history as shaped by the revisionary thrusts of the past forty or so years, rather than the methods of economic history.

The first section focuses on the spaces and structures of the London art market, mapping the cultural geography of the art market as it emerged at mid-century, grew into a major international centre in the late nineteenth and early twentieth centuries, and came to a grim, albeit temporary, halt in the late 1930s. The section begins with the emergence of commercial galleries and professional dealers specializing in the sale of fine art at mid-century, and traces the development of the recognizably modern gallery system, which pioneered many of the elements still familiar today, including changing rosters of exhibitions, detailed exhibition catalogues, a regularized commission structure, and an international network of dealers, galleries, and clients. This emergent system showed considerable volatility as it underwent rapid change in the opening decades of the twentieth century. Typically the story of the rise of the avant-garde in London is a heroic narrative of rebellion against bourgeois convention and materialist concerns. The account offered here demonstrates a much more deliberate engagement between modernist or avant-garde artists and the structures of the marketplace. The final essay in this section by Andrew Stephenson tracks the market in the inter-war years, when the rise of the department store and the reconfiguration of home furnishing boutiques changed the dynamic of the marketplace dramatically, allowing for the rise of a new lower-middle-class patron, who contrasts sharply with the major collectors who dominated the pre-war period.

The second section of the book expands the parameters of the art market beyond the retail world of the commercial gallery to investigate the connections between the art market and its supporting contexts. The market for paintings remained closely tied to the sale of reproductive engravings for much of the period under consideration, a fact that had important implications for both dealers and artists. The burgeoning art press played a critical function in the dissemination of information about galleries and artists, as well as being one of the primary mechanisms by which the value of the art object was established. Art critics, editors, and scholars in the emerging field of art history were key arbiters of taste in this period and it is essential that their relationship to the marketplace, often concealed, be laid bare. These writers, working in a dynamic relationship with dealers and other retailers of art, helped to define and educate art audiences and to establish significance for particular artists and art works. The rise of museum collections of modern art added yet another layer of evaluation, as dealers, curators, and artists worked to secure the imprimatur of the museum.

Building upon this cultural geography and dynamic relationships, the third section focuses attention on individual agents' negotiation of this cultural terrain. The changing topography created new challenges for artists who were given greater opportunities for exhibition but, simultaneously, less assurance of a guaranteed path to success. Artists both collaborated with and resisted these overtures by critics and dealers when seeking to establish their own professional identities. Pricing structures and mechanisms, modes of display, and advertising and marketing could become major preoccupations for the modern artist. Revealing how artists engaged with these concerns complicates the paradigm of the modern artist working in feverish isolation, unconcerned with the outer world.

Within this final section is located a revisionary account of the Pre-Raphaelites, as re-conceptualized in the essays by Warner, Rix, and de Montfort. Some scholars have wanted to situate the Pre-Raphaelites as a British avant-garde, a framing that implies taking an opposing position to the marketplace.[82] The essays on the Pre-Raphaelites gathered here suggest entirely otherwise, demonstrating that these artists thoughtfully and anxiously attended to the market and were keen to adapt to changing circumstances created by the expansion of the print market, the rise of the commercial art dealer, the growing sphere of influence of art critics, and the increasingly competitive field. This revision offers one example of how the study of the art market might shift art-historical narratives.

Important themes cut across these three sections of the book, most notably that of identity formation for the dealer, artist, critic, curator, and even museum trustee. The dealer, for example, at mid-century, was the subject of anxiety and suspicion, Westgarth explains, because of his capacity to dominate trade, stereotypes of dishonesty, and possession of ostensibly hidden knowledge. The latter emerged as the dealer's trump card and, as tracked in the essays by Fletcher, Helmreich, Robins, O'Neill, and MacGilp, the dealer emerges as a new kind of professional, possessing a highly desirable expertise. This new professional, while perhaps more willing to move into new aspects of taste and the market than was the museum, was nonetheless, by and large, risk averse, as is demonstrated in the essays by Warner, Rix, de Montfort, and Nunn. The boundaries of the museum field were highly blurred and permeable as demonstrated by the hybrid careers of individuals such as Roger Fry, described by Robins, and Hugh Lane, described by O'Neill.

The London art world that emerges from this volume is neither provincial nor isolationist. The essays gathered here reveal that it was immediately and always embedded in a larger circulation of goods and consumers that extended from Great Britain to North America, the European continent, and the far reaches of the Empire.[83] It was a key node in a far-flung network formed by agents including artists, dealers, critics, curators, and consumers. This network demonstrated an amazing capacity to accept an increasing flow of traffic and to weather the vagaries of economic change as well as to police itself and to realign as necessary. We look forward to further studies that interrogate the historical processes of this network formation and consider its implications for the configuration of today's marketplace. In addition to such macro-level studies, the field would also benefit from microanalyses that assemble and investigate the data available in the archives described above in order to offer a balance between the quantitative and the qualitative. By thus expanding the boundaries of both our modes of analysis and our conceptual frameworks, we will more fully and accurately describe and critically examine the life of objects within London's art market, the roles of that market's many agents, and the artistic and aesthetic practices it allowed.

Notes

1 Ball and Sunderland, *Economic History of London, 1800–1914*, p. 4.
2 For more, see Crook, *Nouveaux Riches*.
3 Perkin, *Rise of Professional Society*, p. xii. Plutocrats were distinguished from the landed classes, who lost substantial social, political, and economic power, as well as income, beginning in the 1880s, leading them to sell off 'non-agricultural' assets, including art. See Cannadine, *Decline and Fall*.
4 Rappaport, *Shopping for Pleasure*, p. 7.
5 Rappaport, p. 10.
6 Fletcher, 'Creating the French Gallery'.
7 For more on this topic, see Edwards, *Turning Houses into Homes*.
8 Walsh, 'Department Store', pp. 47, 62. See also Edwards.
9 Cassis, *Capitals of Capital*, p. 83.
10 Cassis, pp. 94, 83.
11 Michie, 'City of London', p. 41.
12 Michie, p. 43.
13 Michie, pp. 76–7.
14 Michie, p. 78. Cassis, 'Introduction', in *International Financial Centres*, eds. Cassis and Bussière, p. 1.
15 Crouzet, *Victorian Economy*, pp. 54, 56.
16 Henry and Schmitt, 'Introduction', in *Victorian Investments*, eds. Henry and Schmitt, p. 12.
17 'The Art Season', *Art Journal*, September 1864, pp. 259–60.
18 *The Year's Art 1911*, p. 342.
19 Maas, *Gambart*, pp. 135, 201.
20 'The Winter Exhibition', *Art Journal*, February 1855, p. 65; cited in Maas, *Gambart*, p. 69; *Winter Exhibition of Pictures, Watercolours and Engravings of the English School … at the Gallery, No. 121 Pall Mall East* (London: W. S. Johnson, 1855); 'The Art Season of 1856', *Art Journal*, September 1856, p. 276.
21 'What Becomes of the Pictures?' *Tinsley's Magazine*, April 1868, p. 288.
22 Chu, 'The Lu(c)re of London'; Morris, *French Art in Nineteenth-Century Britain*, pp. 127–43.
23 Quoted in *The Year's Art 1887*, p. 64.

24   Solkin, ed. *Art on the Line*; Trodd, 'Representing the Victorian Royal Academy'; Fletcher, 'Consuming Modern Art'.

25   On the complex status of the Royal Academy as both public and private, see: Trodd, 'The Authority of Art', and Trodd, 'Representing the Victorian Royal Academy'.

26   *The Exhibition of the Royal Academy of Arts* (London: William Clowes and Sons, 1860), pp. 3, 5.

27   Hutchison, *Royal Academy*, p. 101. *Exhibition of the Royal Academy* (London: William Clowes and Sons, 1865), p. 5.

28   To give some idea of the volume of sales, in 1860, 152 works were sold for £7,435; and in 1869, 189 works were sold for £14,905. Hutchison, pp. 99, 112.

29   Hutchison, pp. 143, 192, 204.

30   Codell, 'Artists' Professional Societies'.

31   Codell, 'Artists' Professional Societies', p. 172.

32   *Society of British Artists: The Thirty-seventh Annual Exhibition* (London: [The Society], 1860); Smith, *Professional Watercolourist*, p. 156.

33   A commission of 10 per cent is listed in: *Society of British Artists: The Thirty-seventh Annual Exhibition* (London: 1860), p. 3; *The Year's Art 1883*, p. 42; *The Year's Art 1887*, p. 71. A commission of 15 per cent is listed in *The Year's Art 1893*, p. 86; *The Year's Art 1894*, p. 86; and *The Year's Art 1898*, p. 105.

34   *Society of British Artists: The Thirty-seventh Annual Exhibition* (London: [The Society], 1860), p. 3.

35   *The Year's Art 1883*, p. 42; *The Year's Art 1894*, p. 90; *The Year's Art 1898*, p. 10.

36   *The Year's Art 1883*, pp. 64, 66; *The Year's Art 1893*, p. 132; *The Year's Art 1911*, pp. 211, 213.

37   John Brett to F.G. Stephens, 31 October 1884, F.G. Stephens Letterbook, MSS. Don.E.81, Bodleian Library.

38   Baron, *Perfect Moderns*, p. 24.

39   Piggott, *Palace of the People*.

40   'The Crystal Palace Picture Gallery', *Art Journal*, August 1862, p. 175; *The Crystal Palace Penny Guide* (Sydenham and London: Crystal Palace Company, 1864), p. 22.

41   'The Crystal Palace Picture Gallery', *Art Journal*, August 1862, p. 175.

42   'Minor Topics of the Month', *Art Journal*, January 1863, p. 19; 'Minor Topics of the Month, *Art Journal*, November 1864, p. 347.

43   *The Year's Art 1883*, p. 47.

44   For example, see: *The Fourth Annual Exhibition of Paintings on China by Lady Amateurs and Artists* (London: Howell & James, 1888); 'Exhibition of Paintings on China', *Truth*, 5 July 1877, p. 12.

45   Advertisement, *Daily Telegraph*, 20 May 1909, p. 7.

46   The National Art Library, London, has extensive holdings of exhibition catalogues from both venues.

47   For more on the seventeenth-century London auction trade, see Cowan, 'Art and Connoisseurship' and Ohashi, 'The Auction Duty Act of 1777'.

48 *The Year's Art 1887*, p. 202; *The Year's Art 1911*, p. 341.

49 Helmreich and Holt, 'Marketing Bohemia'.

50 Helmreich, 'Death of the Victorian Art Periodical'.

51 Frith, *Autobiography*, I, p. 58.

52 Frith, I, p. 62.

53 Frith, I, pp. 229–30.

54 'Minor Topics of the Month', *Art Journal*, October 1862, pp. 208–11.

55 Maas, *Gambart*, p. 186.

56 The Center for the History of Collecting in America, The Frick Collection, has created a very useful archives directory for the history of collecting in America: http://research.frick.org/directoryweb/home.php. Accessed 21 February 2010. For a detailed analysis of a single set of the Tooth stock books, see: Bayer and Page, 'Arthur Tooth'.

57 Patricia de Montfort, 'International Networks, Periodical Publication and the London Art Market', unpublished paper delivered at the Association of Art Historians Annual Conference, London, April 2008.

58 For more on luxury, see: Berg and Clifford, eds. *Consumers and Luxury*.

59 Brewer and Trentmann, 'Consuming Cultures', p. 13.

60 Trentmann, ed., *Making of the Consumer*; Macleod, *Art and the Victorian Middle Class*.

61 For more on retail geography see: Wrigley and Lowe, eds. *Retailing*.

62 See, for example: Bakoš, ed., *Artwork through the Market*; De Marchi and van Miegroet, 'Art, Value and Market Practices'; Montias, 'Cost and Value'; Montias, 'Socio-Economic Aspects of Netherlandish Art'; North, *Art and Commerce*; North and Ormrod, eds. *Art Markets in Europe*; van Miegroet, 'Recent Publications'; van der Woude, 'Volume and Value'.

63 De Marchi and van Miegroet, 'Introduction', in *Mapping Markets*, eds. De Marchi and van Miegroet, p. 11.

64 Warren and Turpin, eds. *Auctions, Agents and Dealers*.

65 Ormrod, 'The Origins of the London Art Market, 1660–1730', in *Art Markets in Europe*, eds. North and Ormrod, pp. 182–3.

66 See, for example, Brewer and Porter, eds. *Consumption*; Berg, *Luxury and Pleasure*.

67 Solkin, *Painting for Money*, p. 2.

68 David Solkin, '"This Great Mart of Genius": The Royal Academy Exhibitions at Somerset House, 1780–1836', in *Art on the Line*, ed. Solkin, p. 8.

69 David Solkin, 'The British and the Modern', in *Towards a Modern Art World*, ed. Allen, p. 6.

70 Brigstocke, *William Buchanan*; Lippincott, *Selling Art in Georgian London*.

71 White and White, *Canvases and Careers*; Boime, 'Entrepreneurial Patronage'; Gee, *Dealers, Critics, and Collectors*; Green, 'Circuits of Production'; Green, 'Dealing in Temperaments'; Rabinow, ed., *Ambroise Vollard*; and Ward, 'Impressionist Installations'. See also the essays by Christian Heumer, Patricia Mainardi, and Oskar Bätschmann in the collection *Artwork through the Market*, ed., Bakoš. The

questioning of paradigms derived from the French context that inspired this volume has also led to groundbreaking work with respect to other geographic contexts as in the case of Jan Dirk Baetens's study 'Vanguard Economics, Rearguard Art'.

72 For Jensen's explanation of his use of the phrase, see *Marketing Modernism*, pp. 15–16.

73 See, for example: Athill, 'International Society'; Barlow and Trodd, eds. *Governing Cultures*; Birchall, 'Tate Collection 1897–1914'; Denis and Trodd, eds. *Art and the Academy*; Gillett, *Worlds of Art*; Hemingway and Vaughan, eds. *Art in Bourgeois Society*; Hutchison, *Royal Academy*; Smith, *Professional Watercolourist*. On dealers and galleries, see, for example: Casteras and Denney, eds. *Grosvenor Gallery*; Denney, *Temple of Art*; Ford, *Ackermanm, 1783–1983*; Fletcher, 'Creating the French Gallery'; Helmreich: 'Art Dealer and Taste'; Maas, *Gambart*; Newall, *Grosvenor Gallery Exhibitions*. Commercial dealers have also written their own histories, see, for example, Agnew, *Agnew's, 1817–1967*; Agnew et al. *Agnew's 1982–1992*; Garstang, *Colnaghi, 1760–1984*.

74 See, for example, Hermann, 'Peel and Solly'; Macleod, *Art and the Victorian Middle Class*; Holt, 'Eddie Marsh'; Korn, 'Exhibitions of Modern French Art'; Morris, *French Art in Nineteenth-Century Britain*.

75 Dreschsler, *Zwischen Kunst*; Fyfe, 'Art Exhibitions and Power'; Whiteley, 'Exhibitions'. See, also: Bennett, *Birth of the Museum*. Of the three characteristics of the exhibitionary complex set forth by Bennett – spectacle (p. 65), 'involvement of the state in the provision of such spectacles' (p. 66), and 'a context for the *permanent* display of power/knowledge' (p. 66) – the essays here attend far more to spectacle and the production of knowledge than the role of the state and the execution of disciplinary power.

76 Guerzoni, 'Reitlinger's Data Revisisted'.

77 Geurzoni, 'The British Painting Market', p. 100.

78 See, Bayer, 'Marketing of Genius'; Dyson, *Pictures to Print*; Zablotney, 'Production and Reproduction'.

79 Tedeschi, '"Where the Picture Cannot Go"', p. 19.

80 Tedeschi, 'How Prints Work'.

81 Roberts, 'Exhibition and Review'; Brake and Codell, eds. *Encounters in the Victorian Press*; Clarke, *Women and Art Criticism*; Codell, 'Spielmann'; Fletcher, 'Consuming Modern Art'; Flint, *Victorians and the Visual Imagination*; de Montfort, '"Atlas" and the Butterfly'; Prettejohn, 'Professionalization of Victorian Art Criticism'; Spatt, 'Aesthetics of Editorship'.

82 See Macleod, *Art and the Victorian Middle Class*, pp. 140, 150. For a broader discussion that examines nineteenth-century British art, including the Pre-Raphaelites, see Barlow, 'Fear and Loathing'.

83 See also: Stephenson, 'Edwardian Cosmopolitanism'.

I

Structures

1

'Florid-looking speculators in Art and Virtu': the London picture trade c.1850

Mark Westgarth

The period after 1850 saw the emergence of the modern commercial art gallery in London; distinctive galleries such as the French Gallery and Agnew's isolated the practice of selling of contemporary fine art as a discrete consumer activity. As Pamela Fletcher discusses here and elsewhere, these new commercial art galleries disseminated contemporary artworks to a metropolitan public through innovative exhibition strategies, new marketing techniques, and the professionalized practices of the modern art dealer.[1] The new gallery system also radically changed the established traditions of contemporary art practice, supplanting the artist-and-patron commissioning model with a complex of intersecting relationships, interests, and practices. These new 'modern art' dealers were principally involved in the primary (production, or first sale) art market, although it is important to highlight that many of these new dealers also continued to operate in the secondary (re-sale) art markets and the established practice of retailing 'Old Master' paintings when the opportunity arose. Thomas Agnew & Sons, for example, who were already well known to collectors of contemporary art at their gallery in Exchange Street, Manchester (appropriately named 'The Repository of Arts' after Rudolph Ackermann's famous premises at 101 Strand in London) opened their new gallery at 5 Waterloo Place, London, in 1860, selling contemporary artworks alongside Old Master paintings.

Prior to the transformation of the modern commercial art trade in the 1850s, however, the dominant activities of picture dealers had been in these secondary markets. This history has been hitherto unexplored; this essay discusses the secondary market for pictures in London during the period up to and around 1850 in order to highlight the significance of the role of the picture and curiosity dealer in these earlier networks of exchange and circulation.

The chapter focuses on a number of significant dealers operating in London prior to 1850, mapping the relationships between the London trade and their activities on the Continent and outlining their role in the mechanisms and channels of distribution. Situated in discrete locations in London, these dealers neatly illustrate the complex patchwork of overlapping trades and practices which constituted the 'picture trade' in this period. The art market in the decades up to 1850 was dynamic and complex; the picture and curiosity shop, both as a pragmatic facilitator in the wider distribution of pictures, curiosities, and antique objects, and as a discrete cultural site, played a critical role in these new and evolving patterns of consumption.

The expansion of the art market

In 1976 the historian Francis Haskell drew attention to the important role that the art market has played in the changing fashions for collecting art.[2] Haskell's text paid particular attention to the post-revolutionary period in France and England, when, as he suggested, 'flocks of dealers and agents'[3] emerged in response to the commercial opportunities that had been set in motion by the French Revolution and the Napoleonic Wars. This political and economic instability catalysed the initial development of a vigorous market for pictures and curiosities on the Continent in the first quarter of the nineteenth century.[4] The writer and art critic Louis Clément de Ris, writing in 1864, mused rather nostalgically on the potential opportunities in these post-revolutionary markets: 'Times were good! The storm of the revolution had dispersed to the four winds and thrown out on the side of the road a myriad of objects ... which over centuries, had been amassed in princely palaces, religious communities, secular corporations, and the mansions and homes of rich individuals'.[5]

The expansion in the British economy in the second quarter of the nineteenth century, and the increasing wealth of the metropolitan public, resulted in the art market being sustained far beyond this initial flood of material. Indeed, several scholars and historians have drawn attention to the importance of the expansion of consumer activity for the development of London in the early nineteenth century.[6] Whilst there was considerable economic growth in manufacturing production in Britain during the period (particularly located in northern cities, such as Sheffield for metalwork and Manchester for textile manufacturing), London remained the primary locus where the activities of consumption were played out. The expanding art market was a significant part of the growing consumer economy in the capital. By the 1830s, for example, the desire to own paintings was no longer the preserve of the aristocratic and gentry classes and was becoming much more widespread. The writer Edward Bulwer-Lytton recounted an observation from a friend who was shown a house in London by an agent; 'when the dining-room is completely furnished' stated the agent, 'handsome red curtains, sir – and twelve good "furniture pictures" – it will be a perfect nonpareil'.[7] Pictures, as a kind of cultured wall-furniture, were now becoming an essential part of an increasing and self-consciously aware, middle-class metropolitan consumer culture.

Estimates for the volume of pictures imported into England during the period were the subject of much speculation. Official figures were available; pictures, as well as a range of other antiques and curiosities, were subject to import duty and the Custom House in London kept (relatively) accurate figures on importations. An anonymous writer in *Chambers's Edinburgh Journal* in 1845 speculated that, 'within the last five years, somewhere between 60,000 and 70,000 "ancient" pictures have been imported into England, paying duty at the customhouse in London'.[8] The art theorist, writer, and 'Professor of Perspective at the East India Company', T.H. Fielding provided more accurate information in his *Knowledge and Restoration of Old Paintings* (1847), recounting the annual official Custom's return for 1845 which indicated that 14,901 pictures had been imported into England during that year. Fielding estimated that there could have been as many as 290,000 pictures imported into England between 1825 and 1845.[9]

Clearly, however speculative the figures may have been, the desire for pictures considerably expanded in the period. The rapid rise in the numbers of individuals involved in the picture and curiosity trade was both a reaction to, and a continuing catalyst for, this expanding consumption. During the period 1820–40, for example, the numbers of picture, curiosity and antique dealers in London multiplied by more than 1600 per cent, rising from less than ten dealers listed in trade and Post Office directories in 1820 to at least 160 listed in directories by 1840. In addition to the dealers in the capital there were a considerable number of provincial dealers in many British urban centres, as well as a large number of picture and curiosity dealers on the Continent, where the British trade acquired much of its stock of paintings and objects.[10]

Paris, for example, was a consistent resource for the London trade and scores of dealers made their way to the shops of dealers such as Carle Delange, who was located at Quai Voltaire in the 1840s and 1850s, and M. Cousin, trading at Place de la Bourse in the 1840s. During the 1840s Cousin had significant business transactions with the London picture dealer and agent for Lord Hertford, Samuel Moses Mawson, and sold a number of pictures at auction in Paris in conjunction with Mawson.[11]

The London trade also made regular buying trips to dealers in Italy, especially in Venice and Florence. The latter location was the home of the picture dealer Tito Gagliardi, 'the best dealer in Florence and well known in London', according to the writer and collector Herbert Byng Hall.[12] Frankfurt in Germany and Vienna in the Austrian-Hungarian Empire, the locations of the Goldschmidt dynasty and the Lowenstein brothers respectively, were also regular haunts for the London trade in the middle decades of the nineteenth century. These metropolitan locations on the Continent served as crucial networks for the assembly and supply of the constant stock of pictures, curiosities, and antiques required by the London art markets.

Auction sales of pictures and curiosities, either through the periodic sale of individual collections or trading stock of dealers, were also an important catalyst in the evolving markets in London in the period. 'Importation Sale' became a common auction sale classification during the second decade of the nineteenth century, a reflection of the extensive activities of the dealers on the Continent. Domestically, the trade continued to rely heavily on well-established channels such as auction sales to quickly redistribute large quantities of imported stock. Auction sales were also a critical part of the wider market structure throughout the period because they provided important opportunities for the extension of credit facilities within the trade itself, no doubt an important condition for continued and successful trading given that the contemporary money economy was structured over extended periods of credit based on the circulation of bills of exchange.

The dealer in the picture trade as a hybrid category

Whilst 'Picture Dealer' was a discrete listing in the trade and Post Office directories in the decades up to 1850, the number and range of other trade categorizations illustrate the hybridized character of the art market in the period. 'Picture Dealer & Curiosity Dealer', 'Picture Dealer & Jeweller', 'Importer of Paintings, China and Curiosities', 'Dealer in Ancient Furniture, Paintings and China', were all common categorizations. The boundaries between picture dealing and other trades were extremely fluid and picture dealers trading in curiosities and antique furniture were the convention rather than an exception in the early nineteenth-century art markets.

In the 1830s and 1840s some specialist picture dealers in London made selling paintings, drawings and prints their sole trading activity; Samuel Woodburn at St Martin's Lane and John Smith, trading in Bond Street, are among the most famous examples. Nonetheless, on the whole, picture dealing in the period up to 1850 was far from a uniform, discrete trade practice. The dealer in modern pictures was still a relatively rare phenomenon; private patronage, individual commissions, and the occasional fee-charging public exhibition remained more effective strategies for artists and were the dominant modes of exchange before the appearance of the modern commercial art galleries after 1850. For the vast majority of dealers the practice of picture selling operated alongside a range of other retail trading.

Even those picture dealers well known to us, such as Paul and Dominic Colnaghi or Thomas Emmerson, sold a range of objects, such as antique furniture, ancient armour, and curiosities, alongside paintings. Dominic Colnaghi, recognized as one of the most important picture dealers in the period, was also known for his knowledge of ancient armour and was a regular buyer of ancient armour and other curiosities at auction sales during the 1830s, 1840s, and 1850s. He sold a large collection of twenty-three suits of ancient armour and other arms to the antiquary and collector Sir Samuel Rush Meyrick for £2,000 in 1818[13] and continued to be a regular supplier of such ancient material into the 1850s.[14] Thomas Emmerson, who was listed as a 'Picture Dealer' at Watford Place in the *Post Office Directory* for 1825 before moving to Stratford Place by the early 1830s, supplied paintings to several notable collectors and also regularly combined resources with the picture dealer John Smith to purchase pictures.[15] Alongside his picture dealing activities, however, Emmerson sold a number of articles of antique furniture and decorative objects to collectors such as William Beckford and George Lucy of Charlecote House, Warwickshire in the 1830s and 1840s.[16] By the 1850s, as the new 'modern' picture galleries began to emerge, Emmerson appears to have begun to specialize exclusively in pictures, albeit selling Old Master paintings rather than contemporary art.[17]

Alongside these metropolitan cultural pursuits, the consumption of pictures was also part of the evolving antiquarian culture in the period. In 1855, at the auction sale of the collection of the antiquarian Ralph Bernal (1783–1854) for example, his picture collection, substantial as it was, was considered to be of limited artistic significance when compared to his collections of antiques and curiosities. As the antiquarian J.R. Planché suggested in his brief introduction to the auction sale catalogue, Bernal's pictures had 'avowedly not [been] selected for their value as paintings, but for their illustration of costume'.[18] Bernal had collected his pictures, mainly portraits, for their historical significance in relation to the 'stories' his historical objects and curiosities embodied; they were 'contexts' rather than objects for aesthetic contemplation.

The market for historical, antiquarian pictures was considerable in the period and for a collector such as Bernal there were a large number of dealers in the chains of supply. Horatio Rodd, trading in Great Newport Street during the 1820s–40s, was well known for producing catalogues of his stock. Listed in Rodd's catalogue published in 1842 (figure 1.1) were several pieces of ancient

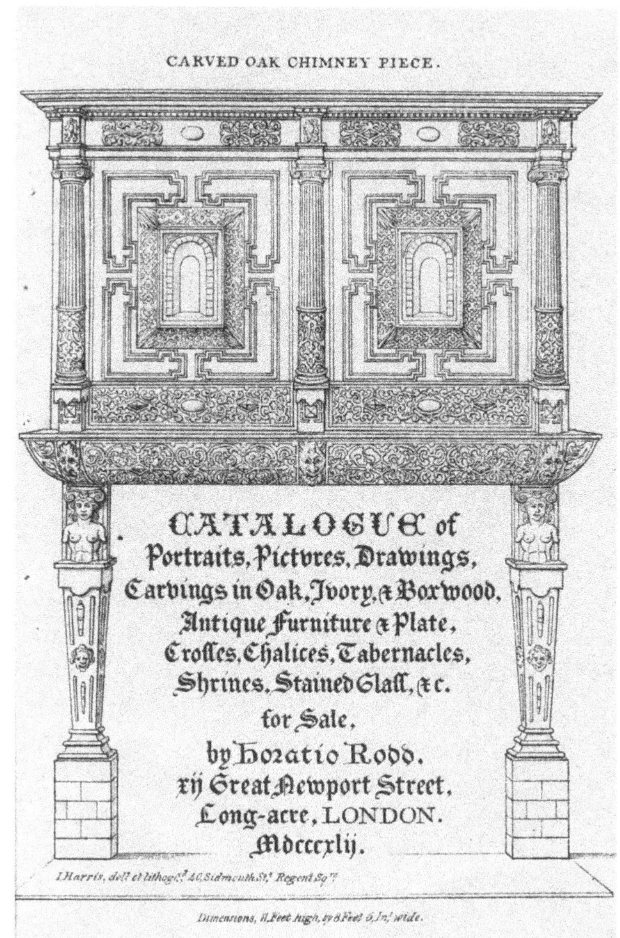

1.1 Title Page from Horatio Rodd catalogue (1842).

oak furniture and other curiosities as well as a range of British portraits and topographical prints of British counties. As both a picture dealer and a curiosity dealer Rodd was keen to highlight the antiquarian aspects of his stock and included a separate category of 'portraits' as one in which he specialized. Collecting 'heads' or 'effigies' was an established tradition and had been practised since at least the mid-seventeenth century among print collectors, but had moved beyond the small, wealthy and leisure-rich social groups of the eighteenth century to become a much more expansive pursuit by the 1840s.

The trade in pictures also comprised individuals associated with art practices such as 'Picture Restorer' and 'Picture Cleaner' as well as furnishing practices such as 'Upholsterer and Picture Dealer'. The furniture makers Town & Emanuel, trading from New Bond Street in the 1830s and 1840s, for example, were regular buyers of pictures at auction and advertised as 'Dealers & Manufacturers of Antique Furniture, Curiosities & Pictures' in the trade directories. Many of the most well-known specialist picture dealers emerged from associated craft trades. The Bond Street picture dealer John Smith began his career in 1794 as a carver and gilder and picture framemaker, and he continued supplying frames into the early 1830s before devoting his time to becoming a specialist dealer in Old Master and contemporary paintings in the late 1830s.[19] Nicholas Green has observed that in Paris the dealer in contemporary pictures also emerged from a similar 'artisanal route', evolving from a patchwork of trades such as picture cleaners, copyists, gilders, and frame-makers, to become gallery owners by the middle decades of the nineteenth century.[20]

As the evidence presented here suggests, the picture trade was composed of a complex series of overlapping trades and practices during the middle decades of the nineteenth century. This is not to say, of course, that those individuals involved in the trade did not perceive their activities to be discrete. Whilst it would be problematic to suggest that the picture trade in this period amounted to a 'profession', evidence that the trade was beginning to forge a discrete commercial and social identity certainly exists. Horatio Rodd, for example, the Great Newport Street dealer, was one of the first members, as well as being at one stage the Hon. Secretary of The Virtuosi Fund (also known as The Dealers in the Fine Arts' Provident Institution). The fund was established in 1842 for the assistance of members and their wives and children who 'had kept shop, showroom, or gallery, principally for the sale of works of art'.[21] The Dealers in Fine Arts' Provident Institution also provides us with an insight into the kinds of objects a 'dealer in works of art' sold in this period: 'Paintings, sculpture and drawings', obviously, but also 'stained glass, armour, antiquities, carvings, china, shells, coins, enamels, fossils' — in fact nearly the whole range of art and curiosities sold by the picture and curiosity trade.[22]

The cultural geography of the picture trade, c.1850

The diversity of commercial locations of those involved in the London art market illustrates the wider patterns of circulation of art objects, which in turn reflect the changing social base of consumption in the period. Locations such as Regent Street and New Bond Street, for example, allowed the new picture and curiosity dealers to draw on the cachet as well as the clientele of trades associated with the social elites, such as fashionable tailoring and other high-class services and goods. Chris Breward and Jane Rendell have demonstrated that, during the opening decades of the nineteenth century these discrete locations became associated with leisure, consumption, and cultured patronage.[23] As Pamela Fletcher and Anne

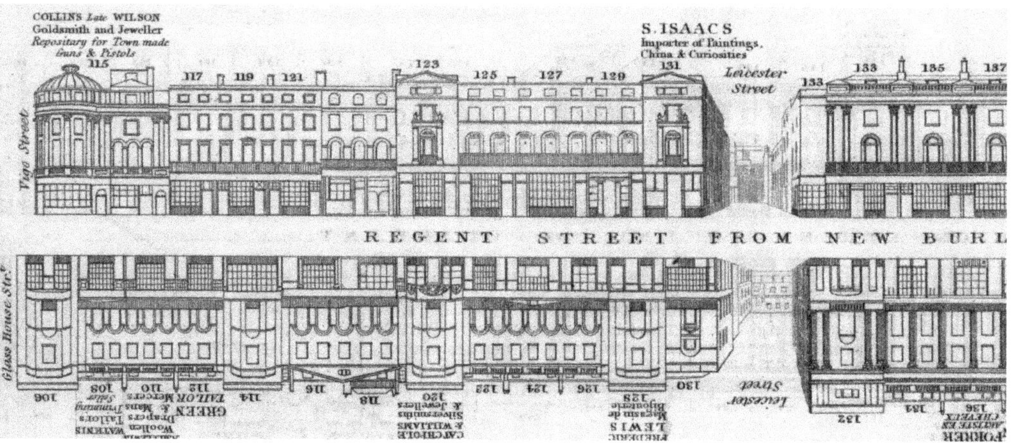

1.2 Part of Regent Street showing the shop of Samuel Isaacs 'Importer of Paintings, China and Curiosities', 131 Regent Street, London, c.1838–40; *John Tallis's London Street Views 1838–1840.*

Helmreich discuss in this collection, Regent Street and Bond Street continued to function as significant sites for the luxury commodity trade.

One of the distinctive features of the picture trade at mid-century was that dealers in curiosities often displayed their stock alongside objects of high cultural value, such as paintings, sculpture, and decorative and collectable porcelain. Such marketing strategies also illustrate the overlapping commercial practices of picture and curiosity dealers and the production of fashionable mercantile goods in the period. Samuel Isaacs, trading at 131 Regent Street as 'Importer of Paintings, China & Curiosities, and Dealer in Jewellery and Bronzes' (figure 1.2), was just one example of a number of dealers operating in this segment of the art market. The appearance of so many of these new picture and curiosity dealers in the new spaces of modernity and commerce in the metropolis draws further attention to the evolving patterns of consumption of pictures and curiosities in the period. It is, in part, through these new consumer spaces in the metropolis that 'curiosities', which had conventionally been associated with uncertain or indeed problematic cultural value, were assigned increasing levels of social significance as they were presented for sale in these distinctive locations.

This discrete consumer market for pictures and curiosities was not just a part of the West End luxury consumer culture. William Neate, 'Jeweller, Curiosity and Picture Dealer', at 3 Sweetings Alley, Cornhill, in the city of London, was also part of this expanding market. Neate produced a trade card, dating from c.1825–35, with a fascinating pictorial representation of the interior of a picture and curiosity dealer's shop (figure 1.3). As we can see, pictures

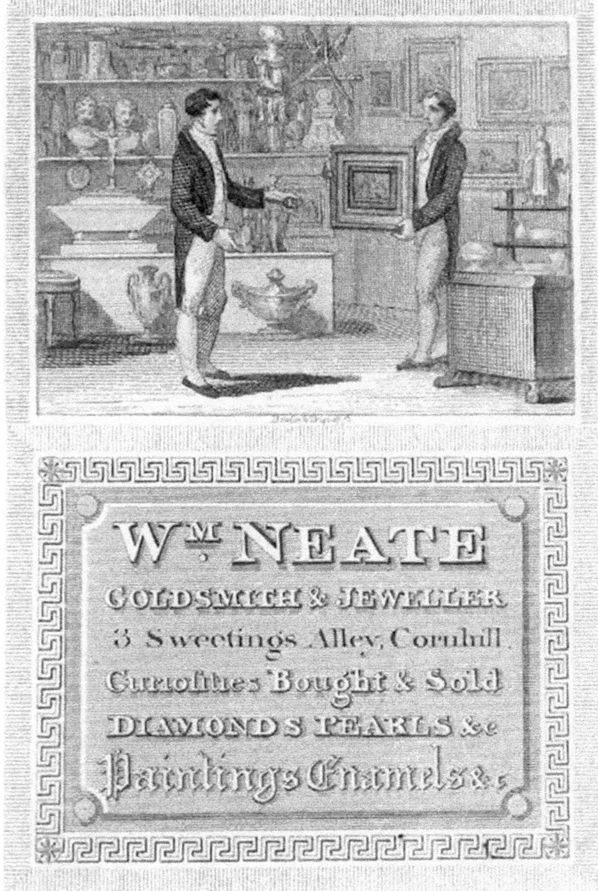

1.3
Trade Card of William
Neate, c.1825–35.

were just one part of a whole range of goods offered for sale, from jewellery, enamels, classical sculpture, medieval relics, and swords, to curiosities and even a stuffed crocodile.

Dealers such as Neate operated across the full range of discrete consumer spaces in London. The furniture shops of Oxford Street had their fair share; James Robinson at 27 Oxford Street is one example of numerous traders and his entry in the trade directories as 'dealer in ancient furniture, pictures, bronzes, sculpture, armour, carvings, books, china, musical clocks and natural and artificial curiosities' encapsulates the multifariousness of objects circulating in these markets and, at the same time, highlights his own desire to advertise the full range of material available at his shop.

As well as in the new consumer spaces of the capital, the picture and curiosity trade also continued to exist in far less prestigious locations in and among the second-hand brokers around areas such as Holywell Street and Seven Dials. The fact that many picture and curiosity dealers were trading from these locations demonstrates the extent to which the art market in the period was heavily segmented. In these liminal spaces picture dealing was a marginal activity as evidenced by testimonies gathered in the reports of some of the court cases heard at the Old Bailey. James Adams, trading in Holland Street, off Wardour Street, for example, described himself as a 'picture dealer', but, perhaps with a degree of envy at the networks of the more established dealers such as Horatio Rodd, also stated that he dealt 'in anything I can get a living by'.[24] The spaces of such picture and curiosity shops were evidently less glamorous than the galleries of dealers in Regent Street and Bond Street. Richard Gale, a 'picture dealer' trading at 47 High Holborn in the 1840s, provides a brief insight into the interior spaces of what must have been an average picture and curiosity dealer's shop in the period. In the testimony he gave at the Old Bailey in 1848 Gale stated, 'I live at 47 High Holborn, and am a picture dealer – it is my dwelling house – I have a gallery at the back of my shop up one pair of stairs – I keep some of my pictures in that gallery – I have also a small back room, up another flight of stairs, in which I keep other pictures.'[25]

One of the most significant locations within London for the picture and curiosity trade was Wardour Street. Indeed, within the specific patterns of commercial zoning in the metropolis in the first half of the nineteenth century, Wardour Street was invested with distinct social and functional connotations. It appears consistently in contemporary accounts of the picture and curiosity shop; it figures in trade literature and descriptive reports from visitors to the metropolis and is a constant presence in letters and other exchanges between dealers, collectors, architects, and designers. Whilst we can say that the emergence of the scores of picture and curiosity dealers throughout Britain during the first half of the nineteenth century was a development of considerable significance, Wardour Street completely overshadows the myriad of other individual locations in the cultural biography of the picture and curiosity trade.[26]

By the mid-1840s Wardour Street had the largest concentration of dealers in Britain and continued to be a centre of the trade until well into the 1870s. During the period 1820–70 at least 75 of the 124 shops on Wardour Street were at some stage occupied by picture and curiosity dealers. In the 1830s and 1840s, when the trade in Wardour Street was at its height, over 50 per cent of the premises in the street were picture and curiosity shops. Wardour Street was a primary location for the range of pictures, curiosities, and ancient furniture gathered by dealers from all over the Continent to be first delivered to the market. Although Wardour Street may not have been as discrete a consumer space as New Bond Street or Duke Street in the period, it was the location of some very prominent picture and curiosity dealers, including William Pollentine, Benjamin Kebble, and Richard Goldring.

Henry Farrer, trading at 14 Wardour Street by the early 1830s, was perhaps the most famous picture and curiosity dealer to have occupied premises in the street and his activities as antiquary, art expert, dealer in ancient and contemporary paintings, and curiosity dealer fully represent the extensive overlapping practices and activities of a significant dealer in the period. Farrer was both a member of the Society of Antiquaries and a member of the Archaeological Society of Great Britain. He was sufficiently well known to have been mentioned by Anna Jameson in her *A Handbook to the Public Galleries of Art in and near London* (1842); he is recorded in George Stanley's revised version of Michael Bryan's *Dictionary of Painters* (1849) as the 'eminent picture dealer'[27] and also appears in Gustav Waagen's survey of picture galleries in 1854, offering, as Waagen suggested, a 'good selection of pictures and objects of virtu'.[28] It is clear that Farrer had an enviable reputation as a connoisseur and an expert judge of pictures. The painter William Powell Frith described the dealer Henry Farrer as one who 'knows so much about old masters that his opinion is constantly asked, paid for, and considered conclusive; his charge ... is one guinea for a single picture, and ten for a collection'.[29]

Farrer is first listed as 'picture dealer' at 13 King Street, Soho in 1822, but moved to 14 Wardour Street by 1834, trading as 'curiosity and picture dealer'. He was joined by his artist brother William Farrer in 1836, and Henry's son, the artist Henry Thomas Joseph Farrer, also operated as a picture dealer at 111 Wardour Street by the early 1840s. Farrer's network of customers reads like a who's who of mid-nineteenth-century collecting; the Duke of Buccleuch, Lord Northwick, Lord Lowther, Sir Samuel Rush Meyrick, Lord Penrhyn, and Joseph Gillot were all supplied with pictures and curiosities by Farrer. He also acted as commission bidding agent at auction for, among others, Queen Victoria, purchasing 'Anne Boleyn's Clock' at the Strawberry Hill sale in 1842 for the Royal Collections. Farrer sold several paintings to the National Gallery in London, including *Philip IV hunting* by Velazquez (£2,200) in 1846, and *Portrait of a man* by J. Van Eyck (£365) in 1851.[30] Farrer was a prominent collector of pictures, ancient furniture, and curiosities; he loaned ancient furniture to the Marlborough House exhibition in 1852 and to the Gore House exhibition in 1853 and sold several curiosities to the South Kensington Museum, including a crystal cross made by Valerio Belli (1468–1546) in 1864.[31]

As well as dealing in 'ancient pictures' and curiosities, Farrer dealt in contemporary art. He made several purchases directly from the Pre-Raphaelite artist John Everett Millais, including *Ophelia*, which he bought from Millais before it was finished on 10 December 1851.[32] By the time Farrer moved to 106 Old

Bond Street in 1856 (still recorded as a 'curiosity dealer'), he had amassed a large collection of pictures himself. His collection of 'about 300 gallery and cabinet pictures', which was sold after his death in 1866, included works suggested to have been by 'del Sarto', 'Giotto', Botticelli', 'Canaletti, Guardi, Watteau and Lancret' as well as 'a grand landscape by Jacob Ruysdael, from Lord Taunton's collection' and 'Baptism of Christ, by Timoteo Viti, from Prince Ferdinand's collection'.[33] Farrer may have been outstanding, but his activities as both dealer and collector neatly illustrate the complex range of practices and activities of a mid-nineteenth-century picture and curiosity dealer.

The social and cultural identity of the picture and curiosity dealer

As the art market expanded in the period and the picture and curiosity dealer became an increasing presence in the social field, the persona of the dealer was inscribed into the contemporary cultural consciousness. The activities of the picture and curiosity dealer became the subject of much public debate and published discussion. The *Art-Union* (later the *Art Journal*) vigorously campaigned to expose unscrupulous dealers, and whilst not naming any specific individuals, the journal consistently directed attention to the activities of dishonest traders. Essays on the London picture trade with eye-catching headlines such as 'Tricks in the Traffic of Objects of Art' and 'Confessions of a Picture-dealer's Hack' also regularly appeared in publications such as *Chambers's Edinburgh Journal*.[34] Characterizations of the dealer as unscrupulous, dishonest, and the instigator and propagator of forgeries were legion.[35] In 1840 a writer calling himself 'Peter Paul Palette' penned a satirical commentary, 'The Picture-Dealer: A Sketch', that appeared in *Tait's Edinburgh Magazine* and rehearsed the common caricature: 'The picture-dealer ... is a sharp, shrewd, long-headed, wide awake kind of personage, whose business it is to supply lovers of the fine arts – persons of taste and fortune – with the "choice productions" of *deceased* painters chiefly and who has the very unenviable reputation of not being always honest in his dealings'.[36] Specific locations within London became notorious for their associations with the fraudulent activities of the trade. Wardour Street, as one of the centres of the picture and curiosity trade, perhaps inevitably emerged as a significant site in the narratives of deception and duplicity. The criticism of Wardour Street was primarily directed at the trade in curiosities and ancient furniture and involved a complex cluster of evolving ideas. Shifting tastes and fashion inevitably played their part, and there was still the lingering perception by many people that 'curiosities' were of limited historical significance and aesthetic value. But the associations of fakes, forgery, and deceit also spilled over into the picture trade. Indeed, such was the infamy of Wardour Street that its role as a signifier for forgery extended well beyond the metropolitan public of London. An anonymous article entitled 'The Rig Sale' published in *Chambers's Edinburgh Journal*, for example, reiterated the notion that the Wardour Street picture dealer was a propagator of fraud. In an ironic description of the fitting-out of a fashionable home in London, the writer announced the arrival of the 'picture dealer': 'Daubins, who is a picture-dealer in Wardour Street, takes the measure of the walls, and fills every available space with some "exquisite gem of art", manufactured in Brompton or Newman Street scarce a twelvemonth since, but figuring in the catalogue of the Rig Sale as the "choicest productions of the Italian, Spanish, Flemish and English schools"'.[37]

That the activities of the dealer were associated with fraud and duplicity was not in itself new, one need only to look at eighteenth-century characterizations of dealers to understand that such contaminating tropes predate the period under review here. Tobias Smollett's infamous Count Fathom, a dealer posing as a connoisseur, peddling counterfeit objects, whose 'commerce … likewise extended to medals, bronzes, busts, intaglios and old china, and kept divers artificers continually employed in making antiques for the English nobility', is just one example.[38] But the rapid expansion of the art market and the increasing desire for pictures, artworks, and curiosities in the period certainly appear to have led to an increase in the notion of the identity and activities of the dealer as a 'problem'.

The circulation and exchange of fraudulent pictures, and strategies to avoid the acquisition of such problematic objects, went hand in hand in the London picture trade in the middle decades of the nineteenth century. Although the picture dealer was seen as the originator of these fraudulent practices, some enterprising dealers took the opportunity to deflect this barrage of criticism and suggested that the trade itself held the potential for a mitigation of these problems. John Smith, 'Dealer in Pictures', dedicated the first part of his monumental nine-part *Catalogue Raisonné of the Works of the Most Eminent Dutch, Flemish, and French Painters* (1829–42) to the collector and politician Robert Peel, and thus rationalized his project:

> The primary objective, Sir, of this work is, to convey such information to amateurs of Pictorial Art as may prevent, in great measure, the success of frauds and impositions too much practised, and to enable them to pursue the objects of their taste with more certainty of attainment than hitherto; to unmask the means of deception, and to obtain for the honest tradesman in Works of Art, their confidence, and the reward due to his knowledge and integrity.[39]

Smith continued his discussion, describing, in some detail, the dubious and fraudulent activities and practices of some members of the picture trade, including:

placing the name of a first-rate master upon a picture by an imitator, or on a copy [...] to place pictures in an auction, and to run them up to large sums, in order to give them fictitious value [...] the placing of old, or purposely dirtied pictures, at *brokers'*, or old clothes' and other shops, where the venders [sic] appear to know nothing whatever about them; but they tell some simple story of having bought them at an 'old Mansion in the Country'.[40]

Of course a picture dealer such as John Smith offered a strategy of avoidance to guard against such impositions and to 'rescue the respectable part of the profession from the disgrace of being classed with fraudulent *charlatans*'.[41] His solution was simple and straightforward – buyers should seek out 'a dealer of acknowledged respectability', i.e. himself.[42]

Another recurring theme distinguishes Smith's remarks – 'inflated prices', 'running up prices', 'potential bargain'; it seems that 'price' plays a central role in his discussions of the picture trade. Indeed, the nine volumes of Smith's *Catalogue Raisonné* were devoted to the publication of information on the prices at which pictures had been sold over the previous decades. Smith was far from alone in privileging price as a defining characteristic of quality and, crucially, authenticity. Fielding also maintained that 'price' was the most useful and appropriate method for the judgement of the authenticity of pictures. The collector should, wrote Fielding: 'compare for himself the prices of well-known pictures with those of [pictures of] doubtful or unknown character. In short, the low prices alone are sufficient to declare that the vendor does not believe them competent to maintain the name given to them, for when a truly original picture of high character is on sale there is no scarcity of purchasers.'[43] The decade up to 1850 witnessed a rapid acceleration in the publication of auction sale price records for artworks, with consistent notification of prices realized for artworks in the local and national press. The publication of the auction sale results of high profile auctions such as those by H.D. Burn at Strawberry Hill in 1842 and Henry Forster at Stowe in 1848, together with Henry Bohn's publication of the results of the Ralph Bernal auction (1855) in 1857, clearly demonstrated the public appetite for such information.[44]

The London picture trade was expanding during a period when the economy itself became the focus of increasing political and cultural comment. As the links between the economy, politics, and the social body became more explicit, it appears that 'price' became ever more inscribed into the public and private meaning of pictures. As Dianne Macleod has written, 'the link between art and money is inscribed in the unfolding saga of the cultural life of nineteenth-century England'.[45]

The roll-call of dealers listed among the purchasers at auction results published in the press and in the price lists of sale catalogues is a testament to the emerging profile of the dealer as a discrete social and cultural identity. But such information also directs further attention to the increasing significance of the specialist commercial knowledge of the art market. Knowledge of pictures was no longer primarily centred on the expert knowing eye of the art connoisseur (although this was still required), and a new kind of expertise, one based on a detailed knowledge of the fluctuating prices of pictures, was emerging. Whilst many picture dealers espoused the disinterested rhetoric of the 'love of art' as the defining principle for acquisition of a picture, they could not resist pointing out that 'first class' works constantly retained their price in the market.[46]

Price is inevitably a relative rather than an absolute index, but in this expanding market, which was drawing in more and more consumers, many of whom had little knowledge of its mechanisms, the pricing of pictures appeared as a kind of alchemy. In this market the picture dealer was in a privileged position. The publication of auction sale results may have provided the public with a useful index, but the public art auction was only one part of the art market and left a whole range of personal and individual transactions that took place in the shops and galleries of the trade invisible to the new consumer. In this 'hidden' market transactions that took place between dealers and collectors and between dealers and dealers left the prices paid for pictures locked within a series of discrete relationships. Many collectors themselves obviously had intimate knowledge of these transactions, and many more may have been aware of anecdotes and rumours of prices given for pictures, but the majority of consumers could not have the 'inside' working knowledge of the art market of the picture dealers. This gap in public knowledge may be one of the explanations for the consistent criticisms and concern over the activities and practices of the trade in the period.

Whilst the price of a picture was suggested by many commentators to be the gold standard it was also a rather fragile shorthand for quality. The idea that price has a direct relationship to the notion of authenticity hangs by the slenderest of threads. As many of the commentaries suggested, price was subject to manipulation, misrepresentation, and outright fraud, something in which the picture and curiosity dealer in particular was seen to be complicit.

The persistent notion that the dealer signified the fraudulent and dishonest aspects of the art market remained throughout the century. The well-known picture dealer, jeweller, and curiosity dealer John Jarman, for example, is just one more of many dealers who were the subject of such critical commentary. Here is the curator of the South Kensington Museum John Charles Robinson, writing in 1891:

Jarman I knew personally after his retirement, full of years and notoriety. He was a dapper, ferret-eyed little man, dressed summer and winter in a black swallow-tailed coat, full-blown shirt-frill, and Hessian boots with a tassel in front ... he dealt generally in the higher categories of 'virtu', his particular specialities were ancient illuminated missals and historical miniatures. His day was that of the palmist epoch of English miniature-painting, and he found no difficulty in enlisting any number of clever manipulators into his questionable service. Innumerable were the spurious Hilliards, Olivers and Coopers, mostly copied from undoubted originals, which proceeded from Jarman's manufactory, and which still encumber the art world. Jarman's false miniatures are, in fact, well known, and abound in the shops and salerooms of London. Imperfect or comparatively poorly-illustrated manuscripts were, moreover, enriched with additional illuminations, usually copied in facsimile from other books. Jarman's knowledge, however, was not on a par with his audacity.[47]

Even today historians of collecting have regularly aired a note of caution when the dealer makes an appearance in the biography of an object. As the historian Clive Wainwright observed: 'It is a curious aspect of objects which have been in the hands of dealers that if they have ever been suspected of being fakes, or of having been in some way altered or improved, then this reputation clings to them however hard scholars try to dispel it.'[48]

The public perception of the dealer as 'problem' had consolidated in the middle decades of the nineteenth century with the rising presence of the dealer in the public sphere. Dealer activity at the major auction sales highlighted the presence of dealers as speculative buyers and reinforced the public perception of the trade as both competitors in, and controllers of, the art markets. The public auction was a particularly significant platform for the rehearsal of such fears and concerns. The auction is a public event, a 'highly visible theatre of competing desires', as Andrew Miller suggests, one where 'the meanings of goods are developed and reinforced as their purely monetary value is recreated and calculated anew'.[49]

The public auction plays a strategic role in the complex frameworks of the social valuation of objects. Arjun Appadurai, for example, draws attention to the importance of the public auction as a 'Tournament of Value'.[50] For Appadurai, the auction is a periodic 'event' where participation can be seen as a privilege of those in power and an instrument of status contests between participants.[51] As Appadurai suggests, auctions are events where social prestige and economic power can be reinforced and where the relationships between economic value, cultural value, and social status are made explicit.

Collectors obviously played critical roles within these social events, but the consistent presence of dealers themselves became a distinctive feature in the period. The *Daily News* reported on the auction sale of the contents of Stowe in 1848 following the spectacular bankruptcy of the Duke of Buckingham and Chandos; 'the lots are generally purchased by agents, of whom, as before observed, there were many present'.[52] At these important public events extensive numbers of lots were knocked down to the trade and the publication of the lists of purchasers at such sales drew further attention to the significant presence of the trade at these 'tournaments of value'. The *Gentleman's Magazine*, for example, regularly reported the activities of the dealers at auction sales,[53] and publication of sale results following the Strawberry Hill auction sale in 1842, the sale at Stowe in 1848, and the Ralph Bernal sale in 1855, provided a roll-call of dealers, immediately recognizable through the conjunction of name and commercial location: 'Farrer, Wardour-street'; 'Goldring, Wardour-street'; 'Hertz, Marlborough-street'; 'Forrest, Strand; Durlacher, Bond-Street; Jarman, St. James's-street'. The continuous rivalry between well-known dealers such as 'Mr. Farrer, Mr. Emanuel, Mr. Mawson, Mr. Colnaghi and Mr. Durlacher', which was also a regular feature in the London and regional press reports, only reinforced the idea of the trade as a dominant force.

With the constant registering of the active participation of the dealers at such important public events, the role the dealer played in the art markets became the subject of further critical debate. Henry Forster, for example, reporting on the Stowe sale, was disturbed by the activities and presence of some members of the trade:

> During the sale scarcely any respectable persons could enter the mansion without being imported to entrust their commission to persons of this class [brokers]: you were told that the applicant belonged to the 'London Society of Brokers' … that it was no use to offer personal biddings as the brokers attended for the purpose of buying and would outbid any private individual.[54]

It is evident in the descriptions of the picture and curiosity dealers at public auctions that their activities were considered by some commentators to be expressly designed to subvert the desires of the collector. The collector Herbert Byng Hall, writing in the 1860s, noted that 'there appears to be a combination among dealers which utterly upsets the hopes and expectations of an amateur'[55] echoing the threats Henry Forster recalled dealers had made at the Stowe auction sale in 1848. Forster had added, 'the villainy of the system will be judged when we add that four or five of these men generally work together'.[56]

Both Forster and Herbert Byng Hall highlight a particularly challenging activity

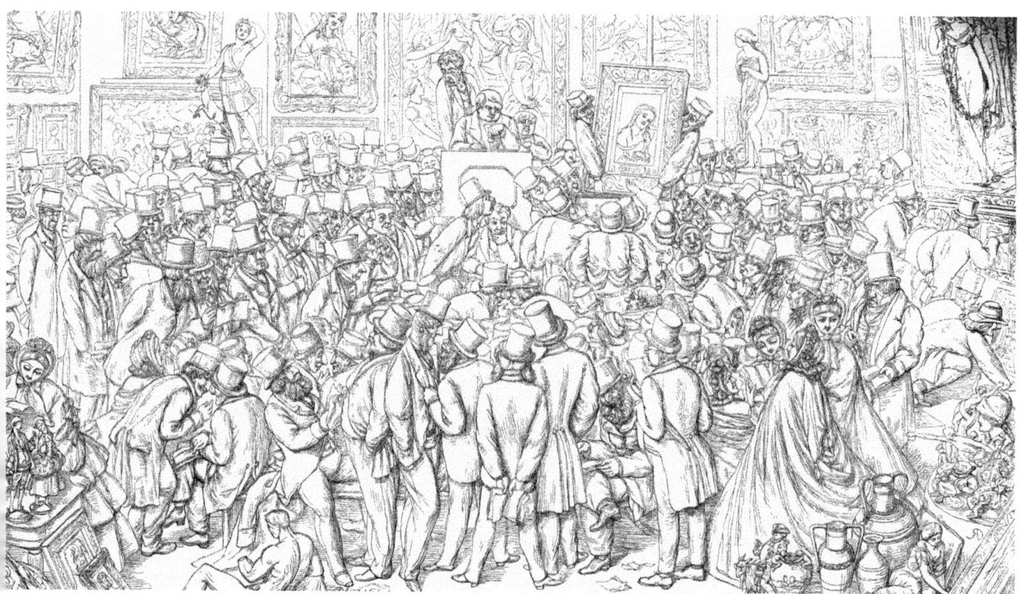

1.4 'Bird's-Eye Views of Society, No. VIII, The Picture Sale', *Cornhill Magazine*, vol. IV, July to December 1861, p. 470.

undertaken by the trade – the 'combination' or 'knockout'. The practice of the 'knockout' (also known as 'the ring') involves a group of dealers agreeing not to bid in competition with each other for an object or number of objects at a given auction sale.[57] The knockout indicates that a subsidiary market for objects operated within the trade, a kind of micro-economy sustained by the members of the picture and curiosity trade itself. This practice was legal at the time, but as the criticism of Henry Forster and Herbert Byng Hall illustrates, it provided a convenient frame through which the distinction between the 'legitimate' practices of the collector and the 'problematic' activities of the dealer could be rehearsed. An anonymous article published in *Cornhill Magazine* in 1861, entitled 'The Picture Sale' neatly encapsulates contemporary attitudes towards the dealer and their activities in the marketplace. The essay was accompanied by a small vignette, one of a series of 'Bird's-Eye Views of Society' (figure 1.4). The conjured scene, an implicit criticism of the overt commercialism of the contemporary art market, knowingly alludes to Johann Zoffany's *Tribuna at the Uffizi* (1772–78). In 'The Picture Sale', however, the aristocrats and their agents who populate Zoffany's painting have been replaced with a heaving mass of consumers, jostling for a place in the market, a potent visual metaphor for the evolving landscape of the secondary art market in the mid-nineteenth century.

Among the crowd, as the commentary indicates, are members of the picture and curiosity trade; 'Musty-looking, dusty-looking dealers are there, prowling about, seeking whom they may bid for ... florid-looking speculators in Art and Virtu'.[58] In mid-nineteenth-century discourse the picture and curiosity dealer may have often been reduced to a stereotype, but that does not diminish the significance of their critical role in the evolving art market in the period.

Notes

This essay is derived from my much more extensive study of the early nineteenth-century antique and curiosity dealer: *The Emergence of the Antique and Curiosity Dealer 1815–1850: The Commodification of Historical Objects* (Ashgate, forthcoming, 2011). I would like to express my thanks to Anne Helmreich for her astute suggestions for improvements to this essay.

1 Fletcher, 'Creating the French Gallery'. See also her essay in the present volume.
2 Haskell, *Rediscoveries in Art*.
3 Haskell, *Rediscoveries in Art*, p. 26.
4 See, for example: Haskell, *Rediscoveries in Art*; Wainwright, *Romantic Interior*, pp. 46, 292; MacGregor, 'Collectors, Connoisseurs and Curators', pp. 7–9.
5 Louis Clément de Ris, *La Curiosité: Collections française et étrangères* (Paris: Renouard, 1864), p. 277. I use the translation here of Janell Watson: Watson, *Balzac to Proust*, p. 10.
6 See for example: Celina Fox, 'A Visitors Guide to London, World City, 1800–40', in *London: World City*, ed. Fox, pp. 11–20.
7 Bulwer-Lytton, *England and the English*, p. 380.
8 *Chambers's Edinburgh Journal*, June 1845, p. 391.
9 Fielding, *Knowledge and Restoration*, pp. 13–14.
10 For more information on the development of the nineteenth-century antique and curiosity trade and biographical details of dealers see Westgarth, *Biographical Dictionary*.
11 Ingamells, ed., *Hertford Mawson Letters*, p. 13, fn. 17.
12 Byng Hall, *Adventures*, p. 199.
13 Lowe, *Sir Samuel Rush Meyrick*, p. 79.
14 Colnaghi is recorded purchasing several 'curiosities' at the auction sale of the collection of Ralph Bernal (1783–1854) in March 1855, including 'a rifle, the stock inlaid with ivory ... and a German inscription and date 1585' (lot 2217, £6 6s 0d). Henry Bohn, *A Guide to the Knowledge of Pottery, Porcelain and other Objects of Virtu ... Comprising an Illustrated Catalogue of the Bernal Collection ... with the Prices at which they were Sold by Auction ...* (London: Henry Bohn, 1857), p. 237.
15 Smith, *Catalogue Raisonné*, part I, p. vi.

16 Wainwright, *Romantic Interior*, pp. 222–3.

17 Waagen, *Galleries*.

18 *Catalogue of the Celebrated Collection of Works of Art … of that distinguished collector, Ralph Bernal … March 1855* (Christie & Manson: London, 1855), introductory remarks by J.R. Planché, p. 2.

19 See Simon, *British Picture Framemakers*.

20 Green, 'Circuits of Production', p. 31.

21 Low, *Charities of London*, p. 273.

22 Printed notice, 'Dealers in Fine Arts Provident Institution' (1846). AJ53, MS139, No. 435. Hartley Library Special Collections, University of Southampton.

23 Breward, *Fashioning London*; Rendell, *Pursuit of Pleasure*.

24 22 October 1838, case reference t18381022–2399; www.oldbaileyonline.org. Accessed 1 October 2010.

25 27 November 1848, case reference t18481127–101; www.oldbaileyonline.org. Accessed 1 October 2010.

26 For further references to the trade in Wardour Street see: Eastlake, *Hints on Household Taste*, pp. 57–8; and Wainwright, *Romantic Interior*, pp. 40–2.

27 Bryan, *Dictionary of Painters and Engravers* (1849), p. 239.

28 Waagen, *Treasures of Art*, III, p. 431.

29 Frith, *Autobiography*, II, p. 247.

30 *Philip IV hunting* by Velazquez is also known as 'La Tela Real' (1632–37), NG197; *Portrait of a man* by J. Van Eyck (1433), NG222.

31 See Wainwright, 'The Banker'.

32 For more on Millais's relationships with dealers see Warner's essay in this collection.

33 *The Times*, 13 June 1866, p. 15.

34 Anon., 'Confessions of a Picture-dealer's Hack', *Chambers's Edinburgh Journal*, July 1851, pp. 56–61; anon., 'Tricks in the Traffic of Objects of Art', *Chambers's Edinburgh Journal*, June 1845, pp. 389–92.

35 See also Fletcher, 'Creating the French Gallery', and Briefel, *The Deceivers*.

36 Peter Paul Palette (pseud.), 'The Picture-dealer: A Sketch', *Tait's Edinburgh Magazine*, January 1840, p. 17.

37 Anon., 'The Rig Sale', *Chambers's Edinburgh Journal*, February 1851, p. 103.

38 Smollett, *Ferdinand Count Fathom*, p. 151.

39 Smith, *Catalogue Raisonné* (9 vols.), part I, p. vi.

40 Smith, *Catalogue Raisonné*, part I, pp. xiv–xvi.

41 Smith, *Catalogue Raisonné*, part I, p. xvii.

42 Smith, *Catalogue Raisonné*, part I, p. xvi.

43 Fielding, p. 34.

44 H.D. Burn, *Aedes Strawberriannae, Names and Purchasers of the Choice Collections of Art and Virtu at Strawberry-hill Villa …* (London: H. Burn, n.d. [1842]); Forster, *The Stowe Catalogue, Priced and Annotated* (1848); Bohn (1857).

45 Macleod, *Art and the Victorian Middle Class*, p. 1.

46 See, for example, Smith, *Catalogue Raisonné*, part I, p. xvii.

47 John Charles Robinson, 'On Spurious Works of Art', *Nineteenth Century*, November 1891, pp. 684–6.

48 Wainwright, 'The Banker', p. 41.

49 Miller, *Novels Behind Glass*, p. 21.

50 Appadurai, 'Introduction: Commodities and the Politics of Value', in *Social Life of Things*, ed. Appadurai, p. 21.

51 Appadurai, ed., *Social Life of Things*, p. 21.

52 *Daily News*, 16 September 1848, p. 3.

53 See, for example the reporting of the sales at The Pryor's Bank in Fulham, the property of the collector and antiquary Thomas Baylis whose collecton was sold in May 1841, and those of the Nottingham collector John Holmes at East Retford in October 1841, in *Gentleman's Magazine*, January 1842, p. 23.

54 Forster, *The Stowe Catalogue, Priced and Annotated*, p. 102.

55 Byng Hall, pp. 197–8.

56 Forster, *The Stowe Catalogue, Priced and Annotated*, p. 102.

57 The practice was only made illegal within civil law in 1927 (1927 Bidding Agreements Act). It has more recently been deemed a criminal act (Bidding Agreement Act 1969). For an outline of the legal status of this practice see Kay, 'Under the Hammer'.

58 Anon., 'The Picture Sale', *Cornhill Magazine*, October 1861, pp. 470–1.

2

Shopping for art: the rise of the commercial art gallery, 1850s–90s

Pamela Fletcher

The commercial art gallery developed as an independent institution in the 1850s and 1860s, as print sellers and dealers who sold works of art along with other items of home décor or artists' supplies began opening galleries exclusively devoted to the promotion and sale of fine art. By the 1880s and 1890s, these commercial art galleries had proliferated across London's West End and become an inescapable force in the art market. As the new form of the gallery took shape, its history was marked by various controversies: was the space an 'exhibition' or a 'shop' (to use the terminology of the period); was the dealer a new kind of patron or a profiteering speculator; would the gallery fragment the ideal national public constituted by the Academy into divisive niche markets? This history of scepticism reminds us that the emergence of the gallery system was a massive transformation of the experience of viewing art; of the economic practices and relationships between artist, dealer, and collector; and of the very criteria of aesthetic value itself. The gallery system was, in other words, a new set of relationships, practices, and expectations, one which embodied the values of originality, distinction, and cosmopolitanism that undergird the familiar narrative of modern art. In this chapter, I chart the history of the commercial gallery from the 1850s to the 1890s, and argue that this new set of structures and practices was well in place by the turn of the twentieth century, forming a network of spaces and associations that created the conditions for the reception of modern art in London in the following decades.

In order to understand this new gallery system, it is necessary to look both at the differences between the commercial gallery and other retail and artistic institutions, and at the distinctions between individual galleries. But this complex typology and cultural geography is difficult to recreate. What kinds of reputations did individual galleries have? What kinds of viewers did they attract, or aspire to attract? How did galleries position themselves in relation to one another, aesthetically, commercially, and geographically? How did they engage with or distance themselves from contemporary retail norms? From artist-run exhibition spaces? What difference did these relationships make to viewers' reactions to the works of art shown in these spaces? How, in other words, can we analyse this new field of cultural production as a dynamic, relational system?

Bourdieu's notion of a cultural field is useful here. Bourdieu defines a cultural field as the system of actors, institutions, norms, and possibilities operating to produce a particular cultural form, such as the fine arts, theatre, or literature.[1] As Lisa Tickner emphasizes in her discussion of the utility of Bourdieu's concept for the study of modern British art, the idea of the cultural field can mediate between an uncritical assumption of absolute autonomous agency and a purely structuralist view.[2] The sum total of the actions of individual agents becomes the terrain on which any individual actor makes his or her choices. So to map any particular historical cultural field, we must simultaneously look for the structures and patterns that characterize the field, and attend to the fact that that field is made up of the acts of agents, each aiming in part at distinguishing him- or herself from those norms. In telling the story of the rise of the commercial gallery in London from the 1850s to the 1890s, then, I will try both to sketch out broad patterns and to trace strategies of differentiation, as I map the basic contours of the cultural field of the commercial gallery at the moment of its consolidation.

The roots of the recognizably modern commercial art gallery lie in the eighteenth-century British history of entrepreneurial art marketing, as artists both exhibited their work privately, and banded together in artist-run exhibiting societies.[3] Dealers, too, frequently exhibited paintings to sell reproductive engravings, but, in the 1850s, there was a significant new development in marketing strategies, as print sellers and dealers began to exhibit paintings in dedicated spaces separated from the reproductive prints that were still the major source of their profits. Ernest Gambart's French Gallery in Pall Mall was one of the pioneers, and Arthur Tooth & Sons, Agnew's, and others quickly emerged as competitors.[4] The challenge for these early spaces was to carve out a reputable niche for the sale of art, differentiated from the itinerant traders and fraudulent dealers that formed the common perception of the art trade. Gambart pioneered one strategy, emulating the Royal Academy annual exhibition with his own annual spring 'French Exhibition' and 'Winter Exhibition' of British artists. These were large comprehensive annual shows with admission fees and educational aspirations, which succeeded in overcoming many critics' objections to reviewing dealers' shows. As even the sceptical *Art Journal* conceded in a preface to a review of a dealer-run gallery in 1860: 'The time has been when almost every work by artists of any eminence regularly appeared in some public institution; but as that is now no longer to be expected, the opportunity of seeing in galleries of this kind so important a portion of each year's Art-produce as is now to be found in the hands of dealers, cannot be neglected.'[5] Breaking from its earlier history of resistance to dealers, the *Art Journal* began regularly reviewing 'private galleries' from this point forward. In 1867 the art critic for the *Saturday Review* also concluded that 'pictures exhibited by dealers ought to be noticed by the press when they were of such quality that the exhibition of them might advance the interests of art', but quickly put conditions on this stipulation: 'however excellent may be the works exhibited, we will take no notice of Dealers' Exhibitions unless the shop character is kept so entirely in the background that members of the ordinary public may be quite sure of studying the pictures at their leisure, without fear of interruption on the part of the dealers and their customers'.[6]

As these critics' changed policies indicate, commercial galleries became both more common and more influential in the 1860s and 1870s. And by the 1880s, as is visible in this series of maps (figures 2.1–2.3), they had spread across the West End of London. These images are drawn from an interactive map that charts the movement of galleries over time and in relation to other spaces, but even in this static form of reproduction, this visualization helps us to see the gallery system as a *system*. The first and most obvious point is the concentration of galleries in the West End over this period of time, particularly on Bond Street and just south of Piccadilly. New galleries opened here, and, perhaps more significantly, as print sellers or frame makers shifted their attention to selling paintings they, too, moved to this area. When the Goupil Gallery moved from the Strand to New Bond Street in 1883, an advertisement explained that they had:

long felt that the situation of their late Galleries has been found too inconvenient to allow of their seeing their patrons so often as they would desire, and they trust that ... their removal to the most famous of West-end thoroughfares, will insure to them not only more frequent visits from their present numerous amateurs, but also that their New Galleries may offer sufficient attraction to draw all interested in the Fine Arts to their Establishment.[7]

In order to attract all those interested in the Fine Arts, it was necessary to move to an area with other artistic attractions.

The result of this concentration was, of course, a huge change in how people encountered art. Bond Street was already an important shopping area for luxury

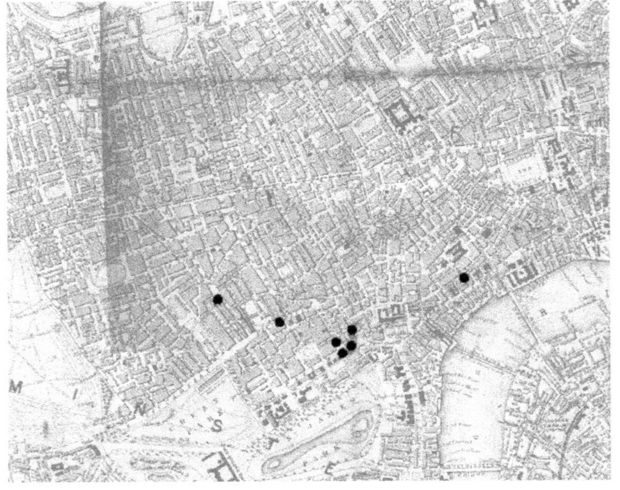

2.1
London galleries in
1865.

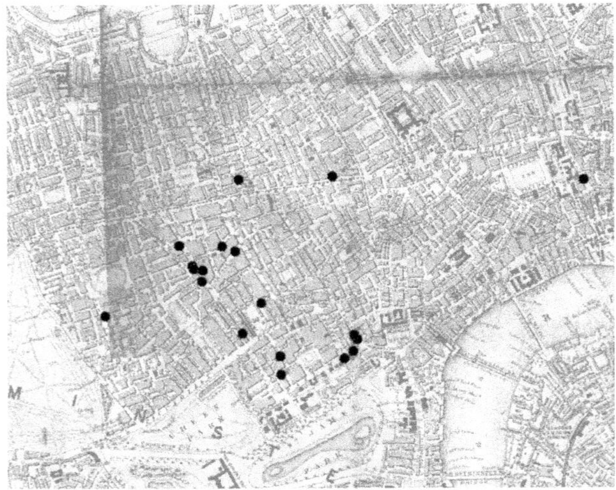

2.2
London galleries in
1880.

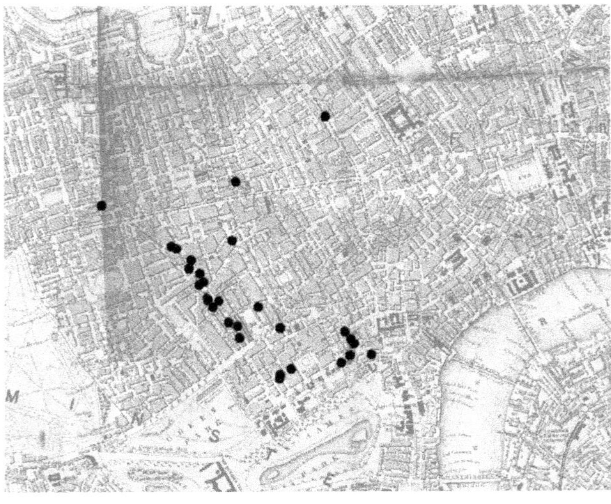

2.3
London galleries in
1895.

goods, and art galleries quickly became one of its identifying characteristics: as a critic for the magazine *Truth* joked in 1905, Bond Street is 'getting more and more like one elongated picture gallery tempered by tea shops!'[8] The entire street became a spectacle of exhibition, as viewing art became one more stop on a shopping (or window shopping) tour of the West End. As early as the 1860s, critics had foreseen the dangers of this proliferation of exhibitions: 'Exhibitions are not mere shops and auction marts for sale: Art has not yet come quite to this last degradation! Exhibitions should be something akin in dignity to those ancient trials of skill and of power, when the fleet of foot and the strong of arm received the laurel crown.'[9] How, then, could galleries distinguish their product – fine art – from other luxury goods, or their gallery from others?

Galleries tried various tactics to lure viewers inside, and to create memorable and distinctly 'artistic' experiences. Henry James offered a marvellous account of this situation in his review of the picture season of 1877:

> The exhibitions in Bond Street, indeed, are legion … In this case I saw by the outside announcements that a great religious work by Sir Noel Paton, RSA, LL.D., was on view within, and … that the picture had, on Thursday, May 10, been conveyed to Marlborough for inspection by H.R.H. the Prince of Wales. Here was a combination of attractions not to be resisted. A religious picture, painted by a baronet, a Royal Scottish Academician, and Doctor of Laws, and further consecrated by exposure to the awful gaze of royalty – a glimpse of such a work was certainly cheap at a shilling.[10]

James goes on to describe paying his fee, entering into the darkened space, with the picture spot-lit and surrounded by draperies, and having the picture explained to him by 'two blond gentleman' in the most insipid terms. This common display technique worked to differentiate – and even sacralize – the gallery space, and reviewers often commented on the experience of 'being guided through a maze of curtained corridors into an apartment pervaded by a dim, religious light, where, as they take their seats they find themselves instinctively talking in a whisper, and, if they are of the sterner sex, removing their hats'.[11] As the satiric tone of these descriptions suggests, however, some critics saw these tactics as artifice aimed at gullible viewers.

Perhaps aiming at this more sophisticated audience, galleries also used a less dramatic, but still effective, transition by creating spaces that looked like luxurious drawing rooms or art galleries in private homes. The Grosvenor Gallery, opened by Sir Coutts Lindsay in 1877, was perhaps the most famous example of this type of aristocratic appeal, and was particularly successful at masking its commercial underpinnings, as Henry James noted in 1877: 'In so far as his beautiful rooms in Bond Street are a commercial speculation, this side of their character has been gilded over, and dissimulated in the most graceful manner.'[12] It is important to note, however, that these different tactics were not mutually exclusive; the exhibition of Paton's religious picture that James described was at Dowdeswell's, one of the more prestigious galleries and home to Whistler's famous exhibition of 1884. As they shaped an identity balanced between the aesthetic and the retail, galleries needed both to create an atmosphere elevated above the ordinary shop and to appeal to the browsing eye.

Not surprisingly, then, it is just as galleries first clustered in Bond Street that we see the development of changing rosters of exhibitions throughout the year. In the early years, galleries' schedules were centred around multi-artist annual exhibitions, generally opening in the spring – to coincide with the Academy's opening – and early winter. As I have noted, Gambart's spring 'French Exhibitions' and his 'Winter Exhibitions' of British artists were early examples of this format. Other galleries adopted this system, including McLean's 'Annual Exhibition of Watercolour Drawings' beginning in 1865, and Goupil's 'Annual Exhibition of High-Class Continental Pictures' beginning in the early 1870s.[13] These early annual exhibitions either focused on Continental art as a counterpoint to the Academy's annual exhibition of British art, or provided a venue for British artists during the 'off' season, exhibiting sketches or water-colours. This model was based on the assumption that artists would save their major oil paintings for the Academy or other exhibiting societies, but they quickly began to send in more finished work to galleries.[14] In 1864 the *Art Journal* noted that 'It is now in the rooms of our most eminent picture-dealers that we must look for those productions of our painters that issue from their studios during the intervals between the exhibitions', and explained that the fashion for smaller pictures meant that artists produced more finished paintings throughout the year than in the days when 'the year was employed on a few works, all of which went to the annual exhibition'.[15]

Indeed, a certain amount of competition sprang up between the Academy and dealers. In the early 1850s, Gambart and other dealers reportedly tried to entice John Everett Millais to exhibit work with them instead of sending it to the Academy, but, according to his son, Millais refused, 'so long as any doubt remained as to the attitude of the Academy', to which he hoped to be elected an Associate.[16] In the early 1860s, Henry Wallis, Gambart's successor at the French Gallery, offered a £150 prize to the artist in his Winter Exhibitions who showed the best work 'painted expressly for the exhibition'.[17] By 1865, the exhibition catalogue for the French Gallery Winter Exhibition specified 'No Picture can be admitted unless contributed by the Painter, the composition being original, and it has not been before exhibited.'[18] And in 1862, in the most widely publicized example of circumventing the Academy, William Powell Frith decided to follow the success of *Life at the Seaside* (RA 1854) and *Derby Day* (RA 1858) by exhibiting his painting *The Railway Station* exclusively with the dealer Louis Flatou. By the early 1880s, it was a common complaint in Academy reviews that artists were sending their best pictures to private galleries.[19] But the Academy exhibition itself was also a site of struggle; many works shown in annual exhibitions were already the property of dealers, who might show the work in their galleries – at least to selected collectors – before the Academy opened.[20]

By the late 1860s and 1870s galleries began to supplement their annual exhibitions with rotating shows opening throughout the year, expanding the art season beyond the spring and summer season when the Academy and other exhibition societies held their large annual shows. At first, most were single picture shows of religious paintings or major works by popular artists, but over time there were increasing numbers of one-person shows. The *Art Journal* singled out an early example of this practice for praise in 1861. Reviewing the exhibition of the work of Thomas Faed at Agnew's, the critic recognized that its form was an innovation, and connected it to the more familiar practice of retrospective exhibitions of deceased artists:

> This is a step altogether in the right direction, and it cannot fail to lead to other assemblages of works of Art upon the same principle. It is both a wise and a gratifying tribute to the memory of a deceased artist, that his works should be assembled and formed into the most impressive of biographies … But there appears to be something, if possible, even more felicitous in the idea of grouping together the pictures which a living and working painter has produced; and while he is still in the midst of his professional labours.[21]

This kind of mid-career retrospective remained relatively rare, and tended to be mounted by larger galleries such as the Grosvenor, which held exhibitions of the work of living artists G.F. Watts (1882), Lawrence Alma-Tadema (1883), and John Everett Millais (1886).[22] More common were collections of recent work by a single artist, and by the turn of the century this kind of show had become a commonplace, as a critic for *Truth* complained in 1900: 'The "One-man show" is no longer a novelty. It has, in fact, been so persistently worked that it has lost much of the attractiveness it originally possessed.' He went on to offer satirical suggestions for new forms, including having multiple artists paint the same subject, imagining 'how London would flock to a Gallery where they could see a view of Windsor Castle, say, … painted by such antithetical artists as Mr. Benjamin W. Leader and Mr. John Singer Sargent, Mr. Sidney Cooper and Mr. J. McNeill Whistler'.[23]

Unless artists were especially prominent, however, single-artist shows were usually justified by a thematic hook, often topographical. As the *Saturday Review* noted in 1886, 'Exhibitions of the work of one man, unless he may have attained a world-wide reputation, are generally advertised under the pretext of illustrating some subject.'[24] For example, over the course of winter and spring 1886 one could see, 'Border Lands' by James Orrock at Dowdeswell's; 'Life in the Bavarian Alps' by Hubert Herkomer at the Fine Art Society; 'The Watering Places of the English Channel' by Tristam Ellis at the Goupil Gallery; and Walter Duncan's scenes of India at the Burlington Gallery. At least some viewers found this endless succession of views of the Lake District, Egypt, and Scotland monotonous – one critic offered the opinion that 'the land of the Pharaohs' had become 'almost as familiar as Piccadilly'[25] – and it seems almost as if the expectation of novelty predated the rapidly changing succession of styles and names that we associate with modern art, as the commercial gallery system created the conditions favouring the new and original without yet the right kind of art to fill it.

The financial model of most early galleries encouraged these kinds of well-advertised rotating exhibitions. Dealers' stock books, correspondence with artists, and auction records indicate that dealers generally purchased works of art outright from artists and at auction. Special exhibitions, however, typically worked on a different financial model. Sheridan Ford disparagingly revealed the mechanics of such travel-themed shows:

> The firm allows a painter a year ... or two ... to prepare the pictures ... He signs legal documents to produce at least forty finished canvases and cash advances to keep him going are made ... The firm pays exhibition and advertising expenses and charges a commission of twenty per cent on sales, pocketing whatever profits accrue from door receipts.[26]

A few things are worth noting here. It is a commission model, and while the dealer takes a significantly smaller percentage than would be the norm today, it was a higher amount than the 5 to 10 per cent more common at exhibition societies in the period. Profits were also generated by the dealer taking door receipts, generally charging a shilling – the same price as the Academy's entrance fee – for admission to these special shows. This was a major source of profit: the sale of daily tickets to the 'Art Patriotic Exhibition' at the French Gallery in 1855 netted £2,223; the first five weeks of the Grosvenor's 1879 season brought in £2,000 in admission charges, and the proprietors hoped to reach £5,000; and if the reported 80,000 visitors to Frith's *Railway Station* each paid their shilling, the total would have reached £4,000.[27] Admission charges also fostered an aura of exclusivity and differentiated the gallery from the shop, as a *Truth* critic's commentary on the subject pointed out in professed admiration for the rare exception: 'Messrs. Vokins, I observe, have the sense to open their exhibition free. Why a picture-dealer should charge people a shilling for inspecting his wares, any more than a hatter or boot-maker, I never could understand. The custom must surely frighten away possible buyers from the less important galleries.'[28] Admission charges for special exhibitions remained the norm until at least the turn of the century, although they seem to have become less common by the early years of the twentieth century.

If these larger patterns of geographic clustering and changing rosters of shows came to characterize all commercial galleries, they were also the means by which individual galleries attempted to distinguish themselves. In the second half of the essay, I will thus shift my focus slightly to the strategies galleries used to position themselves within an increasingly crowded field, including geographic affiliation, the history of individual spaces, exhibition catalogues, and naming.

As I have begun to suggest, geographic location was one of the most important such strategies. The most obvious pattern within the geographic clustering focuses on the Royal Academy, the dominant centre for the exhibition of contemporary art for most of the nineteenth century. As commercial galleries first sprouted up in the 1850s and 1860s, they clustered around Pall Mall and Trafalgar Square, home of the Academy, and when the Academy moved to Burlington House in 1867, a gradual shift is visible as they follow. If it begins as straightforward emulation, though, galleries' positions vis-à-vis the Academy became more complex over the course of the nineteenth and early twentieth centuries, as the Academy's prestige and power was challenged. One sign of this change was the emergence of 'outliers', such as the Chenil Gallery in Chelsea. Moving away from Mayfair seems to have been a self-conscious marker of difference; the Chenil showed Augustus John, Eric Gill, and Spencer Gore, artists setting themselves against artistic and social convention.[29] Remaining closer to the Academy might also signify a kind of allegiance. In 1906, Agnew's held the 'Exhibition of Independent Art of To-day' featuring the work of such modern artists as William Orpen, William Rothenstein, and Walter Sickert. *Truth* welcomed the show as a sign of rapprochement between the 'rebel' artists who had formed the New English Art Club (twenty years earlier) and the Academy, noting that the artists were now closer to Burlington House both topographically and stylistically, and calling Agnew's the 'bridge over which Messrs. P. Wilson Steer, and William Orpen, and George Henry, and Will Rothenstein can pass from the Egyptian Hall [home of the Dudley Gallery, where the NEAC had exhibited] to the palatial Galleries of the Royal Academy.'[30]

The Academy was not the only institution to exert a gravitational pull. Prestigious commercial galleries could also attract this kind of aspirational clustering. As can be seen in figure 2.2, there was a cluster of galleries on New Bond Street from 1880 forward. But in 1875 the only galleries here were the short-lived Marine Picture Gallery and the popular Doré Gallery. The picture changed in 1876 when the Fine Art Society opened, followed the next year by the fashionable Grosvenor Gallery. The latter in particular was an enormous success, perceived as a more refined and aesthetic alternative to the Academy. Over the next several years, other commercial galleries moved to this area: Dowdeswell's opened a new gallery at 133 New Bond Street, cheek by jowl with the Grosvenor, as did others including L'Art Gallery. There is an obvious utility to this: the Grosvenor Gallery drew substantial press attention and significant numbers of visitors (7,000 on the opening day of the first exhibition alone), who might then walk in to browse if something caught their eye.[31] Indeed, even before the Grosvenor opened, the *Art Journal* looked forward to this effect: 'When the Grosvenor Gallery is opened to the public, affording an excellent excuse for killing two birds with one stone, or rather of visiting two galleries for two shillings, it is to be hoped that the arctic paintings [at a nearby gallery] will secure their proper share of public attention.'[32] It is also worth noting that Dowdeswell's and L'Art Gallery seem to be aiming at slightly different factions of the Grosvenor's audience. Dowdeswell aimed to attract the aesthetic crowd, showing the French Impressionists in 1883 and Whistler – a regular and much-noticed exhibitor at the Grosvenor – in 1884 and 1886. (These shows, of course, were nestled among exhibitions of Birket Foster, William Quiller Orchardson, and Sutton Palmer's sketches of scenic Surrey.) In contrast, L'Art Gallery's name suggests an aspiration to an aura of fashion and sophistication, perhaps a little too obviously, as it seems to have closed after a single season.

The location of a gallery in relation to other exhibition spaces at any given point in time was obviously one significant part of shaping an identity and attracting an audience, but the history of a given space over time also carried significance. What things had been shown there in the past? Who organized the shows, and on what lines? One of the major fault lines was between fixed spaces with consistent identities over time and more transitory spaces available for rent. The signal difference was whether or not there was a dealer or firm that guaranteed the work on view. In the early years of the gallery, this was an absolutely crucial distinction, as dealers worked to counter fears of forgery and fraud in the art trade. But this practical assurance to consumers quickly took on other associations, as the meaning and value of one show leached into the works on view at other times. An exhibition of Flemish painting at the French Gallery prompted one reviewer to note that the space, 'with its recent associations, involuntarily subjects the Flemish artists to a comparison with their brethren and sisters from France – ... a comparison which they have scarcely strength to endure'.[33] In more positive light, when Gambart gave Barbara Bodichon her first solo exhibition, her friend George Eliot praised her achievement, writing, 'It is really a step to have your pictures hung together in a regular gallery where you have an illustrious predecessor.'[34] Eliot is referring to a recent show of David Cox's work at the Gallery, and suggesting that the space offered an imprimatur of quality derived from the work previously shown there. As the dealer assumed a gatekeeper role, his taste became a part of what his gallery offered its audience, promising a discerning eye for new art, and an assurance that the unworthy had been weeded out.

As the profession of the dealer gained more authority, a critical point of difference between galleries was how much the dealer was seen to be invested – both financially and symbolically – in the art. Of course, there had always been exhibition spaces for rent by artists, dealers, or societies, and almost all nineteenth-century galleries entered into complex arrangements with artists in which they shared the financial risk. But at the turn of the century we see this question of gate-keeping becoming increasingly important. For example, the Modern Gallery – operating by 1897 – had all the apparatus of an established gallery: a regular space on New Bond Street, an exhibition schedule published in *The Year's Art*, and a logo and house style for its catalogues. But the criteria for getting shown there were purely financial. A note at the bottom of the gallery's advertisement and exhibition schedule in *The Year's Art 1901* indicated 'The Modern Gallery may be rented for "Special" and "One-man" Exhibitions, and for At Homes, Soirees, Lectures, etc. For vacant dates and terms, address: Edward Freeman, Lessee and Secretary.'[35] In contrast, other firms began to suggest some sort of vetting procedure, as in an ad for Dowdeswell's that advised 'Artists desirous of exhibiting their work are invited to call *personally* with specimens.'[36] Reviewers seem to have taken note of the difference. A review of Herbert J. Finn's drawings at the Modern Gallery referred to the artist as 'tenanting' the space, while Dowdeswell's was singled out as one of the best galleries in London because it demonstrated a consistent taste and offered the viewer 'good guidance'.[37] Even if he did not personally like the work on view at Dowdeswell's, the reviewer for *Truth* felt 'quite disposed to admit that there may be another point of view, which I certainly should not were the pictures being shown at some galleries I could mention'.[38]

In addition to location and the reputation of the space and the dealer, galleries had another important tool for shaping audience expectation and experience: the exhibition catalogue. Where the meanings of a dealer's reputation or a gallery's location depended on accumulated knowledge and associations, the exhibition catalogue explicitly instructed viewers in how to look at all these new shows. In the 1850s and 1860s, they were essentially just pamphlets with lists of titles and artists. In some cases, the listings also included Academic titles and honours; for example in the catalogue for the Eighth Annual French Exhibition in 1861, Jean Léon Gérôme was identified as 'Pupil of Paul Delaroche; received third class medal (*histoire*), 1847; second class medal, 1848 and 1855; Chevalier of the Legion of Honour, 14th November, 1855; the first class medal at the Universal Exhibition, 1855.'[39] Like geographic clustering, this reliance on the Academic system of honours indicates that symbolic capital was still flowing through Academic institutions. Artists were quite aware of the financial advantages attached to Academic success; as Frederic Leighton commented upon his election as an ARA in 1864: 'I can't well … conceive it a *great* honour now – but it has material advantages as you see in the case of Gambart – I immediately inferred what you say from the fact of his buying my pictures so readily – he who never bought *anything* of mine before.'[40]

But the source of aesthetic consecration began to shift by the 1870s, as exhibition catalogues relied more and more heavily on quotations from the press to secure prestige. Many exhibition catalogues included a section entitled 'Opinions of the Press' or 'Press Extracts' in which they quoted notices of the exhibition from a wide range of daily papers, art journals, and even Society magazines.[41] Curiously, they don't always seem to mind if the reviews are good or bad – one Burlington Gallery catalogue actually reprinted a critic's opinion that the gallery had 'no significance whatever to lovers of art'; they are just indicating that they have been noticed by the press, a significant accomplishment in itself.[42]

During the 1870s–90s, catalogues also expanded from small folded pamphlets to more substantial booklets with covers, and began to use standard designs – fonts and logos – to create a consistent identity for the gallery across multiple shows. By the early twentieth century, nearly all galleries had some visual identifier. The Dutch Gallery, for example, began using a small tulip logo on its catalogue covers around 1905, and even when the dealer E.J. van Wisselingh dropped the name the 'Dutch Gallery' in favour of naming the gallery after himself, he retained the tulip logo on catalogues up until 1914, continuing the association with Holland, and providing a visual cue of continuity.[43]

As catalogues became more book-like in format, the somewhat indiscriminate reprinting of a wide range of press coverage began to be replaced in the mid-1880s and 1890s by single-authored explanatory prefaces. This practice had existed earlier, as, for example, in Tom Taylor's detailed discussion of *Derby Day* in the catalogue published by Gambart to publicise the engraving.[44] But it began to be common even for more run-of-the-mill exhibitions and events. The Fine Art Society seems to have been a leader in this practice: exhibition catalogues from shows in the late 1870s and early 1880s included explanatory notes or memoirs by well-known critics and artists, such as 'Notes by Mr. Ruskin on his collection of drawings by the late J.M.W. Turner RA, exhibited at the Fine Art Society's galleries' in 1878, and 'Notes by F. G. Stephens on a collection of drawings and woodcuts by Thomas Bewick, exhibited at the Fine Art Society's rooms, 1880.'[45] The historic stature of these (deceased) artists and the credentials of the critics led most reviewers to grant an educational purpose to these treatises and the gallery itself. As the *Art Journal* noted in its review of a Samuel Palmer show in 1881:

> Commercial considerations do not appear to be the sole controlling motive of the exhibitions held from time to time in this gallery. An educational purpose palpably asserts itself on every occasion … For example, with every exhibition comes an annotated catalogue, and generally a memoir of the artist whose works are gathered together, and the visitor is thus enabled on the spot to satisfy himself as to the merits of the works on view. In conformity with so admirable a precedent, Mr. F. G. Stephens has on the present occasion furnished us with a judiciously condensed life of Samuel Palmer, and with certain critical and explanatory notes on his pictures … not only well-written, but almost exhaustive, in their character. To these we would refer the visitor, satisfied that he will find in them whatever is worth saying of the deceased master.[46]

As this last recommendation suggests, such writing threatened to usurp the function of art criticism itself, and as this model of explanatory preface was extended more broadly to contemporary artists, critics chafed at the heavy-handed advertising plugs that could result. After offering praise for the Fine Art Society's exhibition of the work of Giovanni Costa in 1882, the reviewer for the *Portfolio* concluded: 'The descriptive catalogue of the exhibition is of that effusively laudatory description, exhausting the flower-garden of "aesthetic" diction, which appears nowadays to be in vogue. The name of George Fleming appended as the writer is, we understand, in every sense a pseudonym.'[47] Even more direct attacks on the practice appeared as it became more prevalent. The reviewer for *Truth* in 1894 complained 'this surely is the age of art criticism made easy' as shows were accompanied by biographical notices and critical judgement, and warned 'I do not think that it can be considered advisable to ladle out appreciative criticism of this kind with the picture exhibition catalogues, for whilst it is not calculated to stimulate independent praise of the artist concerned, it is not unlikely to make a critic's deprecatory judgment of their works all the more emphatic.'[48] Years before Fry wrote his famous preface 'explaining' Post-Impressionism or Wyndham Lewis published his Vorticist manifesto, then, viewers were accustomed to having the art on view explained to them, and defended, often in very partisan terms.

Exhibition catalogues could also be used to make art more accessible in other than artistic terms. A catalogue for a show of sketches of Australia, New Zealand, Canada, and the United States at the Burlington Gallery included information on where the best shooting was to be had, and one critic identified the intended audience as 'sportsmen who delight in pictures of hunting in all parts of the globe, [rather] than … the usual visitors to picture galleries'.[49] When Arthur Lucas exhibited Herbert Schmalz's religious picture *The Great Awakening*, the catalogue preface by the Rev. John Watson interpreted the picture as 'a work of didactic Art, reinforcing faith and ministering comfort in the straits of life' and encouraged the audience to use the painting as a personal devotional experience.[50] These are rather extreme examples of a larger trend toward dividing the audience for art into niche markets; as a critic for the magazine *Truth* noted in 1907, 'each of the many galleries has an artistic convention of its own to which it always adheres, and which its particular public no doubt regards as the only genuine brand of art'.[51] Such specializations attracted different classes of viewers, and critics sometimes commented on the social tone of the galleries they reviewed; the *Magazine of Art* described the audience at the Doré Gallery as 'country cousins', while the *World* noted the 'chic' private view at the Salon Parisien in 1885 was 'a smart reunion by the French colony in London' with 'a wonderful show of "fashions"'.[52]

The axis of distinction invoked in this comparison – from provincial country cousins to chic French cosmopoles – points to one final strategy by which galleries created their identity or 'brand': the choice of name. One main – and still familiar – strategy was to name the gallery after the dealer; for example, Agnew's, Arthur Tooth's, McLean's, Dowdeswell's, and many others. This strategy emphasized reliability through the reputation of the professional dealer, who invested his prestige and accumulated symbolic capital to secure the aesthetic and economic value of the work of art.[53] A second very common and perhaps more surprising strategy was to claim some sort of international identification. Although the expansion of the late Victorian art market has generally been attributed to a new class of mercantile patrons and their commitment to the work of living British artists, cosmopolitan appeal was critical to the gallery system from its earliest incarnation, when Gambart named his new space the French Gallery. Other dealers followed his lead in trying to distinguish themselves in this way, and a partial and uneven list of such galleries in the late nineteenth century includes the Scandinavian Gallery, the Flemish Gallery, the Belgian Gallery, Salon Parisien, the Continental Gallery, the Japanese Gallery, and the Dutch Gallery.[54]

These names also called attention to the international nature of the goods on display, and the connections between London's art market and other economic centres. Dealers increasingly advertised their connections in other countries, listing foreign branches of their firm even in advertisements directed at the local market. As Anne Helmreich's essay in this volume demonstrates, dealers sent pictures through these various markets in search of a buyer. Reviewers quickly picked up on this aspect of the market. Writing in the *Saturday Review* in 1874, a critic reviewing the many winter exhibitions of foreign art on view, complained 'In these and other like Galleries the contributions often meet the eye as old acquaintances. Pictures in these days are accustomed to make the tour of Europe; they pass from hand to hand as a sort of paper currency, to be changed, on favourable occasions into gold or silver coin.'[55]

As the frank modernity of this last quote reminds us, the second half of the nineteenth century witnessed the development of much of the apparatus of the commercial gallery system as it still exists today: the idea of a named space hosting a changing series of exhibitions; the role of the dealer as consecrator; the symbiotic relationship with the press; exhibition catalogues with prefaces; and, toward the end of the period, a move toward consistent gallery specializations. The logic of the system also remains familiar, with its geography of centre and fringe, its cultivation of sub-publics and rhetoric of exclusivity. In other words, many of the commercial structures and practices that we identify as quintessentially modern were integral parts of the Victorian artistic field. This fact is one part of the ground on which histories of Victorian art and taste need to be based. The muted press reaction to Durand-Ruel's exhibitions of French Impressionist painting in the early 1870s is more comprehensible against the backdrop of the frequent exhibition of foreign art in rented commercial spaces, all clamouring to be noticed by the press. Whistler's famous innovations in gallery design and publicity become logical marketing moves when read against the increasingly (and newly) competitive gallery culture of the early 1880s. Reading these art-historical events against an emergent gallery system does not detract from individual originality, innovation, or even genius, but instead locates such figures within the cultural field upon which they acted, providing a richer context for understanding and evaluating the history of Victorian art.

Notes

I would like to thank the Paul Mellon Centre for British Art, the Getty Research Library, and Bowdoin College for their generous support of the research for this essay.

1 Bourdieu, *Field of Cultural Production*.
2 Tickner, 'English Modernism in the Cultural Field'.

3 Altick, *Shows of London*; Lippincott, *Selling Art in Georgian London*; Pears, *Discovery of Painting*; Codell, 'Artists' Professional Societies'.

4 Fletcher, 'Creating the French Gallery'.

5 'Mr. Morby's Gallery', *Art Journal*, November 1860, p. 349.

6 'Pictures of the Year', *Saturday Review*, 15 June 1867, p. 753.

7 Advertisement, *The Year's Art 1883*, p. 5.

8 'Art Notes: An Artistic Hotch-Pot', *Truth*, 22 February 1905, p. 502.

9 'Society of British Artists', *Art Journal*, May 1863, p. 93.

10 Henry James, 'The Picture Season in London, 1877', *Galaxy*, 1877; reprinted in James, *The Painter's Eye*, pp. 137–8.

11 'Art Notes', *Truth*, 7 February 1895, p. 357.

12 Henry James, 'The Picture Season in London, 1877', *Galaxy*, 1877; reprinted in James, p. 139. On the ways the Grosvenor Gallery established this tone see: Colleen Denney, 'The Grosvenor Gallery as Palace of Art: An Exhibition Model', in *Grosvenor Gallery*, eds. Casteras and Denney, pp. 9–36.

13 *Annual Exhibition of Water-colour Drawings: 1865: The First* (London: T. McLean, 1865); *Catalogue of the Fifth Annual Exhibition of High-class Continental Pictures …* (London: Messrs Goupil & Company, 1879).

14 'The Winter Exhibition, No. 121 Pall Mall', *Art Journal*, January 1855, p. 31.

15 'Mr. Morby's Art-Gallery, Cornhill', *Art Journal*, March 1864, p. 80.

16 Millais, *Sir John Everett Millais*, I, pp. 215–16.

17 'Minor Topics of the Month', *Art Journal*, January 1864, p. 29.

18 *Thirteenth Annual Winter Exhibition* (London: French Gallery, 1865).

19 'The Picture Galleries', *Saturday Review*, 5 May 1883, p. 566; 'Scrutator', 'Chicken and Champagne in the Studio', *Truth*, 19 March 1885, p. 452.

20 On 4 April 1864, Gambart wrote to Gillott offering to show him 'some of the best Pictures going to the Royal Academy'. Quoted in Maas, *Gambart*, p. 168.

21 'Minor Topics of the Month', *Art Journal*, December 1861, p. 377.

22 Allen Staley, '"Art is Upon the Town!" The Grosvenor Gallery Winter Exhibitions', in *Grosvenor Gallery*, eds. Casteras and Denney, pp. 59–74.

23 'Art Notes', *Truth*, 8 March 1900, p. 593.

24 'Art Exhibitions', *Saturday Review*, 13 November 1886, p. 654.

25 Unattributed press cutting in *Exhibition of Water Colour Drawings of Egypt by R. Murdoch Wright* (London: Modern Gallery, 1899), National Art Library, London.

26 Ford, *Art*, p. 21.

27 'The Art Patriotic Exhibition', *The Times*, 6 October 1856, p. 9; Newall, *The Grosvenor Gallery Exhibitions*, p. 34. 'Minor Topics of the Month', *Art Journal*, October 1862, p. 210.

28 'Scrutator', 'The Picture Shows', *Truth*, 26 February 1885, p. 334.

29 On the Chenil Gallery, see Helmreich and Holt, 'Marketing Bohemia'.

30 'New Art in an Old Gallery', *Truth*, 22 February 1906, p. 463.

31 Newall, p. 14.

32 Charles E. Pascoe, 'Art in London', *Art Journal* (New York edition), March 1877, p. 95.

33 'First Exhibition of the Flemish School of the Fine Arts in London', *Art Journal*, January 1857, p. 34.

34 George Eliot to Mme Eugène Bodichon, 27 July 1859. Haight, ed., *The George Eliot Letters*, p. 124.

35 Advertisement, *The Years Art 1901*, unpaginated.

36 *The Year's Art 1910*, p. 13.

37 *Daily News*, 22 November 1898; quoted in *London Art Criticisms on Herbert J. Finn's Drawings Exhibition at the Modern Gallery* (London: Modern Gallery, 1898); 'Art Notes', *Truth*, 22 May 1907, p. 1291.

38 'Art Notes', *Truth*, 22 May 1907, p. 1291.

39 *Eighth Annual Exhibition in London of Pictures, the Contributions of Artists of the French and Flemish Schools* (London: French Gallery, 1861), p. 8.

40 Undated letter from Frederic Leighton to Frederic George Stephens, MS Don.E.69, Bodleian Library; quoted in Maas, *Gambart*, pp. 172–3.

41 For example, the *Seventh Winter Exhibition of the Belgian Gallery* (London: Belgian Gallery, 1878) featured extracts from the *Illustrated London News*, *Pictorial World*, *Art Journal*, *Magazine of Art*, and *Queen*. The *Annual Exhibition of Paintings from the Paris Salon* (London: Continental Gallery, 1895) included 'Press Extracts' from the *Times*, *Morning Post*, *Truth*, *Vanity Fair*, *Echo*, *Observer*, *Glasgow Evening News*, *Daily Chronicle*, *Star*, *Whitehall Review*, *Liverpool Mercury*, *Court Circular* and *Queen*.

42 *Exhibition of Australian and New Zealand, American and Canadian Oil Paintings and Water Colour Drawings* (London: Burlington Gallery, n.d.).

43 *Exhibition of Sketches by A.S. Forrest; the West Indes* (London: The Dutch Gallery, 1905); *Exhibition of Oil Paintings, Water Colour Drawings, and Medals by John Cooke* (London: E.J. van Wisselingh Gallery, 1914).

44 *Mr. W. P. Frith's Celebrated Picture of the "Derby Day"* (London: E. Gambart & Co., n.d.).

45 *Notes by Mr. Ruskin on His Collection of Drawings by the Late J.M.W. Turner, R.A., Exhibited at the Fine Art Society's Galleries* (London: printed at the Chiswick Press, for the Fine Art Society, 1878); *Notes by F. G. Stephens on a Collection of Drawings and Woodcuts by Thomas Bewick, Exhibited at the Fine Art Society's Rooms, 1880* (London: The Fine Art Society, 1881).

46 'Art Notes and Reviews', *Art Journal*, December 1881, p. 377; cited in Faberman, '"Best Shop in London"', pp. 147–8.

47 'Art Chronicle', *Portfolio*, January 1882, p. 132.

48 'Art Notes', *Truth*, 22 February 1894, p. 438.

49 *Exhibition of Australian and New Zealand, American and Canadian Oil Paintings and Water Colour Drawings* (London: Burlington Gallery, n.d.), p. 29.

50 *The Great Awakening by Herbert Schmalz: An Interpretation by Ian MacLaren (The Rev. John Watson MA, DD)* (London: Arthur Lucas, [1898]).

51 'Art Notes', *Truth*, 22 May 1907, p. 1290.

52 *Magazine of Art*, 1880, p. 480; *World*, 21 January 1885; quoted in *Collection of Pictures by Jan Van Beers* (London: Salon Parisien, [1885]), pp. 38–9.

53 Bourdieu, 'The Production of Belief', *Field of Cultural Production*, p. 7.

54 For more on cosmopolitanism and the gallery system, see: Fletcher, 'The Grand Tour on Bond Street'.

55 'Winter Exhibitions', *Saturday Review*, 19 December 1874, p. 796.

3

The Goupil Gallery at the intersection between London, Continent, and Empire

Anne Helmreich

Introduction

Fourteen men are gathered together, posed in two rows (figure 3.1). All the men, carefully suited and wearing crisp collars and ties, stare directly and seriously at the camera, communicating quiet confidence amidst the elegant spaces of the gallery hinted at by the gilt framed paintings visible on walls and the small statuette at the far right. The man seated in the centre of the first row, his arms crossed across his chest, is clearly the focal point of the image and the authoritarian centre as his colleagues on either side lean slightly away from him in gestures of deference. Positioned just behind him in the second row is a man in a military style jacket with epaulettes and metal buttons; 'The Goupil Gallery' embossed on his cap. His uniformed presence, amidst the ordered rows, replete with brand name, makes clear that this is not a social group portrait but that of a corporation – individuals who have come together as employer and employees for the purpose of producing and selling a product, in this case, art.

The seated gentleman at the centre of the image is recognizable as David Croal Thomson, depicted by Philip Wilson Steer in a portrait inscribed 1895 (Tate Britain). At that date Thomson was the manager of the Goupil Gallery, the London branch of Boussod, Valadon & Co., a multi-national print publisher and fine art dealer. The painted portrait commemorated the friendship between Steer and Thomson; the dealer had organized the artist's first one-person exhibition

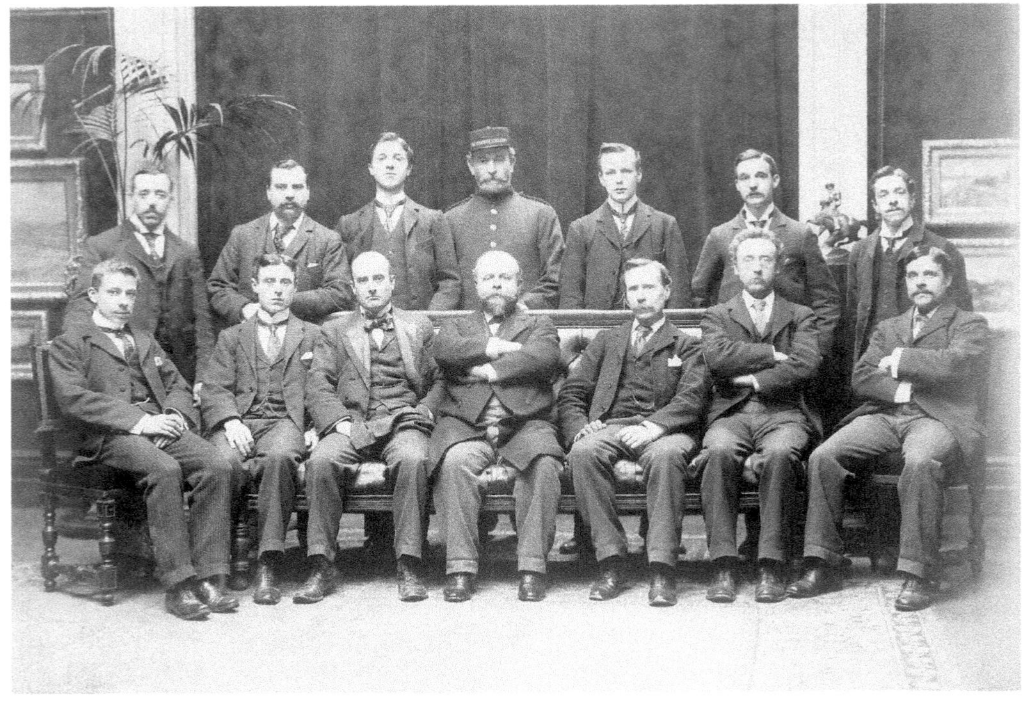

3.1 Goupil Gallery Staff, c.1890–1911.

in 1894, held at the gallery's relatively new premises at 5, Regent Street. The group photograph, one of a series showing Thomson with his staff as well as the gallery itself, was most likely taken upon the occasion of the gallery's relocation to Regent Street from 116 and 117 New Bond Street.

The distinctly corporate appearance of the Goupil Gallery raises questions about the nature of buying and selling art at the turn of the last century. To what degree was such a formation typical or atypical for London at this moment? What advantages or disadvantages did such a configuration have in the marketplace? The London Goupil Gallery is an excellent case study for posing such questions because while it began its tenure as part of a larger financial company, after 1901 it was a singular entity, owned by William Marchant, who had succeeded Thomson as manager in 1898, having previously spent twelve years in the employment of Boussod, Valadon & Co., both in Paris and in London.[1] This essay will investigate the strategies deployed by the Goupil Gallery in both incarnations, which also necessitates considering the networks in which both the gallery and art dealing were embedded. The Goupil Gallery's location in London was essential, it will be shown, for the efficacy of these networks. London, by the end of the nineteenth century had developed a reputation for internationalization (if not globalization), an efficient market economy, a transformed shopping and leisure experience, a burgeoning mass market, and an infrastructure enhanced by technological innovation that made it attractive as a key locus for the ever expanding art market.

History of the Goupil Gallery, London

The Goupil Gallery was originally a branch of the Maison Goupil, which began in the 1820s as the brainchild of Joseph-Henri Rittner, a print seller and print publisher who initially worked for the firm of Giraldon-Bovinet and then collaborated with David-Ferdinand d'Ostervald as he began his own firm. He and Adolphe Goupil entered into partnership on 23 March 1829, with business premises at 12 Boulevard Montmartre. The resulting firm earned a distinctive niche in the marketplace by offering wares of some of the leading artists of the era: Paul Delaroche, Ary Scheffer, and Léopold Robert.[2] In 1841, Rittner passed away and Goupil replaced his business partner with Théodore Vibert, the son-in-law of engraver Jean-Pierre-Marie Jazet, who executed works after Horace Vernet. A third partner, Alfred Mainguet, was added in 1846; in 1856 he was replaced by Léon Boussod who was Goupil's sole partner, Vibert having died in 1850. René Valadon was added as a partner in 1878 and in 1884 the firm was renamed Boussod, Valadon & Co. with Adolphe still participating in the business until 1886 when Etienne Boussod (Léon's son) also entered the partnership. In 1893, both Adolphe Goupil and Léon Boussod died and four years later the business was restructured, separating the art gallery – known as Boussod, Valadon & Co. and under the direction of Etienne Boussod and Renée Valadon – from the publishing firm – initially Jean Boussod, Manzi, Joyant and Company (in recognition of additional partners who had entered the business) and then Manzi, Joyant and Company. The latter ended their business operations in 1917 and the gallery ceased in 1919.[3] As a business, Goupil was technically a private copartnery as opposed to a joint stock company, but its extensive operations endowed it with the appearance of a corporation.

Its scale and volume were characteristic of the nineteenth century and the advent of mass production and were emulated by other print-selling and print publishing firms as well as commercial art galleries. The Goupil firm quickly built up its business, recognizing that art was now securely perceived as a commodity that could be exchanged in the marketplace for a price agreed upon by buyer and seller. Indeed, the print trade was distinctly retail in that prices were typically set in advance as opposed to the negotiations associated with sales of easel painting. But art retained some aspects of the mystique of gifting in that notions of fiscal and aesthetic value were shaped by context – for example, mode of presentation, associations attached to the art object, and the ardency by which the dealer pursued a particular client or artist.

The French firm utilized a number of strategies to create value and to grow their business into a corporate network. They worked with leading artists who had considerable public recognition because of their careers as exhibitors, primarily at the annual Salon. The chief among these was Jean-Léon Gérôme; according to Hélène Lafont-Couturier, Gérôme was particularly profitable 'between 1865 and 1885', when 'the firm was flourishing ... in all sectors, and the artist was at the peak of his popularity', which allowed for speculation in his paintings to the benefit of the firm.[4] In 1887, following the reorganization of the partnership, the firm assessed its holdings, selling off works that had failed to find buyers and, in an attempt to re-gauge the market, ending its contract with William-Adolphe Bouguereau, and signing on the naturalist Léon Lhermitte.[5]

The firm invested in print technology and the means necessary for mass production and marketing. When the firm began, it used the extant techniques of lithography, engraving, etching, mezzotint, and aquatint. In the 1860s and 1870s, it took up the newly available photomechanical processes.[6] These mass-produced goods reached the public through the firm's galleries and shops, but the business was not exclusively vertically owned and managed; goods were also distributed to other print sellers and art dealers.

Closely tied to the firm's establishment of retail premises was its international expansion. Beginning at mid-century, branches opened in important urban centres, including Berlin, London, New York, and Brussels, and the firm absorbed Vincent Van Gogh's gallery in The Hague in 1861. This strategy was emulated by its competition: the Dutch firm of van Wisselingh had businesses in Amsterdam, Paris, and, by 1892, London; the latter called, appropriately enough, The Dutch Gallery. Scottish dealer Daniel Cottier had branches in London, Sydney, and New York. Colnaghi, by the early twentieth century, expanded into the North American market via a close relationship with Knoedler and Company. Arthur Tooth & Sons had a New York branch from around 1900 to 1924. Thomas Agnew and Sons, at various points in the history of the firm, had branches in Manchester, London, Liverpool, Berlin, Paris, and New York; the latter opened in 1925 despite concerns that relations with American dealers on whom they had previously relied might be damaged.[7]

The pattern of international growth of commercial art firms follows the pathways carved out by the development of international finance. London and Paris, over the course of the nineteenth and early twentieth centuries, competed to become the leading international financial centre, with London emerging the winner. By 1870, when the expansion of the international art market began in earnest, New York and Berlin were rising stars, while Amsterdam was in decline although still significant.[8]

The networked model developed by Goupil and others allowed the private copartnery to achieve a hitherto unprecedented scale, which required extensive coordination over great distances and thus heavy reliance on the managerial expertise of the branch managers who were also expected to function as art-historical experts in order to attract business to their galleries. Thomson, for example, in addition to cultivating relationships with contemporary British artists such as Steer, garnered a reputation as an expert on the Barbizon School by both exhibiting the work of these artists and publishing extensively on the topic. Indeed, he is responsible for coining the term 'Barbizon School'.

The retail spaces for Goupil's Paris main house and its international branches were strategically located, revealing a keen understanding of cultural geography. In Paris, the workshops were relocated from rue Chaptal to Asniéres in 1869; the retail premises were located at 19 Boulevard Montmartre, with additional sites at rue Chaptal (1860–93), Place de l'Opéra (1870–84), and 24 Boulevard des Capucines (beginning in 1893), in the fashionable shopping district; thus the working spaces of the business were severed from the exhibiting spaces so that production and display of goods became distinct processes.

In London, agent Henry Gutekunst opened a branch in 1857 which was first located in the Strand, in keeping with its focus on the print and publishing trade. Firms such as Ackermann's Repository of Arts had already established the viability of selling prints and books, artists' supplies, and other items of visual display. In the 1870s, under the management of Charles Obach, the Goupil firm opened a new premise on Bedford Street where they installed a picture gallery. The latter points to the firm's desire to adopt existing practices of exhibition culture to market and to sell their wares. The firm was entering the field late when compared to the activities of their competition such as Ernest Gambart who had already, by the mid-century, organized a system of rotating exhibitions to feature British and Continental art.

By 1883, the firm moved from the Strand to New Bond Street, a social-geographically coded decision that anticipated the relocation of the Paris main gallery to the Boulevard des Capucines in that New Bond Street was located in a highly fashionable shopping district and was emerging as the heart of the luxury trade and the art market. New Bond Street already housed Goupil's leading competitors, including Agnew's, Dowdeswells, the Fine Art Society, and the Grosvenor Gallery. Mrs. E.T. Cook, in her guidebook *Highways and Byways of London* (1903), enthusiastically describes the lavish shop-fronts and window displays, with overtones of imperial spectacle: '"The wealth of Ormus and of Ind" that the shops of Regent Street and Bond Street display, their gold embroideries and wonderfully woven silks, tending to make a kleptomaniac out of the very elect, – these it would be hard to beat.'[9] Her account is of a piece with the representation of London as 'spectacle, marketplace, and commodity'.[10]

In the following year David Croal Thomson, a Scotsman who had previously located to London to work for *The Year's Art* and the *Art Journal*, became the London representative for Boussod, Valadon & Co. and the first director of the Goupil Gallery. Thomson, through his editorial work, had experience in dealing with critics which became increasingly relevant as the firm expanded their roster of rotating exhibitions and added contemporary British art to their repertoire.[11] Thomson was able to use the pages of the *Art Journal* to improve the reputations of artists in his stable, such as George Clausen and James McNeill Whistler, whom he brought into the Goupil fold, as well as the gallery itself.

Around 1893, the firm relocated again, to 5 Regent Street, where it acquired larger premises (figure 3.2). Painter William Roberts recalled the gallery around the turn of the century:

> The Gallery interior was lined throughout with a dark crimson fabric that made a good background to the Steers, Whistlers, Sickerts and Johns hanging on the walls. The entrance and corridor to the inner rooms were guarded by a bespectacled grey-bearded old man in a long faded green overcoat; the finishing touch to this attire was a hat with a shiny peak, his symbol of office, it would seem … At the far end of the Goupil's main gallery, a stair led to an upper room also decorated in dark-toned crimson. It was here that selected paintings were shown to important clients. There was a small round window in this room that enabled Marchant to see and hear what went on the gallery below, without being seen himself. He once referred to the Goupil, meaningly, as a 'regular Whispering Gallery', and he was anxious not to miss a 'Whisper'.[12]

Roberts' description as well as contemporaneous photographs reveal that the Goupil Gallery was luxuriously appointed, fusing together the accoutrements of a wealthy domestic environment with those of a museum or civic gallery. Thus the physical display conveyed a message of status and taste intended to curry favour with potential clients.

In 1897, Thomson left the firm to take a position with their competitors, Agnew's, and William Marchant became manager. Shortly thereafter, in 1901, as the Paris main house entered financial difficulties, Marchant acquired the London business; the terms allowed him to purchase the premises and its furniture as well as a portion of the stock, some of which was still owned by the Paris main house, for whom Marchant functioned as agent, and some of which Marchant sold

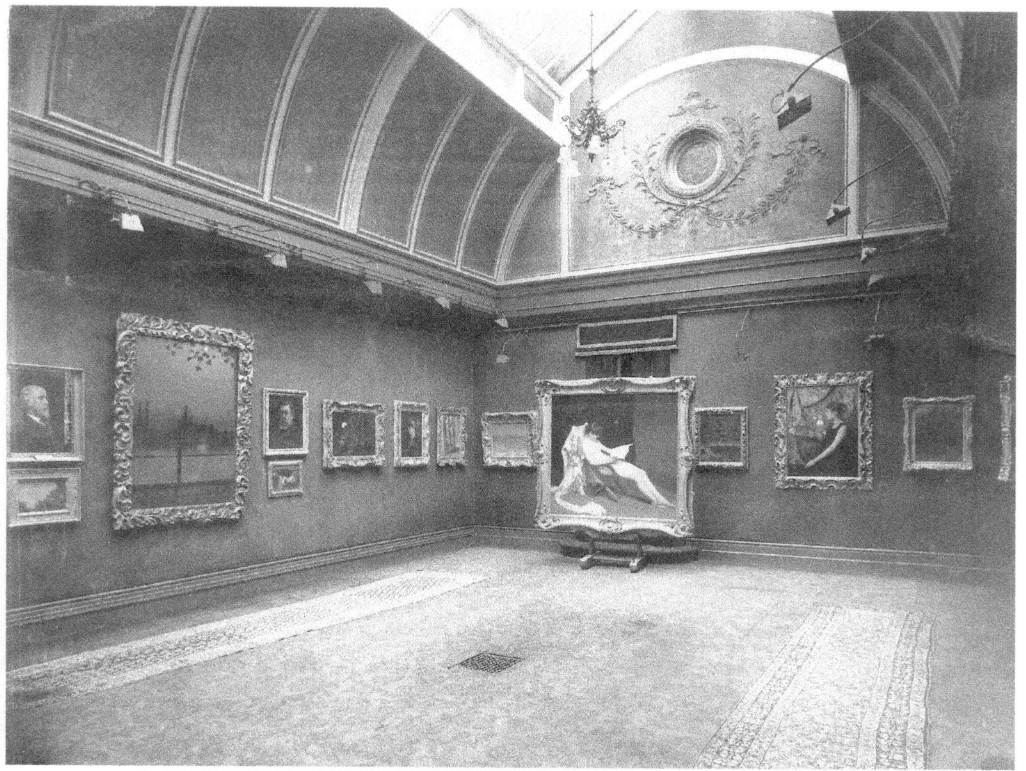

3.2 Goupil Gallery Interior, n.d.

on his own account. For five years he was permitted to refer to his firm as the 'sole agents for the United Kingdom and Ireland of Boussod, Valadon, and Co., successors to Goupil and Co.' Thus the business was converted from a limited partnership to an independent business.

However, several years later Marchant was forced to defend his use of the name 'The Goupil Gallery' in court as Boussod, Valadon & Co. brought an action against him for retaining the title 'Goupil', particularly as they were seeking to re-establish their presence as print publishers in the Strand. The court found in favour of Marchant, allowing him to retain the name of Goupil, which was affixed above the shop in iron letters, arguing that the name was part of the freehold and that 'it was impossible now to suggest that the name Goupil Gallery had not become associated with the defendant's business as carried on there'.[13] This ruling underscores the significance accorded to the names of businesses as brand identities that helped to distinguish them from ordinary retail spaces, as Pamela Fletcher discusses in this collection. The expertise and taste associated with the individual agent, for example, Thomson or Marchant, is now considered inseparable from the space itself, Goupil. That is, the court was allowing for the associative value accrued over time in association with a name – Goupil – to remain in place and forever fixed to the physical locale, a strategy particularly resonant within the luxury trade.

Upon Marchant's death in 1925 his wife Cicely Marchant assumed the business, infusing it with capital by creating a new company 'The Goupil Gallery Ltd.' for which shares were offered. During her tenure she retained the practice of the regular Goupil Gallery Salons, group shows that leavened the offering of one-person exhibitions, a practice that her husband had inaugurated in December 1906 at the point his contract with the Paris house terminated.

Networks

This panoply of strategies by which Goupil built up its business – name brand goods, investment in new technologies, strategically placed and designed retail spaces, an international distribution scheme, rotating exhibitions, and close ties to the art press – was intimately connected to its ability to deploy networks of exchange. These networks took copious advantage of its location in London, a locale with easy access to other distribution points due to its inter-connectedness via rail and shipping routes as well as communication technologies.

As a branch of the Goupil network, the London firm was able to participate in the circulation of goods from Paris to the branches and from branch to branch. Lafont-Couturier describes how prints were produced in Asnières and then distributed to the various outlets, supported by 'warehouses … established throughout the world (Alexandria, Dresden, Geneva, Zurich, Athens, Barcelona, Copenhagen, Florence, Havana, Melbourne, Sydney, Warsaw, Johannesburg …)'.[14]

The stockbooks of the Maison Goupil, now held by the Getty Research Institute, also reveal a history of mobility with respect to oil paintings. In the column marked 'Vendeur' (Seller) are typically found a series of capital letters, often struck through. These capital letters suggestively align with the names of the cities in which the main branches were located – B (Berlin), L (Londres), L.H. (La Haye) – or the Parisian locations – C (rue Chaptal) – and their sometimes rapid succession in the accounting of a single work of art implies that works travelled extensively before a successful sale (figure 3.3). In sum, for singular works of art Goupil moved them in search of a market whereas for reproductions they could saturate multiple markets simultaneously.

When the London branch held its first exhibition in 1875, it capitalized on its connection to the main house in Paris and the branch in The Hague in order to offer, as Vincent enthusiastically described to his brother, 'some splendid pictures:

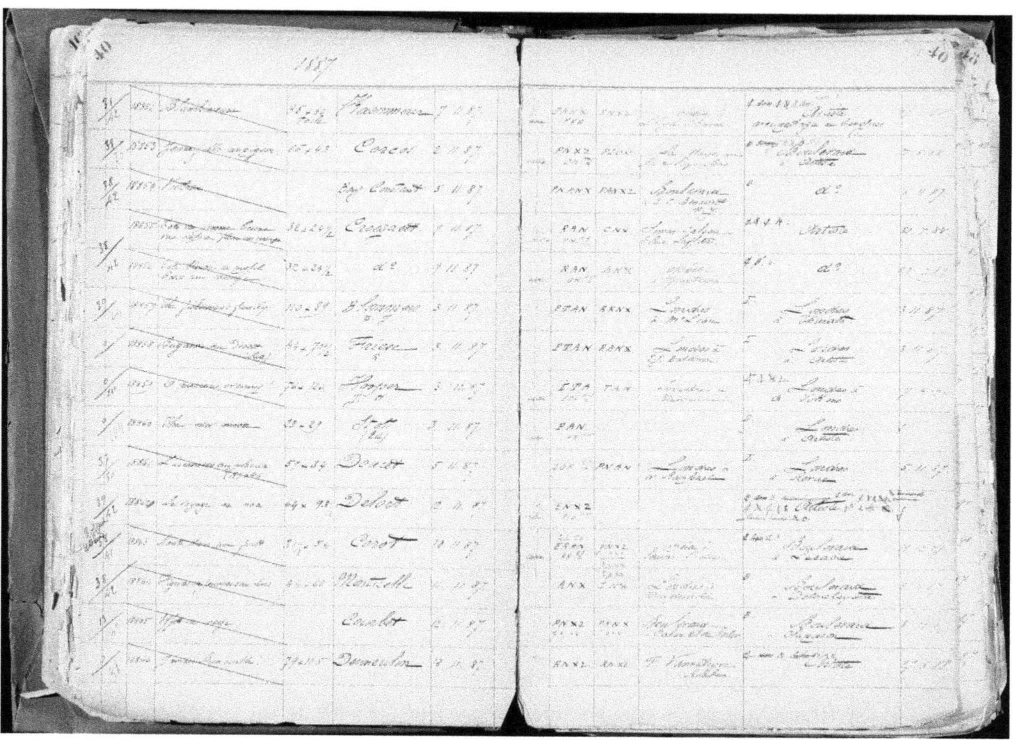

3.3 Goupil & Cie and Boussod, Valadon & Co. Records, Book 12, 1887–91, p. 40.

Jules Dupré, Michel, Daubigny, Maris, Israëls, Mauve, Bisschop, etc. In April we are going to have an exhibition. Mr. Boussod [in Paris] has promised to send us the best things available.'[15] Early reviews indicate that the firm was definitively associated with Continental art; *The Times*'s notice in 1877 snidely described the goods for sale as:

> the most conspicuous successes of the Paris *Salon*, as if painting was gradually bringing down its ambitions and aspirations to the conditions of patronage, and to be renouncing, all but entirely, large dimensions and epic themes in favour of the scale and subjects suited not only to small houses, but to the smaller rooms of small houses.[16]

In addition to French art, the firm garnered a reputation for modern Dutch art; *The Times* concisely reported that 'The successors of Messrs. Goupil (Messrs. Boussod, Valadon and Co.) have every opportunity for forming good collections, whether of this or of any other modern school, and their Dutch pictures are excellent of their kind', citing such artists as Josef Israëls, the Maris brothers, Mauve, and De Bock.[17]

The exhibition history of Goupil London reveals that Thomson's appointment coincided, not incidentally, with the firm's expansion of its roster to include British artists such as Tristam Ellis and A.D. Peppercorn. This direction was reinforced by exhibitions featuring British scenery, as in the case of a display devoted to 'The Norfolk and Suffolk Rivers & Broads' (June 1886); publications concerning British art, as in the case of *English Art in the Public Galleries of London*, and prints after works by British artists such as Luke Fildes.

When part of a larger corporate entity, the Goupil Gallery London had access to a relatively large pool of goods and could benefit from the expertise of other employees in the system. It never, however, exercised a monopoly position, even with regard to the goods in which it specialized, such as the Barbizon and Hague schools or the British and French Impressionists, because of the high level of competition in art dealing in London as well as the multiple exhibiting opportunities afforded by artists' societies. Moreover, dealers, including Goupil, often sold to other dealers, indicating a relative permeability between competitors. In addition, artists would simultaneously exhibit with dealers and artists' societies; indeed, the system encouraged such cross-over activity as the accolades accrued through artists' societies (medals and prizes) could help to raise the fiscal value of their art in the commercial marketplace.

Nevertheless, the corporate network represented a distinct advantage to Goupil in that risk was distributed across the system and thus not borne excessively by any one branch. While major decision making was conducted by the central office, local branches had a relative degree of autonomy that allowed them to cultivate local tastes and talents, although the relationship between the centre and the periphery was occasionally fraught with tension as revealed in Thomson's correspondence.[18] That the branch managers of the Goupil firm worked cooperatively as need demanded is exemplified by the history of James McNeill Whistler's *Arrangement in Grey and Black: Portrait of the Painter's Mother*, 1871. Thomson arranged to have the painting put on view at the Montmartre branch where it was seen by the critic Stéphane Mallarmé (at Whistler's urging) who helped to mount a campaign to have the painting acquired by the French state for the Musée du Luxembourg.[19]

The history of the New York branch of Goupil, initiated by Michael Knoedler who first travelled to the city in 1846, indicates that the relationship between the parent house and its branches could be both formal and informal. The New York retail space opened in 1848 but, in 1857, the firm was sold to Michael Knoedler, who appended the name 'Successor to Goupil & Co.' to his own.[20] The frequent appearance of Knoedler in the pages of the Goupil stockbooks indicates that the New York dealer often acquired works from the Paris house or its various branches and, likewise, the Knoedler stockbooks indicate that works travelled from New York to Paris (albeit less often). These stockbooks as well as the firm's foreign letterbook also show a brisk business between the London branch of the Goupil firm and Knoedler.[21]

Goupil's formal and informal networks could accommodate such a relatively high level of trafficking due to new technologies of communication and transportation that developed over the course of the second half of the nineteenth century. Letters and accompanying photographs of art works could travel between London and New York, for example, in about ten days; telegrams could arrive nearly instantly. The widespread adoption of the electric telegraph came in the late 1860s when the transatlantic cable connecting the United States and Great Britain was put in place. Telecommunication was enhanced in the last quarter of the nineteenth century with the development of the telephone and telephone exchanges. Goods relied on the rapidly increasing shipping trade facilitated by the development of the steamship and the British government readily supported the industrialization of trade. Inland traffic was supported by the swift expansion of the railway, particularly within the United Kingdom.

This infrastructure, combined with Great Britain's free trade environment, concretized by the repeal of the Corn Laws in 1846, allowed the importation of art to flourish. Adam Smith, in his treatise *An Inquiry into the Nature and Causes of the Wealth of Nations* (1776) predicted that free trade between France and England might lead to a 'balance ... in favour of France', but argued against tariffs, underscoring how they encouraged smuggling. Instead, his goal was to 'increase the quantity of gold and silver' which could be accomplished by more circulation of goods. Moreover, he anticipated that imported goods 'might be re-exported to other countries, where, being sold with profit, they might bring back a return equal, perhaps, to the prime cost of the whole French goods imported'.[22] Indeed, this was the case for Goupil London which sold, for example, European-made goods to American consumers as in the case of Whistler's *Battersea Reach*, which was sold to Potter Palmer of Chicago in 1892.[23] London thus provided the ideal framework for Goupil's corporate network as it facilitated the mobility of goods between a trade triangle composed of the European continent, Great Britain, and the United States and also served as the base for sales reaching out into the Empire.

Strategies within and without the corporation

For the remainder of this essay, I would like to consider the role played by the corporate structure as revealed by patterns of patronage, the development of new markets, and the question of speculation that developed during the tenures of David Croal Thomson and William Marchant before the Great War.

As already indicated, the corporate model gave the London branch of Goupil ready access to contemporary Dutch and French art that was particularly prized in the London art market during the last quarter of the nineteenth century. The Hague School, including such artists as Josef Israëls, Jacob and William Maris, and Anton Mauve, was especially in demand, presumably because its rustic and fishing scenes accorded well with the British native tradition; it also appeared to have a genealogical connection with Dutch seventeenth-century landscape painting which had already proven popular among British collectors.[24] The leading collectors in the United Kingdom, Sir John Charles Day, James Staat Forbes, and Alexander Young,[25] can all be found in the Goupil stockbooks; Forbes, for example, favoured the Hague branch but also bought occasionally in London, although he never exclusively patronized the Goupil firm.[26] Thomson helped to attract patrons to the work of the Hague School by hosting periodic special exhibitions as in June and July of 1888 when he organized a collection of pictures of Jacob Maris, supplemented by examples by Matthew and William Maris. Herman Tersteeg, manager of the Hague branch of Goupil, later recalled that 'Goupil had the entire oeuvre of Mauve and Jacob Maris at his disposal for a number of years', an arrangement that Thomson clearly took advantage of —in terms of placing works with patrons but also selling to other London dealers such as Wallis and Sons.[27] By 1880, Dutch scholar Dieuwertje Dekkers explains, 'the monopoly position of Goupil made it necessary that dealers had to acquire their works from The Hague or London branch of Goupil'.[28] Marchant continued to feature the Hague School until around 1906,[29] when his agreement with the Paris house came to an end and, accordingly, the London branch's trafficking in Dutch art dropped off precipitously, leaving the field open to its competitors.

These same patrons also favoured the Barbizon School, an area that Thomson even more assiduously cultivated for the London branch, largely by becoming a recognized expert in this arena. This tactic is indicative of ways in which dealers strove to establish their professional credentials and thus allay fears of unscrupulous profiteering as well as attempt to corner the market. For the first one-person show, of Corot, held at the Goupil Gallery London, Thomson adopted an effective strategy still utilized by dealers today. In addition to selling prints by the artist, the exhibition featured paintings, of which fifteen of the total twenty-one were already owned by leading collectors, such as railroad magnate J.S. Forbes, Alexander Young, and J. Forbes White.[30] The imprimatur of such collectors presumably enticed would-be patrons to purchase currently un-owned works or make an offer, via Thomson, for work already owned. At the very least, the paintings would have presumably helped spur the sale of reproductive etchings.

In the following year, 1890, the Goupil Gallery featured the work of Charles Daubigny, again selling etchings and goupilgravures after the artist's paintings, intermingling works owned by collectors (such as James Staat Forbes and Alexander Young as well as critic W. Cuthberth Quilter and artists H.T. Wells and G.P. Boyce) with un-owned works, and featuring a catalogue essay by Thomson. The difficulty of negotiating the sale of already purchased works, however, is revealed in the exchange of letters between Wells and Thomson. Wells, clearly angered by Thomson's proposition, responded:

You might have told the gentleman, you speak of, that I also, as well as himself, have 'room' for the Daubigny on my walls, and that I allowed it to leave them not for selling but only at your request to help your exhibition. You might have added, with absolute correctness, that up to the present moment of my life I have never parted with a single work of art (except my own productions) that I have once become possessed of. Of course I know pretty much about what has been happening around me in the picture buying way, and know how difficult the rich ones of the north have made it for men of moderate means to resist giving up their dear [?] lambs, but if I even do give up my Daubigny the bribe will have very different figures to the £1200 you mention. The ownership of the picture is almost, if not quite, worth that sum for the sake, alone of engraving or etching.[31]

Thomson's strategy was clearly fuelled by the increasing speculation in works of art that allowed for tremendous increases in their value in relatively short periods of time, thus possibly enticing collectors to part with works. But it was not a practice that Marchant would continue; as in the case of the Dutch artists, the number of one-person exhibitions devoted to Barbizon painters declined during his tenure, presumably because of loss of access to works from the Continent.

The exhibition of Corot's work in 1889 was followed soon after by an exhibition of the work of Claude Monet, a group of works transferred from the Montmartre branch where Theo Van Gogh had previously shown the French Impressionist's work, having begun dealing seriously in the artist's work in 1887.[32] Although the fact that the French artist sold little from this exhibition has often been held up as evidence of the British public's lacklustre interest in Impressionism, it is not entirely clear which works from this collection were actually for sale when it was shown in London although John Singer Sargent did acquire *Landscape with Figures, Giverny*, 1888, at this time.[33]

But perhaps what is most significant about Monet's exhibition is the model that it offered the London branch – of supporting a contemporary artist whose fortunes were on the upswing. Monet had only recently experienced an upsurge of interest in his work in 1881 when Parisian dealer Paul Durand-Ruel was able to support the artist again and aggressively sought out new patrons to the point that Monet was able to play one dealer off another. Whistler emulated this paradigm when he worked with Thomson to organize a major retrospective of his work at Goupil in 1892, *Nocturnes, Marines, & Chevalet Pieces*, and then tirelessly promoted the sale of his work, via Thomson and other dealers, hoping that by pushing up the prices of works already owned he could command higher prices for new works and commissions.

Theo Van Gogh's ability to search out new talent may have also inspired Thomson to support younger contemporary artists working in London as in the case of the exhibition of the London Impressionists, organized by Walter Sickert and held at the Goupil Gallery in 1889. Sickert, who had already worked with Thomson in producing reproductive prints, thanked the dealer for his courage:

> we have all ten appreciated & valued your extremely sympathetic & gracious efforts to do for us, what I, personally believe that probably no one would have had the courage to do for some years to come … we shall all retain the most agreeable recollection of the fearless manner in which you have struck the timeliest & most effective blow in favour of the form of work which we all have at heart.[34]

Thomson's role was arguably not purely altruistic; from the exhibition he forged a working relationship with Philip Wilson Steer, who proved a reliable exhibitor for the Goupil Gallery, extending his tenure beyond that of Thomson himself and continuing to work with Marchant.

Indeed, Marchant continued the practice of supporting new emerging artists, typically in the form of a group show, which retained the association of having been organized by artists rather than dealers. Thus Marchant cast himself in the role of 'facilitator … passing aesthetic authority to a disinterested body of acknowledged art experts' just as Ernest Gambart had done before him.[35] But, in Marchant's case, the desire for detachment may have been driven less by concern about the role of the dealer in what was formerly considered a public good – the organizing of exhibitions – and more by a wish to deflect possible criticism generated in response to progressive painting while concomitantly earning accolades within elite artistic circles for his acumen and bravery. In 1913, for example, Marchant successfully lured away the Camden Town Group from the Carfax Gallery by offering them his larger space and thus fostering an expansion of the coterie, eventually known as the London Group.[36] Just as the London Impressionists show led to a number of 'spin-off' exhibitions so did the London Group display; for example, in 1914 Goupil hosted a paired showing of the work of Harold Gilman and Charles Ginner and in 1919 Wyndham Lewis's show *Guns*.

Another way that Marchant curried favour with the circle around Sickert was by supporting Walter Greaves, Whistler's former pupil and assistant who had fallen on hard times. Marchant held an exhibition of Greaves' early work in 1911 and in 1920 helped to host a fundraising dinner for the artist, organized by William Rothenstein, Augustus John, and William Nicholson.[37] But, in many ways, Marchant's support of Greaves was a miscalculation, perhaps borne out by the lack of oversight from the Paris main house.

Marchant's blunder was twofold: one, to judge that Greaves' works were speculative property and two, to collaborate with Frida Strindberg, who proved unreliable and difficult. Strindberg, then separated from her playwright husband, was attempting to earn money as a collector-dealer and had entered into an agreement with Marchant to sell a collection of works by Walter Greaves. In May of 1911, at the time of the exhibition, Strindberg predicted that 'the Greaves will go up 100 percent' and, indeed, the sales from the exhibition appeared to bear out her prediction. Marchant then took the unsold works and arranged an exhibition of them in New York at the Cottier Gallery, without consulting Strindberg, much to her ire. She eventually filed suit to reclaim more control of the property; Marchant disputed her assertions, countering, in a letter to her lawyers, 'I surely ought to be the one to know what values are to be placed on works of art of which I alone have made a market.'[38] But, by March 1912, the Greaves market was clearly collapsing; Strindberg's lawyers demanded 'that the said pictures should be offered for sale by auction as soon as possible' because 'the interest of the public and of the critics in Greaves pictures roused by the said Exhibition in England [in 1911] shows signs of waning'. Marchant realized that an auction might lead to a disastrous drop in prices and, moreover, during the past year had lent Strindberg money against her share to the point that her loans outweighed any realizable profits. In an agreement of 16 October 1912, Strindberg agreed to allow Marchant to set the prices and to repay his overpayment to her as works sold.[39]

It is instructive to compare this episode to Whistler and Thomson's exchange regarding Whistler's painting *La Princesse du pays de la porcelaine*, 1864. The painting was due to come up for auction on 28 May 1892 and Whistler encouraged both Thomson and Glasgow dealer Alexander Reid to bid for it.[40] Reid was successful at 420 guineas, out-bidding Thomson.[41] But Whistler was angry nonetheless, writing to Thomson:

> Certainly however much I may wish to forgive you, I am sure that you will never excuse yourself – How could you let that splendid picture go for so ridiculous a sum and not either run up the price or secure it yourself? What *did* you risk! ... you knew that you, who are accustomed to investments, would have made a good one in the Princese! [sic][42]

Thomson defended himself by explaining:

> After consultation with our Paris houses were instructed to push it to 10,000 fr = £400. We in London went beyond these instructions to £430 being our bid. The picture was too large for our sale & we want to buy only what we can sell *readily*. Had we been investors you might be *certain* we should have given double for it will be worth £1000 some day.[43]

Thomson's rationale indicates that the London branch of the Goupil firm did not rely heavily on speculative return on investment for income; instead, it appears that quick turnover, accompanied by a high volume of sales generated from prints, books, and photographs, was the formula dictated by the Paris house. This financial paradigm was well suited to the corporate model in which expenses of generating and moving stock through the system were offset by ready profits generated by the profusion of outlets, volume of sales, and ability to place goods with the appropriate market in order to avoid carrying excessive inventory.

When Marchant was no longer linked to Paris, he was able to operate more autonomously and take on more risk, but that risk could come with costs, as in the case of Madame Strindberg. Moreover, while Marchant had clearly established a relationship with the New York firm Cottier in order to place his Greaves exhibition there, he nonetheless lacked the extensive network of his predecessor. Recognition of this absence perhaps propelled him to join in discussions in 1910 with artists to create an organization that would be called, at his suggestion, The Imperial Arts League. The purpose of the organization, located in London but with the aim of membership from across the Empire, was 'to provide a central organization for the Empire, to which all Members ... can appeal for advice or assistance in all matters affecting or connected with the practice of any branch of Fine or Applied Arts'.[44] Marchant's ambitions to participate in the formation of an imperial network were quickly quashed; by the close of the year he was engaged in a public, acrimonious debate with the organization fuelled by the council's decision to restrict membership, rendering 'persons engaged for profit in the business of buying, selling, or valuing works of art or reproductions or materials for the same other than originals or reproductions of their own work ... not eligible'.[45] Marchant, at first, had tried to work from within the group to reverse the ruling, but was banned from meetings and was forced to meet with emissaries. He then resorted to publishing a public letter in *The Times* in which he complained of the rule as insulting and, moreover, running counter to a stated objective of the League 'to promote personal intercourse between artists and others interested in art'. More importantly, he asserted that 'when so many living artists could testify to the advantages they have reaped through their connexion with fine art dealers and publishers, it is almost incredible that any league or society ... should start its career by adopting such an 'Anti-dealer' attitude'.[46] He closed his protest by stating that henceforth no artist associated with the Imperial Arts League would be permitted to exhibit or sell at the Goupil Gallery. On 14 December the Imperial Arts League published its response, admitting that Marchant had been crucial in founding the league but explaining that many artists had refused to join unless dealers were explicitly excluded. It concluded that the organization would not reverse its decision for 'they are responsible for seeing that the artists who are organizing themselves are masters in their own house'.[47]

The fight between Marchant and the Imperial Arts League as well as those between Whistler and Thomson reassert the now familiar antagonism between dealer and artist. But, I argue, the history of the Goupil Gallery proves that the dealer was an invaluable conduit for developing and deploying the formal and informal networks that distinguished the creation of an international art market over the course of the nineteenth and twentieth centuries. That the Post-Impressionist show and not the Imperial Arts League is the most remembered art event of London in 1910 is testimony to the visual and critical impact of exhibition culture – a culture sustained by dealers, who worked collaboratively with artists' exhibiting societies or, in the case of the Goupil Salon, imitated them.

This conclusion regarding the role of the dealer in the formation of an international network consciously and deliberately employs the term 'network'. Networks, as Simon Potter reminds us in the context of his work on the mass media in the British Empire, are 'informal, open, multiple, competing and dynamic'; systems, by contrast, are more formalized, 'restricted', 'entrenched', and able to exert control. Whereas Potter finds evidence of a 'tendency towards systematization' in mass communication as demonstrated by the role of telegraph and newspaper cartels, no equivalent force emerged in the art market.[48] The Imperial Arts League was perhaps the most likely candidate, but by excluding dealers artists had foreclosed on the agents most likely to exert influence in ways and means equivalent to news agencies. As the fate of the Goupil Gallery and Marchant make clear, the dealer, while instrumental in developing these networks, still had to negotiate their constant fluidity and mutability and might even misjudge their direction. The ability of Marchant and his predecessors to survey and to deploy these networks was entirely dependent on their location in London, an increasingly significant node in the circuitry of international and imperial trade, communication, and finance.

Notes

This paper derives from presentations given at the College Art Association annual conference and Northwestern University's Long Nineteenth-Century Colloquium. My thanks to the organizers of these sessions and for the feedback I received. Particular thanks to Chris Bell for her insights.

1 Letter to Clientele of Messrs Boussod, Valadon & Co., 1 January 1890, Goupil Scrapbook II, p. 1. Tate Gallery Archives, 8314.1.5.1.
2 McIntosh, 'Origins of the Maison Goupil', pp. 64, 73.
3 This history is drawn largely from that provided in *Gérôme & Goupil*.
4 Lafont-Couturier, 'Mr. Gérôme Works for Goupil', p. 19.
5 Thomson, 'Theo Van Gogh', p. 76.
6 Lafont-Couturier, p. 14.
7 Agnew, *Agnew's, 1817–1967*, pp. 1, 19, 45, 48, 50.
8 See, Cassis, *Capitals of Capital*.
9 Cook, *Highways and Byways*, p. 299.
10 Rappaport, *Shopping for Pleasure*, pp. 108, 115–22.
11 Helmreich, 'Art Dealer and Taste'.
12 William Roberts, 'Dealers and Galleries', *Five Posthumous Essays*, online source (William Robert Society) www. users.waitrose.com/~wrs/dealers.html. Accessed 28 February 2011.
13 'Supreme Court of Judicature, Court of Appeal … The Goupil Gallery', *The Times*, 21 November 1907, p. 3.
14 Lafont-Couturier, p. 14.
15 Bailey, *Van Gogh in England*, p. 32.
16 'Winter Exhibitions', *The Times*, 29 October 1877, p. 11; see also 'The Goupil Gallery, Bedford Street', *Art Journal*, August 1875, pp. 245–6.
17 'Art Exhibitions', *The Times*, 19 May 1886, p. 6.
18 See both the Thomson correspondence housed at the Getty Research Center and the Whistler-Thomson correspondence contained in MacDonald et al., *Correspondence of Whistler*.
19 MacDonald and Joy Newton, 'The Selling of Whistler's Mother', in *Whistler's Mother*, ed. MacDonald, pp. 75–6.
20 Pierre-Lin Renié, 'Chronology', in *Gérôme & Goupil, Art and Enterprise*, p. 165.
21 Thanks for DeCourcy McIntosh for facilitating my access to the Knoedler archives.

22 Smith, 'Book Four, Of Systems of Political Economy', *Wealth of Nations*, II, pp. 57, 58.

23 For correspondence relating to this sale see Boussod, Valadon and Company to James McNeill Whistler, 28 May 1892, GUW 05742; David Croal Thomson to James McNeill Whistler, 16 June 1892, GUW 05749; James McNeill Whistler to David Croal Thomson, 17 June 1892, GUW 08334; Boussod, Valadon & Co. to J.M. Whistler, 15 April 1893, GUW 05773. GUW numbers refer hereon to record numbers from MacDonald et al., *Correspondence of Whistler*.

24 Bionda, 'The Market for Contemporary Art in the Netherlands', p. 66; Dekkers, 'Goupil', p. 31.

25 Bionda, p. 69.

26 Dekkers, *Josef Israëls*, pp. 107, 108.

27 See, for example, memo of January 14 1896 indicating that W. Peacock from Wallis and Sons 'wishes to see Mr. Thomson as soon as possible re. purchase of 8 Mauves', David Croal Thomson Correspondence, 910126, Box 2, folder 6, Getty Research Library.

28 Dekkers, 'Goupil', p. 33.

29 Ibid.

30 Thomson, *Corot*.

31 H.T. Wells to D.C. Thomson, London, 16 February 1890, Thomson correspondence, 910126, Box 5, Getty Research Library.

32 Thomson, 'Theo Van Gogh', pp. 110–16.

33 Wildenstein, *Monet*, III, p. 458.

34 Walter Sickert, London, [1890] to D.C. Thomson, Thomson correspondence, 910126, Box 4, Getty Research Library.

35 Fletcher, 'Creating the French Gallery'.

36 Baron, *Perfect Moderns*, pp. 62, 67.

37 William Rothenstein to William Marchant, n.d.; William Marchant to William Rothenstein, 17–19 December 1920; printed dinner invitation; William Marchant miscellaneous Correspondence File 1919–22, Tate Gallery Archives 8314.3.1.4.

38 William Marchant to Messrs. Clifford, Turner & Hopton, 20 February 1912, Goupil Gallery Correspondence, Strindberg v. Marchant September 1911–March 1912, Tate Gallery Archives 8314.1.2.15.

39 Goupil Gallery Correspondence, Strindberg v. Marchant, 1909–1911, Tate Gallery Archives 8314.1.2.14; Goupil Gallery Correspondence, Strindberg v. Marchant September 1911–March 1912, Tate Gallery Archives 8314.1.2.15.

40 James McNeill Whistler, Paris, to David Croal Thomson, London, 19 May 1892, GUW 08203.

41 Boussod, Valadon & Co., London, to James McNeill Whistler, Paris, 28 May 1892, GUW 05742.

42 James McNeill Whistler, Paris, to David Croal Thomson, London, 29 May 1892, GUW 08201.

43 David Croal Thomson, London, to James McNeill Whistler, Paris, 31 May 1892, GUW 05743.

44 Imperial Arts League Minutes up to Incorporation 29 April 1909 to 2 May 1911, Memorandum and Articles of Association, 7 April 1911, London Metropolitan Archive LMA/4054/A/05/002.

45 Imperial Arts League Minutes up to Incorporation 29 April 1909 to 2 May 1911, Minutes 2 June 1909, p. 10.

46 'The Imperial Arts League', *The Times*, 9 December 1910, p. 13.

47 'The Imperial Arts League', *The Times*, 14 December 1910, p. 12.

48 Potter, 'Webs, Networks, and Systems', pp. 622, 646.

4

Marketing Post-Impressionism: Roger Fry's commercial exhibitions

Anna Gruetzner Robins

The dramatic impact of *Manet and the Post-Impressionists* (1910)[1] and the *Second Post-Impressionist Exhibition* (1912)[2] on the London art world, the two shows that the critic, painter Roger Fry devised, is well known. The resulting intense critical debate about modern art has been analysed and scrutinized; however, I am not proposing to look at this 'art-quake', as fascinating as it is, in this essay.[3] It is worth pointing out, however, that Fry came up with the term Post-Impressionism as a last minute solution when looking for a way to describe the artists in the first exhibition. Fry certainly understood the power that a style of art described as an 'ism' had within the modern art world; however, the artists in his exhibitions were not the originating source for the term Post-Impressionism because they never formed a cohesive social network like the Impressionists, Fauves, Cubists, or Futurists.

The little known and overlooked fact about Fry's exhibitions is that they were major London art fairs put together with a few works from private collectors and the artists themselves, and a staggering number of pictures, drawings, and sculptures from Paris dealers.[4] This essay examines Fry's use of the commercial art world when putting together the two Post-Impressionist exhibitions. It examines the role of the dealer in forming the canonical reputation of the artists best represented in the show at a moment when a significant number of their works were exhibited in the Anglophone world for the first time. It suggests that the exhibitions had a formative effect on Fry's later writings about the art market.

Both exhibitions were held at the Grafton Galleries, a large commercial space, in the heart of London's elite gallery district, at 8 Grafton Street. The gallery, a few minutes' walk from the Royal Academy on Piccadilly, opened its doors in

1893 by showing Degas's *Dans un Café* or *L'Absinthe* (Musée d'Orsay) which incited a storm of critical abuse and controversy because it represented a down and out man and a sex worker drinking alcohol in a café.[5] The gallery asked Fry to curate an exhibition in autumn 1910 because there was a gap in their programme. As curator of paintings at the Metropolitan Museum of Art, New York, and European adviser to the museum, Fry had established close links with a network of dealers in New York, Paris, and London when buying for the museum.[6] Although he was stepping into a less familiar area when he sought out the great Paris dealers in modern art – Ambrose Vollard, the Bernheim-Jeune Gallery, Daniel Kahnweiler, and the Galerie E. Druet, among others – he made use of his earlier experience of the art market when organizing both Post-Impressionist exhibitions.

Desmond MacCarthy, who acted as secretary for *Manet and the Post-Impressionists* and accompanied Fry to Paris, recalled that 'the first people we went to see were the dealers who had modern pictures' and that they spent 'day after day' looking at pictures while Fry made his selection.[7] MacCarthy was probably referring to the trip Fry made to Paris in September 1910 when he spent a week making arrangements for the exhibition. He was back in Paris the following month when he entered a tantalizing list of dates for 7 October 1910 in his appointment diary, booking an appointment at ten o'clock with Alphonse Kann, an important upmarket dealer and collector who had a large collection that he kept in his apartment at Saint Germain-en-Laye,[8] followed by a two o'clock rendezvous at the prestigious Bernheim-Jeune Gallery, where apparently he made arrangements to visit a private collection, before going on to Ambrose Vollard's gallery at 4 rue Lafitte at half past three.[9]

Manet and the Post-impressionists opened in another four weeks so this must have been a last minute trip to settle some of the arrangements that he had made the previous month. The Bernheim-Jeune Gallery, owned by the brothers Josse and Gaston Bernheim, joined several luminaries from the British art world and a few noteworthy Europeans to form the Honorary Committee.

Fry had met the enigmatic and opportunistic visionary Ambrose Vollard at some point before 1910.[10] Vollard had launched the careers of many of the artists in the exhibition, giving solo shows to Cézanne, Van Gogh, Gauguin, Picasso, Matisse, and many of the Fauves before they gained wider recognition in the art world.[11] Vollard lent eight works by Cézanne, eight by Gauguin, several by the Fauves – Valtat (two), Vlaminck (three), Puy (two), and five bronze sculptures by Maillol to the show.[12]

The London art world was introduced to Cézanne at a large Impressionist show organized by Durand-Ruel at the Grafton Galleries in 1905. Cézanne would probably not have been included on Durand-Ruel's list if Vollard had not supported Cézanne ten years earlier by giving him his first solo exhibition in 1895 at a moment when his work was hardly known in Paris. He had been virtually ignored by other dealers, and Vollard's sponsorship made him the 'first important French artist to forge his reputation within the context of a commercial gallery rather than through public art exhibitions'.[13] Cézanne's exhibition at Vollard's attracted a new circle of admiring artists and critics and his work was soon taken up by a coterie of Paris dealers, including Eugène Druet and the Bernheim-Jeune, all of whom lent works to Fry's show.[14] No one who knew the Paris art world would dispute that Vollard had played an instrumental role in creating the Cézanne 'boom'.

Fry had been championing Cézanne since 1908 and was completely swayed by his French supporters, declaring him 'the great genius of the whole movement'. The consignment of twenty-two Cézannes that came to London was an important feature of the show, where, together with eight Manet pictures, they filled the first octagonal-shaped room and joined works by Gauguin and Van Gogh in the large centre gallery.[15] All the Manet pictures were lent by the Bernheim-Jeune, who formed a consortium for their purchase from the Auguste Pellerin collection with the Durand-Ruel Gallery and the Berlin dealer Paul Cassirer.

Gauguin and Van Gogh, however, were better represented than Cézanne, suggesting that Fry was relying on what the dealers had in stock rather than his own preferences. By 1900 Vollard was Gauguin's principal dealer, and although dealer and artist had an ambivalent relationship, Vollard certainly contributed to the stellar reputation Gauguin acquired after his death in 1903[16] by giving him a solo exhibition that year, and lending a major group of paintings, drawings, and sculptures to the Gauguin retrospective at the Salon d'Automne in 1906.[17]

Once again Vollard's support encouraged an upsurge of interest among other Paris dealers and while Vollard sent a number of Gauguin pictures to London, the Galerie E. Druet was also stockpiling Gauguin pictures. In fact, as the catalogue reveals, the gallery owner, Eugène Druet, followed Vollard's example by investing in a number of other artists whom Vollard first supported. The Galerie E. Druet lent works by Redon and sculpture by Maillol together with works by the Fauves, including their painted ceramics. The idea of using ceramics as a means of disseminating their radical way of painting to cautious collectors had been Vollard's brainchild, and this must have been the purpose of the consignment sent to London.[18]

On the other hand, the Bernheim-Jeune Gallery was cornering the Paris market for Van Gogh (the gallery sent three pictures); however, there was stiff competition from Van Gogh's sister-in-law, Jo van Gogh-Bonger (listed in the catalogue as Mrs. Gosschalk-Bonger), who was the agent for works still in his estate. The critic Felix Fénéon, who managed the new premises of the Bernheim-Jeune Gallery at 15 rue Richepanse (added when Fénéon joined the business in 1906), wrote to Mrs. Gosschalk-Bonger explaining that the aim of the exhibition was to bring together 120 works by Van Gogh, Cézanne, Seurat, and Gauguin. 'Ces quatre mäitres constitutent donc la patrie essentielle de l'exposition', he wrote before asking her to consider lending a dozen pictures by Van Gogh because the exhibition was to be 'la plus importante qui ait jamais été faite en Angleterre dans cet ordre d'idée'.[19] The Bernheim-Jeune also lent works by the Neo-Impressionists Henri Cross, Seurat, Signac (Fénéon was an early supporter of these artists), the former Nabis artists Maurice Denis and Félix Vallotton, and the Fauve painters Friesz, Marquet, and Rouault.

Another smaller group of Gauguin, Herbin, and Picasso came from the dealer Clovis Sagot, one of the first to sell works by Picasso. Sagot offered Picasso drawings for sale and lent his portrait by Picasso to *Manet and the Post-Impressionists*. The loan may have been a way of signalling his early patronage of the artist, at a moment when the bigger dealers were fighting for exclusive rights to Picasso's works.

Daniel Kahnweiler, for example, was making a meteoric rise to fame as a dealer in cubist paintings and was stockpiling cubist pictures by Picasso and Braque. Kahnweiler refrained from sending any works by the cubist giants in 1910, and instead cautiously tested the London market with a few works by Derain, Vlaminck, and Girieud. None of the sixty Picasso pictures he had stockpiled in his tiny gallery by 1910 crossed the Channel that year.

Fry borrowed from the same stable of dealers for the *Second Post-Impressionist Exhibition*; he was taking an increasing interest in contemporary art and had forsaken his first Post-Impressionist artists with the exception of Cézanne, the only dead artist to be included in the second show. Pictures from Vollard and Gaston Bernheim filled the first gallery; however, after the date of the exhibition was extended, some thirty-five works by Cézanne, including five watercolours, were sent over from the Bernheim-Jeune Gallery.[20]

By 1912 Kahnweiler had seen the potential of the international market for buoying up the reputation of Picasso, and to a lesser extent that of Braque, who was never as well represented, and lent nearly two hundred Cubist pictures to a total of eight international exhibitions and dealers' shows outside France that year, including the *Second Post-Impressionist Exhibition*.[21] Kahnweiler remembered the second Post Impressionist exhibition as a group show 'of my painters for the most part' and while this is not entirely true,[22] he did release twenty-four pictures from his closely guarded stock, including thirteen of the fifteen Picasso works on show. Kahnweiler remembered working together with Bell and Fry to select the Picassos and it would be interesting to know whether it was part of the dealer's marketing strategy or a joint decision to display a chronological selection of pictures.[23] The early *Composition: The Peasants* (Barnes Foundation, Philadelphia) came from Vollard and the collector Leo Stein lent another; however, Kahnweiler sent works ranging from the 1904 *Portrait of Suzanne Bloch*, São Paulo Museum of Art, to the most recent Cubist pictures, making the display at the *Second Post-Impressionist Exhibition* a small retrospective designed to introduce Picasso's constantly changing ways of painting to the British public.[24]

The nineteen Matisse works in the 1912 show also illustrated his evolutionary development. Six of these works came from the Bernheim-Jeune; however, the gallery was not giving Matisse its full support, having refused to allow any price increases in his new contract,[25] and, in fact, most of the pictures, sculptures, and drawings came from the artist himself, including some which had not been exhibited before.[26]

These are just some examples of the role that Paris dealers played in Fry's two Post-Impressionist exhibitions. Both exhibitions were modern art markets, and furthermore, most of the hundreds of works in each were offered for sale. When put this way the Post-Impressionist exhibitions were the Edwardian equivalent of an international contemporary art fair although admittedly only Paris dealers were represented. There were virtually no collections of Post-Impressionist art in Britain in 1910 and the Paris dealers, artists, and European collectors were Fry's major ports of call for works of art.

The commercial aspect *Manet and the Post-Impressionists* did not go unnoticed. In a reasonably favourable review, Sickert nevertheless pointed out that Vollard, whose gallery 'cave' where he held dinners for favoured guests was famous in Paris, was largely responsible for the Cézanne boom, which he regarded with great suspicion:

> dealers, and those critics who directly or indirectly depend on them, can to a certain extent hold back or unleash a boom to suit themselves. In Cézanne there were all the conditions most ideal for the practice of great 'operations', as they are called in Paris by the able 'brewers of affairs' who control the winds from their caves full of paintings.[27]

After agreeing to lend his name to the Exhibition Committee, John Singer Sargent publicly disassociated himself from *Manet and the Post-Impressionists* and privately voiced his dislike of the exhibition's close ties with commercial galleries. In a letter which has more than a tinge of anti-Semitism, to the critic D.S. MacColl, another vehement opponent of Post-Impressionism, Sargent singled out the Bernheim Jeune brothers as the worst culprits: 'I am inclined to believe that the sharp picture dealers Bernheim Jeune invented and boomed this new article of commerce.'[28] One of the most vicious attacks appeared in the *New Age* in Huntly Carter's 1911 review of the Salon des Indépendants where he wrote:

The absence of Herbin reminds me that the best work of several new extremists is to be found at the dealers' shops where our own Post-Impressionist exhibition came from … [it] is the standing joke of Paris. It was organised from the dealers, where one may discover many of the bad and indifferent and ancient things that found their way to the Grafton Galleries.[29]

I have not located the account books for the Post-Impressionist exhibitions, and the catalogues do not list any prices. Desmond MacCarthy remembered that his 10 per cent cut of the sales from *Manet and the Post-Impressionists* was £460, which means they sold nearly £5,000 of pictures. The £800 that the Art Gallery in Helsinki paid for Cézanne's *Viaduct at L'Estaque* for which Vollard asked 15,000 francs,[30] accounts for nearly a fifth of this amount. The single Van Gogh, *Factories at Asnières* (Saint Louis Art Museum), that sold from the exhibition accounts for another large part of this percentage.[31] It is unlikely, however, that MacCarthy would have taken a cut from the sale of Gauguin's *Tahitians* that Fry bought for £30 on behalf of the Contemporary Art Society which presented it to the Tate in 1917.[32] Fry's picture was an unfinished work on paper and the prices for Gauguin oil paintings were far higher. The collector Michael Sadler might have been another buyer had he acted more quickly. Listening to Fry lecture on Post-Impressionism inspired him to think about buying a Cézanne and at least two Gauguins, but it was not until the following year that he made his first purchase, buying Gauguin's *Manao tupapau* (Albright Knox Gallery, Buffalo), which he first saw at Fry's show, for £1,400 from Galerie E. Druet.[33] (An increasing wave of recent publications details the British collectors of Post-Impressionist art.[34])

Fry was not naive when it came to the art market. His agreement with the Metropolitan Museum of Art allowed him to take 'a commission of 5% on the paintings purchased for less than £5,000 and 3% on paintings above £5,000; and the liberty to propose to other buyers paintings refused by the Metropolitan Trustees.'[35] Moreover, his dealings with the President of the Metropolitan Museum and millionaire collector, John Pierpoint Morgan, who was relentlessly adding treasures to his private collection (treasures it should be said that he could hardly appreciate), was a salutary lesson for Fry when he later identified what he described as the snobbist tendencies of the rich philistine who was led by fashion rather than aesthetic judgement.

Fry had no interest in economic theory; his writings on the art market sought to identify the various social groups who bought art and many of his ideas about art and commerce must have taken fruit during the period of the Post-Impressionist exhibitions.[36] He later divided his art buyers into four groups, the first being Philistines with bad taste and conformist opinions. Michael Sadler, as a man of culture, a true aesthete and a member of 'that small group of amateurs ... whose influence is profound [in] the survival of works of art', belonged to the second rare group.[37] He had the money to acquire paintings which made a profound impact on him but there were few others like Sadler around at the time of the Post-Impressionist exhibitions and no one in Fry's immediate circle had the funds to buy major examples of Post-Impressionist pictures.[38]

Fry's third group were a rarefied, cultured group who worshipped the past and who would only buy art once it acquired a pedigree. Many of the artists and critics who Fry had known since the 1890s, such as the artists and collectors Charles Ricketts and Charles Shannon whose connoisseurship of Old Master painting easily matched that of Fry, belonged to this cultured group, a group to which Fry too had once belonged. It must have been a shock to Fry when Ricketts publicly denounced him and took him to task for describing Post-Impressionism as 'decorative'.[39] 'I take it that Mr Fry considers that what is too silly to be called painting may be good enough for decoration.'[40] Ricketts was furious that Fry had coerced with Parisian dealers and that he had persuaded three museum directors to lend their name to the Exhibition Committee.[41] He ended his diatribe against Fry by writing: 'I long to see the Grafton decorations bought by the Honorary Committee lest Mr. Fry should stand ashamed before those Parisian dealers who would save us. If the wish is too cruel let the executive, all of whom cannot be wholly innocent, be made to purchase.'[42]

Fry's fourth group of art buyers were the snobs who were led by market value and would only buy new art once it had acquired a fashionable popularity. He realized, however, that this last group were a driving force in the marketplace. Craufurd Goodwin usefully points out that Fry drew up his list of categories of art lovers between the mid-1920s and his death in 1934 when he mulled over the question 'who could generate the demand for true art in the modern world?'[43] Yet, it is more than likely that these ideas first took shape in the aftermath of the Post-Impressionist exhibitions because neither exhibition found a ready London market.

Fry never underestimated the role that the art dealer played in creating the appetite for the work of a particular artist. He expressed this view most clearly in his 1917 review for the *Burlington Magazine* of Vollard's monograph *Paul Cézanne* where he wrote that: 'Vollard has played Vasari to Cézanne and done so with the same directness and simplicity, the same narrative ease, the same insatiable delight in the oddities and idiosyncrasies of his subject.'[44] This linking of Vasari and Vollard, with the assumption that the modern art dealer could play the role of art historian in establishing an artist's legacy, is one example of the almost seamless transition between the marketplace and art history that Fry readily endorsed.

Fry cannily realized that he had his own role to play in the process of giving a mercantile transaction an aesthetic and historical importance. *Manet and the Post-Impressionists* had barely closed its doors for the final time when Fry began an active campaign to give Post-Impressionist art a greater credibility. He used his position as co-editor of the *Burlington Magazine*, which had built its reputation on its scholarly articles about old master painting,[45] by writing an important notice on Cézanne,[46] and publishing articles on Van Gogh by J. Meyer Riefstahl,[47] and on the Post-Impressionists as a group in its illustrious pages.[48]

Fry could have chosen to write about any one of the Cézanne pictures in *Manet and Post-Impressionists*; however, he chose the only one which sold from the exhibition, *The viaduct at L'Estaque* (c.1883), acquired by the trustees of the National Gallery of Helsingfors, now the Helsinki Museum (Antell Ateneum), who also bought *Ulysses and Calypso* by Maurice Denis. Fry set out to canonize these two new works of art which had only just left the marketplace. He rightly tied Denis to 'the great classic tradition of France'.[49] While he admired Denis's painting, Fry had a revelatory visual experience when looking at Cézanne and he sought to explain his perceptual reaction: 'To the inquiring eye new relations, unsuspected harmonies continually reveal themselves; and this is true no less of the subtle, pure and crystalline colour than of the linear construction of the pattern.'[50] Fry continued: 'Cézanne is one of the most intensely and profoundly classic artists that even France has produced', before comparing his picture to the inexplicable mastery of Giorgione's *The Tempest*.[51] This use of aesthetic and historical discourse in a highly respected journal devoted to the connoisseurship of old master painting gave a new importance to a picture that had only recently left the marketplace and secured Cézanne's lineage as a modern artist within an old master tradition.[52]

I am not disputing the overwhelming life-changing importance that Cézanne had for Fry, who became his most important and eloquent spokesperson within the Anglophone world. What has not been taken into account is Fry's use of the art market in cementing Cézanne's reputation. By the 1920s, when the rich industrialist Samuel Courtauld started buying Post-Impressionist paintings for his own collection and gave £50,000 for the purchase of Impressionist and Post-Impressionist pictures for the English national collection, the Post-Impressionist artists were seen to be a 'natural' group, not one that was concocted to describe a mixed bag of artists in a commercial exhibition.[53] Courtauld's collecting patterns can be traced directly to Fry's shows, and, indeed, he bought one of the best-known exhibits in the first exhibition, Manet's *A Bar at the Folies-Bergère* (1881–82), which now graces the walls of the Courtauld Institute Galleries. The purchase suggests that the picture lodged a collective memory of the exhibition. (The dealer Percy Moore Turner, who was part of Fry's circle, sold the picture to Courtauld.) Cézanne's *An Old Woman with a Rosary* (1895–96) was also offered for sale in 1910, and later acquired by Fry's friend Jacques Doucet before being sold to the National Gallery, London, in 1955. As Alexandra MacGilp shows in her essay in this volume, a network of London dealers played a similar role in securing modern works for the Tate collection in the 1930s.

By the 1920s Fry had succeeded in giving Post-Impressionism a canonical status. The solo exhibitions of Van Gogh (1923), Gauguin (1924), and Cézanne (1925) at the Leicester Galleries, and the promotion of Post-Impressionist art at the Lefevre Gallery catered to collectors like Courtauld. In 1926, the year that Fry published his ruminations on the art market in *Art and Commerce* (where he identified the four distinct groups of collectors), Courtauld purchased sixteen modern French paintings, including three works by Cézanne, *The Lac d'Annecy*, 1896 (Courtauld Institute Galleries) alone costing approximately £8,000, nearly a ten-fold increase over what the Helsinki Museum paid in 1910. Was Courtauld one of Fry's 'snobbistes' whose taste in art was formed by Fry's aesthetic campaign or was he a man of culture who, thanks to Fry, regarded the Post-Impressionists as old master artists? The pictures bought with Courtauld's £50,000 bequest were displayed at the Tate in 1926. There is more than a touch of irony in Fry's comment that: 'When one considers how late in the day Mr. Courtauld was able to come to the rescue of our national collection, in the hope of filling a gap which ought never to have existed, one cannot deny that the money has been well spent.'[54]

Many of the pictures in both Post-Impressionist exhibitions were sent to New York for the Amory Show in 1913. The term Post-Impressionism, which Fry used to describe the first exhibition, quickly gained currency within the Anglophone world especially after it crossed the Atlantic and appeared in Jerome K. Eddy's 1915 publication *Cubists and Post-Impressionists*. From this point on it became an established term within the canon of traditional modernism and it acquired a critical and historical meaning that stretched way beyond Fry's original term. Indeed Post-Impressionism – it was always hyphenated – has recently morphed into a new hybrid – Postimpressionism – which suggests that it has the same credibility as the so-called movements of Impressionism, Fauvism, Cubism, and Futurism.

Tracking the use of this term in early twentieth-century exhibition catalogues, art writing, and other publications would cast light on the way in which the best-known artists of Fry's exhibitions – Cézanne, Gauguin, Van Gogh, Seurat, Matisse, Picasso – became imbedded in the discourse of modern art. It would throw light on how the first four artists emerged as Post-Impressionist giants who, together with the two other great moderns, became very expensive artists. The competing and interdependent cultures of Post-Impressionism and commerce have not been studied and yet they had untold effect on twentieth-century museum cultures and academic art history.[55] Indeed it could be argued that Alfred Barr was inspired indirectly at least by the groups of artists that Fry brought together when he started buying for the Museum of Modern Art, New York, in the 1930s.[56] Tracking the early use of Post-Impressionism in the literature would provide an interesting history about the rapid acceptance of the term by dealers, critics, and curators, not to mention art historians. Fry's two commercial exhibitions had a phenomenal influence within the Anglophone world and beyond.

Notes

I dedicate this essay to the memory of David Robins who gave me invaluable support and help when I gave a version of this paper at the conference I co-organized with Victoria Walsh, Tate Britain, on 'The Rise of the London Art Market', 8–9 February 2007.

1 The private view was held 5 November, on Guy Fawkes's day with its explosive fireworks and the exhibition ran from 8 November 1910 to 15 January 1911.
2 The exhibition ran from 5 October 1912 to January 1913.
3 For a useful compilation of critical reviews see: Bullen, ed. *Post-Impressionists in England*, pp. 93–243 and pp. 347–429.
4 For an informative discussion of the Paris art world see: Gee, *Dealers, Critics, and Collectors*.
5 For a discussion of the controversy see: Robins, 'Greatest artist', and Pickvance, '*L'Absinthe* in England'.
6 See Santori, 'European "Masterpieces" for America', pp. 111, 117.
7 The Papers of Roger Eliot Fry, Cambridge, Modern Archive, 4/4/50; Desmond MacCarthy, 'The Art-Quake of 1910', *Listener*, 1 February 1945, p. 123.
8 Alphonse Kann (1870–1948) was of Jewish descent and fled to England in 1938 leaving his collection of around 1,000 works behind. It was seized by the Nazis in 1940. The Kann Association was formed in 1997 to retrieve the collection which was only partly recovered in 1948.
9 See Fry's diary for 7 October, 1910, The Papers of Roger Eliot Fry, Cambridge, Modern Archive, 5/1/2.
10 MacCarthy, p. 124, recalled that Fry already knew Vollard. Possibly Charles Loeser whom Fry knew, and who bought Cézanne pictures from Vollard, would have brought the dealer to Fry's attention or it may have been Ottoline Morrell who introduced the two men.
11 For a fascinating account of Vollard see: Rabinow, ed. *Ambroise Vollard*.
12 Ann Dumas, 'Ambroise Vollard', in *Ambroise Vollard*, ed. Rabinow, p. 21. Dumas suggests that Vollard also lent a Van Gogh to the show. The first version of the catalogue lists Vollard as the owner of (88) *Le gardeur d'oies* by Van Gogh; however,

this appears to be a misprint because two annotated copies of the catalogues (Tate Library and Archive, Tate Britain, and the National Art Library, Victoria & Albert Museum) state that the work was by Gauguin. Belinda Thomson suggests that the work was probably *The Breton goose-boy*, 1889. Wildenstein and Cogniat, *Paul Gauguin I*, p. 367. Dumas also suggests (p. 21) that Vollard lent a Denis to the exhibition; however, if this is the case, the information is not given in any of the versions of the catalogue to the exhibition that I have seen.

13 For Vollard and Cézanne see Robert Jensen, 'Vollard and Cézanne', in *Ambroise Vollard*, ed. Rabinow, p. 29.

14 For a discussion of the Paris dealers' sponsorship of Cézanne, see: Jensen, 'Vollard and Cézanne'.

15 For a list of works see: Anna Gruetzner Robins, '*Manet and the Post-Impressionists: A Checklist of Exhibits*', *Burlington Magazine*, December 2010.

16 For Vollard and Gauguin's relationship during Gauguin's lifetime see: Douglas W. Druick, 'Vollard and Gauguin', in *Ambroise Vollard*, ed. Rabinow, pp. 60–81.

17 Rabinow states that Vollard lent eighteen Gauguin pictures, fourteen drawings, and two wood sculptures to the 1906 Salon d'Automne. Rebecca A. Rabinow and Jayne Warman, 'Selected Chronology', in *Ambroise Vollard*, ed. Rabinow, p. 282.

18 See: Jacqueline Munck, 'Vollard and the Fauves', in *Ambroise Vollard*, ed. Rabinow, pp. 118–29.

19 Fénéon to Mrs. Gosschalk-Bonger, 8 October 1910, Van Gogh Museum Archives, Amsterdam, b 5771 V/1996.

20 The revised version of the *Second Post-Impressionist Exhibition* catalogue shows this to be the case, as I state in Robins, *Modern Art in Britain*, p. 65. However, my research was overlooked in Robbins, *Cézanne in Britain*.

21 See Werner Spies, 'Vendre des tableaux – donner à lire', in *Daniel-Henry Kahnweiler*, ed. Monod-Fontaine, p. 28.

22 In fact, Emil Druet who was probably the son of Eugène lent eighteen works by Friesz, Marquet, Flandrin, and Girieud.

23 See Kahnweiler, *My Galleries and Painters*, p. 75.

24 For a list of exhibits see: Robins, *Modern Art in Britain*, p. 191.

25 For a discussion of Matisse's contractual arrangements with the Bernheim-Jeune see Flam, *Matisse*.

26 For a full list and further discussion of these works see: Robins, *Modern Art in Britain*, pp. 80, 190–1.

27 Walter Sickert, 'Post-Impressionists', *Fortnightly Review*, January 1911; reprinted in Robins, ed. *Walter Sickert*, p. 276.

28 MS John Singer Sargent to D.S. MacColl, Wednesday 12 [December] 1912, MacColl Papers, S49, Special Collections, University of Glasgow.

29 Huntly Carter, 'The Independants and the New Intuition in Paris', *New Age*, 25 May 1911, p. 83. I am grateful to Anne Helmreich for drawing this review to my attention.

30 See: Robins, '*Manet and the Post-Impressionists*: A Checklist of Exhibits'.

31 The picture was bought by the German collector Gustav Robinow who lived at Richmond Hill, Surrey. See Bailey, *Van Gogh and Britain*, pp. 23, 125.

32 This information is taken from the catalogue entry for the picture on the Tate website at www.tate.org.uk.

33 For the most recent account of Sadler's purchases see: Fowle, 'Following the Vision', pp. 104–6.

34 Since the publication of Robins, *Modern Art in Britain*, Bailey, *Van Gogh in England*; Fowle, 'Following the Vision'; and Robbins, *Cézanne in Britain* have looked at the growing taste for Van Gogh, Gauguin, and Cézanne in some detail. See also: Korn, 'Collecting Modern Foreign Art'; Korn, 'Collecting Paintings by Van Gogh'; Korn, 'Collecting Paintings by Matisse and Picasso'; and Korn, 'Exhibitions of Modern French Art'.

35 Santori, 'European "Masterpieces" for America', p. 108.

36 For a selection of Fry's writings about art and commerce and a useful introduction see Goodwin, ed. *Art and the Market*.

37 Roger Fry, *Art and Commerce*, 1926 cited in Goodwin, ed., p. 28.

38 Clive and Vanessa Bell had the funds to make modest purchases and acquired a Picasso, and Fry also acquired a Picasso at some point before 1914.

39 See Charles Ricketts, 'Post-Impressionism', *Morning Post*, 9 November 1910; reprinted in Bullen, ed., pp. 106–8.

40 Ricketts, reprinted in Bullen, ed., p. 107.

41 In fact there were more than three museum directors. The Honorary Committee consisted of: The Rt. Hon. The Earl of Plymouth, The Duchess of Rutland, The Rt. Hon. Lord Ribblesdale, The Rt. Hon. Lewis Harcourt, Sir Charles Holroyd, Sir Edgar Vincent, Claude Phillips, Herbert Cook, James Paton (Director of Glasgow Art Gallery), James Caw (Director of the Scottish National Gallery), Whitworth Wallis (Director of Birmingham Art Gallery), Count Kessler, Princess von Wrede, Madame Cohen Gosschalk-Bonger, Walter Butterworth, Clive Bell, M. Paul Leprieur (Keeper of the Louvre pictures), Le Comte Robert de Montesquiou-Fezenensac, Alphonse Kann, Théodore Duret, Bernheim-Jeune, Auguste Pellerin, and Octave Mirbeau. The Executive Committe consisted of: Roger Fry, Lionel Cust (Keeper of the King's pictures), Professor Holmes (Director of the National Portrait Gallery), Lady Ottoline Morrell, Lord Henry Bentinck, Dr Meyer Riefstahl (Munich), and Robert Dell (Paris).

42 Ricketts, reprinted in Bullen, ed., p. 108.

43 Goodwin, ed., p. 25.

44 Roger Fry, '"Paul Cezanne" by Ambroise Vollard; Paris 1915', *Burlington Magazine*, August 1917, p. 53: cited Dumas, 'Ambroise Vollard', p. 16.

45 See: Elam, 'Roger Fry'.

46 Roger Fry, 'Acquisition by the National Gallery at Helsingfors', *Burlington Magazine*, February 1911; reprinted in Reed, ed. *Roger Fry Reader*, pp. 136–7.

47 J. Meyer Riefstahl, 'Vincent Van Gogh', *Burlington Magazine*, December 1910, pp. 154–7, pp. 160–2.

48 A. Clutton Brock, 'The Post-Impressionists' *Burlington Magazine*, January 1910, pp. 216–19.

49 Fry, 'Acquisition', in Reed, ed., p. 136.

50 Ibid.

51 Fry, 'Acquisition', in Reed, ed., p. 137.

52 The *Burlington Magazine* did publish some articles on modern art especially under Fry's editorship, however, it was devoted to the connoisseurship of old master painting. For a further discussion of its early editorial policy see: Elam.

53 For a full discussion of Courtauld's collection and the Courtauld gift see: House, ed. *Impressionism for England*.

54 Roger Fry, 'The Courtauld Fund', *Nation and Athenaeum*, 30 January 1926; cited in Elizabeth Prettejohn, 'Modern Foreign Paintings', in *Impressionism for England*, ed. House, p. 245.

55 This is a subject of a book I am writing on the cultural and economic infrastructures of Post-Impressionism.

56 For a discussion of Barr's purchasing policy see: Kantor, *Alfred H. Barr, Jr.* Kantor, however, does not discuss the importance of Fry's exhibitions for this policy.

5

Strategies of display and modes of consumption in London art galleries in the inter-war years

Andrew Stephenson

In an article entitled 'Modest Work for Modest Means' published in *The Sunday Times* on 3 October 1921, the art critic Frank Rutter considered the effect that post-war economic conditions and altered domestic situations were having upon the tastes of London's art-buying public. He concluded:

> The London flat dweller, who is the typical representative of the middle class of today, has no space for large pictures and is rarely in the mood or in the position to pay a big price. Yet being educated up to a certain standard of taste, he is anxious to avoid the furniture shops' engravings and to find something personal and distinctive to hang on his walls.[1]

Aware of the subtle distinctions that made the discerning metropolitan purchaser eschew the range of popular prints available in commercial furnishing shops, Rutter observed that younger patrons, favouring simplicity in the domestic setting, were using their reduced incomes judiciously in a period of recession. They now wished to buy small-scale aesthetic objects more suited to the more intimate rooms and limited wall space of the fashionable modern flat. The consequences of these altered domestic and financial conditions upon artists' employment and welfare was most effectively summarized in an article in *The Times* in June 1922 where, under the heading 'Hard Times for Artists', the writer sympathized that 'the artistic professions are feeling the sharp edge of this [economic] truth perhaps more keenly than other occupations, for in hard times, luxuries are the first to go'.[2]

This chapter examines the emergence of these new younger, middle-class art audiences in England and investigates the consequences that this demographic shift had for contemporary artists working in the metropolis. Employing case-studies taken from the arts and crafts exhibition societies and the Lefevre Gallery in the early to mid-1920s; the Arts and Crafts Bureau and the Curtis Moffat Studio opening in the late 1920s; Waring and Gillow's *Modern Art in French and English Decoration and Furniture* exhibition in 1928; the refurbished Mayor Gallery (from 1933); and the Duncan Miller Studio's *Modern Pictures in Modern Rooms* exhibition in 1936, I consider how the evolving customs of presentation developed for temporary art exhibitions in commercial galleries, design studios, and department stores in London in the 1920s and 1930s responded to the taste for simplified, remodelled interiors and developing commercial imperatives. My investigation also illuminates how changing social and economic conditions directed the boundaries of the inter-relationship between painting, sculpture, fashion, design, and interior decoration in the inter-war years. In each case, these innovative displays and the evolving installation aesthetic that they embodied demonstrated a thoroughly modern and metropolitan self-consciousness about presentation and provided for different forms of engagement with twentieth-century interior design and styling. Moreover, these different approaches prevalent in the inter-war years marked out changing attitudes towards commercial consumption in London by highlighting the impact of modern retailing practices and historically changing contexts of consumption upon artists', dealers', and art buyers' thinking.[3]

Writing in *Vogue* in August 1924, Raymond Mortimer, alert to these contemporary attitudes and shifts in taste, condemned what he saw as a tendency 'in recent painting to subordinate everything to decorative effect' and he argued that 'for too long … the art of painting and the art of decoration have been divorced'.[4] Ostensibly reviewing 'Paris Fashions in Furnishing' but, instead, employing it as a way of comparing the advanced tastes of young French women with those of their English counterparts, Mortimer saw the convergence of French art and decoration as a marker of the Frenchwoman's (and France's) cultural superiority. Within the carefully orchestrated, ensemble domestic interior, the fashionably attired single woman could perform her modernity: she 'can read her Proust and her Paul Morand, listen to her Darius Milhaud, and have her Matisses and her Derains. Here she can be not a weak imitation of her great grandmother, but her own exquisite and modern self.'[5]

Mortimer sensed that middle-class French women had learnt the lesson of how to translate personal taste not only into the clothes they wore, but also into the domestic interiors they inhabited as a means to articulate and to reinforce a thoroughly modern and chic sophistication. The subtle placing of contemporary art and design within the home and an up-dated conception of decorative art that abandoned older models of domesticity lay at the heart of Mortimer's francophile admiration of both individuality and discerning feminine taste.[6] Supporting such claims, the late September 1924 cover of *Vogue* reproduced an illustration by Harriet Meserole (figure 5.1) of the young fashionable woman with bobbed hair dressed in the latest Parisian fashions and bejewelled in bold bracelets, long necklaces, and dramatic brooch while looking out from her window. This cover, like others by Georges Lepape, Pierre Mourgue, and Eduardo Benito, reinforces how inter-war mass-market magazines aimed at an international readership, such as *Vogue* and *Vanity Fair* (and from 1929, *Harper's Bazaar*), showcased new role models and innovative tastes for the sophisticated young woman as well as advertising elegant couture from Paris and, with increasing

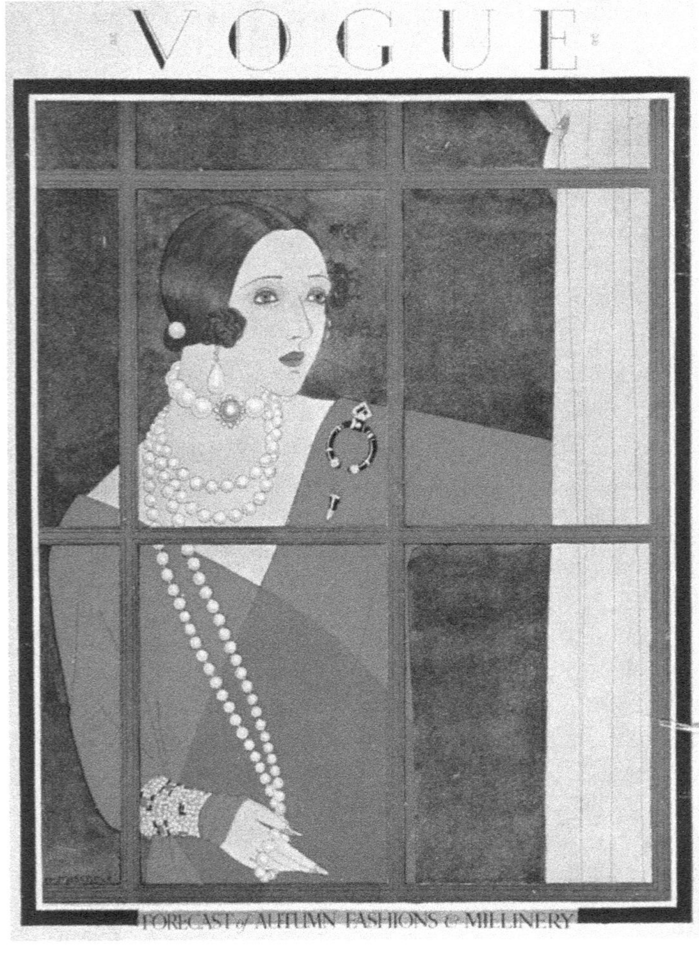

5.1
Vogue (late September, 1924).

emphasis from the early 1920s, from New York.[7] Indeed, as part of Condé Nast's commitment to showing interior decoration alongside couture fashion, *Vogue* interwove different types of information about interior design, fashion, and leisure, thereby demonstrating how interior decoration and fashion had become intimately interconnected within the concept of the modern lifestyle.[8] As *Vogue*'s editorial in May 1925 acknowledged, 'the modern woman ... looks to *Vogue* for the most up-to-date ideas of the modern world'.[9]

In addressing this issue of young women's artistic taste, altered domestic conditions, and modern living, *Vogue* editors, perhaps even Mortimer himself, were alert to recent demographic changes in Britain highlighted by the 1921 census. Following the disproportionate casualty rates of large numbers of middle- and upper-middle-class professional men in the Great War, there was an increasing and disproportionate number of younger, single women from this social background in the United Kingdom. According to Virginia Nicholson, the 1921 census indicated that there were 1,720,802 more females than men (up from 664,000 recorded in the previous census of 1911). Given what newspaper headlines termed 'the Problem of the Surplus Woman', Nicholson argues that middle- and upper-middle-class women had a proportionately lower chance of marriage than their slightly older generation.[10] This imbalance was especially acute for women in the age range twenty-five to twenty-nine years old. By the time of the next census in 1931, 50 per cent of these British women would still be single and 35 per cent of this group would never marry at all during their reproductive years.[11]

The consequences that these demographic changes would carry for art consumption would be considerable, not least because these younger middle- and upper-middle-class women, coming from educated and relatively wealthy backgrounds, had experienced greater employment opportunities during the 1914–18 War and were financially independent. Moreover, they were familiar with the pre-war languages of sexual equality and emancipation that offered new and ambitious possibilities for women both in public and private life. These independent single women were increasingly exposed to less rigid and more cosmopolitan role models in glossy magazines such as *Vogue* and *Vanity Fair* and their interest in fashion, cosmetics, and interior decoration was informed by expanding consumer choices advertised in the mass media and increasingly available in a post-war consumer economy.[12] Women living alone or sharing flats or apartments were increasingly conspicuous in the West End, in areas like Mayfair, Fitzrovia, and Bloomsbury, where newly built or remodelled apartment properties were available.[13] The manager of the Leicester Galleries, Oliver Brown, remembering that modern art exhibitions in the immediate post-war years attracted a different audience from those of the pre-war period, recalled that: 'the visitors at the end of the war were very different in character from those we used to know in 1914. They were much younger and had a much more adventurous outlook, and they increased in numbers ... The new public were intensely interested in our French allies and in the work of their artists.'[14]

As Tony Castle's poster, published in 1927, encouraging travellers to visit the National and Tate galleries by tram underscores (figure 5.2), these twenty-something women, interested in art, could frequently be seen in London's art museums. The 'New Woman' is presented with rouged cheeks, bobbed hair, large modern earrings, cloche hat, and a fashionably streamlined dress in one of the modern art galleries at the Tate Gallery. Having just considered William Hamo Thornycroft's sculpture of a naked adolescent archer ready to despatch his arrow,

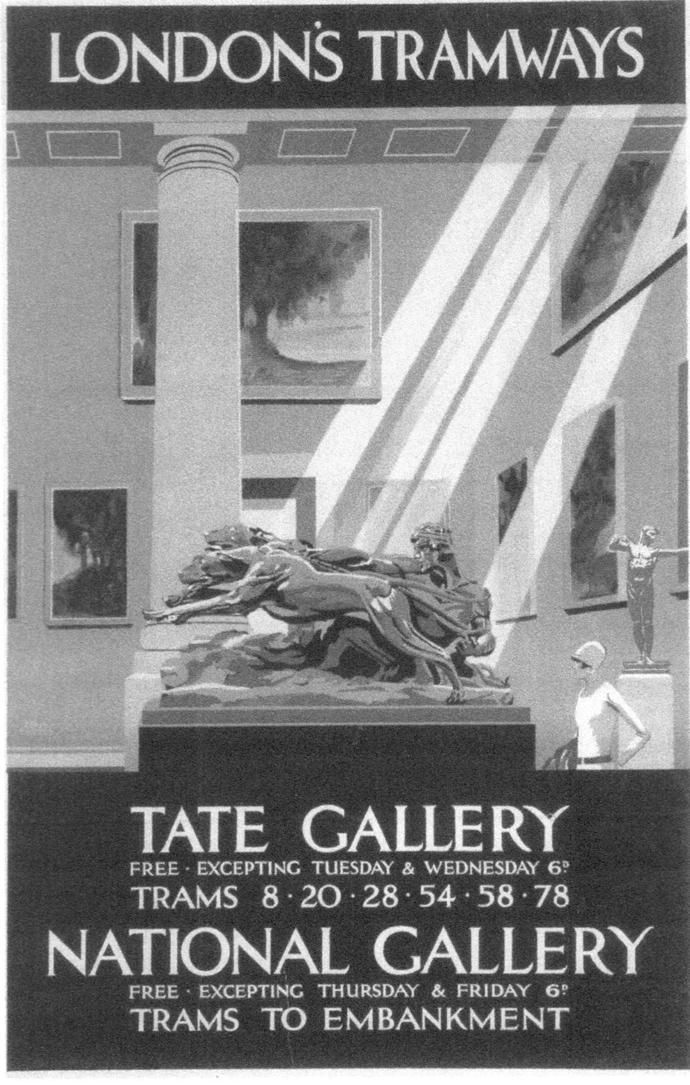

5.2
Tony Castle, *London's Tramways. Tate Gallery*, 1927.

Teucer (1881), she has now turned around and is taken with the life-sized bronze group by Harry Bates entitled *Hounds in Leash* (1889). Looking intently, it seems, at the man's broad back and buttocks, his muscles taut as he fights to restrain the bounding dogs, the woman, it appears, is unperturbed by the male figure's rippling flesh nor ruffled by its manly erotic possibilities. Rather, she seems relaxed with hand on hip and coat under the other arm, as the bright sun-rays play on the surfaces of imagined flesh and muscle, and dramatize the intense struggle between man and hounds. In this gallery setting, the flapper stands confidently and conspicuously as a marker of a modern, self-conscious 1920s sensibility amidst the classicized representatives of an older, more traditional British culture epitomized by the late Victorian landscapes and sculptures on display.[15] As the National Gallery, Tate Gallery, and London's Tramways surely must have been aware, fashion conscious younger women, conspicuous as travellers and art viewers, were eager consumers of the West End's transport, leisure, and entertainment industries.

The arts and crafts exhibition societies and the Lefevre Gallery in the early to mid-1920s

Artists', dealers', and art buyers' commitment to this new affiliation of contemporary art, design, fashion, and decoration was manifested in many different ways in the 1920s. This was not least because of the legacies of the Arts and Crafts movement[16] and the significant role played by the Omega Workshops in fusing the visual vocabularies of the British and Continental avant-gardes with earlier Morrisian social reform ideals.[17] As Paul Nash concluded in his review of 'Modern English Textiles' published in *Artwork* in January-February 1926, although the modern movement in textile design had begun with the Omega Workshops and, under Roger Fry, had laudable aims at elevating personal taste and disseminating modernist aesthetics through the creation of a wide range of hand-made objects for the home – from ceramics to furniture, clothing to rugs, screens and linens – the Omega Workshop's 'marriage of art and craft was not always a successful one'.[18] Indeed, the Omega's demise in 1919 as a manufacturer of interior decoration and furnishing accessories clearly signalled its lack of commercial viability.[19]

From the early 1920s, artists, craft practitioners, and art buyers who supported earlier Arts and Crafts and Bloomsbury artistic positions in which the personalized, the spontaneous, and the artisanal were cherished features were outraged by government attempts to align the modernist crafts with the emerging professional identity of the industrial designer and to force an engagement with commercial mass production methods. This market orientation was fully supported by government organizations such as the Design and Industries Association. Formed along the model of the Deutscher Werkbund, the DIA actively promoted a more commercially engaged alliance of crafts people, designers, manufacturers, and retailers. The British Institute of Industrial Art, established by a Treasury grant in 1920 and active until 1929, similarly encouraged craft practitioners to situate themselves in the evolving commercial contexts of the freelance designer and professional interior decoration market. Economic factors also promoted this direction as the post-war slump forced trained artists and designers into the commercial and industrial sectors. While the immediate post-war years saw the London art market grow substantially, in part due to the market for war memorials and state patronage for national art projects linked to the Great War, from the end of 1920 there were clear signs of depression in the art economy as artists suffered from the withdrawal of state support and falling demand. The *Yorkshire Evening Post* critic, reviewing the London scene in January 1921, recorded that 'the next two or three years will be a terrible time for artists in this country to live through. The first people to feel the breadth of the general slump were the artists. They felt it as early as last April and will naturally be the last to benefit by the recovery.'[20]

By summer 1921, with artists facing the consequences of increased taxation on luxury goods and a substantial decline in demand, the government policy of encouraging artists to produce commercially orientated design seemed appealing. While some artists' exhibiting associations adopted a cheaper pricing policy (notably the London Group from October 1921) and dealers blamed exorbitant taxation, inflated London rents, and high rates for poor sales, there were calls in the art press, supported by artist Leon Underwood, for the Government to establish a Mural Decoration Board. This organization would utilize unemployed artists in public art schemes and commission them to undertake mural paintings in commercial spaces. The *Star*, under the heading 'Art to Brighten Dull Places', reported that 'a wider utilisation of decorative painting would assuredly transform many of our dull commercial offices into charming and attractive places'.[21]

This fall in demand for contemporary British painting and sculpture contrasted with the growing popular demand for modern prints, lithographs, and engravings – a market that was popularly termed 'the poster craze' – that would reach its peak in 1929.[22] Alongside this trend was a growing handicrafts revival with an expanding call for small-sized, modernist craftwork, especially textiles and ceramics, as fashionable additions to an affordable style of sparse contemporary home furnishings. Catering for these were small shops and specialist companies such as Fearnley Limited, designer outlets which 'sold objects of applied art designed to accord with contemporary taste', thereby attracting discerning collectors, many of them women.[23]

One consequence of these shifts in post-war consumption was that the three main arts and crafts exhibition organizations – the Arts and Crafts Exhibition Society (founded in 1888), the Arts League of Service (founded in 1919), and the Red Rose Guild (founded in 1921) – alongside specialist galleries such as the Three Shields Gallery, the New Handworkers' Guild Gallery, and the Little Gallery expanded contacts between artists, designers, consumers, and industry and started exhibiting the arts and crafts alongside each other as part of an integrated modernist aesthetic.[24] In their use of ensemble displays of vernacular objects, the gallery installations adopted what Cheryl Buckley has characterized as an eclectic range of design elements casually arranged in a domestic setting around groups of patterned textiles, batiks, and ceramics, alongside contemporary paintings, prints, and sculptures.[25] Eschewing any sense of clutter or fussiness, these craft societies highlighted their highly personalized, ethical, and non-commercialized approach towards interior design.

A 'truth to materials' philosophy and visible signs of spontaneity in production were distinctive attributes of this modern appreciation of the Arts and Crafts aesthetic invested with a critical and personal edge. Purity in design was especially demonstrated by hand carving, hand block printing, and etching, and evidenced by hand-thrown pots, hand woven abstract rugs, and textiles in needlework and embroidery. The presence of small-scale craftwork, when used sparingly as carefully placed accessories in the domestic interior, signalled a distinctively personalized English 'decorative' sensibility; one that was seen to manifest an intimacy of viewing within a marked informality of display. As Tanya Harrod has defined it, this spare 'eclectic modernism' of the early 1920s stood in sharp contrast to an emerging 'commercial moderne' in the second half of the decade in which designers utilized technology and embraced industrial manufacturing methods. She argues that 'in these relatively under-furnished interiors appropriate crafts had a potential context along with small sculptures, vernacular non-European objects and abstract paintings. We are tracking a domestic rather than a public modernism [that] in its very simplicity could seem subversive in certain situations.'[26]

Given the widening range of outlets for arts and crafts consumption in the early 1920s – through the main exhibiting societies, small specialist galleries, annual society exhibitions that acted rather like bazaars, and local arts and crafts guild shows often incorporating craft demonstrations – it is significant that many were run by women and that such a personalized aesthetic was largely aimed at artistically-inclined, middle- and upper-class consumers.[27] These 'Arts and Crafts People', as the *Manchester Guardian* identified them, were conspicuous at art exhibitions by their 'distinctive clothes' and 'it is still the aim of many, especially the younger set, to express their own individuality by dressing differently from the other people'.[28] Whilst men wore wide brimmed hats and felt hats, the women, the writer observed, dressed in 'bright scarves, short skirts, bobbed hair and russet brown shades' and 'are all in fashion with long coats'.[29]

Responding to these circumstances, by 1925–26, London's modern art galleries were also eager to engage with the crafts revival market and to profit from the growing popular demand for etchings, prints, and wood engravings. To attract these audiences, dealers embraced less formalized layouts, displaying paintings in a prominent position next to smaller-scale sculpture, studio ceramics, batiks, block-printed fabrics and woven textiles. These galleries included the Beaux Arts Gallery, the Brook Street Gallery, and Heal's Mansard Gallery.

Likewise, London galleries that previously had focused on the fine art market diversified to attract a clientele with broader crafts or print interests. For example, in February 1925, the Lefevre Gallery exhibited *Pictures, Sculptures and Pottery by some British Artists of Today*, organized by the Scottish artist J.D. Ferguson. It comprised art by Paul Nash, S.J. Peploe, Ben and Winifred Nicholson, Jacob Epstein, and Frank Dobson alongside pottery by William Staite Murray, Reginald Wells, and Rachel Burnett. Reviewers stressed the common characteristics of the paintings, sculpture, and pottery, discerning a shared aesthetic code of practice that invoked both sensitivity to texture and mark making and a careful respect for the specific quality and nuanced tones of the materials used. Both art and ceramics were, according to Staite Murray, to be judged on equal terms and by the same standards. As he declared: 'Pottery may be considered the connecting link between sculpture and painting for it incorporates both.'[30] Writing in *Artwork* in winter 1926, H.S. Ede reiterated this point, noting that Staite Murray's work had restored to the crafts their ancient dignity since 'pottery is midway between sculpture and painting – the alternating point of abstract and concrete plastic formal expression'.[31]

Later in July 1928, Staite Murray's ceramics were again included in another exhibition at the Lefevre Gallery alongside paintings by Winifred Nicholson and Ben Nicholson. Critics praised Winifred Nicholson's 'exquisite' art for its 'aptitude rather than actual performance' seeing her as a 'genius ... as a flower painter'.[32] Staite Murray's ceramic vessels and Ben Nicholson's paintings (which a later reviewer called 'landscapes reminiscent of embroidered samplers'[33]), demonstrated a complementary approach, sharing a simplicity of technique and truth to materials ethic that was much admired by many English critics and art collectors in the mid- to late 1920s.[34] All three artists were also in the Seven and Five Society whose membership firmly embraced this alliance of contemporary art and crafts. They all exhibited in the group's annual shows at the Beaux Arts Gallery and Arthur Tooth & Sons from 1926, which promoted the possibilities that this craft ideal and context represented for an integrated union of modern arts and crafts practices. As Ede had underscored in *Artwork*, it was evident that 'the three artists form a most interesting trinity, their work is curiously synthetic'.[35]

From what I have argued, it is clear that these galleries increasingly wished to exploit the growing interest in interior furnishings and decorative arts in England in the early 1920s in order to increase fine art sales. Among younger purchasers whose interests engaged prints, posters, ceramics, textiles, and furniture, the categories modern and/or advanced art encompassed many varied and eclectic types of arts and crafts production that could be accommodated within the domestic setting. However, this realignment was problematic for more traditional Arts and Crafts practitioners with their anti-manufacture ideology and liberal, even socialist, allegiances. For them, this collapsing of handicraft practices and fine art categories into ensemble furnishings demonstrated how the arts and crafts had succumbed to market forces and this contributed to a crisis of direction from 1925 to 1927. As the critic Herbert Furst argued, their amateurish craft practices and principles appeared out of step with contemporary times. Highlighting this rift between conservative and more progressive factions, Furst condemned the 1926 Arts and Crafts Exhibition Society annual exhibition as 'smack[ing] too much of hobbies' and warned 'either continue in this traditional way [and take the consequences] or revitalize design'.[36]

In May 1927, this crisis registered again most forcefully in the re-launched *Arts and Crafts* magazine whose editorial called for an updated and revitalized design approach that demonstrated a more professional response to the conditions of the marketplace and to consumer demand. Following criticism of the British Pavilion at the 1925 *Exposition Internationale des Arts Décoratifs et Industriels Modernes* in Paris and responding to recommendations of the British Institute of Industrial Art report published in 1927, the magazine encouraged British crafts workers to distance themselves from outmoded late nineteenth-century Arts and Crafts theories and practices. By being professional, not amateurish, in their approach and by working as freelance designers embracing commercial constraints, modern advertising methods, and altered conditions of work, crafts practitioners were urged to reinvigorate their efforts, organizing themselves on the model of the German Werkbund in order to produce functional, affordable, and aesthetically improved designs. Comparing the Ideal Home exhibition, then on at the national commercial exhibition halls at Olympia in West Kensington, with the Arts and Crafts Exhibition Society's show at the Royal Academy in the previous year, the editorial decried the fact that 'after 38 years of existence' the society could 'only fill three little rooms' and it concluded that 'the Arts and Crafts must get off their aesthetico-theoretical pedestal and come down into the market place'.[37] Put simply, the writer's point was that as a result of shifting market conditions, the place for artist-designers was not 'producing Arts and Crafts novelties'[38] to be displayed at the Royal Academy, but developing viable commercial designs for the exhibition spaces at Olympia and for the mass market.

Earlier, on 16 February 1926, a letter to *The Times* from Laurence Weaver, President of the Design and Industries Association, had supported a call from the Minister of Overseas Trade to encourage trained artists and designers to become involved in industry as 'Art Directors'. In response, the *Building News and Engineering Journal* (a publication approaching these debates from the trade point of view), in an article entitled 'Art and Commerce', had forcefully supported this commercial attitude:

> There are too many artists endeavouring to preserve an independent existence as virtuosi and many of them would be more profitably employed in the design of commercial craftwork, even though such a pursuit would mean sinking their individual identities ... In the present stage of our history and considering the general financial stringency which specially affects the art loving public, there is no opening for a large body of independent painters.[39]

Given the fact that the Arts and Crafts Exhibition Society's membership in 1926 comprised 100 female members to 148 male members, and that by 1927, as many writers acknowledged, women were especially prevalent at the Society's exhibitions and active in all fields, this clarion call seems to be directed at an increasing number of women craft-designers. The increasing involvement of women artists in the post-war art societies, such as the London Group, the Seven and Five Society, and the London Artists' Association alongside those women-only art groups, reaffirmed this visibility. Comprising between a quarter and a half of all members, and attracting attention from critics at the annual Royal Academy and Royal Societies' shows, these 'artist flappers' were gaining considerable success in British art institutions and in the marketplace. By the 1931 census, of the 10,236 people who self-styled themselves as artists, 5,689 were women. More significantly, in London there were 5,521 male artists as against 3,268 women artists.[40]

The Arts and Crafts Bureau and the Curtis Moffat Studio

Against this background and following the model of couturiers in the fashion market, artist-designers and signature-decorators (as the increasingly professionalized interior decorator became known) allowed their exclusive items to be replicated and merchandised by the growing number of specialist design studios and

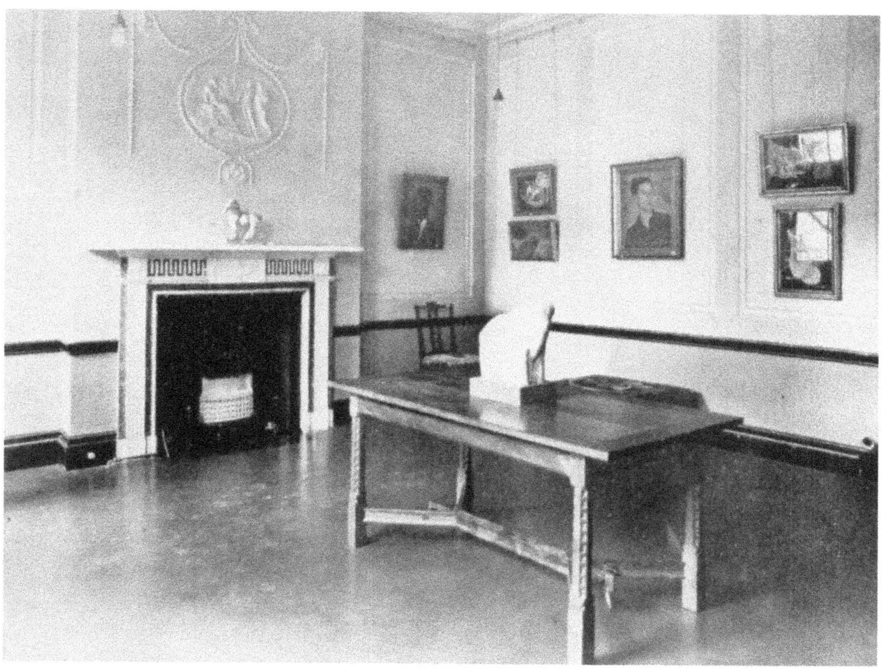

5.3 Photograph of the installation of the Arts and Crafts Bureau, 1928, *Arts and Crafts: A Monthly Review of Arts and Crafts*, 1:1 (July 1928), p. 155.

showrooms opening in London. It is revealing that when the reformed Arts and Crafts Exhibition Society showrooms – its Bureau – opened at 34 Bloomsbury Street, London, in May 1928, its permanent exhibition of contemporary arts and crafts was displayed over three floors and in eight galleries organized as a suite of rooms (figure 5.3). Within an environment of pepper-coloured walls, soft green distempered ceilings, and eggshell green-blue woodwork, paintings, statuettes, pottery, and sculpture by Duncan Grant, Vanessa Bell, John Armstrong, and others were placed on contemporary sideboards and tables, alongside wardrobes and chairs. Incorporated within simulated modern room settings and positioned as contributing to an overall fine art aesthetic, the crafts were placed ready for commercial consumption, enabling a wide range of customers to purchase them.[41]

On 4 July 1929 the Curtis Moffat Studio opened in Fitzroy Square; later it was hailed by the *Studio* as an example of yet 'another modern London gallery … that sets modern pictures as "furnishings"'.[42] Set in a Georgian terraced house refurbished by Frederick Etchells, the press praised it as a 'remarkable work of modernist reconstruction'.[43] Avant-garde paintings, sculpture, ceramics, and textiles were displayed in 'convincing' showroom settings where the Georgian

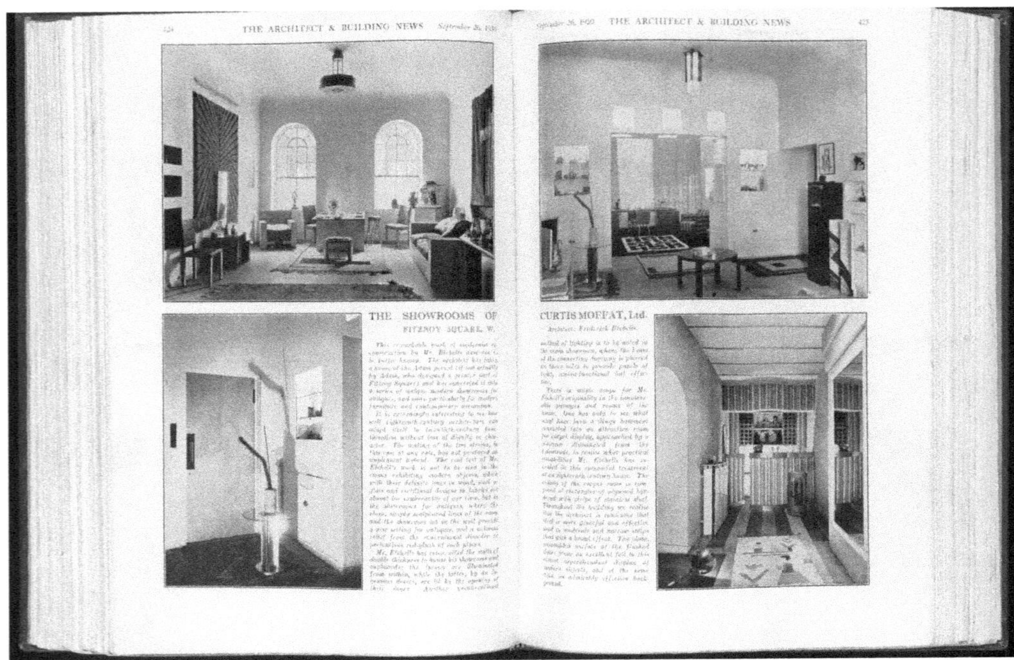

5.4 Showrooms of Curtis Moffat Ltd., *Architect and Building News*, 26 September 1930, pp. 424–5.

interior spaces were exaggerated by large mirrors and the use of focused lighting. Stainless steel mirrors, Perspex tables, a steel cocktail bar, and streamlined furniture were used to highlight and to complement the colourful, woven textiles and modern artworks, notably framed prints, that were strategically positioned (figure 5.4). The innovative lighting (showcases were illuminated from within and handrails were inset with strip-lighting), modern steel fittings, and plywood ceiling were much admired as offering 'a welcome relief from the conventional disorder or pretentious red plush' of many London art galleries.[44] Simplicity of design and minimal detailing marked the renovation as distinctively 'contemporary' in feel. 'The charming display', the *Studio* article continued, 'suggests (of course in a very modern form) the necessary function of pictures as "furniture" – [in a way] which many of the older galleries do not. A picture after all is bought to hang on the walls of the modern small house or flat – and here is both the modern flat and the picture.'[45]

As one of the self-consciously up-to-date art and design studios established in London's West End in the late 1920s, the Curtis Moffat Studio clearly demonstrates the growing commercial interest in and adoption of Continental modernism in architecture and interior design in England. This shift in approach was evidenced not only in the use of reflective surfaces, stainless steel, aluminium, and chromium, but also by adopting a functionalist approach and by maximizing the use of light and, when necessary, installing hidden artificial lighting. Employing plywood with steel and glass partitions as part of an overall functional aesthetic, Etchells, the architect and designer of the Curtis Moffat Studio, was fast gaining a reputation as a fashionable interior design innovator. His Kodak Building for the American photographic company in Kingsway, London, was one of the key modernist landmarks in the capital and in 1930, with Herbert A. Welch, Etchells refurbished the offices of the Anglo-German advertising agency of Sir William Crawford at 233 High Holborn.[46] The project attracted considerable press attention. As the *Architect and Building News* applauded under the heading 'Modernism in London', it was another example of 'modernism gaining force in England' as it 'has already dominated the continent of Europe'. The reviewer continued, 'the most outstanding characteristic is, however, the seeking after fitness for purpose, or what the Germans call *sachlichkeit*'.[47]

Within this process of rethinking what might constitute the modern English interior and in what kind of London environments modern identities might be forged and articulated, the notion of refurbishment was powerful in that it allowed existing exterior architectural styles to be retained while modernist interiors could be economically installed within.[48] Dorothy Todd and Raymond Mortimer's influential 1929 publication, *The New Interior Decoration: An Introduction to the Principles and International Survey of its Methods*, confirmed this direction. It documented a wide-ranging selection of contemporary Continental and American developments in architecture, interior decoration, and design. The book discussed and illustrated key works by Le Corbusier from the recent Stuttgart exhibition organized by the German Werkbund and covered his Laroche flat in Paris, which incorporated paintings by Fernand Léger and Amédée Ozenfant. It presented recent buildings by Walter Gropius at the Bauhaus in Dessau, villas in the South of France designed by Robert Mallet-Stevens, and schemes for apartments by Richard Neutra in Los Angeles and Paul Nelson in Chicago. It also depicted panels for mural decorations in London by Duncan Grant, Vanessa Bell, and Edward McKnight Kauffer alongside 'surrealistic' screens by John Banting, textiles by Phyllis Baron and Dorothy Larcher, mosaics by Boris Anrep, and geometric rugs designed by Marion Dorn. What the book attested to was the increasing speed of dissemination of modernist languages and visual styles among influential metropolitan patrons. It was also instructive about how modern painters, alongside sculptors, designers, craft workers, and architects, now understood their art to be an integral part of an overall fashionable design aesthetic, and to be bought and sold according to patterns of purchasing established in other areas of advertising, merchandising, and marketing. As a result of this greater exposure and commercial accommodation, new possibilities emerged to disseminate a more positive and confident attitude towards foreign-inspired visual languages among this younger audience even if, as Todd and Mortimer complained, 'the public and particularly the rich public is less adventurous in its taste in England than on the continent'.[49]

By the end of the 1920s, the legacies of pre-war Arts and Crafts thinking had been undermined by a more cosmopolitan approach informed by Continental European models and by photographs of such fashionable interiors and buildings being reproduced in mass media periodicals like *Vogue*. Such an up-dated approach to interior decoration was evidenced in the chic and charming showrooms of these London art and design studios and boutiques including the Duncan Miller Studio, the Arts and Crafts Bureau, Betty Joel's Galleries, and the Morris Adam studio. Through exposure to these sets of highly designed modern interior spaces, a wide range of customers, among them a new generation of women consumers, could experience avant-garde art and design first hand, and see for themselves how the artwork they had seen reproduced in photographs in the mass media was perfectly at home in this refurbished urban environment.

'Commercial moderne', Art Deco and the department store

One merchandising feature of the second half of the 1920s and early 1930s was that 'ensemble' interior designs could also be encountered in showrooms in the modern furnishings sections of the city's major department stores such as Harrods, Selfridges, Waring and Gillow, Fortnum and Mason, Peter Jones, and Whiteleys. Increasingly, the vignette style of display and the mock ensemble interior setting were becoming the dominant forms of contemporary merchandising display.[50] As one of the favourite retail marketing devices of the mid- to late 1920s, it was much in evidence in department stores across London's West End (as in other metropolitan centres such as Paris and New York).[51]

As Roland Marchand has argued, the concept of the mock ensemble as an emerging international marketing strategy was premised upon the conscious correlation of all aspects of interior decoration and design, especially of colour, tone, and texture.[52] Crucially, it was linked to the merchandising of a chic and thoroughly cosmopolitan cross-fertilization between art, attire, and lifestyle, and one often featured in the popular press as particularly aimed at reflecting the more casual lifestyle of younger women consumers. At the 1925 Paris *Exposition Internationale des Arts Décoratifs et Industriels Modernes*, the pavilions produced by the French department stores, and the luxury boutiques with their vignette displays reconstructed on the 'rue des Boutiques' had attracted considerable publicity precisely because of the ways in which the French architects and interior designers had simulated lavish modern interiors for the commercial proprietors of the leading Parisian retail outlets as well as for consumption by the exposition's visitors. As Tag Gronberg has shown, these interiors, with their emphasis upon glamour, illumination, and conspicuous display, acknowledged how the commercial sphere had keenly embraced the avant-garde languages of French decorative arts and architecture encapsulated into strikingly modern window displays and interior designs.[53]

More than any other interior decorative style, international Art Deco and its commercialized forms (referred to broadly as 'commercial moderne') penetrated the British interior design mass market in the late 1920s and early 1930s. Its marketability to fashionable young men and women was enhanced by Art Deco's presence in the interior décors of many Hollywood films and in the pages of the fashion magazines, as it became associated with luxurious glamour and celebrity lifestyle.[54] To facilitate its popular consumption, as at the Victoria Street Army and Navy store, London shops employed specialist craftspeople who could properly install the new streamlined interiors, specially made metalwork and mirrors, and complex electrics and high-tech lighting that the style demanded. In supporting an alliance of art and design and commerce, and affirming the role of the artist-designer as decorator, these exclusive retail outlets not only accommodated the work of leading Continental designers, but also promoted the notion of a shared modern aesthetic subscribed to by leading British, American, and Continental artists and designers.

To highlight one example, the Oxford Street furnishings retailer, Waring and Gillow, was particularly significant in the late 1920s in introducing and promoting European, notably French, modern interior décor to London consumers.[55] In 1928, their important exhibition entitled 'Modern Art in French and English Decoration and Furniture' opened comprising sixty-eight rooms, including ten French rooms designed and furnished by Paul Follot (Director of the Modern Art department of their Paris store), alongside ten English suites designed by the store's London equivalent, Serge Chermayeff. It also included a contemporary English flat composed of a study, a drawing room, a double bedroom, and a boudoir.[56] The *Vogue* reviewer, under the title 'The Uncluttered Modern Interior', warned that: 'futurist effects and heavy masses of colour are not essential to modernist decoration … The most characteristically "modern" interior is one that shows a complete absence of unnecessary ornament and design, and contains furniture adapted to the needs and means of today.'[57] Moreover, as *Advertising World* recognized, what was vital was to mark off for the consumer the 'thoroughly modern' approach in contemporary display and window dressing from earlier, more conservative and traditional modes by utilizing mirrored surfaces, focused lighting and non-reflective glass. Employing revealing antinomies, the writer identified these effects as 'accentuating the aluminium over the wooden'; juxtaposing the 'lustrous against the lustreless'; counterpoising the 'beautiful next to the durable' and promoting [American and Continental] streamlining against English 'Pre-Raphaelite principles'.[58]

The Waring and Gillow display also showed a range of artworks by leading British and French artists supporting the claim by dealers and critics that the end of the decade registered a 'boom in British Art'[59] fired by 'young society people [who] now have a new ambition which is to collect small paintings by young modern artists of the advanced kind'.[60] It was precisely this audience that William Gaunt addressed in his article in *Vogue* in October 1930. Although Gaunt's main concern was to contrast a still lively speculative market for contemporary art with the crisis in the stock market, he noted that:

> Wall street slumps and European trade depressions have taken much fun out of speculation in stocks and shares, and amateurs of that pastime have found the share market too dangerous to be profitable ... To those who have anything between £15 and £100 to spend, the judicious buying of pictures can be recommended as a pleasant and, at the same time, profitable investment ... By careful buying, it is possible to become the possessor of a picture of real merit; the value of which will very likely be considerably greater after its owner has had the pleasure of seeing it on his walls for a year or two.[61]

The impact of the Slump upon the rising demand for modern art among younger purchasers and upon speculative investment in the London art market was considerable, forcing a decline in modern art's consumption from around the end of 1929 until the winter of 1933–34, as I have argued elsewhere.[62] Unemployment among artists rose significantly and by the time of the 1931 census, of the 10,000 respondents who identified themselves as 'artists', only 700 confirmed that they supported themselves financially solely from their work.[63] As demand collapsed on the London art market and as calls for government support for British artists along the lines of the American Federal Art Project were refused, many artists were forced to move into the related and more buoyant areas of commercial photography, design, advertising, interior design, and industrial design. As the Report of the Industrial Art Committee of the Federation of British Industries, published in 1931 and arguing for a greater place for the Industrial Arts in art training, concluded, 'Without in any sense desiring to minimise the importance of the Fine Arts, the Committee considers that in the present conditions of world competition and widespread unemployment ... the Industrial Arts ... are equally important from a social point of view and of far greater importance from an economic standpoint'.[64] In response, the Society of Industrial Artists was formed in April 1931.[65]

By the early 1930s, British architects, like artists and craft practitioners, had been forced to adapt to the economic circumstances of the Depression years, which had curtailed building work and limited commissions for Continental-style modern architecture. Smaller-scale, interior renovations and the design of temporary exhibition stands were areas where modernism could still be actively promoted and where increasingly sophisticated modernist styling, new materials, and technical innovation were showcased as part of the refurbishment.[66] These were precisely those arenas in which international languages had revitalized outmoded English visual practices and design cultures, and with which these younger audiences of consumers had become familiar prior to the Depression.[67]

The increasing availability of 'commercial moderne' design and its American version, 'streamlined modern' design in the 1930s, made Art Deco extremely popular, appealing to a broader middle-class audience who encountered its design styling and materials not only in specialist design studios, but also in locales such as cinemas, hotels, beauty salons, cafés, restaurants, fashionable shops and department stores, and on board ocean liners.[68] Emerging at the end of 1933, the drive for this popularization came from the sustained increase in spending power of certain sections of the younger, professional middle classes who had both growing disposable income and an informed interest in interior decoration. Bronwen Edwards has characterized these new metropolitan and suburban consumers as 'a flourishing and broad middle class ... who lavished its prosperity on leisure and consumption, concentrated numerically and culturally in London and the South East [of England]'.[69]

One consequence was that London's commercial exhibition and retailing spaces were now the venues for a number of large, popular shows in which interior design and industrial art featured prominently. The government-sponsored *British Industrial Art in Relation to the Home* exhibition at Dorland Hall, Regent Street, London in 1933; the *Exhibition of Contemporary Industrial Design in the Home*, again at Dorland Hall in 1934; and the *Modern Living* furnishings display, styled in the manner of an exhibition, at Whiteleys department store in Bayswater, London, in 1934, further reinforced this sense of a modernist convergence of art, interior design, and industry. Reviewers also noted how such works could be bought using new credit arrangements developed in retailing and acknowledged the increasing availability of hire purchase agreements and instalment plan credit schemes reflecting Depression-era circumstances.[70]

Reflecting its fashionable and growing appeal to younger consumers, this stark, modernist mode of presentation was quickly adopted by what Clive Bell called 'enterprising and intelligent dealers in London'.[71] By October 1933, the *Daily Mirror* drew attention to the 'outbreak' of many similar exhibitions that included 'ensembles' of modern furniture and fabrics alongside paintings and small-scale 'decorative' sculptures as many galleries vied to attract discerning audiences at keenly competitive prices.[72]

The refurbished Mayor Gallery (1933) and the Duncan Miller Studio's *Modern Pictures in Modern Rooms* exhibition (1936)

The redesigned Mayor Gallery, opening on 20 April 1933 in the refurbished Old Bromhead Gallery, responded to these changes in fashionable metropolitan consumption by adopting Continental, especially German Bauhaus, interior design in which painting and sculpture were displayed to complement this new functional, minimalist aesthetic. The Mayor Gallery showed 'advanced' work by contemporary Continental artists, notably German and French Surrealist art, alongside the work of younger British artists. Its first exhibition was an extensive show designed to place contemporary British art in an international context. Entitled 'Recent Paintings by English, French and German Artists', it featured works by Pablo Picasso, Georges Braque, Fernand Léger, Joan Miro, Max Ernst, Paul Klee, Henri Masson, and Jean Arp next to works by leading British artists Paul Nash, Edward Wadsworth, Ben Nicholson, John Armstrong, and Henry Moore, among others, including the young Francis Bacon.[73] In so doing, the exhibition pointed up the accelerating pace of change in British art and many critics applauded the gallery's vigorous promotion of Continental alliances. The *Weekend Review* saluted the Mayor Gallery for 'filling a glaring deficiency in London for the exhibition of contemporary art'[74] whilst the *Times* praised it as being 'frankly and consistently of the moment' noting that 'the Mayor Gallery is doing the job which should be carried out by the Tate'.[75] Other writers commended it for its daring promotion of German art at a time when it was practically hardly ever exhibited in England.

The Mayor Gallery provided the very latest in interior décor and modern display facilities and this appreciation of the gallery's self-conscious 'cosmopolitanism' extended into discussions of the open-plan layout of the gallery space and its interior decoration scheme designed by Brian O'Rorke. The *Yorkshire Telegraph* and the *Daily Mail* critics respectively acclaimed the gallery as the most 'ultra-modern' in Britain and 'the last word in modernity'.[76] Equally, the refurbishment of the old galleries into the new Mayor Gallery was highlighted as especially significant and cost-effective given the contemporary economic situation, and the design embraced new materials and building techniques. The

Mayor's startling white and orange-vermilion exterior (with Pilkington vitriolite white lettering) was widely applauded in the press. Inside, with its plain, white roughcast walls, split-level layout, hidden lighting and stainless steel furniture, the gallery was, as P.G. Konody endorsed, 'a gay and enlivening atmosphere'[77] and its relaxed intimacy contributed to an exemplary modern environment in which to appreciate contemporary art. Reviewed positively in both *Vogue* and *Harper's Bazaar*, the latter's writer concluded that in all its informal yet self-conscious modernity as evidenced by 'the orange and white façade ... the very interior with a ceiling on different levels, rustless steel furniture, hidden lighting and severe simplicity', it marked out 'the Bauhaus coming to Cork Street'.[78]

The most extensive review of the Mayor Gallery as a space for showing contemporary art was published in May 1934 by Anthony Bertram in *Design for To-day* (figure 5.5). Entitled 'Selling Pictures: An Organisation and a Gallery' and considering the recently formed 'Unit One' group exhibition and its provincial tour, Bertram addressed the issue of the modern artist and his or her commercial market given the altered socio-economic conditions in 1933–34. He argued:

> the aspect of this organisation [Unit One] which is of immediate interest to readers of *Design for To-day* is that it is not a group of painters only; that in its constitution it proclaims the need for co-ordinating the arts, for returning to that older and healthier condition ... in which the present distinction between the fine and applied arts was not drawn.[79]

Turning to consider the Mayor Gallery specifically, Bertram praised the gallery's directors and designer, and continued:

> The colouring of the walls is pleasant but unobtrusive creating a general effect of well-being which may be immediately felt by the visitor though he may find his attention diverted from the pictures to look at their background. The ground floor is off-white, the first floor a subtle and delicate compound of black, yellow white and ultramarine producing a pale green-grey. The exterior since it is designed to attract attention is orange with white lettering. But I think the most important feature of the design is the way in which the gallery has been broken up into small connected compartments and recesses which enable pictures to be isolated into subtle groups and even single pictures to be seen without interference. The gallery feeling is replaced by the room feeling: the pictures so far as it is possible in a gallery which must house changing exhibitions, 'tell' decoratively. They do not compete with one another. They are part of a decorative scheme rather than goods displayed for sale.[80]

DESIGN FOR TO-DAY. MAY 1934

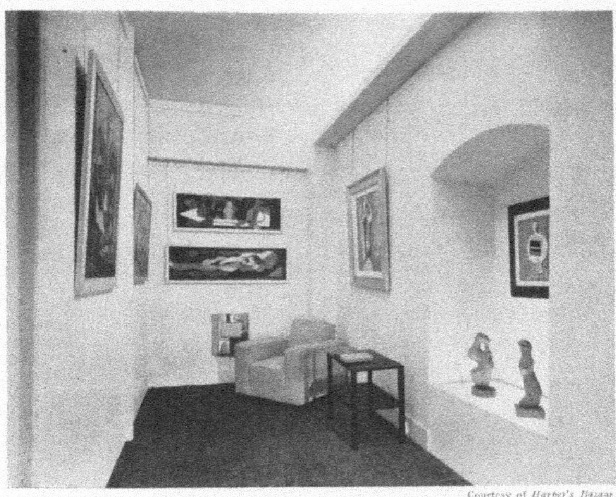

Courtesy of *Harper's Bazaar*

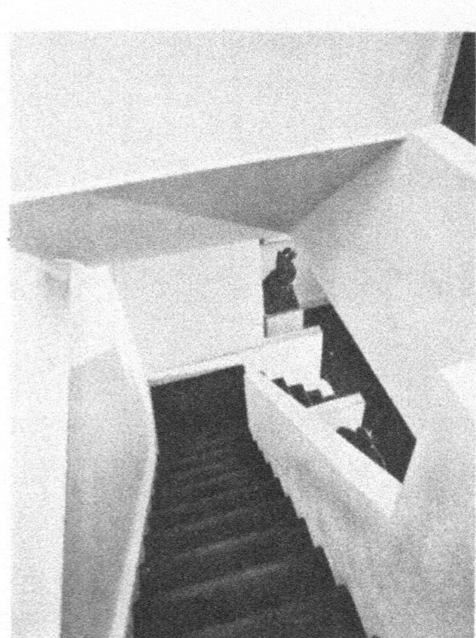

Courtesy of *Harper's Bazaar*

The D.I.A. travelling exhibition has given fresh food ; Unit One will give more. The bookings for both of these are already evidence that the provinces want to know what is happening in London in the nineteen-thirties. In the course of lecturing up and down England during the last six years I have heard no more frequent complaint than "We never see these pictures." I have received essays from students who are enthusiastic about abstract art but have to confess that they know it only in reproduction. This is tragic. England is not so big that such a state of affairs need exist, nor is it so small, nor are time and money so easily available, that everyone who is interested in these things can travel to London for exhibitions.

The importance of this exhibition, therefore, and of the appearance of the book *Unit One*, is not to be measured only in terms of each artist's merits. They represent an experiment which may have enormous results. What some of these may be Read attempts to forecast in his introductory notes, and I cannot end better than by echoing exactly his words. "Having perhaps somewhat unnecessarily characterised the aims of the group in self-seeking terms, I can with an easy conscience proceed to say that from my own point of view, which is that of an independent critic having no status in the group, the formation of Unit One seems to me to have more importance than any event which has happened in the history of English art for very many years."

165

5.5 Mayor Gallery interiors, *Design for To-day*, May 1934, p. 165.

Revealingly, the article is accompanied by photographs of the Mayor Gallery's interiors 'courtesy of Harper's Bazaar' – photographs that would be reproduced again in the next issue of that magazine in the following month, June 1933, and were, no doubt, syndicated widely across its international editions.

This realignment of art and design boundaries and the desire to resituate the artwork as a contributor to the overall interior design aesthetic is reflective of the wider impact of the socio-economic conditions of the Slump between c.1929 and 1933 upon English modernism. The forced involvement of art with economics and the reorientation of modern artists to the commercial imperatives of the marketplace had become even more pronounced as artists and dealers in London had felt the full impact of the art-market collapse as part of the broader recession between 1931 and 1933. Bearing this in mind, the Mayor Gallery's incorporation of many of the décor and styling features of the streamlined, functional environment is significant. By 1933 such fully integrated ensemble interiors were commended in the press for providing what the *Observer* critic called a sense of the unity of aesthetic conception that 'demonstrates that adequately evolved surroundings are desirable if not indispensable so as to get the full ornamental value out of a picture, or a piece of sculpture of the type that is usually referred to as being of an "advanced tendency"'.[81]

In the post-Slump era, these interconnections between affordable modern art, functional interior design, modern-looking furniture, and modernist architecture appeared all the more important because London seemed to many observers in late 1933 to 1935 to be at the centre of an economic up-turn and undergoing a tentative yet discernible artistic renaissance. Douglas Goldring, writing in the *Studio* in February 1934, noted the emergence of a 'large and wholly new type of picture buyer' into the modern art market; 'a vast army of middle class flat dwellers who formerly only aspired towards reproductions [but who are now] beginning to purchase originals'.[82] In September 1935, the *Listener* also highlighted this trend recording that 'the day of the grand private patron is over ... In his place has come a patron, still private but on a much smaller scale. He buys (but rarely commissions) a few pictures (small) that he fancies will look well on the walls of the room of his flat.'[83]

One flaw in this argument was that these keen buyers were not exclusively men, but, as already indicated, included many women who, as part of the professional 'moneyed classes' (as *Advertising World* categorized them),[84] would lead the post-Slump recovery in interior decoration, fashion, and domestic design; they were what market research groups described as the younger, discerning readers of *Vogue*, the *Tatler*, *Harper's Bazaar*, and *Country Life*. It was among this new constituency of middle-class, largely female, consumers that modern British art was divested of its previous connotations of avant-gardism, and increasingly became confused with a fashionable type of interior furnishings style popularized in the growing number of large-circulation fashion, design, and domestic 'ideal home' magazines and promoted by the new design retail outlets such as the Gordon Russell and Duncan Miller studios. As an installation photograph of the exhibition entitled 'Modern Pictures in Modern Rooms' at the Duncan Miller Studio in April 1936 testifies (figure 5.6), this change in taste, embracing lightweight and flexible furniture and open interior layout, incorporated the work of Piet Mondrian, Jean Hélion, and Alexander Calder alongside leading British artists, thereby indicating a transformation had recently occurred in existing boundaries between painting, sculpture, interior decoration, and furnishings.[85] Furthermore, the presence in London of new or refurbished stores with sophisticated shop-fronts, more life-like mannequins, new modes of window display and advertising, as well as up-to-the minute retailing innovations pioneered in New York, Chicago, Paris, or Berlin reinforced the significance of such a modern aesthetic.[86]

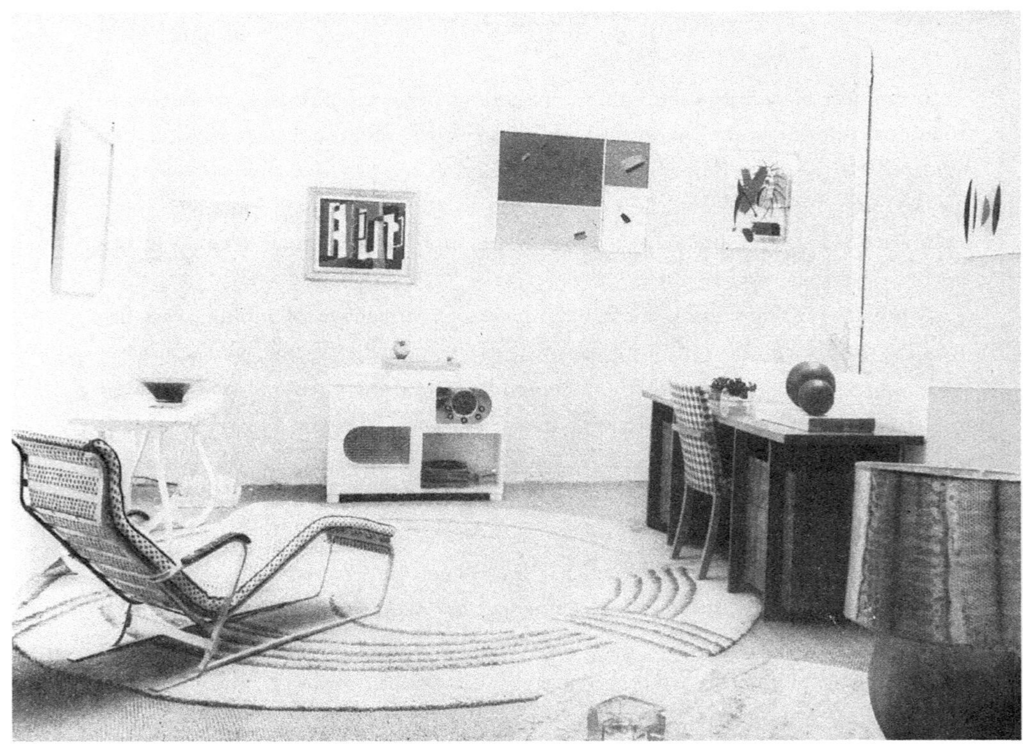

5.6 Photograph of the exhibition installation, *Modern Pictures in Modern Rooms*, from the exhibition catalogue accompanying the Duncan Miller Studio exhibition of the same name (1936).

By January 1935, from the evidence of articles contained in a wide range of fashionable magazines aimed at this younger middle-class readership, this up-dated aesthetic was well established and speculative buying and selling of modern art was making a return in light of a strong demand for contemporary art, fuelling a more buoyant London art market. An article in the *Bystander* enthusiastically reported that 'Now all is changed, *la crise est finie* and there is a new ferment in young Mayfair ... the art dealers know it, the social writers have sensed it and quite nice people are collecting to cover those bare walls ... Now even the doubtful benefits of tubular lights and chromium seats have reached the new suburbs.'[87] What is particularly revealing is that the gossip columnist of a popular magazine like the *Bystander* was carefully monitoring the London art scene. As the same society column had highlighted in November 1934, opening nights at the Mayor Gallery presented famous and fashionable types with golden 'Photo-opportunities' to mingle with other international celebrities and to play up to and to court press photographers' attention.[88]

In September 1935, the art critic of the *Scotsman* complained about the impact these changes in gallery design and art merchandising were having upon the experience of London's exhibition goers. 'These spaces', he lamented 'are so avant-garde and up to the minute that a conservative like myself enters [them] with a feeling of mild dismay. There seems to be something bullying in the very efficiency of the place ... Everything seems valuable for its novelty and soon, it appears, everything will be "dated" and set aside.'[89] By highlighting how economic imperatives, modern retailing methods, popular journalism, and new modes of consumption had reshaped the commercial gallery experience, this critic clearly felt that such collusion had undermined the authority of contemporary British art and threatened its (claimed) aesthetic integrity. Other viewers, among them fashionable young women and men, would, I believe, by the mid-1930s have forcefully disagreed with such an old-fashioned, insular, and out-dated approach.

Notes

1 Frank Rutter, 'Modest Work for Modest Means', *The Sunday Times*, 3 October 1921, p. 7.
2 'Hard Times for Artists', *The Times*, 10 June 1922, p. 9.
3 See also: Stephenson, 'From Conscription to the Depression'; Stephenson, '"Strategies of Situation"'.
4 Raymond Mortimer, 'Paris Fashions in Furnishings', *Vogue* (late August 1924), pp. 27–8.
5 Mortimer, p. 28.
6 Christopher Reed has characterized Mortimer's columns on theatre and literature

in *Vogue* as offering 'a consistent attitude identified as that of irreverent youth' and marking out the emergence, under the editorship of Dorothy Todd, of a queer subcultural identity. See Reed, '*Vogue*', p. 51.

7 See Packer, *Vogue Covers*, and Conekin and de la Haye, 'Introduction'. Also, Magidson, 'Fashion Showdown'.

8 See Sparke, *Modern Interior*, pp. 57–9.

9 'Editorial', *Vogue* (late May 1925), p. liii.

10 Nicholson, *Singled Out*, pp. xiii, 13–14.

11 Nicholson, p. 71.

12 See David, '*Vogue*'s New World', pp. 14, 31–2, and Ross, ed. *Twenties London*, p. 20.

13 Weightman and Humphries, *Making of Modern London*, p. 34.

14 Brown, *Exhibition*, p. x.

15 Zeitz, *Flapper*.

16 Tillyard, *Impact of Modernism*, pp. 47–56.

17 Reed, *Bloomsbury Rooms*, pp. 111–12.

18 Paul Nash, 'Modern English Textiles', *Artwork* 2:6 (January-February 1926), p. 83.

19 Gerstein, ed. *Beyond Bloomsbury*.

20 'A Bad Time for Artists', *Yorkshire Evening Post*, 4 January 1921, p. 4.

21 'Art to Brighten Dull Places', *Star*, 7 February 1921, p. 27.

22 Carey and Griffiths, eds. *Avant-garde British Printmaking*, pp. 13–15.

23 Boydell, *Architect of Floors*, p. 26.

24 Harrod, *Crafts in Britain*, pp. 22–8; Jones, *Studio Pottery*, pp. 59–76. It is noteworthy that these small galleries were established and run or co-run by women, including the Three Shields Gallery, the New Handworkers' Guild Gallery, and the Little Gallery. Harrod, p. 117.

25 Buckley, *Designing Modern Britain*, pp. 73–8.

26 Harrod, p. 115.

27 Harrod, pp. 126–9; Moira Vincentelli, 'Potters of the 1920s: Contemporary Criticism', *Women and Craft*, eds. Elinor et al., p. 76.

28 'The Arts and Crafts People', *Manchester Guardian*, 18 January 1926. The reviews of the Arts and Crafts Exhibition Society shows are derived from the Press cutting albums of the Society contained in the Archives of Art and Design, Victoria and Albert Museum, London: Files AAD 1/120–1980. All subsequent references will be AAD Press cuttings.

29 'The Arts and Crafts People', *Manchester Guardian*, 18 January 1926 [AAD Press cuttings].

30 William Staite Murray, 'Pottery and the Essentials in Art', *Arts League of Service Bulletin* (London, 1923–24), p. 11. I am indebted to Cheryl Buckley for her guidance regarding Staite Murray's pottery and its affiliations with contemporary artists' work.

31 H.S. Ede, 'Ben Nicholson, Winifred Nicholson and William Staite Murray', *Artwork*, 4:16 (Winter 1926), p. 267.

32 'Pots and Paintings', *The Times*, 6 July 1928, contained in the Lefevre Gallery Press cuttings Albums, 1927–36 Tate Archives, London [TAM 9E]. All subsequent references will be LGPA.

33 'Ben Nicholson: Flat-Pattern Painting', *Scotsman*, 7 March 1930 [LGPA].

34 Jones, pp. 60–5.

35 Ede, p. 262.

36 Herbert Furst, 'The Arts and Crafts Exhibition Society at Burlington House', *Apollo* (February-March 1926) [AAD Press cuttings].

37 'Musings at Olympia: The Ideal Home Exhibition and Another', *Arts and Crafts: A Monthly Review of Arts and Handicrafts* (May 1927), p. 25 [AAD Press cuttings].

38 'Arts and Crafts Novelties', *Daily News*, 18 January 1926 [AAD Press cuttings].

39 'Art and Commerce', *Building News and Engineering Journal*, 130:3,711 (19 February 1926), p. 185 [AAD Press cuttings].

40 In the Seven and Five Society, approximately a third of the membership was female. By 1934, women artists comprised 32 per cent of the seventy-two members of the London Group. The Women's Group exhibited at the Lucy Wertheim Gallery, London, from 1933. Katy Deepwell estimates that women artists consistently formed between 25 and 40 per cent within the large open exhibitions during these years. See Deepwell, 'Introduction', *Decades*, unpaginated, and her 'Women Artists'.

41 This account is taken from *Arts and Crafts: A Monthly Review of Arts and Handicrafts*, 1:1 (new series, July 1928), p. 155 [AAD Press cuttings].

42 'Events', *Studio*, January 1931, p. 67.

43 'The Showrooms of Curtis Moffat Ltd.', *Architect and Building News*, 26 September 1930, p. 424.

44 Ibid.

45 'Events', *Studio*, January 1931, p. 67.

46 For more on Crawford see, David Mellor, 'London–Berlin–London: A Cultural History. The Reception and Influence of the New German Photography in Britain 1927–33', in *Germany*, ed. Mellor, pp. 113–30.

47 'Modernism in London', *Architect and Building News*, 19 September 1930, p. 373.

48 See Elizabeth Darling, 'The Scene in Which the Daily Drama of Personal Life Takes Place: Towards the Modern Interior in Early 1930s Britain', in *Designing the Modern Interior*, eds. Sparke et al., pp. 95–105.

49 Todd and Mortimer, eds. *New Interior Decoration*, p. 26.

50 See Wilson, 'Exhibiting Modern Times', pp. 101–2.

51 For the American market, see Friedman, *Selling Good Design*.

52 Marchand, *Advertising the American Dream*.

53 Gronberg, *Designs on Modernity*, pp. 74–5.

54 Sparke, *Modern Interior*, pp. 70–2.

55 'Modern Furniture: The Waring Exhibition', *Studio*, February 1929, p. 131.

56 Buckley, pp. 75–6.

57 'The Uncluttered Modern Interior', *Vogue*, 6 February 1929, p. 32.

58 'Aluminum for Shop Display', *Advertising World*, October 1931, p. 304.

59 'Boom close to a Dull Year', *Daily Express*, 30 November 1930 [LGPA].

60 *Sunday News*, 30 November 1930 [LGPA].

61 William Gaunt, 'On Buying Pictures', *Vogue*, 29 October 1930, p. 58.

62 See my 'Strategies of Situation'.

63 Quoted by Beckett, 'Circle', p. 12.

64 'Declaration of the Aim to Establish State-Aided Industrial Art Education' by the Industrial Art Committee of the Federation of British Industries Report (1931) quoted in *Advertising World* (supplement to the September 1931 issue), unpaginated.

65 An announcement of its formation was published in the *Studio*, April 1931, p. 293. The fullest examination of this trend is Read's *Art and Industry*.

66 My thinking here is informed by Williams, 'Rodney Thomas', which examines how Thomas worked within a circle of modernist artists, designers, and architects operating in the new fields of film and retailing, many of whom were employed by Crawford's Advertising Agency, and how their practices responded to the impact of the Slump.

67 The introduction of the Abnormal Importation (Customs Duties) Act in November 1931 temporarily imposed 50 per cent duty on luxury goods and textiles from abroad, reduced to 20 per cent in July 1932, and encouraged purchasers to buy British-made art and luxury objects.

68 Sparke, p. 103.

69 Edwards, '"Bond Street"'.

70 See, e.g. Mayor Gallery exhibition catalogues and reviews, which are contained in the Mayor Gallery Papers and Press cutting Albums from 1933–35 in the Tate Archives, London [TAM 7B]. All subsequent references will be MGPA.

71 Clive Bell was referring to the Zwemmer Gallery and praising its innovative presentation methods in 'Mr. Zwemmer', *New Statesman and Nation*, 22 December 1934 [MGPA].

72 *Daily Mirror*, 23 October 1933 [LGPA].

73 This exhibition opened on 20 April 1933. The Directors of the Mayor Gallery were listed as F.H. Mayor, Douglas Cooper, and J.F. Duthie.

74 Edward Crankshaw review in the *Weekend Review*, 29 April 1933 [MGPA].

75 *The Times*, 22 April 1933 [MGPA].

76 *Yorkshire Telegraph*, 13 October 1933; *Daily Mail*, 13 April 1933 [MGPA].

77 P.G. Konody, 'Gayest Art Show – Last Word in Modernism – Presents a Puzzle', *Daily Mail*, 20 April 1933 [MGPA].

78 *Vogue* (late June 1933) and *Harper's Bazaar*, June 1933 [MGPA].

79 Anthony Bertram, 'Selling Pictures: An Organisation and a Gallery', *Design for To-day*, May 1934, p. 162 [MGPA]. *Design for To-day* was launched as a monthly journal in May 1933 incorporating both *Design in Industry* and the *DIA Quarterly*.

80 Bertram, p. 162 [MGPA].

81 Review of Zwemmer's 'Artists of Today' exhibition, *Observer*, 4 June 1933 [MGPA].

82 Douglas Goldring, 'Artists and Pictures', *Studio*, February 1934, p. 100; quoted in Beckett, p. 12.

83 *The Listener*, 25 September 1935 [MGPA].

84 H.W. Yoxall; quoted in *Advertising World*, October 1931, p. 252.

85 'Modern Pictures in Modern Rooms – An Exhibition of Abstract Art in Contemporary Settings Arranged by S. John Woods and Duncan Miller', at Duncan Miller Ltd, 10 Lower Grosvenor Place, London SW1. There were works by Constantin Brancusi, Naum Gabo, Alberto Giacometti, Jean Hélion, Ben Nicholson, Eileen Holding, Arthur Jackson, Joan Miro, Moholy-Nagy, Piet Mondrian, Henry Moore, Paalen, John Piper, and John Woods priced from £5 for drawings to £409 for Moholy Nagy's *Architecture V* (1920). The catalogue noted that 'deferred payments can be arranged'.

86 Morrison, *English Shops and Shopping*, pp. 59–60.

87 'Not so Private Views', *Bystander*, 1 January 1935 [MGPA].

88 'Photo-opportunities', *Bystander*, 20 November 1934 [MGPA].

89 *Scotsman*, 30 September 1935 [LGPA].

II

Intersections

6

The art press and the art market: the artist as 'economic man'

Julie F. Codell

The nineteenth-century art press ranged from the populist to the elitist and specialist. I focus on the populist art press (the *Art Journal* and the *Magazine of Art*) which functioned as guides to middle-class, socially aspiring readers hailed both as art consumers and as advocates of national culture. Despite these journals' claims of high-minded educational intentions, they also functioned as trade journals, but in a special way, unlike most trade journals. These two publications were addressed not just to artists, as a trade journal would be, but also to the public. Thus, despite their superficial differences (the *Art Journal* cost more and appealed to a more well-to-do readership), these two journals, by exploring trade issues of art market economics, including artists' own economic needs and art production in the studio, that sanctum sanctorum, exposed insider information to the public. In this way, both journals' candid focus on the art market, meant to encourage the public to buy British art, also served to transform economics into a sign of a successful national culture and to transform art production into a business enterprise conducted by exemplary artists aligned with middle-class social decorum, the Victorian gospel of labour, and Britishness.

In both these journals, business became a paradigm for art production. Economic success symbolized both the work ethic and artists' concomitant good moral character. In the golden age of art consumption in the 1860s, artists profiled in the press donned new roles as contributors to Britain's economic well-being; their own successes guaranteed that they complied with social norms and exemplified Britain's presumed cultural superiority. Economic topics in the art press ranged widely, from advice for middle-class patrons, stories about successful artists, assessments of art's contribution to Britain's gross national product and balance of trade, new sources of income for artists (advertising, 'artistic' postcards, electric fittings, and home furnishings) to recommendations of talented young artists whose works would appreciate over time as worthy investments.

As Stephen Copley points out, the civic humanist and the consumerist accounts of painting emerged together in the eighteenth century; these two strands 'continued to coexist in uneasy symbiosis'.[1] For Victorians economics became a sign of artists' professionalism, not of greed or social climbing, as it had been in the eighteenth century. I argue that the Victorian press significantly contributed to a discourse in which the civic and the commercial were sometimes symbiotic, sometimes merged, but rarely adversarial. As early as 1854 Thomas Skaife defended artists who painted for money.[2] Charles R. Leslie in his biography of John Constable (1843, 1845) stressed Constable's economic knowledge and careful negotiations over money and commissions.[3] These emphases distinguished Leslie's biography from other mid-century accounts of artists' lives but became commonplace from the 1860s on as signs of shared values between artists and new consumers composed of entrepreneurs, industrialists, and the mass public.

Victorians were sometimes uncomfortable about artistic success; John Ruskin attacked artists who dined with patrons or owned expensive carriages. He promoted an ideal of an innocent, childlike artist working outside social and economic demands.[4] But these arguments were countered by periodicals' celebrations of artists' celebrity, wealth, and sociability with endless citations of artists' prizes, commissions, and high prices.[5] To transform economic success into professionalism the art press deployed New Journalism methods – the interview, sensationalism, and the hyperbolic language of advertising. The gossip column provided 'inside' information about works in progress, artists' current activities, sales, and imminent exhibitions to whet readers' appetites and induce spectating and buying. The art press provoked debates about the nude, child prodigies, and other hot art topics. Yet sensationalist New Journalism, while aggrandizing artists, also threatened to commodify art and artists as some critics and artists recognized.

Samuel Carter Hall, first editor and founder of the *Art Journal* in 1839 (then called the *Art-Union*), bragged, '*I had to create a public for Art*' by blending 'information and instruction with interesting and useful intelligence', initially to replace consumers' purchases of Old Masters with acquisitions of works by living British artists.[6] The *Art Journal* (figure 6.1) in 1861 asserted, 'The power of the British Press has been as great as that of the Royal Academy, and it has been much more abused' because of critics' 'unintelligible jargon ... technical slang' and 'empty phrases' of connoisseurship, instead of an art language for middle-class readers.[7] As Pierre Bourdieu argues, art is produced not only by artists but also by art discourses in 'reproductions, catalogues, art journals, museums', whose

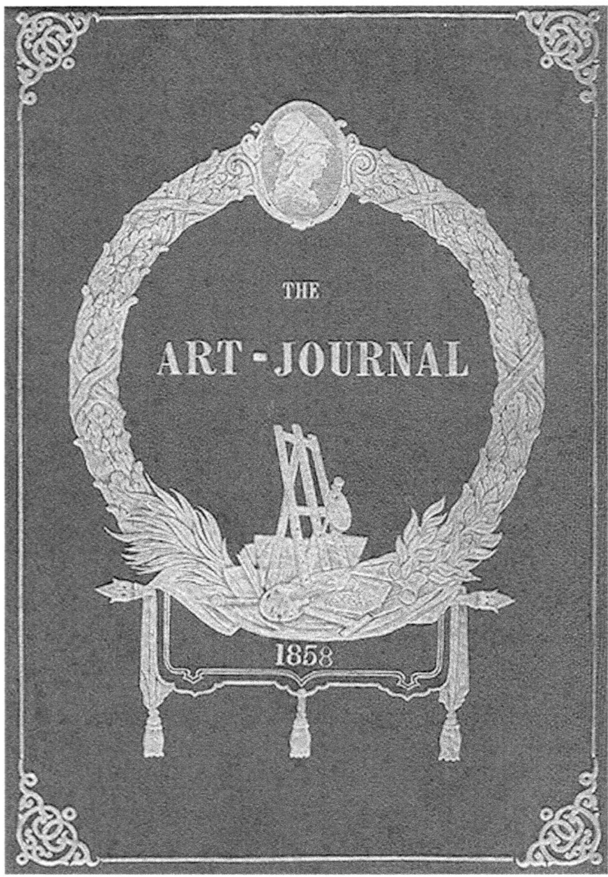

6.1
Art Journal, cover,
1858.

discourses become 'a stage in the production of the work, of its meaning and value'.[8] *All* commentary – criticism, catalogues, biographies, cartoons, media, and exhibitions – competes in 'a struggle for the monopoly of legitimate discourse about the work of art, and consequently in the production of the value of the work of art'.[9] Hall, self-fashioning himself as a producer of art's public, became a co-producer of British art.

The role of the press in the production of art and of its public was extensive. The *Art Journal* claimed that monthly circulation increased from 700 in 1839 to 8,000 in 1850 to nearly 25,000 in 1851.[10] Other evidence of its wide readership was advertising in the journals and in the *Art Journal*'s popular *Art Annual*s appearing at Christmas and Easter. Among the advertisements grouped at the ends of individual issues were illustrated travel books, Osler's Table Glass and China, books on a wide range of non-art topics, artistic cards, prints, furniture, leaded windows, gardening seeds, cough remedies, and cocoa. Such advertising

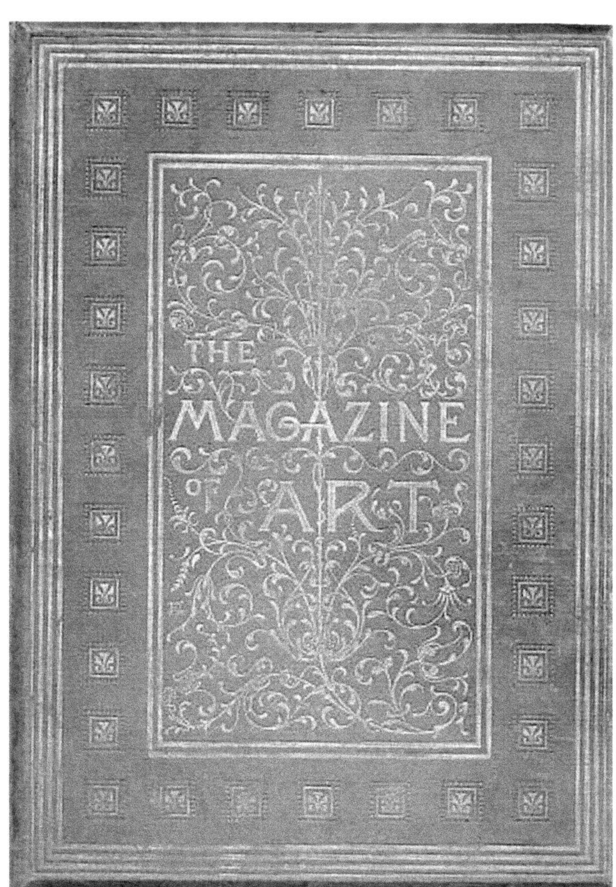

6.2
Magazine of Art, cover,
1878.

reveals the context for art within an enormous sphere of goods that we now consider discrete – one cannot imagine ads for seeds and medicine in today's art publications. Recently scholars have shown that positioning advertising and novels' serialized chapters side by side in the press mutually inflected both genres.[11] Similarly, ads and art criticism co-existing in the same journal inflected each other by blending promotional language with matters of taste.

The *Magazine of Art* (figure 6.2) had a chequered life, first as a short-lived journal published by Cassell's that was part of the publisher's vision of offering a kind of working-class education. Cassell's published the *Illustrated Exhibitor*, an exhibition catalogue for the 1851 Great Exhibition with costly wood engravings, which appeared weekly for 2d, and in monthly parts for 8d.[12] The first number sold out in a day, was reprinted, and sold 100,000 copies by the end of the first month.[13] The *Illustrated Exhibitor and Magazine of Art* was retitled the *Illustrated Magazine of Art* in early 1853, its cover illustrated by George Cruickshank; its writers were non-specialists who knew little about art. It sold for 2d weekly, but failed in 1856. The *Illustrated Exhibitor* emerged for the 1862 Exhibition, but its sales did not justify continuing it. In 1878, the year of the Paris International Exhibition and following a decade of a flourishing art market for living British artists, John Cassell's partners, after his death, began the *Magazine of Art*, catering to the general public in contrast to the more expensive *Art Journal*. The *Magazine of Art* was conservative, endorsed the Academy at every turn, and was ever suspicious of new art from Aestheticism to Impressionism.

In 1898, the magazine still asserted its aesthetic conservatism from which it had a brief hiatus from 1881 to 1887 under editor William Ernest Henley.[14] Henley had avant-garde tastes and promoted Whistler, the Barbizon painters, and Rodin. Hostile to English art and to Ruskin, he hired knowledgeable art critics (Sidney Colvin, R.A.M. Stevenson, Andrew Lang, Cosmo Monkhouse, among others).[15] Despite Henley's editorship, the magazine's interests lay with commercial success, the art establishment, and trade journal topics of economics and technical matters.[16]

When the magazine was turned over to Marion Harry Spielmann in 1887, its editor until its demise in 1904, it returned to its original positions: pro-Academy, insular taste vis-à-vis Continental art, and a Ruskinian moral purpose. Spielmann, steeped in New Journalism, tried to include a range of views to create 'a thorough encyclopedia of the whole subject',[17] and also to sustain controversy and public interest. Nevertheless, French art and its English followers were pilloried by the magazine's Academician authors, and Impressionism was attacked as late as 1904.[18]

The magazine was initially successful, doubling in size in 1880 to 500 pages and moving from pen sketches and woodcuts to photogravure frontispieces and high quality engravings and woodcuts.[19] Its price increased to a shilling in 1881 without a drop in sales. It launched a wide advertising campaign complete with a poster by Hubert von Herkomer, initiating a trend in advertising of employing pictures by RAs. In 1893 the magazine grew to 600 pages, contained full-page colour reproductions and cost 1s 4d, but sales declined from 1897, despite gossip columns ('Notes and Queries' which encouraged readers to write to the editor[20]), sensationalist debates, and supplements. Spielmann's eulogy for the magazine commented on his attempt to take 'a line in art-politics' against new movements, but in the end he failed to keep the public interested in views lagging behind new tastes and currents.[21]

Beyond periodical publication cycles, these journals' Christmas art annuals entered the market as art objects themselves, predecessors of coffee table books, to generate further cultural capital for artists' names as brands that fed buyers' social aspirations. As Catherine Soussloff notes, 'Names and naming in the biographies of artists and the discourse of art history become performative of the process of art making itself.'[22] Anthropologist Mary Douglas considers naming a form of consumption.[23] Biographies indulged in a form of branding by the repetition of artists' traits: tall, manly Millais or Watts the idealist.[24]

Furthermore, many authors of press interviews and articles wrote biographies for popular series on Old Masters and living artists, many published by periodical publishers.[25] So much writing by so few authors meant that some artists appeared repeatedly across the press, books, and print shops, generating their celebrity status as circulating commodities in a tightly controlled network of information. As Laurel Brake explains, critics commonly wrote for several periodicals and newspapers, recycling their articles but modifying tone, style, and politics for diverse audiences.[26] A single critic could mobilize much public opinion: William Michael Rossetti wrote almost four hundred art essays for English and American periodicals from 1850 (when he became critic for the *Spectator*) to 1878.[27] An artist's biography could appear in multiple places: F.G. Stephens wrote biographies of James Clarke Hook for the *Art Journal* which became an *Art Annual* edition, and for the *Portfolio*.

Successful artists were increasingly empowered socially and economically to endow their purchasers with cultural and symbolic capital as artists' very names became bearers of multiple kinds of capital. Bourdieu 'warns against philosophy that considers creativity to be tainted when it is involved in any political, commercial, pedagogic or decorative function and which only exalts pure art forms totally disengaged from other human concerns'.[28] Such philosophy denies the permeable borders between kinds of capital: cultural capital of educational qualifications, social capital from a home well-endowed with cultural capital, honorific capital of civic recognition from a successful life in industrial society, and symbolic capital associated with writers and artists. Combined with economic resources, these forms of capitalism 'form a personal patrimony'.[29]

The art press promoted all of these at once. To do this, it worked in tandem with art markets through gallery advertisements, exhibition announcements, and the promotion of British artists. Although editors made nationalism one ideological justification for promoting British artists, from the 1860s onwards press attention to Continental and colonial art, limited to pan-European realism (e.g., France's Rosa Bonheur, Hungary's Michael Munkacsy, Russia's Ilya Repin, and white artists from Australia, Canada, and South Africa), legitimated British Academic realism as a global language. Thus, one criterion of British artists' success and exemplarity became their global reputations *as British artists* who increasingly exhibited internationally.

The artist's emerging professionalism: money into virtue

Victorian artists were quite open about their economic and social success. Such successes, attacked in the eighteenth century as signs of greed and commercialization, became signs of Victorian artists' respectability that mirrored their public's ambitions. In voluminous letters to critics such as F.G. Stephens (*Athenaeum* critic for forty years) and M.H. Spielmann, artists wrote about works-in-progress that they wanted published, sometimes with a drawing or maquette to titillate the public and to stir potential consumers. Drawings seemed to capture the creative process, a surplus value, as artists represented their adherence to the work ethic as a sign of their Englishness. Artists exploited their networks to gain economic security and social recognition. They insisted that when one artist's prices fell, they all suffered, indicating their sophisticated understanding of how speculative markets work. Artists worked to sustain each other's reputations and market values to their collective advantage. Thus, artists directly intervened in their public image, transforming it from greedy arrivistes or marginalized Bohemians to domesticated paragons of manly Britishness.

Artists 'on the highway to prosperity', as the *Art Journal* described Hubert von Herkomer, became popular subjects of press gossip, 'notes', and biographies.[30] Artists and the press negotiated the dialectic between economic success and aesthetic vision through the concept of professionalism. A profession was a calling marked by autonomy in the marketplace – setting one's own prices. For professionals at mid-century, the overt exchange of money was considered vulgar and ungentlemanly.[31] Paula Gillett argues that Victorians viewed the professional's high remuneration as more 'recognition *of* service rather than payment *for* service', leaving the artist's motives ideal, 'unsullied', and distinguished from businessmen's motives. Sales transactions were handled by servants, dealers, or professional societies' personnel. What artists claimed as their proper rewards were honorific and symbolic capital (awards, titles, museum purchases).[32]

Many outsiders could become insiders by the end of the century.[33] H. Byerley Thomson wrote in 1857 that: 'professions and the professional classes … form the head of the great English middle class, maintain its tone of independence, keep up to the mark its standard of morality, and direct its intelligence'.[34] Professionalism, redefined less by social status than by expertise of knowledge available through expanding educational opportunities, was appropriated by emerging disciplines (e.g., medicine, history, and literature).[35] The first attempt to count professionals was in 1841; artists were first counted in 1861 and totalled 4,643, but ambiguities marked artists' professionalism: 'for none of the "artistic" group … could you lay down exact qualifications: still less could you erect an examination ladder' as was possible in other professions to clearly distinguish professionals from amateurs.[36]

Professionalism synthesized three economic claims: market autonomy to control the cost of services; a 'calling' or vocation motivated by public service, unlike 'labour' motivated by economic need; and a special expertise or knowledge that contained surplus value (public good) not strictly measured by supply and demand.[37] As Magali Larson points out, 'The two dimensions – entrepreneurial and vocational – are *analytically* distinct, but they appear fused in the early modern professions.'[38] The goal of a profession was to idealize its claims beyond 'economic and political power; it meant seizing the "moral and intellectual direction" of the historical process'.[39]

The intangibility of professional products included professionals themselves: 'their product ... is inextricably bound to the person and the personality of the producer ... *the producers themselves have to be produced* if their products or commodities are to be given a distinctive form ... professionals must be adequately trained and socialized'.[40] Colin Trodd notes that 'In the *Magazine of Art* we find representations of the artist authoring himself through ... reproductive technologies.' Many Victorian artists coordinated 'complex systems of production and marketing by fully recognising and exploiting the shape of the modern art world', encouraged by editors like Spielmann, who believed that artists must 'recognise the symbiosis of art and commerce, painting and advertising'.[41]

Marketing the artist: biography, the interview, and the studio home

In a circular logic, successful artists were worthy of being biographical subjects which, in turn, endorsed their material success. At the same time artists were represented as rejecting motivations of fame and fortune. Press biographies and interviews, acting as proto-infomercial genres, produced the producers, allowing artists to construct their own identities publicly and behind the scenes through their close relations to art critics. Voluminous biographies shaped Victorian concepts of art, artists, genius, and aesthetic worth as functions of a blend of classical economics based on production/labour and marginalist economics based on consumption/desire, put to the service of unifying national taste.

One form of art writing, art criticism, directly affected market success or failure. Samuel Cameron argues that critics provide advertisement, define reputations as a form of capital, create markets for their criticism and for artists, and influence meta-preferences by validating consumers' self-image through notions of proper taste.[42] Victorian critics negotiated artists' identities to mirror consumers' identities of nation, race, and class. By the repetitious display of their knowledge of aesthetics and art history, critics created demand and shaped consumers' perceptions and purchases: 'The weight of the canon of received work is a burden on potential consumers', that is 'eased by critics but may conflict with their tendency to promote originality'.[43] Critics lobbied for originality, but situated works within the canon with its 'fallout' values of historical validation, long-term economic worth, and cultural capital.

Biographies were the most popular Victorian art writing. Readers consumed quantities of 'collective lives, biographies in series and biographical dictionaries'[44] and biographies in the press and special Christmas and Easter annuals. This literature produced 'art' and the 'artist' who was constructed as a persona whose production, daily life, personality, and new social role exemplified a national character inseparable from the valuation of art works in particular and of cultural production in general. Artists' biographies negotiated their representation in the context of social formation (hero worship and professionalism), art production and exchange values (living artists v. Old Masters, patronage v. new buyers), and nationalism in an increasingly international market. Artists' biographies participated in a broad national discourse within overlapping topics of capitalist speculation, commercialism, social status, and professionalism.

The nonspecialist *Nineteenth Century* and the *Fortnightly Review* also contained life writings. The *Athenaeum* regularly reviewed biographies, including French and German biographical series. *Art Annuals* published by the *Art Journal* at Christmas and Easter produced a steady stream of artists' biographies thematizing struggle rewarded by success. Articles on Continental artists reflect an international discourse about artists that paralleled the growing international art market. *Scribner's* in America ran a series on British artists. French critic Robert de la Sizeranne in *English Contemporary Art* cited biographies and interviews. Biographies in the *Art Journal* cited the *Revue des Deux Mondes*'s information about English artists.[45]

The *Art Journal*'s first incarnation as the *Art-Union* in the series 'Portraits of British Artists', one-column long laudatory biographies, deployed the promotional language of advertising, e.g. one artist's 'latest production has been always his best'.[46] Equally hyperbolic, another notice proclaimed Daniel Maclise 'a leading glory of the British School', whose fame 'extended throughout Europe'.[47] Engraved portraits by fellow artists accompanied these mini-biographies,[48] whose serialization was paralleled by the series 'Great Masters of Art', linking Old Masters with living British artists, a promotional tactic.

Serialization whetted readers' appetites for subsequent stories and created a cumulative effect on intertwined social and aesthetic values through repeated themes. In 1855 the *Art Journal* series, 'British Artists: Their Style and Character', was illustrated by engravings of paintings by prominent engravers, such as the Dalziel Brothers, J. and G. Nicholls, J.W. Whymper, and Butterworth and Heath, which could be removed and put on walls. This series mapped trajectories of economic success onto moral virtues in 'the progress of a young artist, from the time when he manifests such indications of superiority as to attract especial notice … till he has won for himself an imperishable name', a brand name. This trajectory was mitigated by hard work: 'no man ever became great without working assiduously for his object'.[49] Popularity was now considered a sign that artists were united with the British public through a shared work ethic and meritorious character.[50]

Biographies openly assured readers of investment value: the *Art Journal* constantly referred to its continuous watch over young 'promising' artists 'our eye has ever been upon'.[51] Biographies referred to previous biographies in the same journal as evidence that the journal or critic spotted talent early, making their economic speculations correct, so that 'their' artists' stock rose.[52] Investment over time governed many assessments. Julia Ady's long essay, 'Jean François Millet', described Millet's paintings' rising prices as a slow progress signifying the 'endurance' of his work and its quality as rivalling the Parthenon frieze and Michelangelo's frescoes, typical biographical hyperbole.[53] Investments could fail: some artists 'stopped far short of the point at which we predicted they would arrive'.[54]

Artists' entrepreneurship was a focus of biographies. Elizabeth Butler 'saw at a glance that by the good luck of genius this field lay awaiting her; and this perception has undoubtedly been the foundation of her successes'.[55] Her professional status was initiated 'by entering simply and ingenuously into the market', so that 'she could fairly measure herself with her brothers of the brush'. Butler was redeemed from her own success by being made a professional motivated by a calling ('nobler ambition of fame') not unfeminine ambition.[56] Few women artists appeared in biographies and their economic know-how had to be mitigated by femininity, lest they appear worldly and businesslike, as many were.[57] In the biography of a male artist, prices and market appreciation of works could be more overtly praised.[58]

Despite the persistence of biographies between 1847 and 1904, series changed over time from didactic to professional, from describing artists as embodying moral truths in elevated language, to casual accounts of training, travel, and works. The *Art Journal* 1873 series by James Dafforne, 'the Works of', focused on works. Authors for 'Our Living Artists' apologized for their inability to address life and work in depth and their inadequate estimating of living painters.[59] The cool tone of its series 'Biographies of Artists', 1886–1904, abandoned the moralizing of biographies of the 1850s. The *Magazine of Art* after 1900 had series on photographers, etchers, and younger or 'rising' artists, an investment category. The plethora, decreased length and formulaic treatment turned biographies into a culture industry. As early as 1861 James Dafforne berated artists' overexposure in the press: 'the subject is, in a manner, exhausted, or we run the risk, by re-entering the field of investigation of multiplying words without increasing the information we desire to afford'.[60]

Biographies in *Art Annuals* from 1884 to 1909, saturated with the political economy of art, covered over some uneasiness about artists' economic ambition. Mrs. Lang described Frederic Leighton's RA presidency as requiring 'a man of much social tact, a good businessman'.[61] To represent Englishness properly the artist had to be materially successful while disavowing economic motives. Despite being good businessmen, English artists:

> do not yield to the exigencies of political economy in Art. They are always searching, always advancing, … unsparing of their labour. The journeyman in Art … is too much with us. He has entered the camp of the world, and must sell his labour, at cheapest cost to himself, in the highest market. To counterbalance his influence, Nature provides a constant series of young men, new generations not yet tamed by marriage and the world on one side; and, on the other, such steady followers of Art for her own sake as Mr. Watts, Mr. Burne-Jones, and the President. Their work has a kind of moral value, rising from its individuality and distinction, apart from its quality and defects as painting or sculpture.[62]

Biographies insisted that successful artists were motivated by determination and duty, a 'misrecognition', to use Bourdieu's word, that replaced economic motives with 'higher' ones, or defended successes as manly and even self-sacrificing. Archdeacon Farrar insisted that William Holman Hunt made less money than if he 'merely followed the practice of the ordinary run of painters', and that his high pay for *Finding the Saviour* compensated several years' work.[63] James Little insisted that William Orchardson 'never prostitutes his high abilities to pander to lasciviousness' but paints 'in the manner of a healthy-minded and sane man of affairs and man of the world … his excellent robust virility'.[64] Elizabeth Butler's studio had 'business-like walls'.[65] After 1900, artists' studios and homes were less important and sometimes not even depicted in *Art Annual* biographies, the bourgeoisification of the artist having become commonplace.

Art journalists and artists worked together to promote each other through New Journalism's practices of investigation, interview, and sensationalism. In biographies these practices were folded into ideals of heroism, national identity, and cultural dominance embodied in those artists deemed representative of 'Englishness' by virtue of their domesticity, manliness, or retained femininity despite professional activity and material success.

But as in any market exchange, there was a price to pay: repetitious biographizing turned artist-celebrities into public property:

Every artist who has reached a high position becomes, from the very elevation to which he has *raised himself*, public property ... the public whose favourable suffrage he has won by his works ... desire – and the desire is legitimate and perfectly reasonable – to learn some of his life and history. Such a man can no more expect to escape observation ... that would penetrate even the solitude of his studio and, to a certain extent even the sanctity of his domestic hearth – than a great legislator or a renowned warrior, or a successful author ... This is the penalty ... each pays for his position and popularity; the man himself may be indifferent to the praises or the censures of his biographer; ... but as the history becomes the inevitable result of the reputation, he must make up his mind that when he has himself achieved the one, sooner or later somebody will effect the other for him.[66]

'Suffrage' is an intriguing term; by recognizing artists among other 'self-made' men, the public is enfranchised to deploy biographical scrutiny to oversee cultural production. Artists' lives determine 'history' and defined the age, what Thomas Carlyle envisioned as biography's grand purpose.

Underlying this suffrage was a modern notion of culture, described by Ernest Gellner as:

no longer merely the adornment, confirmation and legitimization of a social order ... culture is now the necessary shared medium ... the minimal shared atmosphere ... For a given society it must be one in which they can *all* breathe and speak and produce; so it must be the same *culture* ... it can no longer be a diversified, locality-tied, illiterate little culture or tradition.[67]

Cultural success was constitutive of civic identification, enabling artists to ascend socially and economically without shame, because the Victorian culture industry replicated industrial capitalism's structures and values to secure readers' identifications with artists. Criteria for cultural legitimacy and criteria for economic achievement were identical – material trappings, philanthropic use of money, hard work, domesticity, etc. Biography became 'another institutional channel through which the modern state can materially produce or reproduce the individual in this world'.[68]

Similar to biographies in their dual probe of the professional and the personal, interviews became a sensational, duplicitous simulation of the artist's privacy. Richard Salmon argues that the interview both represented *and* undermined intimacy simultaneously, making biographical subjects 'products to be circulated and consumed'.[69] The interviewer projected an 'authentic' self, 'revealed' by the biographical subject, whose celebrity was deemed worthy of the 'cultural distinction which the interview confers upon its subject'.[70] Thus, the subject's interviewability turned surveillance into spectacle.

Studio homes were staged representations of such intimacy. In 1880 in the *Art Journal* 'Artists' Studios' appeared complete with floor plans followed in 1883 by the series 'Artists Houses'. Studios and houses exposed a variety of complex, fraught issues. Homes and studios were called shrines; objects and furnishings became embodiments of their owners' personalities.[71] But such projections were especially troubled for artists, given popular beliefs about studios as morally ambiguous sites with unchaperoned models. In addition, biographers debated whether a studio should be luxurious for socializing, or simple for working, a debate articulating artists' inextricably intertwined social, economic, and professional activities.

Helen Zimmern's interview-cum-biography of Alma Tadema redefined the artist's luxurious home into a site of moral virtue earned through labour: 'no superfluous rooms ... All there is, is to be of *us*'.[72] But, Giles Walkley notes, this 'modest residence' had sixty-six rooms, including atrium, billiard room, and cellar for mineral waters, plus studios for his wife Laura and daughter Anna.[73] Zimmern's spin underscores biographies' ideological function regarding Victorian anxiety over studio homes as possible signifiers of greed, ostentation, commercialism, and social ambition. She inscribed Alma Tadema's studio with virtue, masculinity, utility and simplicity, a site of work rather than social ambition, to show that Alma Tadema, not 'led astray by success', was 'self-exacting, self-critical'.[74] Zimmern's language – 'splendid', 'remarkable', 'power', 'superb' – was promotional and hyperbolic.

The *Magazine of Art* ran a series 'The Homes of our Artists' in 1881 in which authors read artists' homes didactically. Leighton's house reflected his character: 'a house of generous and easy yet unpretentious size, not intended to cause astonishment by its proportions and style', a 'charming place, [with] its lucidity and its colour'.[75] Leighton's home was not just a matter of taste, but 'of kindness and courtesy also'.[76] Millais's home reflected English good sense and a *proper* display of prosperity in its lack of 'affectation ... stately and prosperous; and prosperity which is not obtrusive or self-assertive is in itself rather a beautiful thing'.[77] A studio home, sign of economic success, became a sign of virtue, too.

Beyond this, the studio home participated in a curious artistic economy of exchange between artists and buyers. Wilfred Meynell, writing under his pseudonym 'John Oldcastle', equated the sale of artists' works to a loss with homes as substitutions for this loss:

An artist chiefly serves others by his power; the picture ... is destined to be the possession of strangers for ever after ... he must endure many pangs of parting. Some of those dear children … have fallen into the hands of the Philistines … in return for all this diffused good and pleasure, he has won for himself the pleasure of following his own altogether unfettered choice in the building of his home.[78]

The artist's home was a return investment for contributing to others' pleasure, a sacrifice of pictures that were metaphorically the artist's secrets and children. This exchange had economic resonances, too. If the work appreciated in value later, artists were often unable to buy back their works, even though they 'bore' them. The home became fetishized as a substitute for artists' lack.

As Walkley argues, home studios symbolized social and economic forces and marked artists as professionals. Studios, part of the home and separate from it, embraced domesticity and work. Their domesticity rebutted Bohemian studios' moral ambiguity in fiction and inscribed on art production a nostalgic pre-industrial cottage industry: 'the heavenly, all facilitating studio represented both an inspirational tool and material proof of the professional approach' and also 'removed the suspicion of amateurism'.[79] Victorian artist and administrator Richard Redgrave promoted 'a model house of the professional suburban artist'.[80] Artists moved to upmarket areas and competed to build elaborate homes, and women artists were among studio house clients.[81] Models came up the servants' stairs, so artists could separate themselves spatially from morally troublesome models to assure the public that art production was respectable and that artists' status mirrored the status of their patrons.[82] Valentine Prinsep and Leighton became 'virtual nouveaux-riches members of the middle classes' through property rents and merchant shipping; their homes served to 'distinguish the paintings they produced in them', a kind of social cleansing that distanced art from commerce.[83] The home studio symbolically synthesized economic success, moral well-being, hard work, and professionalism. As biographies were reduced in number and importance in the *Art Journal* and the *Magazine of Art*, professional topics – professional societies; distinctions between artists and amateurs; articles on artworld social events and rituals, such as the RA banquet, or the studio smoke – began to dominate from the mid-1880s though biographies continued in truncated forms.

Marketing art: commerce, surplus value, and art as gross national product

Economics directly saturated professional art discourse in the press. In the *Art Journal*'s 'Art Gossip and Reviews', purchases were announced and the government frequently condemned for failing to raise the funds to purchase a worthy work for the Nation, whether Old Master or modern British.[84] The *Art Journal* also advised artists on economics: in 1888 an anonymous essay 'The Business Side of Art' recognized an excess of supply over demand in art and recommended expanding the art market by dividing it into coteries, something the professional societies were already doing after 1880.[85] The author, suggesting that poor artists avoid the Academy exhibition and go for mass production, believed the masses were 'keenly alive to beauty, simplicity and truth ... repelled by the too evident parade of affectation in Art', from which they sought common sense and sanity.[86]

Attention to economics was consistent with what the *Art Journal* called 'art commerce'. Hall wanted to show 'the commercial value of the Fine Arts', that '"beauty is cheaper than deformity", that it is sound policy as well as true patriotism to resort to native artists ... in every branch of Art-manufacture'.[87] Like most art press editors, he argued for better fees for painters.[88] The *Art Journal* regularly published the year's sales, detailing objects' prices, owners, buyers, and dates of auction sales.[89] Knowledge of the market was part of artists' professional knowledge, but was now also available to the public. Perhaps the need to present the insider trade information to the public represents the complex and atypical nature of artistic professionalism in which there is no absolute certification – amateurs sell on the market in competition with professional artists, and the public considers itself adequate to judge aesthetic merit, even without expert knowledge.

The professional art discourse tallied art's contribution to the national wealth, as well as artists' symbolic capital generated by biographies. The press recognized beauty as a surplus value and taste as a commodity. P.L. Simmons argued in 'Art-Aids to Commerce' that 'taste is a marketable commodity, which being of so much value is worth getting honestly, and by fair purchase'. Thanks to art, the 1871 balance of trade was in the black through consumption of 'artistic' goods that elastically included opera-glasses, artificial flowers, and other non-art goods.[90]

The populist art press, acting like a trade journal, attended to market fluctuations, annual auction sales (figure 6.3), copyright laws, advertising, and marketing new popular forms, such as artistic postcards, that combined aesthetics with commercial viability. Walter Shaw Sparrow insisted that artists should rightly earn a living without criticism for doing so: 'the practice of every art is bread-winning as well as aesthetic adventure, and attacks on bread-winning are crimes against citizenship when they cannot be justified by sufficient evidence'.[91] This statement, moreover, implied that the ability to earn inscribed citizenship and masculinity ('bread-winning') on artists. Culture and consumption constructed each other and neither was merely a base for the other: artists' wealth marked their civic status, since 'being denied the access to goods is a form of disenfranchisement'.[92]

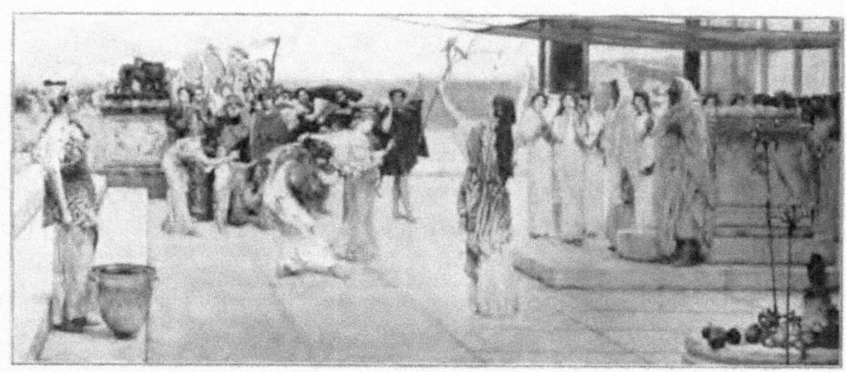

DEDICATION TO BACCHUS (5,600 GUINEAS).

By Sir L. ALMA-TADEMA, R.A. By Permission of Messrs. T. Agnew and Sons, the Purchasers, and of Messrs. H. Lefèvre and Sons, the Owners of the Copyright.

THE COLLECTOR.

PICTURE SALES OF 1903.

By W. ROBERTS.

IN several ways the past season of art sales has been one of considerable interest, although it will not perhaps rank among the great years. In the first place we have had a record day's sale, in the second we have had an unusual number of important sales of works by modern artists, and in the third there have been more than the average number of "surprises" in the way of big prices, for both pictures and objects of art. I do not indeed remember a season which has been so fruitful in what may be generally termed romances of the auction room ; some of these romances have been published widely, and have lost nothing in travelling, whilst others, perhaps quite as remarkable, have been very carefully suppressed. The season's sales have included no such remarkable dispersals as those of Gibson-Carmichael, Bardini, and Dunn Gardner, which so considerably helped to swell last year's total, and the Dudley jewels of that season still maintain the record in that particular class of sale. If one were permitted to examine Messrs. Christie's ledgers, it is possible that these eminent auctioneers would describe the season of 1903 as of a somewhat lean character ; that it has not been of a starvation type may, I think, be gathered from the following list :

Old masters, Vaile collection, etc., May 23, 86 lots	£105,845
Jewels, Gordon-Lennox, and others, April 30 and May 1, 253 lots	58,293
Modern pictures, R. T. Hamilton Bruce, May 16, 153 lots	31,057
Modern pictures, E. Gambart, May 2 and 4, 289 lots	31,014
Modern pictures, H. J. Turner, April 4, 166 lots	29,126
Old French furniture, Page Turner, and others, February 20, 128 lots	26,609
Modern pictures, Sir H. D. Davis, and others, June 27, 151 lots	23,613
Pictures by old masters, April 25, 142 lots	18,201
F. Litchfield's stock [sold by Foster] July 13 and six days, 1,424 lots	17,393
Old Masters, Page Turner and others, Feb. 21, 126 lots	16,808
Modern pictures and drawings, Gurney and others, July 11, 149 lots	15,942
Old Porcelain, etc., Sir Hugh Adair and others, Feb. 27, 142 lots	13,434
Modern pictures, Robert Orr, June 13, 152 lots	10,528
Early English engravings, J. Holland, May 6-8. 604 lots	10,214

6.3 W. Roberts, '"The Collector": Pictures Sales of 1903', *Magazine of Art*, 1904, p. 343.

This justification did not end debate on economic matters. Edward Poynter in his 1871 lecture 'Systems of Education' complained that English art students wanted to sell before they were adequately trained (indicating that consumers failed to distinguish between amateurs and professionals). French critics also denounced English artists as market driven.[93] But G.D. Leslie claimed that money inspired artists, condemning the Academy for forbidding students from selling their works while they attended its schools.[94] He argued, moreover, that making money did not harm their work, that Old Masters 'by no means despised the remuneration', and that geniuses often sprang from humble circumstances and so appreciated 'the advantages of wealth'.[95]

The long-range cultural capital of fame itself was often more prized than immediate wealth for artists. Economists B.S. Frey and W.W. Pommerehne note that for most Victorian painters 'the real monetary rate of return on paintings lies below that of financial assets, whereas the risk is higher'.[96] In light of this, Victorian artists' market behaviour was often calculated to serve long-range goals – reputation, social bonds with patrons and other artists, and posthumous fame – rather than immediate rewards; these interests marked them as professionals, not labourers. As Viviana Zelizer argues, the market is cultural, not just economic. Commodification does not destroy subjectivity, because consumption is a cultural resource, not just a cultural process, and thus generates new meanings.[97]

Some artists advocated the business of art. Prinsep noted that successful artists possessed excellent business skills in their dealings with collectors and dealers. They:

> displayed a knowledge of the world which secured them an independent position without which an artist is at the mercy of others. How many painters are there who, lacking this businesslike talent, remain without recognition? The combination is indeed rare; for the artistic temperament, being poetic and impractical, is somewhat antagonistic to the precision and method which, combined with shrewdness, forms the stock-in-trade of the successful man of the world.[98]

Marketing the artist: economics and national exempla

Both artists and consumers needed to feel comfortable in the art marketplace as members of an enterprise society and conveniently juxtaposed market knowledge with an aesthetic high ground. The language of the political economy of art in the *Art Journal* and the *Magazine of Art* became the obverse of 'aesthetic' or socially uplifting artist's mission. Frederic Leighton in his 1888 Presidential Address at the Liverpool Art Congress argued for a national role for artists in his blend of nationalism ('greatness', 'pride') and economics ('national prosperity'). By raising public taste and knowledge, artists made the public better consumers of art and thus contributed to national prosperity. He argued further that art should not be divorced from 'industrial production'.[99] Consumer demand needed to be shaped and educated by artists.[100] He called the public 'purchasers' and artists, 'suppliers', and directly mentioned the market, applying the emerging Victorian marginalist economic model and encouraging artists to actively shape consumption.[101]

Leighton, G.D. Leslie, and Prinsep advocated artists' participation in economics as professionalism that distinguished artists from amateurs and from artisans. Jonathan Freedman argues that aestheticism synthesized oppositional demands – aesthetics and commodification – by positioning artists as professionals through constant renegotiations between notions of art production, economics and the social[102] 'to accomplish the commodification of "culture" itself'.[103] This positioning created 'a sphere of autonomous high culture' accessible not only through the exercise of innate taste or a rigorous education, but also, directly, 'through the acquisition of goods whose possession would confirm the high cultural status of their consumers'. Ironically, 'some of the most crucial of these goods turned out to be artefacts that critiqued commodity culture itself'. Freedman characterizes Anglo-American aestheticism, as distinct from Continental versions, by 'its complete but complex entanglement with the development of a cultural apparatus at once thoroughly professionalised and wholly commodified'. Bearing a 'monopoly of knowledge', the artist appeared disinterested, while staging a successful choreographed career.[104] In biographies, this success 'proved' artists' disinterestedness by insisting that popularity revealed the inherent (or naturalized) cultural unity of national taste and moral character that explained high sales.

The *Art Journal* and the *Magazine of Art* condemned avant-garde artists – English and French Impressionists – for using novelty merely for commercial success, echoed in Ruskin's attack on Whistler for flinging paint 'in the public's face' – a conflation of canvas with consumers.[105] To call Impressionism ephemeral, as W.P. Frith did, was to signal to readers that buying such art would be a poor investment.[106]

But as late as the 1880s, when the art market struggled economically, the arts were still deeply suspect. The 'decorous British public perceives a certain aroma of social and moral laxity in the atmosphere of the studio, a kind of blended perfume of periodical impecuniosity, and much tobacco-smoke'.[107] Increasingly powerful commercial venues (dealers' galleries, advertising, the press) threatened artists' claims that art making was a 'calling', while amateurism undermined artists' assertion of their special expertise. The populist art press strained to appeal

ELECTRIC LIGHT FITTINGS OF TO-DAY DESCRIBED AND CONSIDERED. 59

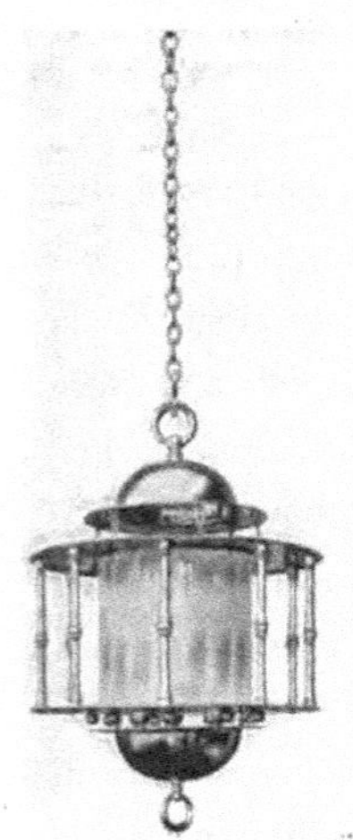

HANGING LAMP.
DESIGNED BY W. A. BENSON.

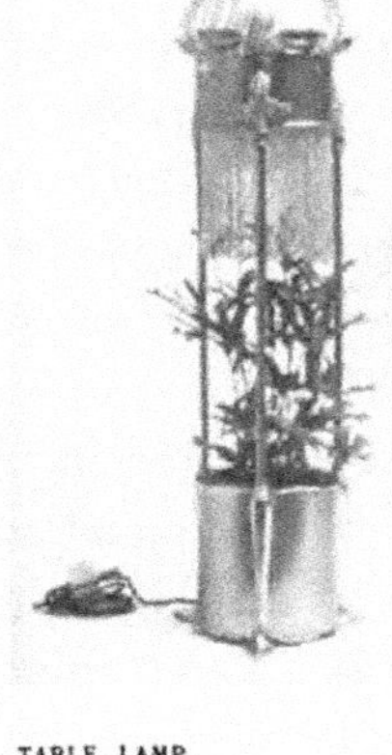

TABLE LAMP.

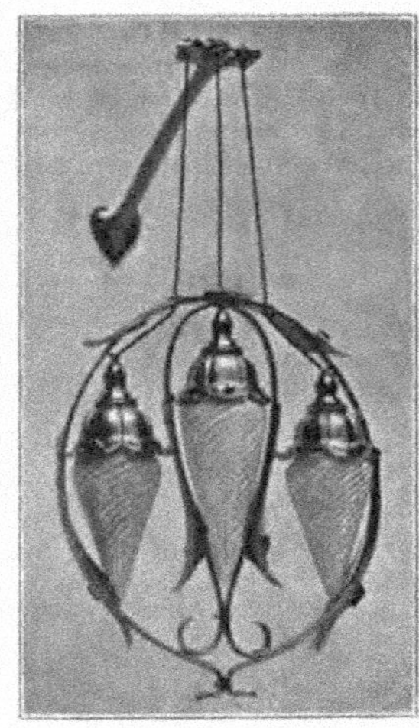

WALL LAMP.

allowing the finished products to appear until he has approved them—that is to say, he does what he can to secure success; and though it is doubtful whether as many masterpieces are likely to be produced by the unassisted invention of one brain as by the employment of several minds in the fashioning of designs, an individual manner is likely to distinguish productions upon which so much individual attention is lavished. This is the more likely when the designer holds strong theories as to the proper mode of treatment of any special material used in manufacture. Mr. Benson's revolt against the over-massiveness of those electric light fittings which were adapted from designs made for use with gas or candles, and his perfectly reasonable contention that their design should be marked by greater lightness both in appearance and substance, have led to a certain wiriness of design which is not always pleasing. One is glad to see that the large un-modelled surfaces of burnished copper, so characteristic of his design of some years ago, and the uninteresting leaves of the same material, which were so often quite out of scale with their surroundings, have almost disappeared, and have given place to a different treatment of the thin metal. There is, too, more fancy displayed in the shapings of the receptacles for the bulbs within which the glowing filaments are preserved.

The wall-lamp illustrated, which was shown at the last Arts and Crafts Exhibition, is a fresh and unusual treatment of a group of three lights, and serves its purpose well. A table reading-lamp, which is convertible for hanging on the wall, is much less successful in the former than the latter position. Used as a table lamp the curves of the stand appear unnecessary and rather weak, but when hung on the wall their resilience is very effective, and gives a reason for and a meaning to the position of the bulb and the shade. The idea was ingenious, but the result shows how exceedingly difficult it is to design a thing which shall be equally satisfactory in several positions. A table-lamp with a receptacle for a fern below is another idea, and though in reproduction it inevitably suggests a shower bath, in its proper place on the table it looks very well. The circular hanging lamp is also acceptable in execution, though it would have been better had the knop in the centre of the balusters been higher, or if there had been a slight frieze-like member below the upper plate. The screen for the light is of silk, which is really the best material for electric light shades, but unfortunately it soon gets dirty in the atmosphere of cities.

A good many fittings in the historic styles have been designed by Mr. Aubrey C. Williams for Messrs. Frank Suter, but not to the exclusion of a more modern form of design. He shows great aptitude in assimilating what is good in the movement to which the impulse for the production of most of the fittings which have here been illustrated is due, while generally avoiding

6.4 F. Hamilton Jackson, 'Electric Light Fittings of To-Day Described and Considered', *Magazine of Art*, 1904, p. 59.

simultaneously to consumers, artists, and *cognoscenti* by promoting British artists, promoting art at both professional and trade levels, and expanding coverage to crafts, home décor (figure 6.4), colonial art, artists who painted with their teeth, and the US market.

But neither the *Art Journal* nor the *Magazine of Art* could compete successfully with an omnipresent Victorian visual culture embracing everything from museums to department stores and advertising. Nor could they maintain a niche in the changing world of the art press itself. By the 1880s, the art world was becoming decentralized: new market niches were being shaped by professional societies overtaking the monolithic Academy and by burgeoning specialist galleries catering to consumers' diverse interests and financial resources. Specialized publications proliferating in the 1890s ranged from the well known (the *Savoy*, the *Studio*, the *Yellow Book*, and the *Century Guild Hobby Horse*[108]) to obscure periodicals (the *Parade*, the *Pageant*, the *Rose Leaf*, the *Cameleon*, the *Quarto*, the *Poster*, the *Butterfly*[109]) that served consumers' and artists' new aesthetic identities. The *Magazine of Art* ended in 1904, the *Art Journal* in 1912, both replaced by specialist publications that disguised economics beneath a new veil of aesthetic mystifications of the market in the demise of trade content for artists and for the public.

Notes

1 Barrell, *Politics of Culture*, p. 7, referring to Copley, 'Fine Arts'; see also and Pears, *Discovery of Painting*.

2 Skaife, *Exposé*, p. 35.

3 Codell, *Victorian Artist*, Chapter 4.

4 Codell, *Victorian Artist*, pp. 79–96, on artists' presumed innocence in economics.

5 Codell, *Victorian Artist*, Chapter 2.

6 Hall, *Retrospect*, pp. 197, 199.

7 'Exhibition of the Royal Academy', *Art Journal*, 1861, p. 161.

8 Bourdieu, *Field of Cultural Production*, pp. 10–11.

9 Bourdieu, p. 36.

10 *Art Journal*, 1851, p. 301; Landow, 'There Began to Be a Great Talking about the Fine Arts', p. 30.

11 E.g. Steinlight on advertising and the Victorian novel.

12 Rumbaugh, 'Magazine of Art', pp. 11ff. on the early history of the magazine.

13 Nowell-Smith, *Cassell*, p. 32.

14 Anon., '"The Magazine of Art" – Its Majority: A Retrospect', *Magazine of Art*, 1898, pp. 316–20.

15 The publishers disliked Henley and in 1881 appointed as Art Director Academy-trained Edwin Bale, R I, leaving Henley in charge of literature.

16 The *Magazine of Art* had technical how-to articles written by RAs for young artists; Rumbaugh, p. 204.

17 Anon., '"The Magazine of Art" – Its Majority: A Retrospect', *Magazine of Art*, 1898, p. 320.

18 Julie Codell, '"The Artist's Cause at Heart"', and Codell, 'Spielmann'.

19 Rumbaugh, pp. 31–2.

20 Rumbaugh, p. 59.

21 'Valedictory', *Magazine of Art*, 1904, p. 461.

22 Soussloff, *Absolute Artist*, p. 35.

23 Douglas, *In the Active Voice*, p. 29.

24 M.H. Spielmann, 'Mr. G. F. Watts: His art and his mission', *Nineteenth Century*, 41 (1897), p. 161.

25 George Newnes published a biographical series, *Newnes Art Library* and the *Strand Magazine*; George Virtue published the *Art Journal*, its *Annual*s biographies, and book biographies; Richmond Seeley published the *Portfolio* and reprinted the *Portfolio*'s biographies as a series, *The Portfolio Artistic Monograph*; Seeley, Jackson and Halliday published the *Portfolio*'s series as 'English Painters of the Present Day' in 1871; Cassell's published the *Magazine of Art* and a biographical series, *Gems of Art*; Otto Limited published biographies from the *Connoisseur*.

26 Brake, *Subjugated Knowledges*, pp. 10–11.

27 Thirlwell, *Other Rossettis*, p. 123.

28 Cited in Douglas, p. 126.

29 Douglas, p. 129.

30 *Art Journal*, 1880, p. 109. Codell, *Victorian Artist*, Chapter 3.

31 Reader, *Professional Men*, p. 37. Perkin's *Rise Of Professional Society* offers an historical view but does not address artists as a group.

32 Gillett, *Worlds of Art*, p. 54. Gillett addresses conflicts between gentlemanly status and technical knowledge for RA members (pp. 43–68).

33 Reader, p. 98.

34 H. Byerley Thomson (1822–67) in *The Nature of Professionalism in England*, cited in Reader, p. 1.

35 Thomson, *Choice of a Profession*, p. 5.

36 Reader, p. 148. The number of artists went from 4,000 in the 1860s to 11,059 between the 1880s and World War I, compared to actors (4,600); authors, editors, journalists (3,434); and architects (6,900).

37 Elliott argues, 'professional goals are not simply individual but social' in *Sociology of the Professions*, p. 101.

38 Larson, *Rise of Professionalism*, p. 61.

39 Larson, p. 91.

40 Larson, p. 14.

41 Trodd, 'Academic Cultures', p. 187.

42 Cameron, 'Critics in the Culture Industry'.

43 Cameron, p. 329.

44 Nadel, *Biography*, p. 13.

45 *Art Journal*, 1855, p. 47.

46 *Art-Union*, 1847, p. 164.

47 Ibid.

48 Maclise by Edward M. Ward and Frith by Augustus Egg, *Art-Union*, 1847, p. 165.

49 Biography on Edward Ward, *Art Journal*, 1855, p. 45.

50 Biography on Edward Ward, *Art Journal*, 1855, p. 140.

51 *Art Journal*, 1855, p. 45.

52 *Art Journal*, 1859, p. 205.

53 Julia Ady, 'Jean François Millet', *Nineteenth Century*, 1888, pp. 433, 437, 438.

54 *Art Journal*, 1855, p. 45.

55 *Magazine of Art*, 1879, p. 258.

56 *Magazine of Art*, 1879, p. 260.

57 E.g., Kate Greenaway, Helen Allingham, Henrietta Rae, Rosa Bonheur, and Elizabeth Thompson Butler.

58 E.g., Biography of Frith, *Magazine of Art*, 1879, p. 81.

59 *Magazine of Art*, 1878, p. 241; *Magazine of Art*, 1880, p. 73.

60 *Art Journal*, 1861, p. 133.

61 Lang, *Sir F. Leighton*, p. 7.

62 Lang, p. 32.

63 Farrar and Meynell, *William Holman Hunt*, p. 16.

64 Little, *The Life and Work of William Q. Orchardson, R.A.*, p. 15.

65 Meynell, *The Life and Work of Lady Butler (Miss Elizabeth Thompson)*, p. 23. Meynell was Thompson's brother-in-law!

66 *Art Journal*, 1856, p. 41. Italics mine.

67 Gellner, *Nations and Nationalism*, pp. 37–8.

68 Epstein, *Recognizing Biography*, p. 67.

69 Salmon, 'Signs of Intimacy', p. 159. See Codell, *Victorian Artist*, and White and White, *Canvases and Careers*.

70 Salmon, p. 162.

71 Salmon, pp. 164–6.

72 Zimmern, *L. Alma Tadema, Royal Academician*, p. 30. Italics mine.

73 Walkley, *Artists' Homes*, p. 129.

74 Zimmern, p. 29.

75 Wilfred Meynell, 'The Homes of Our Artists: Sir Frederick Leighton's House in Holland Park Road', *Magazine of Art*, 1881, p. 170.

76 Meynell, 'The Homes of Our Artists: Sir Frederick Leighton's House in Holland Park Road', p. 176.

77 John Oldcastle (pseud. W. Meynell), 'The Homes of Our Artists: Mr. Millais' House at Palace Gate', *Magazine of Art*, 1881, p. 290.

78 Oldcastle (pseud. W. Meynell), 'The Homes of Our Artists: Mr. Millais' House at Palace Gate', p. 295.

79 Walkley, p. xxiii–xxiv.

80 Walkley, p. 34.

81 Walkley, pp. 63, 113–14.

82 Walkley, p. 50. Grand studios mimicking rich patrons' homes typified eighteenth-century portraiture practices.

83 Walkley, p. 56.

84 The *Art Journal* condemned the government for not purchasing Stanhope Forbes's *Wedding* for £650 but praised it for purchasing Herkomer's *The Chapel of the Charter House* for £2,200 ((1889), p. 192).

85 Codell, 'Artists' Professional Societies'.

86 'The Business Side of Art', *Art Journal*, 1888, p. 249.

87 Hall, p. 210.

88 Spatt, 'Aesthetics of Editorship', p. 53.

89 E.g., Alfred Beaver, 'Art Sales of 1884', *Art Journal*, 1884, pp. 261–4; Walter Rowlands, 'The Art Sales of 1887', *Art Journal*, 1887, pp. 294–5.

90 P.L. Simmons, 'Art-Aids to Commerce', *Art Journal*, 1872, p. 296.

91 Sparrow, *Memories*, p. 245.

92 Street, 'Fear of fridges', p. 157.

93 Stephenson, 'Leighton', pp. 228–9.

94 *Art Journal*, 1882, p. 71.

95 *Art Journal*, 1882, pp. 71–2.

96 Frey and Pommerehne, *Muses and Markets*, p. 113.

97 Zelizer, *Money*, p. 628.

98 V. Prinsep, 'Personal Recollections: James McNeill Whistler, 1834–1903', *Magazine of Art*, 1904, p. 577.

99 Barrington, *Leighton*, II, pp. 343–4.

100 Barrington, II, pp. 350–1.

101 Barrington, II, pp. 358–61.

102 Freedman, *Professions of Taste*, p. xii. This is also a theme in Gagnier, *Idylls of the Marketplace*.

103 Freedman, p. xii–xiii.

104 Freedman, p. xix.

105 M.H. Spielmann, 'The Paris Salons', *Magazine of Art*, 1898, p. 535, and Anon., 'Royal Academy Exhibition: II', *Magazine of Art*, 1898, p. 465.

106 William Powell Frith, '"Realism" vs "Sloppiness"', *Magazine of Art*, 1889, p. 7.

107 Escott, *England*, p. 322.

108 Codell: 'Moderate Praise'; 'Constructing the Victorian Artist'; 'Righting the Victorian Artist'; and 'Serialized Artists' Biographies'.

109 Rumbaugh, p. 241.

7

The call of commerce:
the *Studio* magazine in the 1920s

Ysanne Holt

In his 1928 'Retrospect and Prospect' of the *Studio: An Illustrated Magazine of Fine and Applied Art*, the young William Gaunt reflected on the changing role of the magazine since its foundation in 1893 by the retired Bradford business man and Arts and Crafts devotee, Charles Holme.[1] Appearing monthly at a single price of 6d with a striking launch cover design by Aesthetic movement illustrator Aubrey Beardsley, the *Studio* rapidly became one of the most influential art periodicals in Europe and the United States, disseminating knowledge and appreciation of the latest national and international tendencies across art, architecture, and design. Gaunt's essay acknowledged the shifts in the magazine's evolution and fortune — but pointed to what he regarded as its continuity of purpose. 'Throughout its history', he wrote:

> runs the unbroken thread of an ideal … By striving to spread an appreciation of arts and crafts and encouraging an interest in the work of both English and foreign artists it helps to promote both national and international goodwill. It disseminates widely the refining and civilizing influence of art. It suggests alternatives to the deadening monotony of mechanical labour. It emphasizes the unity which should exist between artists and art lovers whatever the class (or the nation) to which they happen to belong. And its battle cry is still, 'The Age we live in and its artistic needs and aspirations'.[2]

That ideal of unity, appeal to the civilizing influence of art, and opposition to the deadening monotony of labour are all worthy of both Ruskin and Morris in the latter quarter of the nineteenth century, but are made here in the context of the inter-war period when the social and economic circumstances of everyday life and national and international relations were entirely different.

The concern in this essay is to explore how, amidst the complex changing conditions of the 1920s, the *Studio* effectively negotiated models of artistic identity; how it represented the growing interaction between diverse areas of practice across visual and material culture; how and why its articles and reviews endorsed certain forms of past and present-day practice; and how its strategies related to wider critical discourse around recent and contemporary art and design. A key interest is in how the magazine's particular emphases corresponded to emerging tendencies amidst the endlessly proliferating societies and institutions, the private and public galleries, and increasingly diverse commercial venues for the display and consumption of art in London. The ambition is that this study of one arts magazine will contribute to our wider understanding of the dynamics of the art market and patterns of taste in the early twentieth century and contribute, too, to the revision of a dominant idea of the 1920s as singularly insular and parochial and marked by an excessive nostalgia for the past – a view often maintained in art-historical writings that are heavily reliant on perceived distinctions between the avant-garde and modernist coteries of the period in British art c.1910–14.[3] That view is productively countered by examining the broader intersections between late nineteenth- and early twentieth-century visual and material culture, and the very specific and evolving modern contexts in which they emerged. From this perspective we find a culture, and a market, which is far more dynamic, outward-looking, and internationally focused, than has been generally proposed.

Gaunt's emphasis at the end of the 1920s on the *Studio*'s continuity of purpose and its acute sense of the 'spirit of the age' was endorsed in Clive Ashwin's and Peter Rose's accounts of the magazine in its earlier years. As they noted, from its beginnings in 1893 with its first two editors Joseph Gleeson White and C. Lewis Hind – both of whom had direct connections to the Aesthetic movement and Art Nouveau, the *Studio* successfully distinguished itself from the established *Magazine of Art* and the *Art Journal*, not simply in its opposition to their rather more conservative academicism and in its own broader commitment to the applied and decorative arts, but also, in design terms, in the quality of its reproductions.[4]

An emphasis on handicrafts in early issues reflected an increased middle-class leisure time and taste for civilized amateur pursuits, as indicated in the lengthy reviews of metropolitan and provincial Arts and Crafts exhibition societies as well as the popularity of the regular *Studio* competitions – the best amateur photograph, best cheap cottage design, best design for a damask tablecloth etc. All of these sustained interactions with a growing readership – both male and female – and underlined participation in a refined cultural milieu; one which drew together enlightened producers and consumers from across Europe, notably from Scandinavia, Holland, Germany, and Austria, and from the United States.[5]

From the 1890s to the First World War articles on contemporary painting and sculpture often focused on those associated with secessionist groups like, in London, the International Society and the New English Art Club, and reflected antipathy to the vulgar philistinism with which dominant, rival institutions like the Royal Academy were associated.[6] The prevalence of articles ranging from the subject of landscape painting, both national and international, and advice on suitable painting grounds, to reproductions of simple Cotswold-style furniture, the decorative designs of Walter Crane, and the vernacular architecture of Charles Voysey, reflected the widespread middle-class anti-urbanism of the period.[7] Charles Holme himself, one-time resident of William Morris's Red House, had a garden designed in 1908 by Gertrude Jekyll for his house Upton Grey, Hampshire, which had been partly restored by guild architect Ernest Newton – all seemingly underscoring a characteristic 'Englishness'.[8] The *Studio*'s emphasis on international commonalities in taste, however, counters a dominant retrospective view of the period as one of entrenched, often jingoistic cultural nationalism.[9]

The *Studio* sustained a distinct aura of cultivated discernment. Commercial enterprise was always a presence, indeed was regarded as a necessity to be handled appropriately, not simply to be shunned. Education and the dissemination of 'good taste' (later 'good design') were constant concerns, underlined in Art Nouveau designer Arthur Heygate Mackmurdo's call 'to render all branches of the art [of interior decoration] the sphere no longer of the tradesman but of the artist'.[10] From the 1870s, Charles Holme was already in pursuit of objects that met his aesthetic criteria, trading overseas and 'bartering carpets, rugs and embroideries in exchange for the products of Bradford'. He was, to Gaunt, the 'old type ... of "East India" merchant [with] the far-seeing imaginative vision of the explorer-Englishman'.[11] That explorer-exoticism, and developing metropolitan, middle-class trends in consumption, coalesced perfectly in the Regent Street store Liberty's, a physical manifestation of the sensibility of subscribers to the *Studio*, with a similar ambition of providing 'utility and good taste with modest cost' and with clear Arts and Crafts and Art Nouveau connections by the 1890s alongside a predilection for Japanese art and design.[12] The magazine consistently underlined this Japanese taste in subsequent years. For Holme the 'Oriental artist and craftsman' shared that Arts and Crafts ideal of (as Gaunt wrote in 1928): 'giving grace and interest to even the smallest article made for personal or domestic service'.[13] The connecting aesthetic was in the degree to which Japanese craftsmen, like the designers of simple Arts and Crafts objects, reject and eliminate superfluous ornament – all of which appealed to the taste of the magazine's readers and, at the same time, privileged the vision of the designer. Little scope for the messy interventions of individual clients or consumers here; taste was carefully circumscribed in the provision of a 'total work of art'.

In its breadth of interest and the cultivation of its market, the *Studio* was unique among British art magazines before the Great War. The *Magazine of Art* closed in 1904, the *Art Journal* in 1912, and the *Burlington Magazine for Connoisseurs* (begun in 1903) ventured little beyond its scholarly studies of painting and sculpture, while the *Connoisseur* (begun 1901) focused most particularly on antiques and Old Master collections – despite a modest attention to contemporary painting. Those few pre-war modernist art magazines provided little, if any, overt acknowledgement of the special requirements of a commercial world. *Rhythm*, for example, launched in 1911 with an overt commitment to a vital new art for the modern world and strongly influenced by Bergsonian aesthetics; its incorporation of advertising from its second issue jarred to a degree with its editorial emphasis on unfettered creativity and spiritual intuition.[14]

Despite, however, some tensions in maintaining distinction from obvious commercialism, there are connections between the *Studio* and developments in those other art magazines. Julie Codell's essay in this volume points to the emergence in the *Art Journal* and the *Magazine of Art* of a discourse that could acknowledge and respond to market forces whilst still retaining the 'aesthetic high ground'.[15] Artists, like all professionals, developed their expertise and pursued a vocation that was increasingly, certainly by the 1880s, perceived to be operating in the public good through providing aesthetic pleasure and raising standards of taste.[16]

The artist and designer's public role and responsibility was increasingly debated in the period of the First World War when the *Studio*, now including articles on war art exhibitions, commemorative panels, and memorial sculpture, adopted a very specific stance. The October 1915 'Lay Figure' debate between 'the Critic and the Man in the Red Tie' on the 'Artistic Impulse in the War' maintained that art reflects the spirit of the nation which produces it and 'after the war new responsibilities and obligations' will fall upon artists. The positive effects will be to 'purify and strengthen the national sentiment [to] purge and develop our art'.[17] Sue Malvern has observed that the effect of the war was to produce a 'new renaissance' in modern British art and a sense of public purpose among artists in which immediate pre-war factionalism was irrelevant. As Malvern states, a new consensus and collectivism emerged – in accord with Lloyd George's 1918–20 coalition government – geared through benevolent state guidance to build the health and wealth of the nation anew.[18] The *Studio* was to develop a clear sense of its own role and purpose in this respect.

As Gaunt recounted, throughout the war years, its revenue halved and production costs soaring due to increased costs of paper and printing, the *Studio* was permitted to continue publication, its role regarded as of 'national importance'.[19] But, as the *Times* later recorded, its readership declined from a pre-1914 circulation of 40,000 at a shilling a copy with a considerable international (especially Austrian) clientele.[20] 'After 1918, the price doubled and, with central Europe bankrupt, its circulation dropped to a quarter of the old figure.'[21] It was, as Gaunt put it, 'a strange new world this world of after the war — a ruined, shattered, hopeless place ... *The Studio* was no longer the beloved international magazine but an English magazine, thin at that, which would have to fight its way back in the face of war prejudice and national feeling.'[22]

Amidst these circumstances Charles Holme's son Geoffrey assumed editorship and, along with his business partner, F.A. Mercer, set about restoring The Studio Ltd.'s fortunes, first by expanding the book publishing side of the company. Before 1914 Geoffrey Holme had travelled in Egypt, Japan, India, and the United States with the decorative artist and designer George Sheringham whose work frequently appeared in the *Studio* in the 1920s. After the war, he travelled again, setting up — or in some cases reforming — offices in Rome, Leipzig, Milan, and New York.[23] Through sound marketing the business grew and, crucially, diversified. Large folio volumes with colour plates on 'Modern Painting' were produced (the first in 1921 on Laura and Harold Knight for 7s 6d), alongside special supplements. Increasingly diverse advertisements appeared including, for example, notices about correspondence art classes and studio rentals, inserts on artists' materials offering free trials of the newly popular medium of tempera, descriptions of etchers' tools — and advertisements for Aquascutum women's sports suits and 'fadeless carpets and textiles from Harvey Nichols'. All of which demonstrates the wider significance at this point of advertising and magazines; Jeremy Aynsley has characterized the situation as the evolving interdependence of publicity and promotional industries and the pressures to convert readers into consumers.[24] Decisions about layout, typography, and the placing of advertisements — as well as the content of articles — are as much the result of social and economic factors as aesthetic ones and, as both Aynsley and Marie-Louise Bourallius assert, a magazine is a physical object and 'a commodity as well as a cultural artefact'. Its design assumes a specific value for a specific readership and market at a specific time.[25] Here then we might infer a primarily metropolitan, artistically inclined market with an aesthetic, yet practical, concern for the domestic interior — and an eye on high quality fashionable dress appropriate for open air activities. It is tempting to assert a primarily female audience, although this was not actually the case. In any event we might imagine the ideal reader/consumer in the early 1920s as one of those sturdy young women with bobbed hair enjoying a stiff holiday breeze on a Cornish headland, as seen in Laura Knight's pictures of the period.

A key commercial strategy for the magazine – and widely practised – was its purchase of competitive publications. *Commercial Art* (later renamed *Art and Industry* and edited by F.A. Mercer) and *Drawing and Design* were taken over; the successful *Year-Book,* begun in 1906, was renamed *Decorative Art: The Studio Year-Book* in 1927, relaunches being another trend. The *Times* obituary for Geoffrey Holme, however, chose to remember 'a complete aesthete and in no way a business man'. He had 'capital and good taste' and 'unerring judgement in works of art'. 'He was a master of mise-en-page and devoid of artistic snobbery, although his bias was a little too heavily on the side of the applied arts and he sometimes lost readers by over-emphasis on objects of use.'[26]

This bias was of ever greater relevance. The continued editorial tone of the magazine perfectly corresponded to the ethos of young organizations like the British Institute of Industrial Art (BIIA) (formed in 1919 via the Board of Education and Board of Trade) and the Design and Industries Association (DIA). The latter was formed in 1915 under the influence of the Deutscher Werkbund to 'combat the unpractical influences in British design and industry' through the creed, 'Fitness for Purpose'.[27] The essential requirement was – once again – an aesthetic of simplicity, borne from the desire to reduce excessive ornament for the fundamental forms that dominate tendencies in early twentieth-century modernism across visual culture. As we have seen, all of these characteristics had been expressed in the *Studio* since its inception.

In an important study '"Strategies of Situation": British Modernism and the Slump', Andrew Stephenson clearly demonstrates the extent to which the social and economic experiences of 1929 to 1934 and the effective collapse of the London art market contributed to declining sales for modernist easel paintings and to the necessity for modernist artists to diversify into related areas of industrial and commercial activity. This led to widespread calls for the re-organization of fine art education and training – appeals very often heard in the *Studio*.[28] Whereas, as Stephenson shows, Bloomsbury artists with their doctrine of 'civilised individualism' maintained their distance from commercial practices and 'ordinary' patronage, others, like Paul and John Nash, Wadsworth, and Burra, moved into areas like commercial illustration, poster design, and interior decoration.[29] Paul Nash, in an often cited 1932 article on the precarious position of the artist, made a virtue out of the situation, suggesting that 'it might be possible to regard the artist, in a new light, that of a member of a community or even what is called a useful member of society, wherein his potentialities … may become a matter of general interest'.[30]

If we look back, however, through those very early 1920s *Studio* articles, editorials, and 'Lay Figure' columns, and note, too, the advertisements inviting artists to provide illustrations for advertisers (lured by promises that 'men or women artists with the right training will be able to live in comfort and save money'), we see that the grounds for the concept of the artist as one engaged with public, commercial life and needs and concerned to raise aesthetic standards were already clearly prepared.[31] This vision of the artist was underscored by wartime experience and the immediate post-war economy, but drew fundamentally on the professional model as developed in the late nineteenth century – reflected in the persistence of an Arts and Crafts ideology in the journal throughout the inter-war period.[32] The difficulty in the early to mid-1920s was to play down, or rather to update, connotations of amateurishness, hobbies and handicrafts, and the occasional over-cultivation of the artistic interior – and to render the public role of the artist a more acceptable concept, without alienating the loyal and original readership.

The 1920 *Studio Year-Book of Decorative Art*'s article on 'Decorative and Applied Art' emphasized the value of artistic training in practical affairs and the need for efficient encouragement to producers at a time of keen competition, acute economic crisis, and a drive to improve exports.[33] The importance of training and of appealing to *young* artists is referred to emphatically; for example, 'It is extremely unlikely that an artist who has been working for years on one aspect of painting will produce a successful design. He or she needs to be caught young and be ready to *adapt* [my emphasis] to the limitations of some applied art.'[34] Adaptability, then, like diversification, becomes a key term in this early part of the decade, underlining the importance of an ability to turn from easel painting to mural design, to designs for pots, carpets, furniture, textiles, and stained glass.

In this the developing career of Frank Brangwyn is exemplary. He was a continual presence in the *Studio* from the 1890s to the 1920s and in the *Year-Book*. From the first account of his art by James Stanley Little in 1897, to a reproduction of a 'Decorative Painting' in 1922, to C.G. Holmes's review 'Frank Brangwyn's Designs for British Industry' (1930), he was the subject of numerous articles, book and exhibition reviews, 'Studio Talk' references, and exhibition advertisements and, on occasion, wrote for the magazine himself.[35] Praised continually for his 'prodigious output and masterly achievements in so many branches of art' – oil and water-colour painting, etching, lithography, murals, and furniture and applied arts design – his trajectory was symptomatic in its move from the 'oriental splendour' of his colouring in earlier 1890s paintings emphasizing decorative effect, to what was seen as the 'dignified composition' and the 'deliberate preservation of simplicity' of his mural paintings for Christ's Hospital Chapel in 1915,[36] to his Industry-regenerating furniture and carpet designs shown at Pollard's exhibition in 1930. This artist-designer embodied the ideals, and the ideal adaptability of the *Studio*. If we view the magazine itself more widely across this longer time frame,

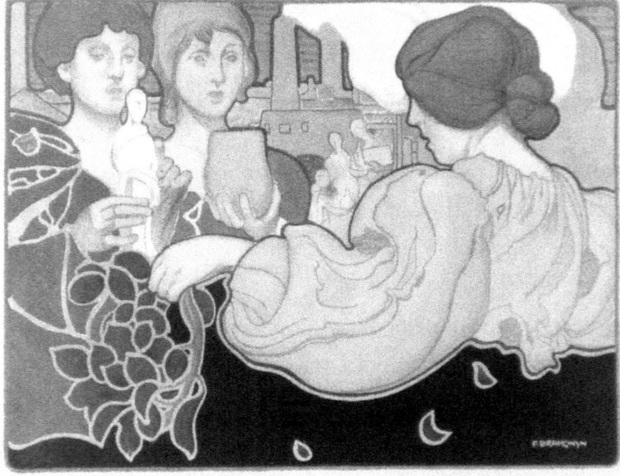

7.1
Poster designed by Frank Brangwyn for *The Studio*, 1899.

with less emphasis on the war as a crucially re-defining watershed and with a broad view of its contents – art, architecture, decorative and applied arts, works reviewed, and opinions disseminated – we see that Brangwyn was not alone and that all artists – modernist and traditional – needed to be highly attuned to the social, cultural, and economic (modern) pressures of their period.[37]

A sense of increasingly devout, at times Utopian, public mission emerges from Geoffrey Holme's *Year-Book* editorial in 1921.[38] Current restrictive public spending led him to re-assert DIA principles of 'fitness for purpose', 'a fundamental essential in every artistic thing' requiring sound construction, recognition of the limitations of materials, and the elimination of shoddy work and superfluous 'plastered over' ornament. Art and Technical schools had an important role and the close association of design and production was crucial. Only then would artists be able to offer manufacturers good quality design. The magazine would contribute to this ambition, educate the public and undo the harm done to popular taste in the past, and illustrate the best examples of recent work from, for example, Sweden and Germany. There are echoes here of the campaigning spirit from mid-Victorian design reform and Arts and Crafts appeals for honest craftsmanship, and a foreshadow of the zeal with which Utility designers like Gordon Russell seized the opportunities presented by Second World War economic restrictions to reform the standards of taste of 1930s suburbia. Russell is an especially interesting example; influenced by Gimson, his designs for Heal's also appeared in the *Studio* in the 1920s, 'freely acknowledging the value of traditional influences [yet] individual in character and modern in spirit'.[39]

Holme, in his 1921 editorial, asserted that both the *Studio* and *Year-Book* would 'help matters by appropriate propaganda' with relevant illustrations of work to merit attention.[40] These included bungalow designs by Maurice Adams, Baillie Scott's designs for country homes, a Heal's dresser, and Liberty and Foxton fabrics. From this point circulation steadily improved, foreign correspondents were re-established, and the quality of illustrations continually enhanced. To the six colour plates and numerous half-tones a section of photogravure was added. In 1922 the *Year-Book* reiterated its state of the nation message in a feature on the new Roehampton Estate. Taxation, the demands of organized labour, and unstable foreign exchanges were seen to be seriously affecting the progress of art. The rich were less rich and the future clearly lay with the multitude – whatever regret might be felt for the passing of the old order of things.[41] It was ever more important at this juncture for the *Studio* to eliminate any remaining residue of other-worldly aestheticism and to openly position itself as an agent of democracy at the behest of social and economic circumstance and government imperatives.

From the start of the decade an important opportunity for the artist/designer to unite principles of beauty and fitness was seen to lie in the 'decoration and furnishing of small rooms', the title of a 1920 article by Shirley Wainwright. At this time of reconstruction, the modest home was not simply the domain of the working class; following higher taxation, inheritance tax, and the scarcity of domestic servants, members of the business and professional classes were now also looking to smaller houses. As noted, the *Studio*, and *Year-Book*, had reproduced examples and run competitions for the design of these for some time. An article in the issue on 'Concrete Homes' found them 'suited to the requirements of educated people, for whom large houses are no longer desirable'. With smaller scale and new innovations many 'cherished traditions', alongside 'the meaningless collection of fragile tables and cabinets staggering under loads of rubbish', were simply redundant.[42] In this regard the magazine also reflects what Paul Overy described as a post-1918 European modernist faith in the physical, emotional, and

DESIGNS FOR BUNGALOWS

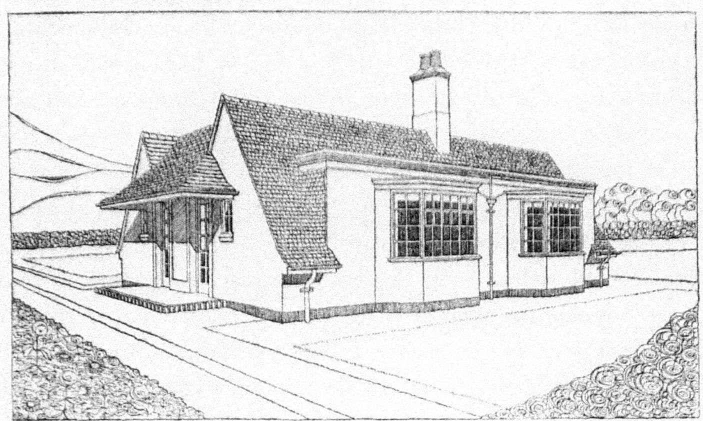

THREE BUNGALOWS
DESIGNED BY MAURICE
S. R. ADAMS, A.R.I.B.A.

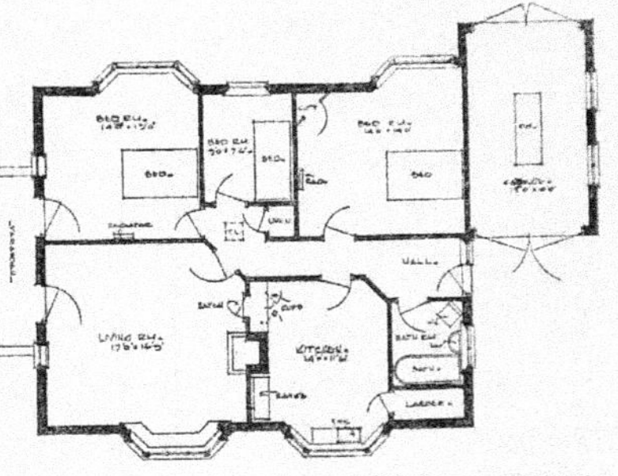

IT is in the house of moderate capacity, on a free and open site, that the full advantages of the bungalow, or single-floored house, may be realised. Very large bungalows are apt to become rambling in plan, expensive to build, and costly to maintain; while small houses, on two or more floors, are necessarily more cramped and box-like and do not engender the same sense of freedom. Bungalows are only suitable where a site of generous size is available, which is necessary not only to prevent the rooms being overlooked, but also to allow unrestricted light and air to all the rooms. If carefully arranged, the bungalow plan may be more compact, while being more spacious than the two-storied house of similar accommodation, and as regards convenience and labour-saving the bungalow form has undoubtedly the advantage.

The three bungalows illustrated here were designed to meet post-war conditions and limited expenditure; the greatest economy of space, cube and material was therefore essential. The buildings were planned to

39

spiritual efficacy of sunlight, fresh air, openness, and health, which he observed in the design of sanatoria in the Netherlands. In the contemporary literature of hygienicism 'ornament and decoration were proscribed as enemies of the hygienic and healthy home'.[43]

Frank Brangwyn's general compliance with the developing tone is clear in his own later introduction to the 1925 twentieth-anniversary issue of the *Year-Book*. He reiterated those dominant themes of adaptability and utility, the fundamental duty of artists to common life, and the need for manufacturers to employ artists. No anti-commercialism here: 'No art can ever be vital that does not get into the homes of the people. And good art is always good business. France and Germany recognised this many years ago. How long will it be before Great Britain sees it too.'[44] The *Studio*, for Brangwyn, is showing the way forward with artists now called upon to satisfy the needs of a growing and varied audience in public places.[45] Within this context the notions of decoration and 'decorative art' were variously understood, generally referring to a range of activities from mural painting to book illustration and to small paintings of the kind produced by the Decorative Art Group. This formed in 1916; examples of its panels, pastels, and paintings, including Brangwyn's, and Nancy Smith's and Frank Potter's decorative paintings, and other works, like George Sheringham's schemes for interior decorations, frequently appeared in the *Studio*. A review in 1920 of their exhibition at the new Dorien Leigh gallery noted their defining character as the elimination in their 'schemes of the 3rd dimension, the illusion of which is created by shadows[;] these artists in their paintings and appliqué hangings, posters and stencilled designs restrict themselves more or less to two dimensional design [recognizing] the supreme importance of rhythmic colour and line in decoration'. This was decorative art appropriate for the 'furnishing of small homes' and for altered domestic situations.[46]

If artists now sought new audiences, this was often in novel commercial venues away from the traditional art market which, the *Studio* had asserted in 1919, was typically 'concentrated within the half-mile from the Piccadilly end of Bond Street'.[47] One striking example was Derry and Toms' department store on Kensington High Street which had held exhibitions for the previous three years, often favouring the Decorative Art Group. A Derry and Toms exhibition notice appears in the October 1919 issue, listing several of the Group's favoured artists, including Walter Bayes, Jacob Epstein, Jacob Kramer, Nevinson, Ernst and Dod Proctor, Anne Estelle Rice, and Ethelbert White – all artists whose works could complement the ceramics, textiles, and glass on display throughout the store.[48] Ambrose Heal's store in Tottenham Court Road had opened its Mansard Gallery in 1917 and, like Derry and Toms, often exhibited those 'adaptable' artists capable of working across a variety of art forms, seen for example in its 1919 show,

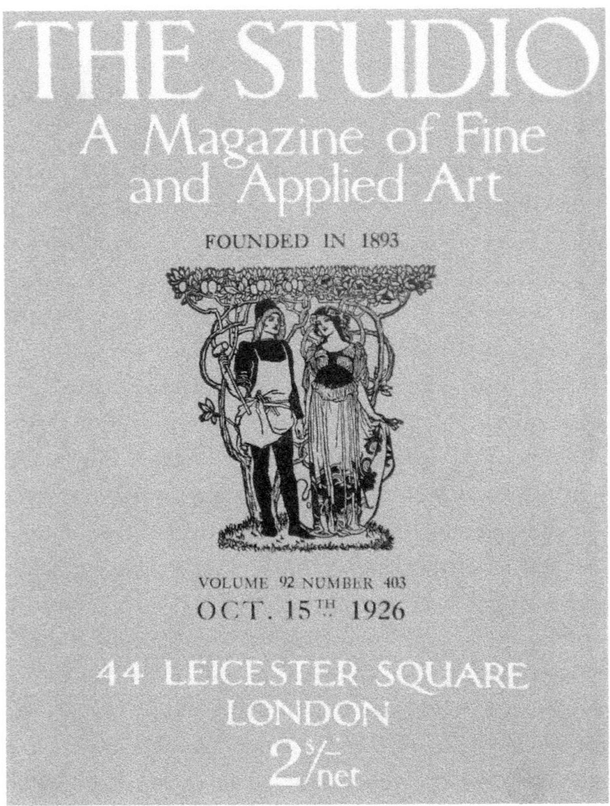

7.3
Cover design for *The Studio: A Magazine of Fine and Applied Art*, 15 October 1926.

also reported in the *Studio*, of works by Claude Lovat Fraser, including posters (Fraser frequently designed Heal's posters) alongside examples of his watercolours, drawings, stage scenes, fabrics, and costumes – the variety of product to be expected in such a context.[49] Similarly in April 1920 Heal's staged a memorial exhibition of that prime early *Studio* artist Walter Crane, of his illustrations, paintings, murals, and textiles.

Studio advertisements also appear from the early 1920s urging readers to visit new art galleries at some distance from the West End including, notably, the Hampstead Art Gallery in North London's Finchley Road – the advertisement supplied bus and tube directions. The October 1920 issue described its inaugural exhibition of works by Alfred Wolmark (painter, and theatre and stained glass designer), noting that the gallery was providing a rallying point for the many artists living in the locality. It was at the same time, of course, catering to the local market looking for home furnishings. In yet another development of the period, other new galleries away from the West End chose, like department stores, to vary their merchandise. In February 1920 an advertisement appears for the Chelsea Book Club in Cheyne Walk, announcing the sale of not only English and foreign literature, but also paintings, prints, and drawings, including works by Derain, Picasso, Signac, and Eric Gill.

Better known but in the same vicinity was the Chenil Gallery. In 1923 its proprietor Jack Knewstub took out an advertisement in *Colour*. This magazine ran from 1914 to 1932 and included numerous illustrations – often, of course, in colour and frequently featuring *Studio* artists like Brangwyn, Dulac, and W. Russell Flint – alongside a modest number of book and exhibition reviews and a larger number of poems and short stories.[50] *Colour* was a less experimental, more commercial version of *Rhythm* and *Blue Review* with conceivably lower advertising rates than those at the *Studio*. Knewstub's advertisement claimed that excessive rates in West End galleries had resulted in declining profits. His remedy was decentralization and what was ultimately, in his case, an overly ambitious degree of diversification. The New Chenil Galleries, heralded in *Colour*, along with artists' studios and materials shop, as well as a theatre, dance hall, and restaurant, finally opened in 1925 – and closed two years later.[51] There was a delicate balance to be struck between unique exclusivity and adequate commercial appeal.

The *Studio*'s focus on relations between art and commerce naturally extended to interest in commercial art with, in July 1926, the announcement that the magazine *Commercial Art* was now part of its group and the byline '"Commercial Art" is Above all things practical. It illustrates Beauty in Everyday things.' The first issue included articles on 'The development of the new poster', 'The Curwen Press', and 'The Advertising of Shell'. At one shilling, and so half the price, it nevertheless featured articles by several of those who wrote for the *Studio* – e.g. Gabriel Mourey on 'French Mannequins', S.B. Wainwright on 'Poole Pottery', as well as articles by designers themselves, for example Horace Taylor on 'The Westminster Press'. Interrelations between the magazines were clearly maintained for the potential of accessing sufficiently different readerships – *Commercial Art* therefore advertised the *Studio*'s forthcoming special supplement on 'Art as Publicity'.

A revival of poster design comparable, it was noted, to the success in the 1890s of the Beggarstaff Brothers (painters and poster designers James Pryde and William Nicholson) was perceived in relation to the commercial enterprise of London Underground – underlining the perpetuation of tradition, rather than radical new innovation. The spring *Studio* in 1923, complaining of 'acres of ghastly poster hoardings', went on: 'and yet when the Rolls Royce is unavailable and we go home by tube we can see in the Underground how, sometimes, the right thing is done'.[52] The art was now being taken seriously; even, the 'Lay Figure' noted in 1924, the Royal Academy was 'condescending' to take up poster design. Edward McKnight Kauffer, frequently praised, for example, for his posters for Derry and

A NEW ENTERPRISE

COMMERCIAL ART

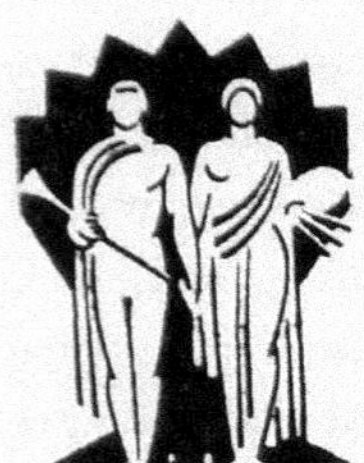

Realising the need for a special publication to serve the mutual interests of business man and artist, the proprietors of "The Studio" have purchased "Commercial Art," hitherto published by Drawing Ltd.

Its main purpose is to be of real use to the commercial world and to the artist and designer by securing their efficient co-operation. It will treat of art as a selling factor from every point of view and will interest all who desire beauty in everyday things by showing the products of those who are trying to serve them.

MONTHLY

1/- NET

Published on the first of the month.

Annual Subscription

16/- post free

THE FIRST NUMBER OF THE NEW "COMMERCIAL ART" WILL APPEAR ON JULY 1st

"COMMERCIAL ART"
WILL BE ABOVE ALL THINGS PRACTICAL

DRAWING AND DESIGN

MONTHLY

1/- NET

Published on the first of the month.

Annual Subscription

15/- post free

N.B. — Please note this magazine is reduced from 1/6 to 1/-

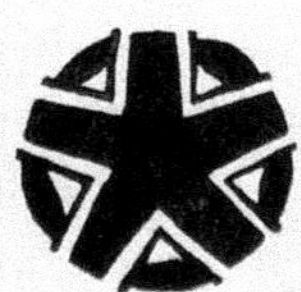

The acquisition by "The Studio" of "Drawing and Design," the well-known art periodical, is an event of importance.

It will appeal to artists, art students, and the cultured lay public; in fact, all those who wish to follow the movements of art.

It will illustrate both old and modern work, with the aim of making clear both principles and processes.

It will act as a continual inquiry into the ways by which form can be expressed.

It will help to create standards of appreciation by which art may be judged and enjoyed.

THE FIRST NUMBER OF THE NEW "DRAWING AND DESIGN" WILL APPEAR ON JULY 1st

"DRAWING AND DESIGN"
WILL NOT BE A DUPLICATE OF
"THE STUDIO"

ORDER JULY ISSUES EARLY

Published by
THE STUDIO LTD., 44 LEICESTER SQUARE, W.C.2.

7.4 Advertisement in *The Studio* for 'Commercial Art' and 'Drawing and Design'.

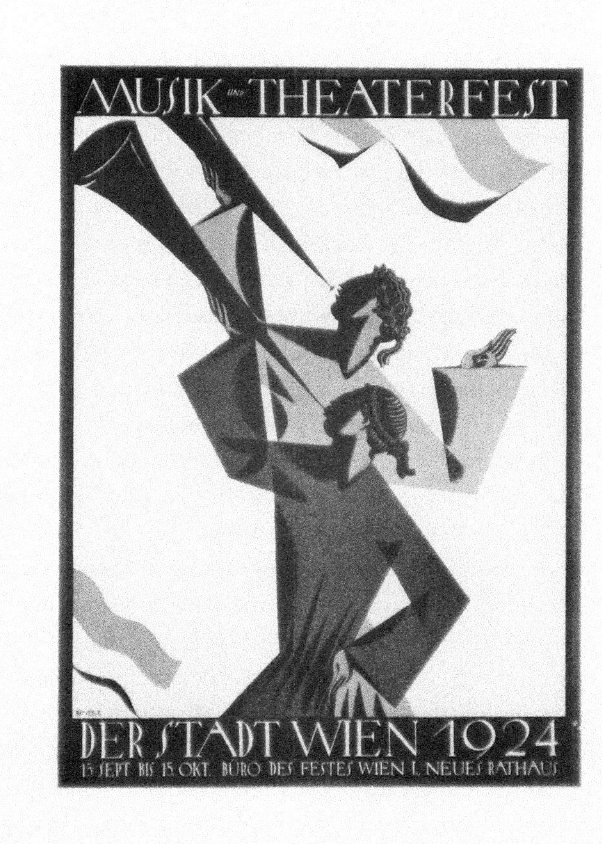

7.5
Josef Binder, Poster for
'Musik und Theaterfest,
Der Stadt Wien, 1924',
The Studio, 15 May 1926,
p. 337.

Toms and for London Group exhibitions at the Mansard Gallery, was a central figure – alongside the Viennese designer Josef Binder – in the *Studio*'s special 1926 edition 'Posters and Publicity', demonstrating that 'the union between art and publicity grows closer and stronger every day'.[53]

That same year, the year of the General Strike, Shirley Wainwright reported that 'Of late, artists have been surrendering to the lure of pattern designing for textiles.' Paul Nash, Phyllis Barron, Dorothy Larcher, and Enid Marx – subjects of his article – were all members of the 'Modern Textiles' cooperative experiment producing dress and furnishing fabrics, with premises on Beauchamp Place, but now facing 'the apathy of the public towards aesthetic enterprise ... at a time of social discouragement and economic distress'.[54] The *Studio*'s support, together with its ability to sway the market, was to be increasingly critical for artists struggling in the current crisis, as much as for national standards of production and consumption in general.

Amidst crisis came a corresponding need for order. In this McKnight Kauffer and Marion Dorn's account in a 1929 *Studio* article on modern carpet design is interesting. 'The design of a rug [Kauffer argued] should follow the architect's conception of the ground plan – this will suggest a motive that can be applied – all in line with a sense of order so important in the present day.'[55] The pattern should suggest the horizontal, restful line and be self-contained; preferably it should be concentric, not eccentric. There is a sense here of Bauhaus-inspired understandings of the symbolic, associative properties of line and colour, and a foreshadow of similar assertions by Herbert Read in the context of mid-1930s international modernism with its dominant appeal for a classical spirit of calm regulation rather than romantic turbulence.[56]

This emphasis on order and architectural proportion was essentially the aesthetic espoused by Frank Rutter in the 'Triumph of Design' chapter of his influential 1926 study *Evolution in Modern Art*. Rutter was a frequent contributor to the *Studio* from the later 1920s and his book was advertised in the magazine. Outlining the importance of the DIA in countering Victorian ornament, Rutter also described the shift within British art from typical 1880s and 1890s preoccupations with 'atmosphere' in versions of Impressionism towards an emphasis on a quality of 'rhythm', and a 'clear, clean hewn type of picture with the accent on design, construction and proportion'.[57] This tendency he perceived in modern British watercolour, wood engravings and woodcuts, and contemporary murals and in a shift towards paintings that pursued decorative rather than illustrative ideals.[58] These tastes and ideals dominate numerous *Studio* reproductions and articles about artists such as Algernon Newton, praised by James Laver in the magazine that same year, 1926, for the harmonious stability of his designs, his 'passion for straight lines' seen in 'the symmetry of eighteenth-century streets', and the 'Great simplification in the forms', in spite of considerable precise detail that refers us back to eighteenth-century topographical draughtsmen. Yet, for Laver, the artist belongs to his own time and shares 'the modern dislike of vagueness'; he is free of sentimentality and knows that 'beauty is a matter of proportion'.[59] If the *Studio* sought to continually reflect 'the spirit of the age', this, precisely, was 'the new spirit' of the 1920s which, for Rutter, 'increasingly animated the fine arts, manufacture and industry'. In this, '"decoration" does not mean some added and usually unnecessary ornament, but the whole mode of conception and manner of treatment of a work of art'.[60] We can of course extend this conception from the work of art out into the whole interior in which the work hangs.

In 1926, a *Studio* advertisement announced its acquisition and re-launch of *Drawing and Design*, assuring readers that '"Drawing and Design" is not a Duplicate

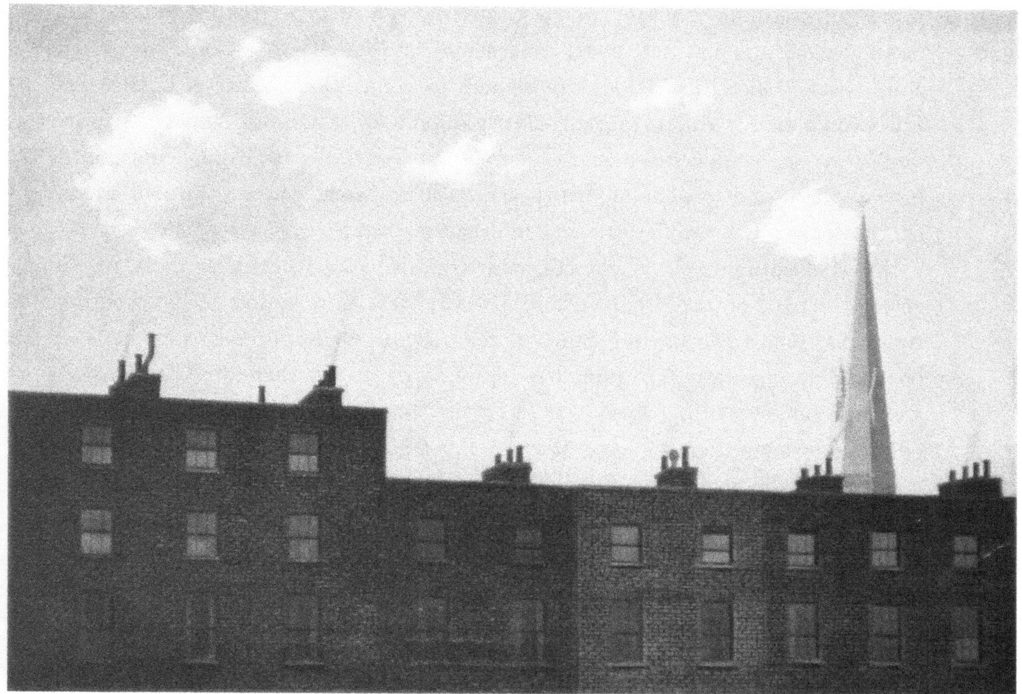

7.6 Algernon Newton, 'From a London Window', 15 October 1926.

of "The Studio".' Nevertheless, as with *Commercial Art*, several of the same writers inevitably appeared in its pages with, for example, an October article on 'Paul Nash' by William Gaunt (two years before his *Studio* retrospect).[61] The new magazine's editorial for its first issue in July announced:

Its special function will be one which no other journal has assumed to any considerable degree – that of dealing with the methods and principles of art old and new in such a way as to establish a comparative standard of appreciation ... we go to the caves of France and find that prehistoric man knew about significant form ... art seeks the fundamental essence that lies beneath style and tradition ... Drawing and Design, therefore, can fill a very useful place in the scheme of criticism.[62]

For David Peters Corbett, this policy of relating present art to past traditions indicates what he regards as the adaptive, compromise modernism of the 1920s.[63] By contrast, a less negative view emerges via a long view from the later nineteenth century up to the writings of Read in the 1930s; considering the relations between visual culture more generally; and acknowledging a clear persistence in the tenor of the *Studio* and its now 'sister' magazines and 'stable' of associated writers and artists. *Drawing and Design*'s references to connections between English and European artists, past and present, clearly implies an optimistically new, outward sensibility once understood in the context of assertions regarding continuities between past and present in British art made to assert native traditions in the context of insidious anxieties about internationalism.

In establishing its views, the magazine was also keen to criticize those widely revered artists of the 1920s whose practice was now found to be wanting. Augustus John's works on show at the Chenil Gallery possessed 'signs of boredom', suggesting 'Mr John has better work to do than this.'[64] Hardly a welcome review as the gallery was struggling to avoid bankruptcy. Similarly, its editorial welcome for the new Modern European wing at the Tate in August, condemned the inclusion of 'too many Sargents and an awful Mancini'.[65] A seemingly excessive degree of attention to modern European art and design at times in *Drawing and Design* caused resentment among certain readers. Especially interesting was the effect of the magazine's initial inclusion of a letters page; an effort, like the *Studio*'s competitions, towards open interaction with its readers. The departure backfired, however, as one letter writer expressed annoyance at that over-representation of foreign work. Despatched from 'The Alison Studio' in St. Ives, the letter criticized the magazine's 'cold, aloof, superior and carping tone [which] depresses to extinction ... our only too delicate and introspectively sensitive English temperament'.[66] The reader was annoyed by an implied criticism of Laura Knight's drawing and felt that French and German magazines did a better job for their own art workers, recognizing as they did that 'judicious praise and encouragement of what good there is produces better results than any amount of nagging criticism'. An editor's note reassured readers that the field of English art would be examined extensively. This was clear evidence of the consumers' ability to influence and potentially re-form content, although, perhaps predictably, the letters page soon came to an end.

A shift in tone began to emerge. No longer could these magazines primarily dictate taste from above; they needed to respond and re-form, following the demands of readers who were now (in part because of the *Studio*'s very existence since 1893) increasingly well-informed, sophisticated consumers and producers, but finding themselves in harsh social and economic conditions. The July 1928 editorial, 'Art and the Machine Age', therefore adopted Utopian rhetoric: 'And yet this is a marvellous period in which to live. There is a certain amount of disorder which is inseparable from the creation of new things; but there is a romance in the present day, both in its life and art for which there is hardly any parallel in the past.'[67] Adaptability again was key and this extends beyond purely national economic imperative to a positive connection with Europe and America, faced of course with similar economic circumstances but now 'setting an example … England must not lag behind content to repeat formulas which are unsound because they have lost their meaning.'[68]

Internationalism, for the purposes of personal and collective physical, moral, and spiritual well-being, now overtly shaped the magazine's agenda. For example, the *Studio*'s September 1928 issue containing Frederick Etchells' essay 'Le Corbusier: A Pioneer of Modern European Architecture' asked whether British artists and designers might also be pioneers. In 1930 the *Studio* special number by Joseph Duveen, 'Thirty Years of British Art', claimed the number of professional artists in Great Britain and Ireland had increased from 10,000 in 1907 to near 20,000 in 1927. Not just financial support but a real purpose to their existence was required and, again, the models were France and America, 'where artists' importance as agents of culture and their influence upon the education of the masses is popularly recognised'. For Duveen, the British press would surely help in this 'desirable crusade', alongside promoting several new ventures in international exhibitions and displays.[69] The *Studio*, certainly its spokesman William Gaunt, would no doubt argue that it had been performing exactly this function since 1893, its battle cry always 'The Age we live in and its artistic needs and aspirations'.

Looking back at the magazine from a 1953 issue, Clyfford Musgrave noted that the natural affinity between Japanese decoration and functional design was also the basis of the modern movement in architecture and furnishing. Similarly, for Clive Ashwin (following Pevsner), the new spirit in the domestic architecture of Voysey and Baillie Scott promoted throughout the early *Studio* reinterpreted rural vernacular in its sparing use of surface decoration – so allowing the simple geometry of the building to speak for itself as an expression of 'fitness for purpose', presaging early twentieth-century modernist architecture as well as wider attitudes towards ornament in the decorative and applied arts.[70] The connections were frequently made through instructive juxtaposition in 1920s. As Read and others established in the 1930s, the simplicity of Leach pottery provides a connecting link between Japanese and native vernacular ceramic traditions and modernist forms. Gordon Russell furniture, as we have seen, connected Gimson's cabinet making traditions to modernist forms. Continuities at various times are indeed made to speak for an innately native tradition (although the *Studio*'s persistent discussion of American and European craft traditions balances that assertion). In painting too, as noted, Algernon Newton's pictures are seen to evoke the cool linearity of an eighteenth-century watercolour tradition. The striking simplicity and boldness of contemporary poster design harks back to the Beggarstaff posters of Pryde and William Nicholson in the 1890s, just as the 1920s landscape paintings of William's son Ben, are seen to possess the elegant simplicity of William's own pre-1914 paintings of the Downs. The editorial in that first issue of *Drawing and Design* asserted:

> By taking the wide view, by placing the old and established in juxtaposition with the experimental ... with the defining view of rationalising and co-ordinating[,] ... the comparative method – a continual enquiry into the ways of representing form – to which drawing and the fundamental forms of design specially lend themselves is to be ... our policy.[71]

With all of these examples and assertions of continuity, native and international, a continual emphasis is laid upon the ideal artist/designer/craftsman or woman's social role and responsibility and a continual privileging occurs of those adaptable individuals capable of working in a variety of forms appropriate to an ever evolving market amidst rapidly changing social and economic conditions. By acknowledging all these circumstances and with a broader view of the interrelations between forms of visual culture and from the perspective of the pages of the *Studio* and its sister magazines in the 1920s, it becomes possible to revise and contradict more typical assertions about modernism in Britain between the wars.[72]

Notes

1 William Gaunt, '"The Studio"', 1893–1928, Retrospect and Prospect', *Studio*, January 1928, p. 10. For brief overview of the early years see: Woodham, *Modern Design* and Houfe, *Birth of The Studio*. See also Brothers, *A Studio Portrait*; and Leonard, 'Internationalist in Spite of Themselves'.

2 Gaunt, p. 10.

3 David Peters Corbett's *The Modernity of English Art* is an important revision of critical orthodoxies in relation to early twentieth-century British art but does maintain a particular overview of the 1920s that largely confirms that dominant perception of the decade as one of retreat and insularity.

4 Ashwin, 'The Founding of the Studio', in *High Art and Low Life*, ed. Ashwin, pp. 4–8. See also Peter Rose's essay in the same catalogue.

5 According to Brown University and University of Tulsa 'Modernist Journals Project' website, the American edition was entitled the *International Studio*. Until 1921 a proportion of the magazine was printed in England with an added American section. In 1922 it was taken over by International Studio inc. and then produced entirely in America, see http://dl.lib.brown.edu/mjp/periodicals.html. Accessed 22 October 2010.

6 Royal Academy annual exhibitions were reviewed, although the works were generally found to be rather tame and repetitive. The growing consensus, too,

was that New English shows were becoming increasingly hard to distinguish from those at the Academy.

7   The *Studio* clearly participated in that contemporary culture of ruralism, the Simple Life and Back to the Land movements, reflected in magazines like *Country Life*, begun in 1897 and in the founding of the National Trust in 1895. For more discussion of this ruralism see: Holt, *Modernist Landscape*.

8   Holme's house and garden is discussed in Helmreich, *English Garden and National Identity*, pp. 202–4.

9   For a recent discussion of the developing international outlook in modern British art and design after the turn of the twentieth century, see Stephenson, 'Edwardian Cosmopolitanism'.

10   Cited in Schmutzler, *Art Nouveau*, p. 41.

11   Gaunt, p. 3.

12   On Liberty's see: Escritt, *Art Nouveau*.

13   Gaunt, p. 4.

14   Those most commonly reproduced in *Rhythm* included J.D. Fergusson, Ann Estelle Rice, Derain, and Matisse – artists working in a typically decorative and hedonistic form of Post-Impressionism.

15   See Julie Codell's essay in this volume.

16   Codell also cites here Freedman, *Professions of Taste*.

17   'The Lay Figure', *Studio*, October 1915, p. 76. The 'Lay Figure' ceased c.1925–26.

18   Malvern, *Modern Art, Britain and the Great War*, p. 93.

19   Gaunt, p. 9.

20   Figures from: 'Obituary of C. Geoffrey Holme', *The Times*, 14 December 1954, p. 10.

21   Ibid.

22   Gaunt, p. 9.

23   See: 'Obituary of C. Geoffrey Holme', *The Times*, 14 December 1954, p. 10.

24   Aynsley and Forde, eds. *Design and the Modern Magazine*, pp. 8–9.

25   Aynsley and Forde, eds. *Design and the Modern* Magazine, p. 18.

26   'Obituary of C. Geoffrey Holme', *The Times*, 14 December 1954, p. 10.

27   The quotation is from C. Collins Baker, cited in Rutter, *Evolution in Modern Art*, p. 141.

28   See: Stephenson, '"Strategies of Situation"'.

29   On the dominance of Bloomsbury aesthetics in the inter-war years, see also: Stephenson, '"Anatomy of Taste"'.

30   See Paul Nash, 'Going Modern and Being British', *Weekend Review*, 12 March 1932, pp. 322–3, see also: Nash, *Room and Book*.

31   The quotation here is from an advertisement, 'A Golden Year for Artists', *Studio*, 1920, AD.IX.

32   For an interesting study of the persistence of Arts and Crafts ideology into 1920s English modernism see, Chris Stephens, 'Ben Nicholson', *The Geographies of Englishness*, eds. Corbett et al., pp. 225–47.

33   The article begins on p. 59.

34   See 'A Golden Year for Artists', *Studio*, 1920, AD.IX.

35   James Stanley Little, 'Frank Brangwyn and his Art', *Studio*, October 1897, pp. 3–20; *Studio Year-Book of Decorative Art*, 1922, p. 91; and C.G. Holme, 'Frank Brangwyn's Designs for British Industry', *Studio*, December 1930, pp. 440–5.

36   Arthur Reddie, 'Mr Brangwyn's Mural Paintings in Christ's Hospital', *Studio*, December 1915, pp. 151–63.

37   In a chapter 'Revisionist Modernism in the Twenties' in *The Modernity of English Art, 1914–1930* (pp. 82–92) David Peters Corbett describes an 'adaptive modernism' (p. 86) in the 1920s. In this, he argues pleasurable, non-controversial subjects were dominant and a new emphasis on formal qualities, the rigour of design, produced a compromise aesthetic replacing the pre-war radical critique of the avant-garde with a form of modernism which enabled the artist and the culture at large to evade the conditions of its own modernity. Evade and compromise imply a degree of failure; the ambitions of a small body of pre-war avant-garde painters now in ruins, modernism could survive the following decade only through redefinition as design. The *Modernity of English Art* considers the *Studio*'s role in these terms in the late 1920s. My argument, however, is that from the wider perspective and time frame of the *Studio* stress on a pervasive conservatism in the 1920s is less instructive. The distinction regarding an art that adapts itself to changing modern conditions rather than an adaptive modernism is, I think, important.

38   Holme, *Studio Year-Book of Decorative Art*, 1921, pp. 1–4.

39   On Russell see for example: *Studio*, March 1924, p. 132.

40   Holme, 1921, p. 4.

41   Sydney R. Jones, 'The Roehampton Estate', *Studio Year-Book of Decorative Art*, 1922, pp. 37–55.

42   'Concrete Homes', *Studio Year-Book of Decorative Art*, 1920, pp. 49–53.

43   Overy, *Light, Air and Openness*, p. 68.

44   Frank Brangwyn, *Studio Year-Book of Decorative Art* editorial, 1925, pp. 1–4.

45   For recent studies on the artist see the essays in Horner and Naylor, eds. *Frank Brangwyn*.

46   *Studio*, 'Studio Talk', July 1920, pp. 191–2.

47   *Studio*, 'Studio Talk', November 1919, p. 76.

48   *Studio*, July 1920, p. 34. Amidst the growing trend for amalgamations, 'Studio Talk' laments that Barker and Co., having now bought the store – although keeping its name – had discontinued the 'excellent exhibition gallery' at the top of the former firm's premises which for the past two or three years had been devoted to 'various manifestations of modern art'.

49   Heal was a founder of the DIA.

50   The information on *Colour* here is drawn from the 'Modernist Journals Project' website (see n. 5).

51   For more discussion, see, Helmreich and Holt, 'Marketing Bohemia'.

52 *Studio*, special spring number, 1923, p. xiv.

53 Sydney R. Jones, 'Editorial', special number of the *Studio*, 1926, 'Posters and Publicity', p. 1.

54 Shirley Wainwright, 'Modern Printed Textiles', *Studio*, December 1926, p. 394.

55 *Studio*, January 1929. 'New Rug Design by E. McKnight Kauffer and Marion Dorn: A Conversation with a '"Studio" Representative', pp. 37–8.

56 See, for example, Herbert Read's *Art Now* (1933). For discussions of Read see: especially Paraskos, ed. *Re-reading Read*; and Read and Thistlewood, eds. *Herbert Read*.

57 Rutter, *Evolution in Modern Art*, p. 134.

58 Rutter, along with Laurence Binyon and Geoffrey Holme, traced this tendency back to eighteenth- and early nineteenth-century British traditions and to figures like Cozens and Cotman.

59 James Laver, 'The Paintings of Algernon Newton', *Studio*, October 1926, pp. 231–2.

60 Rutter, *Evolution in Modern Art*, p. 142.

61 William Gaunt, 'Paul Nash', *Drawing and Design*, October 1926, pp. 111–12. For Gaunt, Nash 'looks back to English tradition with reverence ... [but] is capable of adapting it so as to express the range of new conceptions that has swept over the modern world.'

62 Editorial, *Drawing and Design*, July 1926, p. 1.

63 Corbett, *The Modernity of English Art*, pp. 86–7.

64 *Drawing and Design*, October 1926, p. 28.

65 Editorial, *Drawing and Design*, August 1926, p. 37.

66 'Letters', *Drawing and Design*, September 1926, p. 108.

67 Editorial, 'Art and the Machine Age', *Studio*, July 1928, p. 3.

68 Ibid.

69 *Studio*, Autumn 1930, pp. 101, 105, from Duveen's letter to Stanley Baldwin.

70 Clyfford Musgrave, *Studio*, April 1953, p. 139; Ashwin, 'The Founding of the Studio'.

71 Editorial, *Drawing and Design*, July 1926, p. 1.

72 See: Alan Powers, 'The Search for a New Reality', in *Modern Britain*, eds. Peto and Loveday, pp. 18–39.

8

Decorative politics and direct pictures: Hugh Lane and the global art market, 1900–15

Morna O'Neill

In her important study *Civilizing Rituals: Inside Public Art Museums*, Carol Duncan argued that public art museums are not isolated from the 'real' stories of politics, economics, and religion; instead, they belong at the centre of 'a broader international history of bourgeois culture'.[1] Duncan highlights the crucial roles played by wealthy collectors in the creation of public art museums in Europe and America in the late nineteenth century as the aristocratic and idiosyncratic habit of collecting and displaying art became a public, professional practice. As Duncan acknowledges, the development of the international art market enabled this revolution. Art dealers, however, are largely overlooked in her study and in subsequent scholarship, even though they were vital agents in the creation of museums. As Helen Rees Leahy explains, to acknowledge that 'a work of art is for sale to the highest bidder' is to negate 'the myth that individual owners are custodians of a shared heritage whose meaning and value exceeds the boundaries' of private property.[2] It could be argued, however, that art dealers functioned as diplomats, brokering deals that allowed for the construction of local and national identity through the creation of museums and galleries. Although the goals of the museum would seem to be in conflict with those of the art dealer, each needs the other.

The Anglo-Irish art dealer and philanthropist Hugh Lane is an ideal figure through which to explore the intersection of museum and marketplace. A successful dealer of Old Master pictures and collector of modern art based in London, Lane occupied a unique place in the Edwardian art world as a founder of public museums: the Municipal Gallery of Modern Art in Dublin, the Johannesburg Art Gallery, and the Michaelis Collection in Cape Town.

The network of London-Dublin-Johannesburg-Cape Town suggests the central importance of the British Empire to Lane's conception of the art dealer. The movement of the 'centre' culture to these 'periphery' markets of the British Empire contributed to the dominance of a London-based art market in the early twentieth century. Formerly known as the 'workshop of the world', Great Britain became, by the end of the nineteenth century, the 'shipper, trader, and intermediary in the world's system of payments', according to historian Eric Hobsbawm.[3] Within this context, scholars have charted the migration of artwork from British private collections into American 'plutocrat' collections.[4] This history is often isolated from a parallel narrative involving equally plutocratic 'Randlord' collectors, those businessmen who had earned their wealth in diamond and gold mining ventures (the latter centred in Witwatersrand or 'the Rand') in South Africa.[5] Lane broadened the scope of the art market beyond the one-way flow of goods and services from Europe to America.

Most accounts of Lane's career focus on the saga of his gallery of modern art in Dublin, and they invariably explain the Dublin project biographically: Lane was a member of the Anglo-Irish gentry, a nephew of the Celtic Revival leader Lady Augusta Gregory, and a friend of the Yeats family.[6] Because of this family history, the plans for the municipal gallery in Dublin are often considered in isolation from Lane's work in South Africa, even though these projects were, in some senses, just as philanthropic. That these efforts coincided with the rapacious 'new' imperialism of the Edwardian era, often defined as the 'capitalist expedient to exploit the rest of the globe', makes a global interpretation of his efforts all the more pressing.[7]

According to Lane, the municipal art gallery presented an ideal focus for the art-loving dealer. As he explained, 'I never sell a picture until I am driven to it. And if I sell to some millionaire it is lost. I don't see it again, it may not give any very great pleasure to him and it is lost to everyone else. But if I give a picture to a gallery, that is really good business. It is as much mine as ever, I still possess it. I can see it when I like and everyone else can see it too, so that's no waste in the matter.'[8] In this remarkable explanation of his business philosophy, Lane expresses disdain for his clients and conflates philanthropy with the market imperative. This essay will discuss the way in which Lane positioned himself in the art market as a gentleman dealer and how this professional identity informed his own collecting and philanthropy. His public galleries, like his success as a dealer, relied upon values that underpinned the international art market: the individual vision and discernment of the connoisseur. Yet these same qualities prompted others to contest his role as cultural interpreter, and Lane could not sustain his identity as both 'dealer' and 'philanthropist'. As I will discuss, whether in Dublin, Johannesburg, or Cape Town, Lane's galleries were embroiled in national and imperial political debates tinged with a growing suspicion of public gallery schemes.

Hugh Lane, picture dealer

Hugh Lane died in 1915, when German torpedoes sunk the *Lusitania*. He had travelled to New York on behalf of Lloyd's of London to file an insurance report in a claim involving works owned by Duveen Brothers, and the trip also provided him with an opportunity to court American clients.[9] Obituaries praised his selfless devotion to art and his atypical business practices in equal measure. The artist Henry Tonks, writing in the *Burlington Magazine*, described Lane as 'a picture dealer', but 'never in romance or real life has there been such a dealer before. If he had ambitions, it would be very difficult to say what they were; at least they were not those of a dealer.'[10] The critic D.S. MacColl noted in 1909 that Lane was 'a sort of dealer', while to the historian and collector Michael Sadler, Lane seemed 'an adventurous buyer of works of art' with 'an extraordinary intuition for what is good'.[11] Lane carefully constructed the professional identity of gentleman dealer suggested by these comments.

By 1909, Lane had been in business for more than fifteen years.[12] He began in the professional art dealer trade in 1893 with an apprenticeship at Martin Colnaghi's Marlborough Gallery, a position obtained through an introduction from Lady Gregory. Lane did not stay long, and he began to buy and sell as an independent agent in 1895. The following year, he joined the dealer E. Trevelyan Turner, manager of the Carlton Gallery, in a business venture: Turner would provide gallery space for the display of works acquired by Lane for a percentage of the sale price, and he would engage Lane as a 'finder' or 'buyer' of Old Master paintings. This arrangement also soured quickly, and Lane established his own rooms in Pall Mall in 1898, first on Pall Mall Place, and then later 43 Duke Street, and, finally, 93 Jermyn Street. Although his premises were at the heart of the London art dealer trade, Lane was eager to distance himself from 'the trade'.[13] By 1906, he was also sharing space with the artist William Orpen in South Bolton Gardens, storing and displaying works adjacent to the artist's studio.[14] He conducted his business along 'gentlemanly' lines, forgoing written contracts in favour of verbal agreements and, eventually, relocating his pictures to his home.[15]

Lane moved his business into his home in 1909, when he acquired Lindsey House, part of a former seventeenth-century mansion at 100 Cheyne Walk in Chelsea. The move from the commercial West End to the more bohemian Chelsea further removed Lane's business from the usual trade. According to his friend and biographer Thomas Bodkin, Lane was an inveterate decorator, and Lindsey House became his show piece.[16] While it was not unusual for dealers such as Paul Durand-Ruel and Duveen Brothers to set up apartments or devise mock domestic situations in which to invite clients to view works, it was unusual for the dealer himself to live on those premises as his home.[17] Lane settled at Lindsey House, and he commissioned decorative paintings from Augustus John for the front hallway (these were never fully realized, much to Lane's dismay), while the rest of the home displayed his taste for the seventeenth and eighteenth centuries: carvings by Grinling Gibbons above the mantelpiece, a prized cabinet designed by William Kent for Burlington House, and Jacobean oak panelling. These provided a backdrop for his collection of Chinese and Japanese ceramics as well as paintings in his holdings. According to his friend, the architect J.M. Solomon, Lindsey House evoked a range of artistic references: the bay window overlooked the Thames in a way that suggested 'Whistler's nocturnes' while the light in the room recalled the art of Rembrandt and Goya; Lane himself looked like an El Greco.[18] He courted potential clients by inviting them to tea, spilling out into the back garden designed by Edwin Lutyens; the dealer knew that such events were 'good for trade'.[19]

The movement of his business practice into his home in Chelsea contributed to Lane's identity as a 'gentleman dealer', one who 'formed a collection to please his own taste'.[20] This role seems to be Lane's own invention, although there are models for this type of behaviour among eighteenth-century antiquarians and connoisseurs.[21] This rationale explains his habit of buying from and selling to other dealers, as 'each new item was paid for from the proceeds of the sale of something rejected to make way for it'.[22] The quality and coherence of his collection was the primary concern: Lane was a scrupulous curator of his collection.

Lane's role as gentleman dealer, however, led his contemporary Joseph Duveen to dismiss him as an 'amateur'.[23] The gentlemanly domesticity of Lane's practice distinguishes him from competitors. Duveen, for example, drew upon a range of museum professionals and 'experts' such as Bernard Berenson, Wilhelm von Bode, and Robert Langton Douglas to authenticate works, often for a percentage of the profit.[24] Lane, in contrast, styled himself as an aesthete, and he used this reputation as a marketing tool that subverted the regularized commission structures and contracts. While Duveen stage-managed the firm's outposts and sold paintings alongside tapestry, furniture, ceramics, and enamels, Lane's clients would, quite literally, buy works of art from off the walls of his home.[25] The grandeur of Lindsey House performed a kind of alchemy: each work became a prized part of a gentleman's collection.

Lane's lack of academic training, as well as his disinterest in the developing field of academic connoisseurship, meant that his judgements often remained based on his 'sixth sense': his eye for art.[26] Auctions proved to be a profitable source of pictures: he often purchased mis-attributed works or those in poor condition to clean (he sometimes did this work himself) and sell at a higher price.[27] Martin Colnaghi advised Lane that the most important training for a dealer was viewing as many works of art as possible in person; with this in mind, Lane toured country houses in Ireland throughout 1903. Lane's family background gave him access to aristocratic collections in Ireland, and it put him in a position to negotiate sales for impoverished Irish aristocrats.

Many of Lane's sales were enabled by two inter-related factors: the influx of paintings from British private collections onto the marketplace and Lane's background in the Irish 'Ascendancy'.[28] In the period between the 1880s and the 1930s, historian David Cannadine argues, the supply of aristocratic art collections and the demand of wealthy American collectors fuelled the art market.[29] The novelist George Moore recalls that one prominent Irish collector insisted on describing Lane as 'a London picture-dealer' and suspected that he 'had come to Ireland to see what he could pick up'.[30] A number of Irish families sought Lane's advice on selling works from their collections.[31]

With such sales, Lane became a purveyor of aristocratic provenance, and, accordingly, contemporary accounts of his sales blur the boundaries between dealer and gentleman collector. A notice of the sensational sale of Titian's *Portrait of Philip II* (c.1550, Cincinnati Museum of Art) to Mrs. Thomas J. Emery in Cincinnati makes it sound as if Lane were not an entrepreneur whose business was the sale of works of art – Mrs. Emery's friend Mary Morgan Newport visited Lane's home in London and noticed the Titian: 'I asked Sir Hugh if the painting could be bought. He replied in the affirmative.' The article describes the dealer as 'a noted English art connoisseur'.[32] Furthermore, a knighthood in 1909 from Edward VII in recognition of Lane's 'services to art' enhanced his status as a gentleman.[33]

Although their means and methods may have differed, Lane, Duveen, and other dealers, attempted to 'align' themselves with their customers as collectors and philanthropists.[34] According to Lane's biographers, the James Staats Forbes collection first piqued Lane's interest in French art, and he focused his own collecting on Impressionist art.[35] The Irish painter William Orpen had introduced Lane to the work of Édouard Manet and the Impressionists during a single day's visit to Paris in 1904. Lane described the dynamic between his roles as dealer and collector as 'selling pictures by old painters to buy pictures by living painters',[36] even though he rejected an invitation from the dealer Felix Fénéon to consider more recent work by Cézanne, Van Gogh, and Matisse during one visit to Paris.[37] He relied upon the dealer Paul Durand-Ruel for most of his purchases, including his first acquisition: the larger version of Pierre Puvis de Chavannes's *Beheading of John the Baptist* (c.1869, National Gallery, London).

According to art historian Philip McEvansoneya, his subsequent collecting in this area often put him in competition with wealthier buyers, including the American collectors Louisine Havemeyer and Dr. Albert C. Barnes.[38] However, many works remained beyond Lane's budget, especially since he was also adding to his dealer's holdings during trips to Paris. For example, during one visit to the city, he purchased a painting by Edgar Degas from the Henri Rouart collection at a much publicized, multi-day sale, as well as works by El Greco, Anthony Van Dyck, and Thomas Gainsborough. Lane's purchases expanded his personal collection of French Impressionist pictures: in 1907, he acquired Pierre-Auguste Renoir's *The Umbrellas* (figure 8.1; 1881–86, National Gallery, London), among others, and he later purchased another group of Impressionist pictures in 1912.[39] For the most part, Lane's personal collection was not hung in his home; those works purchased before he announced his Dublin gallery were often placed on long-term loan with friends. William Orpen, for example, kept Manet's *Portrait of Eva Gonzalez* (1870; National Gallery, London) in his studio. Art acquired after the gallery opened was sent directly to Dublin. By locating his pictures for sale in his home, and then establishing a museum in Dublin for his personal collection, Lane effectively confused the categories of dealer, collector, and philanthropist.

Lane first suggested a gallery of modern art in Dublin in 1905 when he organized a temporary exhibition that included works from the Staats Forbes collection, and it opened to the public in temporary premises in January of 1908, displaying 280 works of art. The French Impressionist and other pictures that are now known as the 'conditional gift' of 39 paintings to be given to the city once the Corporation established a permanent home for the collection are the best known, but his collection also included British art, Irish art, and portraits that Lane hoped would be the beginning of an Irish National Portrait Gallery. Most accounts of the gallery scheme focus on the disagreement between Lane and the Corporation of the City of Dublin over provisions for the collection.[40] Some critics accused Lane of seeking 'personal glorification' and a 'tremendous advertisement' for his business as an art dealer.[41] The rejection of his proposed scheme in 1913 by the Corporation led Lane to change his will and leave the pictures to the National Gallery in London. An unsigned codicil from 1915 transferred the pictures back to Dublin.

The contested legacy continues to this day, with the 'conditional gift', including the prized Impressionist pictures, shared by the National Gallery in London and what is now called 'Dublin City Gallery The Hugh Lane'.[42] Art historian Fintan Cullen has suggested that Lane's gallery courted controversy because he envisioned an Irish identity beyond the boundaries of the British Empire. Lane wanted his gift to promote a 'national school' of Irish art, but his choice of modern French art moves beyond parochial notions of Irish identity and Irish art.

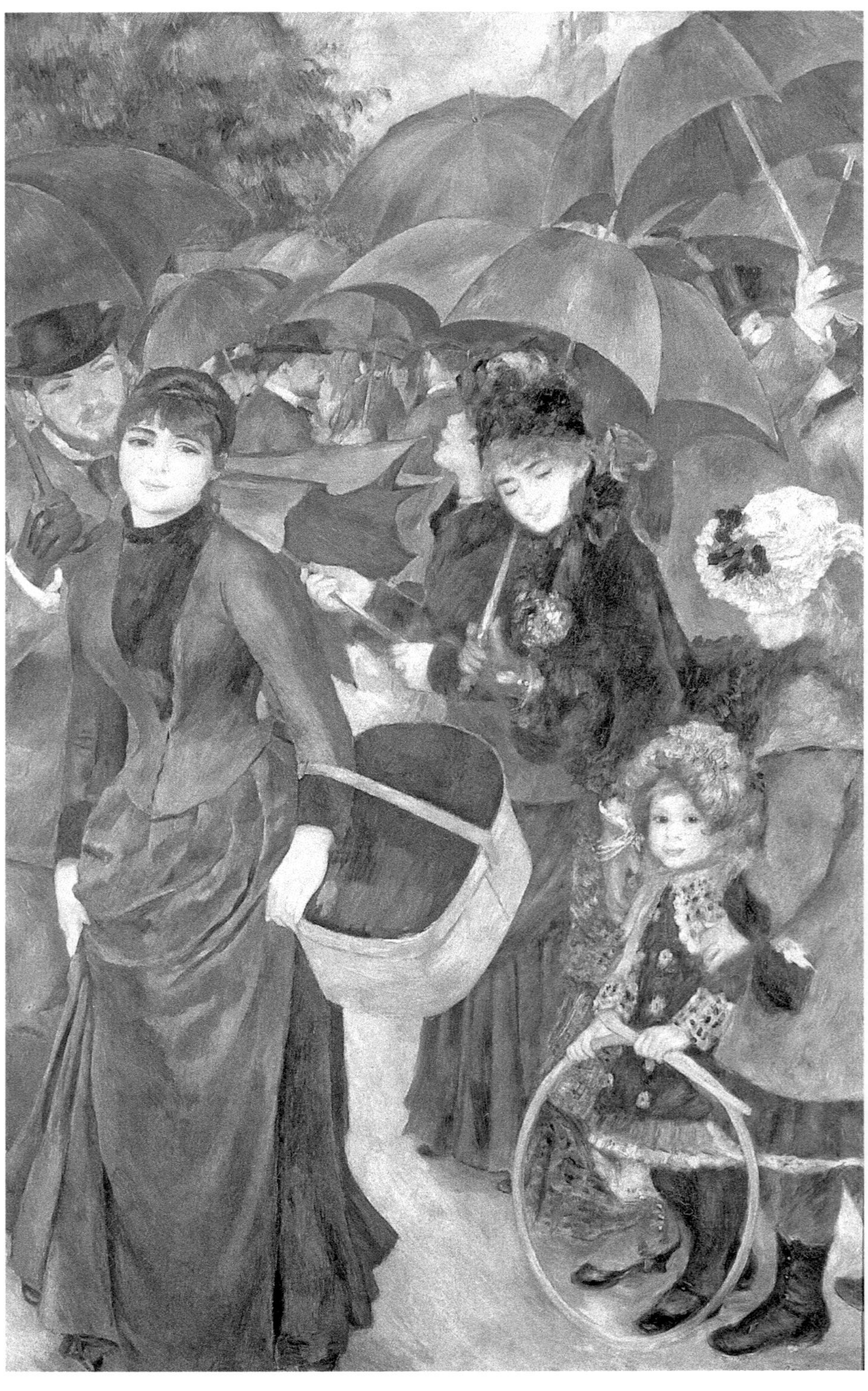

8.1 Pierre-Auguste Renoir, *The Umbrellas*, 1881–86, National Gallery, London.

Thus, according to Cullen, Lane posited a cosmopolitan, European identity.[43] I would suggest, however, that in his public comments and publications, as well as his organization of exhibitions, Lane presented his gift as complementary to Irish identity. With his proposed gift of modern art to Dublin, Lane created an Irish identity for his French pictures by presenting them as part of a decorative tradition that included Celtic art.

Decoration in Dublin

Lane's interest in Irish art coincided with his introduction to the Celtic Revival circle of his aunt Augusta Gregory, and he organized a successful exhibition to aid the Royal Hibernian Academy in Dublin in 1902. He tried, unsuccessfully, to exhibit a collection of Irish art at the World's Fair in St. Louis in 1904.[44] He showed those pictures at the Guildhall in London that same year. In a prefatory notice to the catalogue, Lane praises the artistic production of the Irish 'of early times', especially what he calls the 'perfect forms' of twelfth-century decorative practices.[45] He praises the decorative 'Irish race instinct' in literature, and suggests that 'it can hardly be absent in the sister art'.[46] This 'racial' view of Irish art was apparent to many critics who visited the exhibition, since 'the art they saw there was not Irish, but all those who produced it had Irish blood in their veins'.[47] He goes on to suggest that a gallery of modern art in Dublin would lead to the development of 'a distinct school of painting in Ireland'.[48]

Lane was not unique in his appreciation of the 'race instinct' in Irish art. This view can be traced back to rise of ethnography in the 1850s, and George Stocking pointed out the 'close articulation, both experiential and otherwise, between the domestic and colonial spheres of otherness' in his important *Victorian Anthropology*.[49] Within a Celtic context, Matthew Arnold's 1867 text 'On the Study of Celtic Literature' was perhaps the best-known Victorian exposition of this topic.[50] Arnold hoped to reconcile the 'Celtic' identity of the British people with the 'Teutonic' (and 'Norman'). By 1900, 'every educated Britain knew in outline the "racial" history of the British nation'.[51] Popular texts such as John Beddoe's *Races of Britain* from 1885 popularized this history even as it transformed mid-Victorian ethnocentrism into racism.

The novelist and evolutionist Grant Allen, however, suggested the radical value of 'the Celt' in an essay from 1891. Allen applied Arnold's notion of the 'Celtic Genius' to the visual arts, in particular the painting *The Rose Bower* from *The Briar Rose Series* (1870–90, Faringdon Collection, Buscot Park, Oxfordshire), by the nominally Celtic Edward Burne-Jones. Allen believed in 'the Celtic wave of influence' that would overtake the 'Teuton' in English identity. These categories were probably influenced by the French art critic Ernest Chesneau, who first opposed the abstract nature of 'Latin art' to the realist impulse of 'Saxon art' in 1868.[52] Allen fuses these terms with his own socialist politics. Thus Burne-Jones's exemplary 'Celtic product' champions intricate fretwork pattern, overall design of a composition, and poetical, symbolic subject matter, in opposition to realistic, fact-based painting engendered by the industrialism and materialism of contemporary English life.[53] Allen summarizes this Celtic artistic instinct as 'decorative', a tradition superior to and distinct from what he calls the 'imitative' and 'Teutonic' artistic impulse nurtured in England by the Anglo-Saxons.[54] For Allen, the Teutonic desire for 'technical mastery' too easily approaches the industrial imperatives of the late Victorian era.

The Celt in Britain 'like Mr. Burne-Jones's enchanted princess, has lain silent for ages in an enforced long sleep' but it has returned with a vengeance, 'bringing [...] the Celtic characteristics into the very thick and forefront of the actual fray in England' which will lead to an eventual 'Celtic upheaval'.[55] Thus the 'Celtic temperament' has the potential to transform not only British art, but also British culture and British politics through socialism and Home Rule agitation. If, as contemporary authors suggested, the decorative art of a people reflected their character, then the Celt is an aesthete, who values beauty above all. As Allen concludes, 'To the Celtic type of artist, the picture itself, as a lovely and glorious thing, is the end and aim of all.'[56] Given Lane's reputation as an aesthete, it would not be surprising if he found Allen's ideas appealing.

Lane, it seems, invested in this notion of Celtic decoration: in fact, he acquired Burne-Jones's *The Sleeping Princess* from the first *Briar Rose Series* (c.1872–74, Dublin City Gallery The Hugh Lane) at an unknown date, and he made it the centrepiece of the British room in his Dublin gallery (figure 8.2). Lane may not have offered interior decoration as part of his business, but he oversaw the adornment of each room of the gallery, including eighteenth-century furniture, ornamental ceramics, and floral arrangements.[57] This decorative impulse further confused domestic space and gallery space, especially since the gallery occupied a Georgian townhouse in Harcourt Street. Lady Gregory recalls that Lane gave her and other ladies flowers at the opening and directed them to pose in certain corners of the galleries to add to the 'decorative effect' of the pictures.[58] The 'decorative' display of his galleries harkened back to a 'gentlemanly' form of display popular in the seventeenth and eighteenth century that, according to Carol Duncan, 'subordinated individual works to larger decorative schemes, often surrounding them with luxurious furnishings and ornaments'.[59] He also devised a scheme to decorate his gallery with mural painting depicting important events from Irish folklore and history.[60]

In Dublin at least, modern art merged with Celtic ornamentation: according to one (exasperated) Irish critic of Lane's gallery, 'we hear so much nowadays of the desirability of a school of distinctive Irish art. The man who draws intricate designs of interlaced ornament is looked on as an evangelist.'[61] Lane's exhibition efforts were often connected with Arts and Crafts activities as vernacular expressions of decorative art thought to embody 'Celticness'.[62] Dermot Robert Wyndham Bourke, the seventh Earl of Mayo, the honorary president of the Arts and Crafts Society in Ireland, spoke at the opening of Lane's 1905 exhibition and explicitly connected the dealer's efforts with those of the Arts and Crafts group.[63] Invitation cards to the opening of the gallery in 1908 were printed in Gaelic and English, as were labels and the catalogue.[64] Furthermore, Stephen Gwynn of the Gaelic League spoke at this event and declared Lane's project 'sympathetic' to the goals of the nationalist League.[65] Irish nationalists reclaimed the ethnographic notion of 'the decorative Celt', and both the 'Irish Ireland' brand of nationalism and the Celtic Revival promoted the innate artistry of the Irish people, as evident in the 'Derry Horde' of Celtic gold discovered in 1896 and the celebrated Book of Kells.

Decoration thus provided a 'Celtic' context for the prized Impressionist pictures. Scholarly focus on the perceived modernity of the 'modern' pictures in Lane's collection, and their subsequent place in a teleological history of modern art, has overlooked the way in which decoration allowed Renoir's *The Umbrellas* (figure 8.1), for example, to take its place alongside Edward Burne-Jones's picture from the *Briar Rose* series (figure 8.2) as 'decorative'. The term was a critical lynchpin in the late nineteenth century, deployed in numerous contexts to describe a diverse array of artistic production.[66] Meaning shifted depending on its context, but in discussions of both Renoir and Burne-Jones, it was used to denote an emphasis on colour and patterning of the painted surface as well as attention to the overall 'design' of the composition.[67] A number of artists in the Lane Collection were considered 'decorative' in outlook: Renoir and Monet, as well as Puvis de Chavannes, Giovanni Segnatini, and Auguste Rodin, to name a few.[68] Despite a later modernist denial of decoration, scholars have argued that the decorative can be found in the very patterns, vivid coloration, and flowing lines that motivated the art of pure form.[69] I would argue that Lane gravitated to Impressionism as a marketable form of modernism that could be legitimized historically in Ireland through decoration.[70]

The ethnographic link between an Irish state, however ancient or imaginary, and a decorative Celtic art became a part of nationalist rhetoric in Ireland.[71] Lady Gregory argued for Lane's gallery scheme as a nationalist project in an editorial published in Gaelic in the Gaelic League weekly paper *An Claidheamh Soluis*.[72] The League and the paper became known as the mouthpiece of 'Irish Ireland', a term popularized in the 1890s.[73] Yet the final Corporation vote on the gallery divided Nationalist members.[74] Members withdrew their support from Lane, exasperated

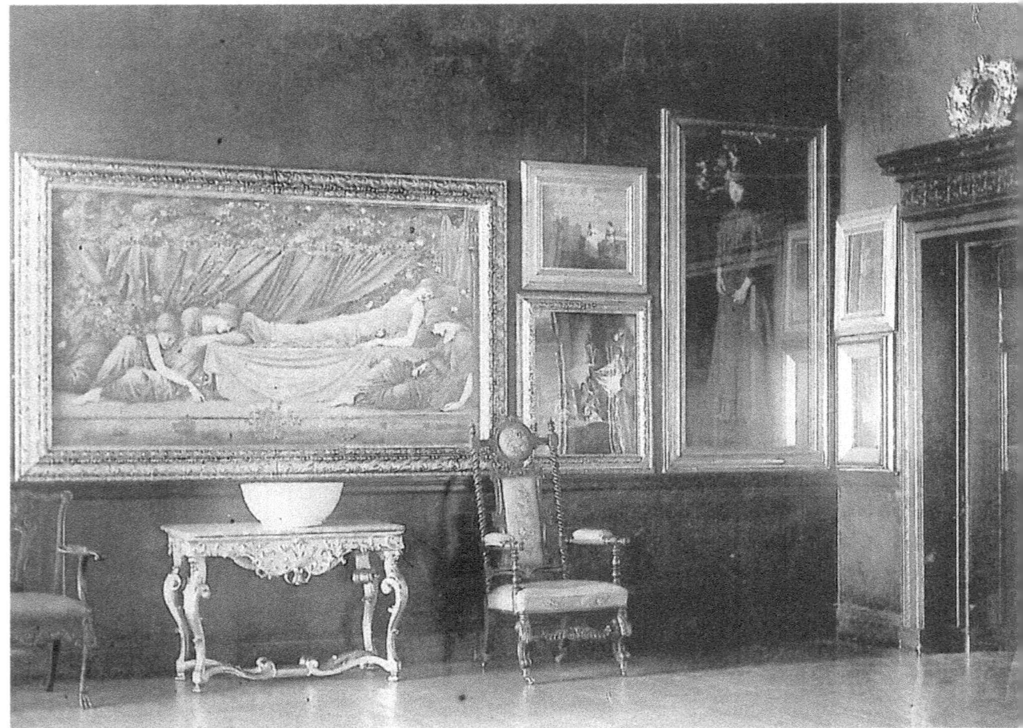

8.2 View of the British room, with Edward Burne-Jones's *The Sleeping Princess* (c.1872–74), Municipal Gallery of Modern Art, Harcourt Street, Dublin, c.1910.

by what they saw as his desire for a monument to himself.[75] As his Dublin scheme courted controversy, Lane turned his attention to South Africa. Most discussions of Lane's career separate his work in Dublin from his two projects in South Africa. By isolating these projects, however, historians and art historians have lost the full imperial context for Lane's work. Ireland and South Africa were vital 'areas of interaction' since both agitated for modern nation-states in the first decade of the twentieth century, and commentators often paired 'Irish' and 'South African' concerns.[76] Lane's galleries, then, present us with an ideal case study to illuminate the cultural dynamic of imperialism. In contrast to the European identity and 'Irish Ireland' nationalism suggested by Lane's gift of modern art to Dublin, both Johannesburg and Cape Town remain firmly within the imperial context. Through collections for museums in Johannesburg and Cape Town, Lane and his sponsors negotiated imperial identities for South Africa in the decade after the South African War (more popularly known as the Boer War) by drawing upon notions of a shared cultural heritage among the white populations of South Africa.

Direct pictures for South Africa

Lane's involvement in South Africa came through Florence Phillips, wife of Lionel Phillips. As a manager of Eckstein and Co., the South African arm of the banking firm Werner, Beit, and Company, Phillips was a member of the Randlord elite. Lane met Florence Phillips in 1909 during one of her visits to London, and he may have approached her as a potential client. South African mining magnates were caricatured as 'plundering Randlords', enterprising men made rich through gold and diamond mining and eager to accrue markers of taste and status. Many channelled their wealth into art collections, although most of these collectors did not make significant donations of artwork to South Africa, preferring instead to settle their collections in Great Britain. Lionel Phillips suggested that a philanthropic attitude towards the collecting of art for South Africa might best counter the stereotype of the Randlord: 'if one considers the profit taken out of this country and the comparatively little spent in those voluntary institutions which in other countries [...] contribute to people's enlightenment and contentment, one realizes how it is that the absentee capitalist is so disliked'.[77] Florence Phillips played a central role in the establishment of museums in Johannesburg and Cape Town, and Lane assisted in assembling these collections.

These efforts should be considered part of the British reconstruction of South Africa in the decade after the South African War. Although the peace settlement named Dutch as the official language of the colony and the British agreed to pay war damages, they secured control over the former Boer republics and were free to shape a new South African state.[78] Subsequent policy emphasized that Great Britain and South Africa would be 'partners' and focused on uniting disparate groups of white South Africans. The races should work together 'for the good of South Africa as a member of the greater whole'.[79] The 1907 memorandum by High Commissioner Lord Selborne outlined the goals of the 'closer union movement' based on the affinity of the two principal 'races' of South Africa – British and Dutch. Eugenic discourse pervades the text, especially in the discussion of the shared Teutonic heritage. As the *Memorandum* continues, 'the fusion between them is merely a matter of time, as it was with the Saxons and the Normans who were related to one another in a similar degree of kinship'.[80] In the wake of this acknowledgement of racial affinity, Jan Smuts negotiated the return of self-government in the Transvaal in 1907, and with the support of Boer nationalist delegates from the Orange Free State, obtained a constitution for South Africa, ratified by Edward VII in 1909.

Against this backdrop, Lane suggested a collection of modern art for Johannesburg, a city increasingly important to British colonial policy and business interests. Jillian Carman's *Uplifting the Colonial Philistine* gives a full account of the establishment of the Johannesburg Art Gallery, and the roles played by Florence Phillips and Hugh Lane in its foundation. She situates the gallery as part of a broader effort to create a stable civil society in South Africa in the aftermath of the South African War. Cultural activities, many of them spearheaded by Lady Phillips, bolstered the 'Closer Union' movement and sought to establish the cultural agenda of the new state. The Johannesburg Art Gallery, Carman argues, '[implied] a symbolic link between the centre and the periphery of the British Empire' through the public display of a collection of modern British art.[81]

Lane's roles as dealer and collector complicated his involvement in the Johannesburg Art Gallery since he did not actually sell modern paintings, but rather collected them for himself and for his own gallery in Dublin. Lane himself noted the conflict of interest in purchasing modern art for Johannesburg and Dublin. 'I find that I cannot buy for two galleries (not the same sort of thing) and I want all the *bargains* for Dublin.'[82] He acted as a finder for Phillips, locating affordable works and purchasing them on her behalf or on the behalf of other donors. While Lane's Dublin gallery was 'the first real attempt at a representative collection of Modern Art'[83] in the British Isles, the Johannesburg Art Gallery was the first collection of modern British art outside of the British Isles. The 'Modern' art purchased for South Africa included French Impressionist painting and works by artists affiliated with the New English Art Club.[84] The first works acquired for the museum at Lane's suggestion, set the tone: three paintings by a leading 'English Impressionist' Philip Wilson Steer.

Some South African donors debated the appropriateness of this type of modern art for the colony. The delicate coloration and technique associated with Impressionism seemed inappropriate for South Africa. Randlord and collector Julius Wernher took Lane to task for considering Henri-Joseph Harpignies's *Last Days of Summer* (figure 8.3; 1863, Johannesburg Art Gallery) for the gallery since 'it is far too poetic for that material place'.[85] He declined to purchase the painting, and Lane persuaded the mining magnate Friedrich Eckstein to fund the purchase. Wernher's doubts about the appropriateness of this elegiac landscape for Johannesburg aligned with contemporary debates about the purpose of colonial museums. London-based critics such as Roger Fry praised the aesthetic coherence of Lane's selection as 'far more representative of the whole scope of modern British art than anything that we have in England'.[86] South African donors, in contrast, viewed the art in an instrumental way, since the museum would play a vital role in the formation of South African civil society.[87]

Wernher also questioned his gift of a John Everett Millais painting, asking Lane 'whether for a beginning one shouldn't buy to a greater degree what I would call "direct pictures"'.[88] Wernher probably refers here to Millais's *Cuckoo* (1880,

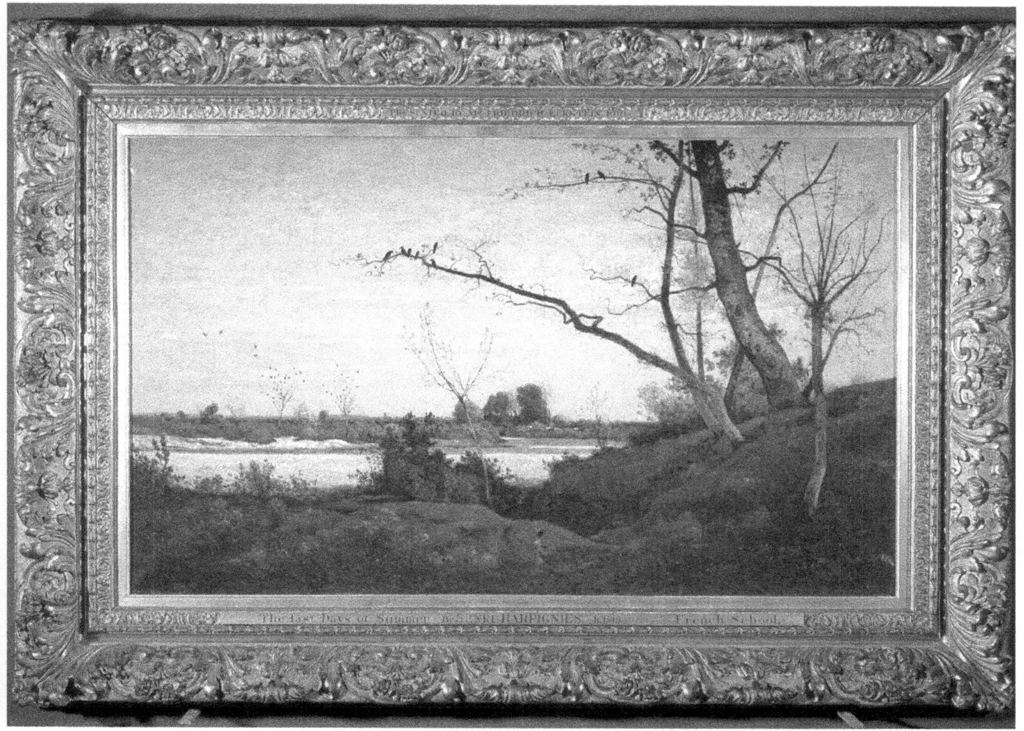

8.3 Henri-Joseph Harpignies, *Last Days of Summer*, 1863, Johannesburg Art Gallery.

Johannesburg Art Gallery), a study of two girls sitting in the woods that the artist exhibited at the Royal Academy in 1880. With the formulation 'direct pictures', Werner suggests that *Cuckoo* is not a direct picture: it evokes a mood rather than tells a moral. Lane countered Wernher's critique by combining instrumentality and aesthetics: Johannesburg needed 'poetic' pictures as a counter to the 'material' reality of the place. When he spoke at the opening of the gallery on 29 November 1910, Lane quoted the socialist George Bernard Shaw, noting that 'it is the duty of the rich to provide luxuries to the poor; the necessaries of life they are likely to fight for themselves'.[89] The gallery, then, is a philanthropic project, and the art dealer plays a crucial role in enabling these efforts; he is the conduit for 'luxury' in the lives of all, rich or poor. Yet the question of aesthetics and the issue of 'direct pictures' would come to the fore in Cape Town.

Florence Phillips also recommended that Lane look into the possibility of an art collection for Cape Town in the hopes that a donor would come forward to purchase it for the city. It is thought that the Boer leader Jan Smuts gave Lane the idea to assemble a collection of 'the golden age' of Dutch art for this purpose. According to an early Lane biographer, the dealer visited South Africa in 1910 to oversee his Johannesburg project, and Smuts suggested a collection that would 'recall the Dutch population of the Dominion [to] the glories of their past civilization in the days when they first colonized South Africa'.[90] In a letter to Lady Gregory, Lane reports that 'it is a just satisfaction to me to have created an "old master" gallery for a continent as it wants one so badly'.[91] A gallery of seventeenth-century Dutch art would unite Boer and Briton a decade after the bitter South African War through 'the representation of the art in which the Dutch and English first met in spirit'.[92] For Cape Town, Lane drew upon the 'Teutonic' heritage of mutual British and Boer admiration for Dutch art and provided a collection of seventeenth-century Dutch art as a gift of 'direct pictures' for the 'materialist' city. In each city, the art selected by Lane posited a relationship of centre to periphery. Johannesburg united Britain and South Africa in the present, while the Cape Town project suggested the continuity between past and present.

Lane's efforts on behalf of Cape Town played a vital role in this construction of a new, united South African identity, as discussed by art historian Michael Stevenson.[93] Max Michaelis, formerly of the Cape Diamond Company, purchased the collection assembled by Lane of forty-two seventeenth-century Dutch and Flemish master paintings for £76,000 and donated it to Cape Town.[94] Initial newspaper reports emphasized Lane's largesse and even suggested that the dealer had not assembled the Dutch pictures with this gallery in mind, but instead 'was willing to dispose of his Dutch pictures provided they were purchased for a public gallery'.[95] By all accounts, Lane sold Michaelis the paintings 'at cost' to guarantee the creation of the gallery, which he modestly claimed as 'my' third public gallery.[96] Michaelis finalized his gift to the city in 1914.

The New York Times reported that the Michaelis gift constituted nothing less than 'A National Art Gallery for South Africa'.[97] The critic for the *Times* emphasized the Dutch heritage of the Cape Colony, one of the reasons Michaelis himself cited for the gift.[98] The gift signified the importance of South Africa to the British Empire, even as it marked a departure from the popular Royal Academy products usually found in colonial museums such as the Art Gallery of New South Wales, founded in Sydney in 1871. Dutch art placed South African identity within a European context; as the *Studio* reported in 1919, 'Cape Town is proud of its association with the enterprise of the old world. It has never ceased to regard itself as an outpost of Europe.'[99] The works were put on display in Cape Town's Old Town Hall, which dated from the 1770s. The gift of Dutch art to Cape Town defined South African identity in a new post-Union way.

The art collection would have a particularly salutary effect on the 'Cape Colony Dutch' or 'The Cape backveldt Dutch', who were considered 'more ignorant, more backward than their fellows in the other three Provinces'.[100] It was thought

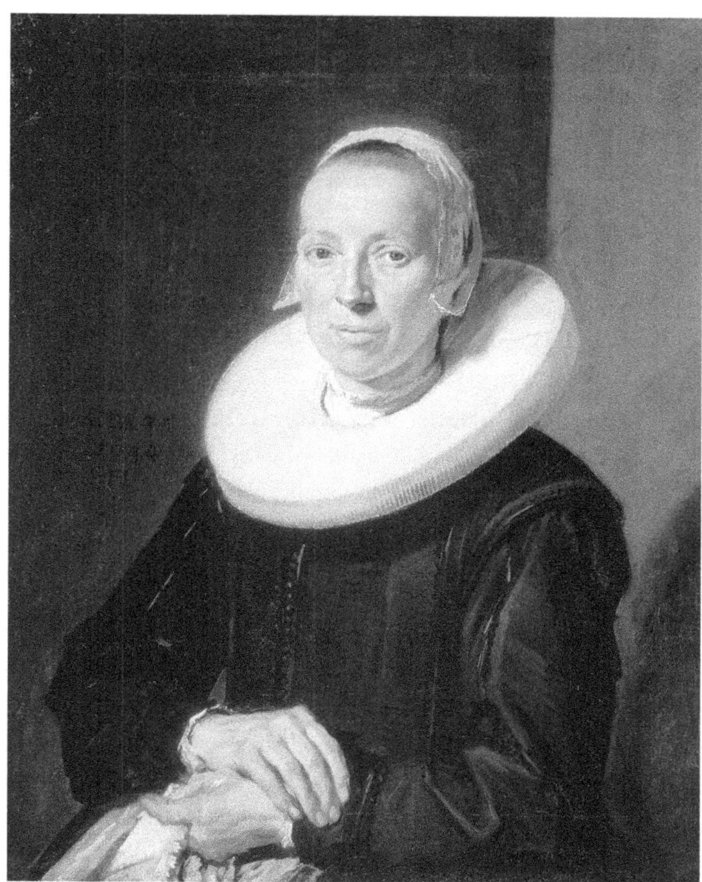

8.4
Frans Hals, *Portrait of a Woman*, 1644, The Michaelis Collection.

that they would identify with the strong Teutonic impulse on display – Grant Allen's description of technically perfect, detailed, and moralistic paintings. Frans Hals's *Portrait of a Woman* (figure 8.4; 1644, Michaelis Collection, Iziko Museums of Cape Town), bought by Lane from Duveen in 1909, exemplifies the serious, middle-class portrait thought appropriate for the Cape Town viewing public. In her unadorned 'Sunday' dress, she exemplifies a modesty not observed in the Randlords but desired in their employees, while *vanitas* subjects seemed to temper the sumptuous lifestyles of the Randlords with an underlying moral message.[101]

Both London critics and Afrikaner nationalists, however, were unimpressed with the Michaelis gift. When Lane showed the collection at the Grosvenor Gallery in 1913, it touched off a bitter and public disagreement over his attribution of works to Rembrandt and Hals.[102] South African nationalists wondered why Michaelis chose Cape Town over Pretoria as the recipient of his munificence.[103] Such discussions hinted at the growing rivalry between the

Cape and the Transvaal for leadership of the 'new' South Africa. Editorials suggested that the collection should go to Pretoria, the capital of the former Boer South African Republic and the administrative capital of the new Union of South Africa.[104] Unlike Lane's bilingual Dublin Gallery, the catalogue and labels were available in English only at the Old Town Hall. In both Ireland and South Africa, Lane elided nation and race; or, rather, he interchanged these two terms. This gambit worked against the imperial project in Dublin, as the assertion of a 'Celtic' race matched the desire for an Irish nation. In Cape Town, the assertion of a unified 'Teutonic' race only highlighted the fissures in this recently united 'nation'.

In each city that benefited from Lane's practice, the donation of art raised troubling questions about the relation of the individual to the larger social structure. A public gallery takes art out of circulation as private property and transforms it into public good. Some critics portrayed the exhibition of works of art in public galleries as a form of 'emancipation' – a phraseology that echoes Lane's own comments on the 'loss' of works of art that are sold to millionaires. Yet Lane faced criticism in his role as 'arbiter' of local, national, and imperial taste. How could he presume to collect for museum visitors in Dublin, Johannesburg, and Cape Town? According to historian Jordanna Bailkin, the first decade of the twentieth century witnessed a crisis in the 'material culture of Liberalism',[105] a growing suspicion of the public good posited by municipal museums, art education, and town planning. The fact that 'national' and 'imperial' culture rested in the hands of a few exacerbated this debate. Furthermore, modern aesthetic theory no longer viewed art as an instrumental social good.[106] As Carol Duncan has discussed, the museum in the early twentieth century shifted from the Enlightenment ideal of a place to 'enlighten and improve its visitors morally, socially, and politically' to the twentieth century ideal of 'the aesthetic museum'.[107] Lane attempted to fuse these two elements, investing moral, social, and political purpose into the aesthetic. Yet he found that he could not supplant the aristocratic owner of a work of art without being subject to the same critique. Lane could not sustain his identity as both 'dealer' and 'philanthropist', someone who, in his own words, would 'never sell a picture' unless he was 'driven to it'.[108]

Notes

1 Duncan, *Civilizing Rituals*, p. 3.
2 Leahy, 'Desiring Holbein', p. 77.
3 Hobsbawm, *Industry and Empire*, p. 125.

4   See, for example, Boime, 'America's Purchasing Power', p. 129; Roberts, 'Collecting'.

5   Fraser, 'Randlord'. Accessed 10 October 2009.

6   See Foster, '"A Family Affair"'.

7   Torrance, *Strange Death of Liberal Empire*, p. xvi.

8   Lane, as quoted in White, 'Sir Hugh Lane', p. 116.

9   See: O'Byrne, *Hugh Lane*, p. 208.

10 Henry Tonks, 'Sir Hugh Lane', *Burlington Magazine*, June 1915, p. 128.

11 Michael Sadler typescript in Tate Archives, TD 28 October 1909 visit with D.S. MacColl to Augustus John and P.W. Steer, 8221.5.4. My thanks to Anne Helmreich for bringing this source to my attention.

12 For Lane's biography, see O'Byrne.

13 Lanes's gallery at 93 Jermyn Street does not appear in *The Post Office London Directory for 1908* (London: Kelly's Directories, 1908).

14 O'Byrne, p. 97.

15 Lane had no written contract for his work in South Africa. As discussed in Carman, *Uplifting the Colonial Philistine*, p. 141.

16 Bodkin, *Hugh Lane*, p. 70.

17 Ward, 'Impressionist Installations'.

18 J.M. Solomon, 'Sir Hugh Lane: A Memoir', *Country Life in South Africa*, 1:3, June 1915, p. 11.

19 Bodkin, p. 70.

20 Bodkin, p. 3. The phrase is Bodkin's.

21 See Myrone and Peltz, eds. *Producing the Past*.

22 Bodkin, p. 3.

23 As quoted in O'Byrne, p. 93.

24 See Samuels, *Bernard Berenson*, pp. 192–3, and Simpson, *Artful Partners*, p. 87.

25 As described by Secrest, *Duveen*, p. 51. See also: Bailey, *Building the Frick Collection*, pp. 59–60.

26 Gregory, *Hugh Lane's Life*, p. 27.

27 As noted in O'Byrne, p. 23.

28 See: Foster.

29 Cannadine, *Decline and Fall*, p. 113.

30 Moore, *Hail and Farewell!*, II, p. 259.

31 Peter Mandler referred to this practice as 'maximizing the assets' of landholders. See Mandler, *Fall and Rise of the Stately Home*, p. 119.

32 'Mrs. Emery Buys a $400,000 Titian', *New York Times*, 20 December 1913, p. 1.

33 Gregory, p. 158, as quoted in O'Byrne, p. 117.

34 See, for example, Lapine, 'Asher Wertheimer', p. 46.

35 See: Morris, *French Art in Nineteenth-Century Britain*, pp. 242–3.

36 Morris, p. 164.

37 Uncatalogued Hugh Lane letters, National Library of Ireland, Acc. 5073.

38 McEvansoneya, 'Lane's Choices', p. 37.

39 McEvansoneya, p. 40.

40 See Dawson, 'Hugh Lane's Pictures', and Sharp, 'The Wrong Twigs for an Eagle's Nest?'.

41 As noted in 'Dublin and Sir Hugh Lane', *Weekly Irish Times*, 25 January 1913, p. 10.

42 McDiarmid, *Irish Art of Controversy*, pp. 38–9.

43 Cullen, 'The Lane Bequest'.

44 See Bowe, 'Vernacular Expression', p. 16.

45 Lane, *Irish Painters*, p. ix.

46 Lane, p. x.

47 'Pictures and Picture Galleries', *Weekly Irish Times*, 31 December 1904, p. 16. For the 'Irishness' of this art, see also P.G. Konody, 'About Art. New Municipal Gallery at Dublin', *Observer*, 26 January 1908, p. 10.

48 Lane, p. x.

49 Stocking, *Victorian Anthropology*, p. 234.

50 Arnold, *Celtic Literature*. These essays first appeared as 'On the Study of Celtic Literature' in the *Cornhill Magazine* in 1867.

51 Urry, 'Englishmen, Celts, and Iberians', p. 83.

52 As discussed in Mainardi, *Art and Politics*, p. 163.

53 G. Allen, 'The Celt in English Art', *Fortnightly Review*, 1 February 1891, p. 267.

54 Allen, p. 268.

55 Allen, p. 267.

56 Allen, p. 271.

57 For museum décor, see Waterfield, *Palaces of Art*, pp. 49–65.

58 Gregory, p. 49.

59 Duncan, p. 25.

60 O'Byrne, p. 171.

61 'Gallery of Modern Art in Dublin', *Cork Examiner*, 8 March 1907 in MS 35,827/6, Scrapbook compiled by Ruth Shine, 1885–1907, National Library of Ireland, Dublin.

62 See Bowe, 'Vernacular Expression', and Bowe, 'Romantic Nationalism'.

63 In an article entitled 'The Art Movement in Dublin' from 18 April 1905, a correspondent for the *Dublin Express* relates that the Earl of Mayo connected Lane's efforts to the Arts and Crafts movement. MS 35,827/6, Scrapbook compiled by Ruth Shine, 1885–1907, National Library of Ireland, Dublin.

64 Bodkin, p. 19.

65 Press clipping from the *Dublin Express*, MS 35,827/6, Scrapbook compiled by Ruth Shine, 1885–1907, National Library of Ireland, Dublin.

66 For cogent summaries of this issue, see Auther, 'Clement Greenberg'; Cheetham, *Rhetoric of Purity*.

67 For Renoir, see Herbert, *Nature's Workshop*, p. 66. For Burne-Jones, see Arscott, *Interlacings*, pp. 203–24.

68 See, for example, Herbert, 'Monet's Cathedrals'; Levine, 'Claude Monet's Art'; Shaw, *Dream States*.

69 As discussed by Anger, *Paul Klee*, p. 2.

70 Jensen, *Marketing Modernism*, p. 3. See also Galenson and Jensen, 'Careers and Canvases', accessed 23 March 2008.

71 See, for example, Larmour, *Arts and Crafts Movement in Ireland*; Sheehy, *Rediscovery of Ireland's Past*; and Theiding, 'Anxieties of Influence'.

72 Reprinted in Gregory, pp. 62–4.

73 Lyons, *Ireland Since the Famine*, pp. 320–1. See also MacCartney, 'MacNeill and Irish Ireland', p. 77.

74 See O'Brien, *'Dear Dirty Dublin'*, p. 56.

75 As quoted in McDiarmid, p. 27.

76 As noted in Torrance, p. xvi. Scholars have also discussed 'imperial affinities'; see Cook, *Imperial Affinities* and Lennon, *Irish Orientalism* as well as Nagai, *Empire of Analogies*.

77 As quoted in Stevenson, 'History of the Collection', p. 30.

78 Marks and Trapido, 'Lord Milner'.

79 As quoted in Dubow, 'Colonial Nationalism', p. 57.

80 As quoted in Dubow, 'Colonial Nationalism', p. 68.

81 Carman, p. 239.

82 As quoted in Gutsche, *No Ordinary Woman*, p. 260. Emphasis in Lane's original letter.

83 P.G. Konody, as quoted in Carman, p. 177.

84 See Goldin and Keene, eds. *Da Corot a Monet*.

85 National Library of Ireland, MS 13,071/2: Julius Wernher to Lane, 30 August 1910, as quoted in O'Byrne, p. 136.

86 Roger Fry, 'Reviews and Notices: Catalogue of the Municipal Gallery of Modern Art, Johannesburg', *Burlington Magazine*, June 1911, p. 178.

87 As discussed in Carman.

88 National Library of Ireland, MS 13,071/2: Julius Wernher to Lane, 30 August 1910, as quoted in O'Byrne, p. 136.

89 H. Lane, 'Prefatory Note', in Ross, *Gallery of Modern Art, Johannesburg*.

90 Bodkin, p. 29. For museums in Cape Town, see Tietze, 'Classical Casts'. For the history of museums in South Africa, see Carman.

91 Letter from Lane to Lady Augusta Gregory, dated 13 November 1912, the Henry W. and Albert A. Berg Collection of English and American Literature, the New York Public Library.

92 As quoted in Stevenson, 'History of the Collection', p. 32.

93 Stevenson, pp. 29–43.

94 See Stevenson.

95 'Collection of Dutch Masters Bought for South Africa', *Scotsman*, 11 November 1912, p. 8.

96 As quoted in Stevenson, p. 32.

97 'ART TREASURES IN AFRICA; Shipment of $400,000 Worth of Canvases Reaches Cape Town', *New York Times*, 28 August 1916, p. 15.

 98 Michaelis as quoted in Bax, 'History of the Building', p. 20.
 99 T. Martin Wood, "The Michaelis Gallery, Cape Town," *Studio*, May 1919, p. 93.
100 General Louis Botha, first Prime Minister of the Union of South Africa, as quoted in Lowry, *South African War*, p. 10.
101 See Hochstrasser, *Still Life and Trade*.
102 Slive, 'Michaelis Collection'.
103 Dubow, 'Imagining the New South Africa', p. 91.
104 See Gutsche, pp. 289–90.
105 Bailkin, *Culture of Property*, p. 3.
106 Minihan, *Nationalization of Culture*, p. 167.
107 Duncan, p. 16.
108 Lane, as quoted in White, 'Sir Hugh Lane', p. 116.

9

Matthew Smith, the Tate Gallery, and the London art market

Alexandra MacGilp

This study explores the Tate's collecting of works by the English painter Matthew Smith from the late 1920s until the outbreak of the Second World War in order to elucidate the Tate's patterns of collecting and relationships with dealers. It examines the institution, the artist-dealer system, and the social and professional networks operating in the broader framework of the London art world. It sheds new light on the career of an artist often neglected by art historians because he eschewed the group memberships that were such a crucial feature of his time. Early twentieth-century artist groups, including the New English Art Club, the Camden Town Group, the Bloomsbury Group, the London Artists' Association, the Seven and Five Society, and Unit One, helped garner attention in the marketplace and bypassed art dealers. Smith, by contrast, preferred unofficial affiliations, which proved to be, in his case, more powerful and long-lasting. Smith's career demonstrates the significance of networks created by artists as well as those created by dealers and the need to exercise more than one network at any given moment in order to achieve artistic prominence and fiscal success.

Smith was working in a moment when these networks underwent tremendous change because of the increasing significance of a new type of patron – the museum. The Tate Gallery opened in 1897, the industrialist and philanthropist Henry Tate providing the foundation collection and the funds for the building. For its first two decades, the gallery housed only recent British works and was subordinate to the National Gallery. In 1917 it gained its own director and trustees and became the home of modern and historic British art as well as modern foreign art.[1]

The acquisition of Smith's paintings by the Tate provides a well-documented case study of the functioning of the London art market, and how the museum intersected with yet another network – that of the press. Reviews of Smith's exhibitions in newspapers and specialist art periodicals were key to circulating knowledge about his practice, establishing his reputation, and enhancing the desirability of his works. His paintings were regarded as challenging but recognized as worthy of a place in the national collection, which led to their grudging acquisition by the institution. Crucially, the Tate was dependent on commercial galleries to introduce Smith to the public and garner critical press attention. It could not, however, openly acknowledge this mutually beneficial arrangement for fear of the perceived stain of the commercial sphere on its purportedly transcendent and edifying work. The Tate trustees were hamstrung by their anxiety over following the lead, or taking the advice, of art dealers, with whose expertise they could not compete.

Matthew Smith and his networks

In April 1926, Smith, at age 47, had his first solo exhibition at the Mayor Gallery. The gallery, run by Freddy Mayor, had opened the year before and was building a reputation for its exciting programme of contemporary art. Smith had studied at the Slade, lived in France where he briefly attended the Atelier Matisse, and been encouraged by Jacob Epstein and Walter Sickert to exhibit with the London Group. At the Mayor Gallery Smith showed his bold nudes and clamorous, strongly coloured Cornish landscapes, as well as flower pieces; all priced from twenty to fifty guineas. The show was a financial success with three-quarters of the works sold, and caused shock waves on the London art scene. The press response characterized Smith as modern, colourful, and sensuous but also abnormal, violent, and excessive. The critic P.G. Konody, an early supporter of Smith, was attracted to the painter's exuberant sense of colour, and wrote in the *Observer*: 'The fierceness of Mr Smith's pouring of vivid, though invariably well-harmonised, hues over the whole surface of the canvas is ... exciting and disturbing'. Like several other reviewers, Konody doubted Smith would receive general recognition because he was 'too aggressively daring to "go down" with the general public'.[2]

The critics were required to coin a new vocabulary in order to describe Smith's work, a task they evidently relished. Smith's extravagant use of colour was considered his defining characteristic but seen by some as a flaw. The *Morning Post* imagined Smith stepping into a 'blind alley where he sees little else than ungracious-looking women mostly arrayed in ruddy gore red, emerald green, and grimy brown'.[3] Smith's choice of larger models was criticized for not conforming to conventional standards of beauty. Newspaper reviews were rarely illustrated and black and white reproductions could not do Smith's paintings justice so these critics' accounts were of particular descriptive value. Musical comparisons were frequently employed; the *Saturday Review* heard 'a thundering of colour which rolls over our senses like some rich and sombre passages of Beethoven'.[4] The press played a vital role in publicizing Smith's work and emphasizing his audacious use of colour as his unique selling point, whether or not it met with their admiration.

The most important outcome of this exhibition for Smith was a laudatory review from the influential critic Roger Fry in the *Nation and Athenaeum*. Two years earlier Fry had purchased a pair of uncompromising nudes from Smith in Paris for £35, one for the Contemporary Art Society (CAS), the other for his own collection. Fry now heralded Smith's achievement as a point of national pride: 'Those who are bold and optimistic enough to believe in the future of an English school of painting will gain fresh confidence from Mr Matthew Smith's pictures.'[5]

The critic T.W. Earp praised Smith: 'one of the most interesting and important young English painters has obviously assimilated much from the French Post-Impressionist schools. But he has welded his origins into coherence and added the stamp of mastery.'[6] Richard Wyndham, an early collector of the painter's work, recalled the vital support Smith received from his fellow artists, Jacob Epstein and Augustus John, who purchased works.[7] Smith's critical reputation as that rare phenomenon, an English painter who had successfully digested the lessons of the French avant-garde, was being launched.

Smith followed his success at the Mayor Gallery with a solo show at the Reid & Lefevre Gallery in December 1927. Here the painter exhibited nudes, flower paintings and Cornish landscapes. Among the purchasers was the respected collector Edward Marsh who bought *Woman Reclining* for £75.[8] The Tate would have been aware of Smith's spectacular debut but this second show was the moment when they officially noticed his work. The director of the National Gallery wrote to Tate director Charles Aitken, tepidly noting two flower pictures he felt to be 'successful in size and colour', but adding that he did not care for the nudes.[9]

Six months later, in July 1928 the Tate purchased its first Smith, *Peonies* (c.1928; figure 9.1) from the Godfrey Phillips Gallery. The sale came about with the help of Epstein, now a close friend of Smith and keen collector of his work. There had been some discussion of Epstein loaning a Smith work from his collection to the Tate but he was unwilling to do this if it would prejudice their purchasing a painting. The sculptor recommended Aitken visit Phillips to examine his Smith paintings. Phillips ran the gallery with his wife Dorothy and the couple were friends of Epstein. Despite the fact that his seven-year tenure as an artist-trustee on the Tate Board had ended a year earlier, it was Muirhead Bone, a friend of

Epstein, who visited the gallery on Aitken's behalf and reported that he liked the paintings and felt the Tate should get one. The trustees selected *Peonies* over another flower piece and a reclining figure they viewed; the price was reduced from £90 to £75.

It was not entirely disinterested of Epstein to introduce Aitken to the Godfrey Phillips Gallery. In the autumn of 1928, Epstein held an exhibition there from which the Tate would acquire his bronze bust of Dorothy Phillips, presented through the National Art Collections Fund, and two drawings, which they purchased.

Here was a demonstration of an artist's network in action, which set the pattern for Smith's relations with the Tate. Epstein had successfully exploited his connections with the Tate to the benefit of his protégé Smith, his gallerist friend Phillips, and himself. Despite his controversial reputation Epstein was able to broker a deal to facilitate the acquisition of Smith's work. The value of his own collection of his friend's work increased as a by-product of the transaction. This transaction was typical of the Tate Board's lack of a coherent acquisition

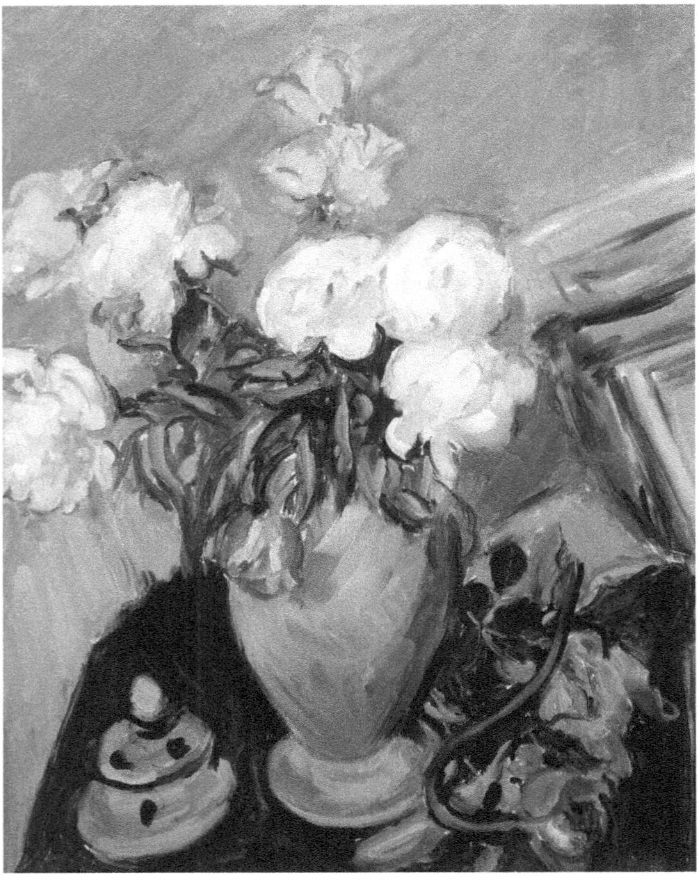

9.1
Matthew Smith, *Peonies*,
c.1928. Purchased 1928.

policy, which relied on personal enthusiasms to ensure important works entered the collection.

The Tate's selection of *Peonies* was an unexciting but safe choice. Smith's flower paintings were popular and easily palatable. The *Morning Post* decided that whereas in the past Smith's paintings 'might have been designed to decorate an abattoir, so gory was their colour' his works at the Lefevre were 'almost normal', while one flower painting possessed 'the lyric spontaneity and charm of a song by Burns'.[10] It was established that even art world citizens who did not care for Smith's 'red' nudes could appreciate his flower subjects.

In 1928 Smith joined the gallery Arthur Tooth & Sons, the same year as Augustus John. In the mid-1920s the new director Dudley Tooth had re-branded his gallery, founded in 1842, expanding to deal in progressive contemporary art and had appointed Ralph Keene to liaise with his new stable of artists. The artists were given a solo show every two and a half years. Tooth's dealt with the entirety of their artists' output, taking a commission of 33$^{1}/_{3}$ per cent on the selling price. The artists bore the costs for publicity, advertising, and framing but relinquished control of these areas to the expert, their dealer, as they were of vital importance to the sale of paintings.[11]

When Paul Nash was considering a contract with Tooth in 1933, the dealer explained to Nash the main attraction of his firm: 'you will have the most powerful selling organisation in London behind you – and your work will be "pushed" to the limit'. In exchange they asked that at least 75 per cent of Nash's works be 'what is generally recognised as Landscapes, Still Lifes, etc and not Abstract subjects'.[12] Tooth's proved themselves to be a powerful selling organization and they placed several works by their artists in public collections. This letter strongly emphasizes the power of the dealer network, which worked alongside artists' networks in the acquisition of Smith's work by museums and city galleries.

Tooth's launched Smith with a successful 1929 retrospective and his reputation was enhanced with further solo shows in 1932 and 1934. Smith's paintings sold to critics and collectors, including P.G. Konody, Sir Michael Sadler, Kenneth Clark, and Edward Marsh. In 1929 his work entered a provincial collection for the first time when the Belfast Municipal Gallery purchased *Daisies and Pears* for £95. In 1931 Manchester City Art Gallery bought *Dahlias* for £200 and Southampton Art Gallery purchased *Roses and Lilies* for £150. Flower pieces were the preferred choice for provincial galleries. By 1934, however, Manchester had built up to a nude and purchased the daring *Model Reclining*, for £150.

Of the three networks – artists, dealers, and critics – perhaps that of the critics appears the least powerful, but in fact they held the vital role of educating the public and the trustees and creating demand for the work. Moreover, key players from the artists' and dealers' networks sought to publish accounts in the press to support Smith. Much to Smith's irritation the press enjoyed characterizing him as a wild man and their ambiguous coverage contributed to the Tate's anxiety about his work. Without press support more conservative works were purchased. Smith continued to be considered a difficult and 'foreign' artist. *The Times* commented in 1930: 'The musical comparison is to Wagner, with the emotional excess implied. One can understand why he is said to be Mr Jacob Epstein's favourite English painter.'[13] The press found it easier to define artists in groups and so allowed Epstein's notoriety to rub off on Smith. Although he would never suffer the same levels of abuse, Smith was accused of subscribing to a cult of ugliness alongside Epstein. It was not until January 1935 that the Tate made its second acquisition of Smith's work, another flower painting, *Cyclamen* (c.1920; figure 9.2) that had been shown in two of Tooth's mixed group shows in 1932. *The Times* had praised its 'magic of colour' and compared Smith to Delacroix.[14] The painting belonged to Tooth, who had bought it at Sotheby's and was keen to sell it, but not to the Tate, whom he would have preferred to purchase a more important work.

The circumstances surrounding the Tate's acquisition of this work are very revealing. The Board Minutes are sparse so circumstances have to be reconstructed

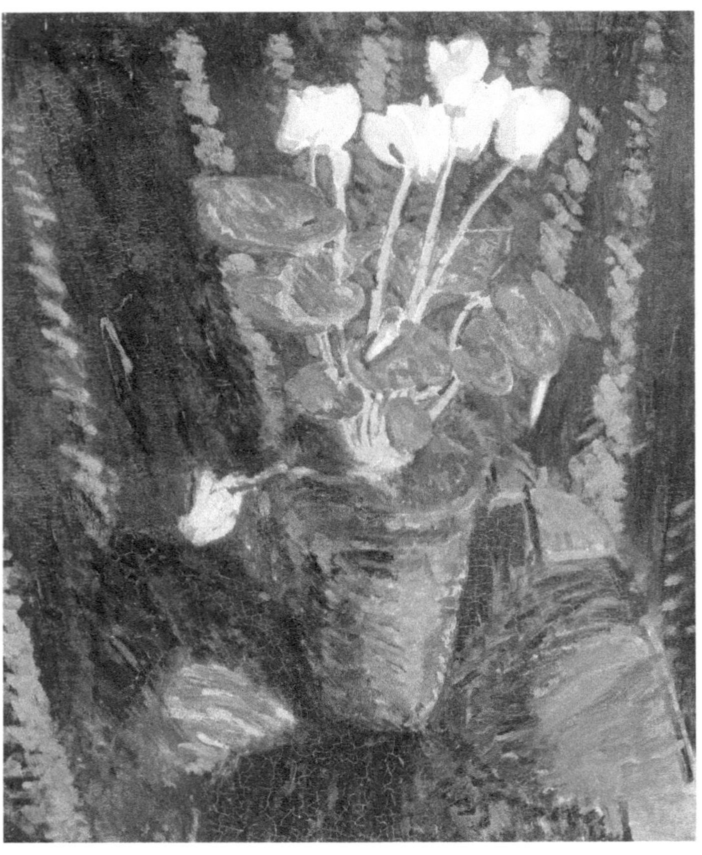

9.2
Matthew Smith, *Cyclamen*, c.1920. Purchased 1935.

from trustee and dealer correspondence. The staff at Tooth's had been monitoring Tate director J.B. Manson's laissez-faire attitude towards acquisitions and decided to take matters into their own hands. They asked John, a Tate trustee since 1933, to participate in an elaborate charade. They knew they could rely on John's friendship and admiration for Smith. In June 1934 Keene wrote candidly to John:

> I wonder if you could suggest to Manson that we should send down one to two of Matthew Smith's pictures for consideration at the next meeting? I have spoken to Dudley Tooth, who says that it would be wrong for us, as dealers, to approach Manson direct.
>
> I am sure you will agree that Smith deserves to be better represented at the Tate – and so many people have remarked about this that we feel it is time an effort was made to secure one of his more important pictures for the nation.
>
> Manson has not been in to Smith's Exhibition and we should very much appreciate it if you could … suggest to him that he should come in to see the pictures … If he has not time to do this, we could select two or three ourselves to send down.[15]

Keene had to seek John's collaboration as a negotiator because etiquette forbade a dealer to approach a public institution directly and be seen to manipulate its acquisition policy. The dealers demonstrated a great deal more passion, initiative, and entrepreneurial spirit than their museum counterparts. They were also scrutinizing public perceptions of the Tate's role and analysing its failings. Keene assumed that John would use his powerful position to educate the public for the mutual benefit of artists and dealers in the face of the ignorance and bureaucracy of officialdom.

Keene tried another tactic in his mission to improve Smith's representation when he wrote an appreciation of his work for the *Artist* in September 1934, praising Smith's intensely individual vision. This he viewed as part of the reason Smith has waited so long for recognition, alongside the 'artist's strong personal distaste for publicity or "business methods" of any sort in the marketing of his paintings'.[16] This aversion was genuine on Smith's part but also fitted the dealer's need to make his artist seem apart from the marketplace in order to proclaim his genius. Keene declared that Smith would never be a popular painter. This was the ultimate accolade in a subtle marketing strategy. Keene explained: 'His pictures are too disturbing for that, too pregnant with the stress and turmoil of a highly sensitive temperament striving to break through the limitations of mundane existence to fix a moment's ecstasy. The majority of people require of the arts that they shall lead them into a world of sweet make-believe, decorously romantic. But

Smith, like Van Gogh, is of the company of those who fight for beauty with a sort of fierce desperation. Such artists inspire admiration – but seldom popularity.'[17] Keene noted that appreciation of Smith's work was increasing: 'Especially amongst artists, less prone to be upset by lack of conventional prettiness'.[18] Keene attached a certain snob-value to Smith's work, by cultivating his reputation as 'an artist's artist'. He thus implied that only the exceedingly discriminating collector could appreciate the painter.

By December, Sir Evan Charteris, chairman of the Board, had decided to put *Cyclamen* to his trustees. He considered this painting 'of the most admirable quality and just what we need at Tate'.[19] Charteris and Manson had selected it from fifteen unidentified paintings that Tooth had shown them. Charteris now needed to assemble a majority vote in its favour. Tooth wrote to John asking for his support, emphasizing that he would be doing Smith a good turn. Charteris successfully recruited the support of trustees the Earl of Sandwich, the Rt. Hon. William Ormsby-Gore, and Kenneth Clark in favour of the acquisition.

Tooth relayed the Board's decision to Smith who was very unhappy with the Tate's choice and wrote: '"Cyclamen" though not a bad canvas ... is more or less an isolated one and does not it seems to me give much idea of my painting in the main; not in fact representative, I should have thought it their business to be careful to choose one that is ... "The Model Turning" to think of one off hand. I am frequently being told how little the one at present there represents me and that makes already one flower piece.'[20] Smith was concerned that his artistic reputation was being distorted by his poor representation in the national collection and felt that the Tate was not fulfilling its role.

In response Tooth repeated to Smith what Charteris and Manson had explained to him:

> that members of their Committee are extremely difficult to handle where Contemporary Art is concerned and that it would be hopeless for them to submit ... anything but a very easily understood straight-forward Flower picture, and that there is no possible chance of their getting votes in favour of your figure subjects or landscapes at present. I agree with you that it is hardly representative of your painting in the main. They are anxious to have your work better represented at the Tate and therefore selected the best picture which they thought there was any chance of their very conservative confreres accepting.[21]

This is a damning assessment of the Board's tastes but the only member of the Board at this time who might obviously have been classified a 'conservative confrere' was the Royal Academician Sir William Reid Dick, a sculptor of portrait statuary. The trustees Sandwich, John, and Clark had all recently purchased landscapes by Smith for their own collections. With the exception of John, the trustees, however, preferred to err on the side of caution and refrain from challenging each other.

John wrote letters to Charteris, Manson, and Smith to disapprove of *Cyclamen*, saying that Smith would be represented by another immature work. He also added that Smith would not benefit financially from the sale and implied unfairly that Tooth merely wanted to off-load the work. But despite his protests, the *Cyclamen* purchase went ahead with the price reduced from £175 to £150. Tooth was pragmatic and told John he was sorry he did not approve of the painting, but explained that 'besides liking this one, Manson felt it would be difficult to get the Committee to pass any of the more recent ones, so it was a question of this picture or nothing at all'.[22] Keene's intervention and deployment of John as a broker had been only a half-success, a compromise on his initial aim of securing an important picture for the nation. It is interesting that Tate policy rendered dealers taboo but assumed that artists and patrons would make disinterested trustees, when they were in fact frequently friends with, or collectors of, the artists whose works were under consideration.

Everyone involved seemed aware that *Cyclamen* was not a representative work but the Tate Board and Tooth were more easily resigned to the disappointing situation. Tooth was patient and knew that flower paintings had an easier appeal. His tactic was to encourage public galleries to purchase these initially to prepare the way for them to acquire nudes later. Manson was happy to appease the more conservative elements on the Board and was a flower painter himself.

Smith was in the best company as the Tate's first acquisition of the work of Pablo Picasso in 1933 was *Flowers* (1901; figure 9.3), acquired from Reid & Lefevre who, only two years earlier, had held a magnificent retrospective of the artist's work. It was this acquisition, in conjunction with the critical press response to the reopening of the ultra-modern Mayor Gallery which drove the critic Geoffrey Grigson to call for an institution like New York's Museum of Modern Art in London. He wrote acerbically of the new Picasso acquisition: 'I do not say that it is not an interesting Picasso, and I must admire the astonishing labour which the Tate officials evidently went through before they got it. They searched and searched, and found a naturalistic Picasso of flowers in a pot, which can offend no one terrified of modern art – a Picasso so rarely untypical of his great importance that it must wrongly impress all who see it, and do not know who Picasso is or what he paints.'[23] He accused the Tate of failing to do its job: 'The Tate, it seems to me, is gravely unaware of its public duty; and I would put much of this down to the art-criticism permitted and encouraged by the daily and weekly press.'[24] He commended the enterprising Mayor Gallery for fulfilling the Tate's

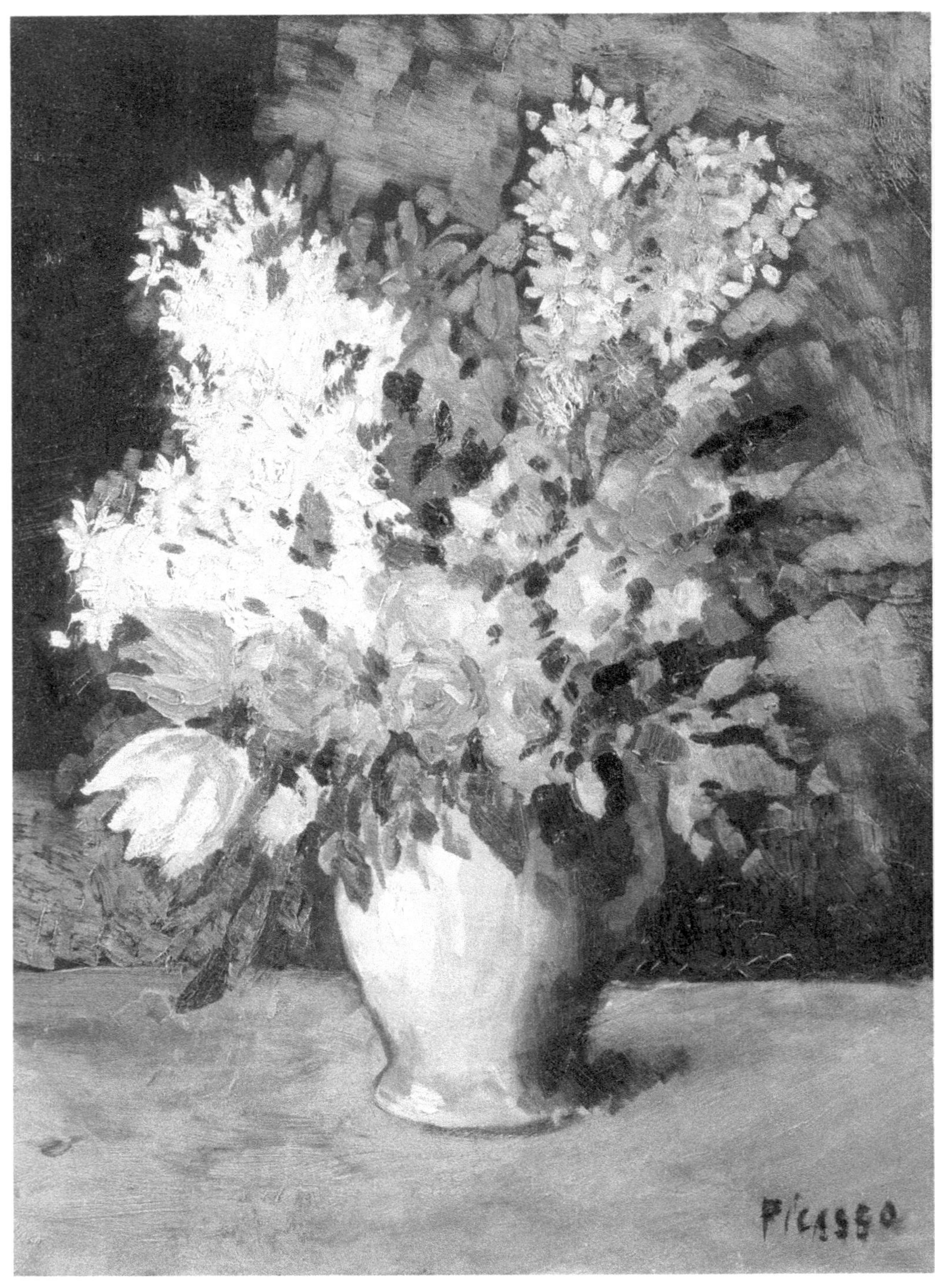

9.3 Pablo Picasso, *Flowers*, 1901. Purchased 1933.

role of educating the public in the recent developments in European and English art. He also felt keenly the press's inability to take modern art seriously, which contributed to the Tate's conservative acquisition policy.

Smith's solo show at Tooth's in November 1936 was another success with two-thirds sold on the first day. Several Tate trustees purchased works: Charteris a flower painting, Sandwich a still life, and Clark a landscape and a still life. During the mid-1930s, Tooth reported Clark's regular purchases and praise for Smith to the artist with relish, and Smith was duly delighted. The young and glamorous director of the National Gallery was an extremely influential arbiter of taste during this period.

Smith's exhibition prompted Sandwich to write to Manson declaring it was time for the Tate to acquire a Smith, as he was 'one of the very best of the younger generation'. Sandwich said he himself had been slow to appreciate Smith due to his limited subject range but now the artist was painting landscapes he ought to be in the national collection. He seemed to have forgotten about the two flower pieces and the fact that Smith had been painting landscapes for several years. Sandwich urged Manson to hurry because Smith's works were selling very quickly. He pointed out that Clark had just bought the show's best landscape and added that Smith was 'one of the few English artists that the French appreciate'.[25]

Manson agreed with Sandwich that Clark's landscape was very desirable and they should acquire one too, adding that he had known Smith for twenty-eight years and watched his remarkable development with interest. Thus the Board's refusal of the CAS's offer of Smith's landscape *Environs D'Antibes* in July 1935 is further evidence of disorganization and lack of a coherent policy at the Tate. Charteris also agreed with Sandwich that the Tate should have another Smith, adding that the artist was unhappy with his representation. Charteris admitted: 'I am fortified in my liking of him by the fact that John has 8 and Epstein 12 of his works … I myself have had one for about 10 years.'[26] Charteris had indeed purchased *Dahlias* from Reid & Lefevre in 1927. That Charteris felt reassured in his liking of Smith because two great artists collected his work again demonstrates the power of artists' networks.

Although Sandwich proposed the Board wait a year to acquire a good landscape, in November 1936 the Tate purchased the nude *Model Turning* (1924; figure 9.4) for £250. This was the canvas Smith had suggested at the time of the *Cyclamen* purchase. *Model Turning* had been shown at Tooth's three times: at his solo shows of 1929 and 1932 and in *Pictures for Collectors* in 1932. It had taken the Tate several years to build up to it. Finally here was a painting representative of Smith's achievements.

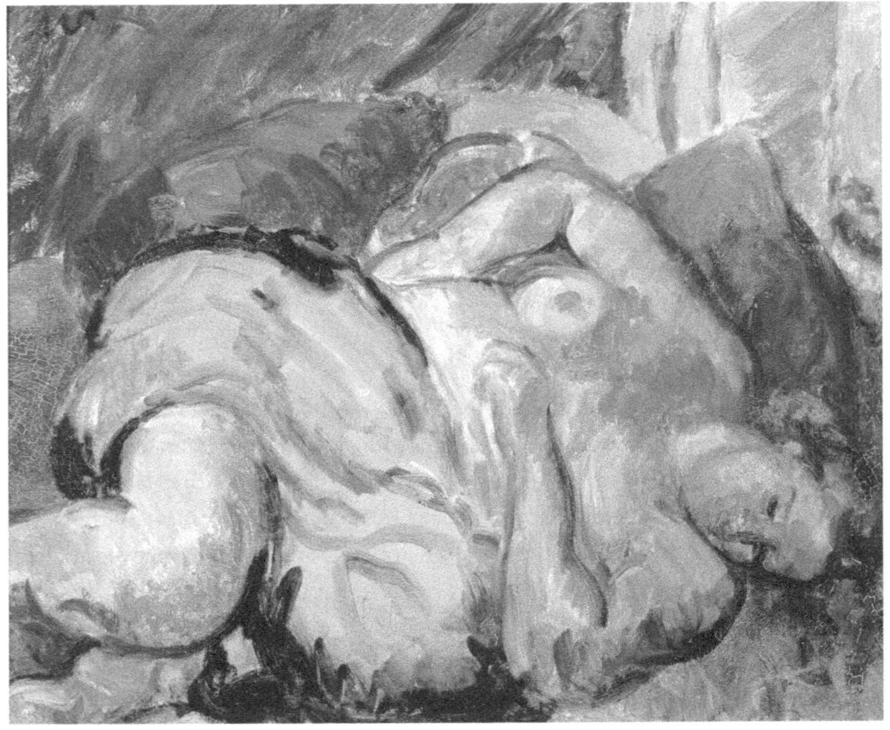

9.4 Matthew Smith, *Model Turning*, c.1924. Purchased 1936.

The Tate Gallery

The Tate Board consisted of the directors of the Tate and the National Gallery, ex officio, and 'a selection of gentlemen with a knowledge of or interest in modern and contemporary art'.[27] From 1920 four artists were added to the group of aristocratic collectors, two of whom were to be Royal Academicians. Members of the all-male Board during the 1920s and 1930s included Lord Balniel, Lord Bearstead, Lord Henry Cavendish-Bentinck, Sir William Burrell, D.Y. Cameron, Samuel Courtauld, Viscount D'Abernon, Francis Dodd, D.S. MacColl, Sir William Nicholson, Glyn Philpot, Sir William Rothenstein, Sir Philip Sassoon, Charles Sims, Lord Howard de Walden, and Sir Robert Witt.

Art dealers were not considered appropriate trustees although Robert Ross, who had managed the Carfax Gallery, had been appointed in 1917 and served until his death the following year. Of course the Tate could never escape this stain of association with dealers when so many of its galleries had been paid for by the Duveen dynasty.

A Tate publication of 1927 reviewed the Board's performance: 'As a National Gallery is the possession of all, a certain width of view in forming the National Collections would seem to be desirable, and the criticisms that have occasionally occurred both from the "left" and the "right" wings, to the effect that interesting developments in painting are not being adequately represented, and, on the other hand, that dangerous modern experiments are being encouraged, would seem to indicate that a discreet *via media* is being pursued.'[28] The Board clearly followed a 'middle course' policy. They feared bad press and opprobrium from the public but failed to define their own educational role. They perceived the British public to be hostile to contemporary art and, furthermore, were worried about being duped. Their anxiety was stoked by the general press conviction that modern art was a hoax. The report declared that it was better to risk occasional mistakes while prices were low than to have to fill gaps later at great expense. The Board as a group, however, lacked confidence in its ability to judge work by living artists and neglected to follow its own advice. It eschewed the role of boldly introducing modern art to the public with characteristic examples. The Board repeatedly failed to define a clear acquisition policy and the collection consequently grew in an arbitrary fashion with decisions being made on a case-by-case basis. An artist's representation in the national collection relied on whether they had an influential trustee, such as John or Clark, willing to promote their work.

The chairman was the most influential member of the Board; D'Abernon, ambassador to Berlin and a close friend of Duveen, served from 1923 to 1934, succeeded by Charteris, who served until 1940. Aitken praised D'Abernon for understanding 'the maximum progress possible without hostile reaction'.[29] This phrase precisely sums up the Board's overly cautious attitude to acquisitions.

In 1935 Sandwich addressed the Board's dearth of a clear policy head-on in a memorandum. He noted that in most cases the Tate had acquired works too late in an artist's career or only after death, with the result that very high prices were paid for works that could have been purchased years earlier for a fraction of the price. He reiterated 'that if private collectors are able to judge the moment when a painter of repute has arrived, surely the same judgement should be possessed by a body of men especially selected for their knowledge of painting'.[30] He argued that there was 'undoubtedly a period during the life of a rising artist of obvious eminence' when both dealers and the public were satisfied that they were 'ripe for buying'.[31] This was the moment, he declared, when a public gallery should do the same. The Tate had succeeded in acquiring Smith at this ripe moment but not the right work. Sandwich recognized the market's vital role in establishing value for an emerging artist and as the most appropriate arbiter of taste. This suggests the waning influence of artists' networks in comparison to the dealer network.

It is striking to hear such clear criticism emanating from the heart of the Tate Board. Sandwich proposed making a desiderata list of artists missing from the collection and creating a sub-committee to pursue their acquisition by actively seeking assistance from artists and dealers. This sensible idea was not acted upon.

The trustees were also hamstrung by a chronic lack of funds. For British art the National Gallery allocated to the Tate from 1918 the Clarke Fund of £576 a year, replaced in 1938 by the Knapping Fund of £1,170 a year. From 1922 the Duveen Fund for drawings and watercolours generated £200 a year. Gifts sometimes filled the gaps but would-be donors were often given no encouragement and they could not feel confident their gifts would be welcomed. As well as failing to buy interesting works, the Board frequently declined offers of high quality gifts, bequests, and loans. London-based Dutchman C. Frank Stoop would eventually leave his collection of modern masterpieces, including works by Cézanne, Picasso, and Matisse, to the Tate in 1933. But in the preceding years he did not feel encouraged by the Tate or its reputation. In 1929 he told Manson that he was tempted to leave his collection to the more enthusiastic Rijks Museum: 'From so many sides I hear of discouragement given to friends of modern art by the selection committee of the Tate that I do not wish to risk my pictures being refused or at best accepted with demur.'[32]

During the 1920s and 1930s the trustees repeatedly requested an acquisition grant, but they would wait until 1946 to receive it. The excuse given by the Treasury for denying the Tate a grant was that it received works purchased by the Chantrey Bequest, a private benefaction worth about £2,000 a year. The problem was that the Bequest was administered by the Royal Academy who used it to purchase dull works by Academicians at inflated prices. The situation was an ongoing scandal and, in 1933, art critic Frank Rutter noted that the CAS had spent less than a tenth of the amount spent by the Chantrey Bequest and had purchased works of considerably higher aesthetic value.[33]

The National Art Collections Fund, founded in 1903, and the CAS, founded in 1909, both funded by voluntary subscriptions, also supplied the Tate with artworks. The policy of the CAS made an instructive contrast to the Tate Board; it selected one buyer from the executive committee each year to make purchases to their own taste, unhampered by compromise. During the 1920s and 1930s the CAS had £500 a year to spend and amassed a strong collection, which they distributed to public galleries.[34]

As already described, the Tate relied heavily on private benefactions; funds for its buildings were provided by Henry Tate and the Duveen family and funds for much of their contents were supplied by Hugh Lane and Samuel Courtauld.[35] Francis Watson, in his polemic *Art Lies Bleeding*, examined the government's funding of the arts in the late 1930s. The National Gallery and the Tate had

£35,136 a year from the Government for running costs, of which £7,000 was earmarked for National Gallery acquisitions. No money was provided for Tate acquisitions.[36] The Clarke Fund, allocated by the National Gallery to the Tate, was a private benefaction. Of the state's £350,000 a year, allocated for allowing the public to see art across its galleries and museums, only £600 was spent on buying from living artists, the majority of this sum by the Victoria & Albert Museum.[37] Watson reports dryly: 'the Government is not divided upon an aesthetic issue. It is simply not interested. If the State spares no money for Surrealists, neither does it spare any for the Does-'Oo-Like-Butter School. It is admirably impartial.'[38]

The Tate Board did not always spend its meagre funds wisely, unlike Sir Edward Marsh. This long-standing CAS committee member and eventual Tate trustee demonstrated what a forward-thinking collector could achieve. He built his collection on an average annual expenditure of only two or three hundred pounds and turned his flat into 'a sort of Museum of Modern British Art', to quote a 1947 article. The writer also recalled the courage it had taken to purchase modern art when 'to condone even the artistic activities of Matthew Smith ... was a sure sign of cultural, if not of mental, aberration'.[39]

The poor state of the Tate's collection was partly due to the lack of enthusiasm and enterprise, and limited knowledge and taste of its directors, Charles Aitken 1911–1930, J.B. Manson 1930–38, and John Rothenstein from 1938. The institution was understaffed with one Director/Keeper and two Assistants responsible for both the British and Modern Foreign collections. The director needed to possess skills in administration, accountancy, public relations, fundraising, curating, research, and writing as well as diplomacy, initiative, professionalism, creativity, passion, dedication, good health, a thick skin, and good contacts. All these demands accorded with paltry pay and little recognition, thus finding trained staff was an ongoing headache for the Tate.

The most problematic director was Manson, who had joined the Tate as a clerk in 1912. He was a painter in an Impressionist style associated with the Camden Town Group and the London Group but his taste extended no further. Clark described Manson as: 'a man of great charm, with a flushed face, white hair and a twinkle in his eye; and his twinkling eye got him out of scrapes that would have sunk a worthier man without a trace ... Manson was so confident in his charm that he used to appear drunk at Board meetings.'[40] Sandwich felt that Charteris allowed Manson too much freedom and came into conflict with the director when Manson declared the only artist whose work the Tate should acquire was Constable.[41] Manson was arguably unsuited to his role but it was the government that was guilty of appointing the wrong man to the job.

The nadir of Manson's career came in 1938 when he refused to recognize Brancusi's *Sculpture for the Blind* as a work of art in order to save it from import duties when it was being shipped from Paris to an exhibition at Peggy Guggenheim's Cork Street gallery. This caused a scandal in the press. St. John Hutchinson wrote to the *Daily Telegraph*: 'We know that Mr J.B. Manson is an artist himself, but we know that Herr Hitler painted water-colours, and the fact that the latter has announced that Cézanne and Van Gogh are degenerate lunatics and can only be exhibited as a warning to others, shakes our complete trust in the artist as the best judge of what works we should be allowed to see.'[42] Manson was forced to back down on the issue, and retired shortly thereafter.

H.S. 'Jim' Ede was an Assistant at the Tate 1921–36. He had much more advanced taste in art than Manson, with whom he clashed. Ede befriended many artists, including Picasso, Brancusi, Miró, Ben Nicholson, and Barbara Hepworth. In 1928 Ede made an unsuccessful attempt to redefine his role, appealing that he ought to have time within official hours to make himself conversant with the progress of contemporary art, which would require research at home and abroad, visiting exhibitions, and studying catalogues and prices. He felt that a gallery professional should digest contemporary criticism and know more than the critics, so he could form his own opinions.[43] He also advocated befriending collectors and was influential in persuading Stoop to loan works from his collection to the Tate in 1929 and later to bequeath them.

It was not until Rothenstein, who had previous experience directing public galleries in Leeds and Sheffield, took over that Ede's ideas became the norm. Rothenstein was the son of the artist William Rothenstein and a dedicated art professional with a doctorate in Art History. He inherited a deeply dysfunctional institution and his primary ambition was to make the British collection more representative by filling gaps among the senior contemporaries and strengthening the representation of the emerging generation, few of whom had yet entered the collection.

Rothenstein invited loans to improve the Tate's collection without spending funds. In 1939 he borrowed three landscapes and a flower piece by Smith, which balanced out his representation.[44] Meanwhile Tooth's were keen to further Smith's reputation abroad and helped organize an exhibition at Galerie Bing Paris of Christopher Wood, Sickert and Smith. The Jeu de Paume expressed an interest in purchasing a Smith canvas but the deal did not come to fruition.

The case study of Smith at the Tate reveals that in the London art world of the 1920s and 1930s, dealers, not the museum, were the nurturers of avant-garde artists. They took on the role of educating the public – a task that museums have assigned themselves today – as well as assuming the risks and giving emerging artists vital support and exposure. Until Rothenstein took over and began to institute changes, it was not possible to see works in Cubist, abstract, or Surrealist

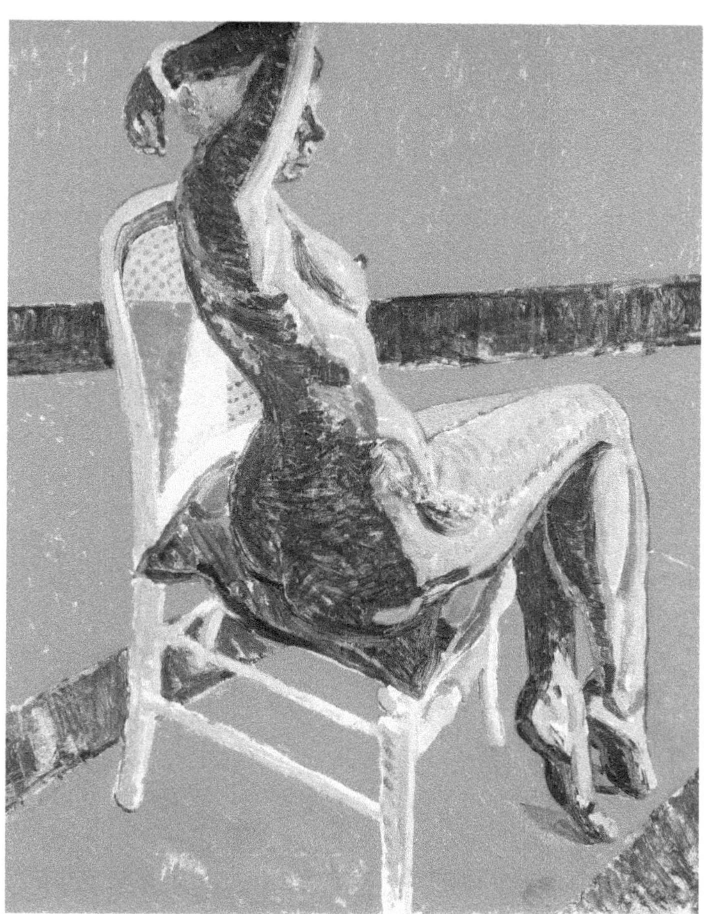

9.5
Matthew Smith,
Nude, Fitzroy Street, No. 1,
c.1915. Purchased 1952.

styles on the walls of the Tate. In this context, Smith, who may have been characterized as difficult but was still a figurative artist, was an excellent means by which to introduce modernism into the gallery given that by the 1930s his work was regarded as more acceptable to the public.

As we have seen, the Tate cautiously collected artists who had built up a market reputation, through favourable reviews of commercial gallery shows and the private collections they entered. This case study illustrates how print culture and the museum offered systems for attaching value to artworks, seemingly independent from, but inextricably linked to, the commercial sphere. Writers working with dealers helped to educate art audiences and establish worth for particular artists. In turn, works entering public collections added value to artists for the dealers. The development of the Tate's collection added another layer of evaluation as dealers, curators, and artists worked to secure the authority of the national museum. Once an artist was represented in the national collection, despite its flaws, more timid collectors and critics gained confidence to purchase or praise, and the artist was set on the path to general acceptance. Prices rose accordingly; Smith sold nudes for £17 in 1924, £100 in 1927, and £250 in the 1930s.

While the Tate's staff and trustees limited the intellectual reach of the institution, the state further restricted the mobility of the institution by limiting the Tate's funding. The gallery did not have the resources to offer patronage to artists and, moreover, expected to be offered discounted prices for works. This state of affairs would change during the war with the activities of the War Artists Advisory Committee, the British Council, and the Council for the Encouragement of Music and the Arts, and later with the Arts Council.

But we should not position the dealers solely as heroic innovators. While dealers of avant-garde art had to regard their stock as a long-term investment given the slow pace of sales, they also needed to pay their rent, often considerable given their premises in expensive areas of central London. In short, they could not cover their overheads by selling only the works of young artists. Thus established galleries such as Tooth's and Reid & Lefevre also dealt in nineteenth- and early twentieth-century French works to keep their business profitable.

The idea that a commercial gallery might fill the gap in the patronage of contemporary art represented by the Tate is manifested by the plans of Peggy Guggenheim, heiress, dealer, and collector who ran Guggenheim Jeune on Cork Street during the late 1930s. Her gallery made a loss of £600 a year so she decided 'if I was losing that money I might as well lose a lot more and do something worthwhile' and initiated plans for a Museum of Modern Art in London with Herbert Read as director.[45] Guggenheim's scheme was fuelled by her troubled relationship with the Tate: in 1938 Manson had attempted to sabotage Guggenheim's exhibition of modern sculpture and Rothenstein had only grudgingly accepted the Kandinsky offered to the Tate by Guggenheim's sister; and in 1939 the Tate rejected Guggenheim's offers of works by Yves Tanguy and Geer Van Velde. Sadly, lack of funds and the outbreak of the Second World War scuppered Guggenheim and Read's plans.

These episodes underscore the unique conditions of the London art scene. The London art world was an intimate place, with much overlap between the roles of trustee, collector, dealer, artist, critic, and curator. Art critics and scholars, who functioned as arbiters of taste, were deeply involved in the art market. Reliant on such individuals as well as commercial dealers, lacking an explicit acquisition policy, and with limited funds, the Tate, unlike the Museum of Modern Art, became a follower rather than a leader of taste, dependent upon the market to guide its choices.

Notes

1 See Spalding, *Tate*, for full history.
2 P.G. Konody, 'The Mayor Gallery', *Observer*, 11 April 1926, Mayor Gallery Press cuttings Album on microfiche, Tate Archives, London, TAM 7A [MGPA].
3 J.G., 'A Pair of Moderns', *Morning Post*, 12 April 1926 [MGPA].
4 Anthony Bertram, *Saturday Review*, 24 April 1926 [MGPA].
5 Roger Fry, 'The Mayor and Claridge Galleries', *Nation and Athenaeum*, 1 May 1926 [MGPA].
6 T.W. Earp, 'The New English Art Club', *New Statesman*, 19 April 1926 [MGPA].
7 Richard Wyndham, 'Matthew Smith', *Horizon*, 6:32 (1942), pp. 108–12.
8 For more on Edward Marsh as a collector, see Holt, 'Eddie Marsh'.
9 MS Letter Charles Holroyd to Charles Aitken, 8 December 1927, National Gallery NG 16/215/4.
10 'Eccentricity in Art: Matthew Smith's Colour Schemes', *Morning Post*, 6 December 1927, Alex Reid & Lefevre Gallery Press cuttings Albums 1927–31 on microfiche, Tate Archives, London, TAM 9E.
11 MS letter Richard Smart to Paul Nash, 30 May 1933, Tate Gallery TGA 7050/1296.
12 Smart to Nash, ibid.
13 'Five English Painters', *The Times*, 21 February 1930, p. 12.
14 'At Tooth's Picture for Collectors', *The Times*, 15 January 1932, p. 10.
15 MS letter Ralph Keene to Augustus John, 1 June 1934, Tate Gallery TGA 20106, The Records of Arthur Tooth & Sons, 1880s–1970s.
16 Keene, 'Matthew Smith', p. 23.
17 Keene, 'Matthew Smith', p. 24.
18 Ibid.
19 MS letter Evan Charteris to Earl of Sandwich, undated 1935, Tate Gallery TGA 707.
20 MS letter Matthew Smith to Dudley Tooth, 12 December 1934, Tate Gallery TGA 2000/9/1.
21 MS letter Dudley Tooth to Matthew Smith, 14 December 1934, Tate Gallery TGA 2000/9/1.
22 MS letter Dudley Tooth to Augustus John, 17 January 1935, Tate Gallery TGA 20106, The Records of Arthur Tooth & Sons, 1880s–1970s.
23 Geoffrey Grigson, 'Brief Chronicles: Art. Unit One, Herbert Read, and the Mayor Gallery', *Bookman* (October 1933), Mayor Gallery Press Cuttings Scrapbooks, Mayor Gallery, London.
24 Ibid.
25 MS letter Earl of Sandwich to J.B. Manson, 5 November 1936, Tate Gallery TGA 4/2/970/1.
26 MS letter Evan Charteris to Earl of Sandwich, November 1936, Tate Gallery TGA 707.

27 *National Gallery, Millbank*, pp. 8–9.

28 *National Gallery, Millbank*, p. 10.

29 Tate Records Board Minutes, 23 June 1930, Tate Gallery TGA 1/3/3.

30 Papers of George Charles Montagu, Earl of Sandwich 1934–44, Tate Trustee (1934–41), 'Lord Sandwich Memorandum: Suggestions as to Procedure in Selection of Works of Art for the Tate Gallery', 25 January 1935, Tate Gallery Archive, TGA 707/19.

31 Ibid.

32 MS letter C.F. Stoop to J.B. Manson, 17 February 1929, Tate Gallery TGA 806/1/887.

33 Frank Rutter, *Sunday Times*, 27 August 1933; quoted in Committee Meeting Minutes, Contemporary Art Society, London, 12 October 1933, Tate Gallery TGA 9215/2/2/1.

34 Bowness, *Contemporary Art Society*.

35 For more detail, see Spalding, *Tate*.

36 Watson, *Art Lies Bleeding*, pp. 78–83. The Victoria & Albert Museum did not have a clear policy but its departments of Painting, and Engraving, Illustration, and Design did acquire contemporary works, spending an undisclosed sum of not more than £500 a year out of a £16,000 a year purchase grant.

37 Watson, *Art Lies Bleeding*, p. 83.

38 Watson, *Art Lies Bleeding*, p. 84.

39 Denvir, 'Edward Marsh', p. 132.

40 Clark, *Another Part of the Wood*, p. 233.

41 Montagu, 'Reminiscences', 1961 unpublished manuscript, pp. 38–9. Thanks to Richard Shone for allowing me access to this manuscript.

42 St. John Hutchinson, 'Letter to the Editor', *Daily Telegraph*, 24 March 1938, Press Clippings Scrapbook, 000501 Peggy Guggenheim Foundation Papers, M0002. Solomon R. Guggenheim Archives, New York, NY.

43 MS H.S. Ede 'List of Duties for Assistant', undated 1928, National Gallery Archive, NG 16/215/5.

44 The Smith works were *Landscape*, *Flowerpiece*, *Landscape at Cagnes*, and *Landscape near Cagnes*, lent by Mrs. Arthur Bliss and Miss Barbara Bliss. Tate Records Board Minutes, 20 June 1939, Tate Gallery TGA 1/3/4.

45 Guggenheim, *Confessions*, p. 196.

III

Negotiations

10

Millais in the marketplace: the crisis of the late 1850s

Malcolm Warner

Looking at the career of John Everett Millais *as* a career – in the professional sense – opens up a fresh perspective on his development as an artist and tells us much about the economics of the Victorian art world.[1] The most dramatic years of Millais's life from this point of view were the late 1850s, a time of crisis in the art market as a whole. Thanks to the letters he wrote to his wife and others about the trials of selling the paintings he showed at the Royal Academy exhibitions of 1857 and 1859, we have a detailed picture of the frustrations leading up to what his son and biographer John Guille Millais rightly called 'the turning-point in the life of the painter'.[2]

The early Victorian period was a golden age for the patronage of modern British art, owing largely to the appearance on the scene of the rich middle-class collector. In the words of Lady Eastlake, 'The patronage which had been almost exclusively the privilege of the nobility and higher gentry, was now shared (to be subsequently almost engrossed) by a wealthy and intelligent class, chiefly enriched by commerce and trade; the note-book of the painter, while it exhibited lowlier names, showing henceforth higher prices.'[3] Soon after the middle class arrived in the art market, so did the middle man – the dealer – and the 1850s saw the rise of the Titans of the dealing business, Ernest Gambart and Thomas Agnew and Sons. The dealers became central figures in the Victorian art world, and Millais's career well illustrates the benefits and drawbacks of their growing influence.

Though still a young man, turning thirty in 1859, Millais had tried a good number of the means by which an artist could make a name and a living, and knew from experience the ways of patrons, collectors, and dealers. While still a student at the Royal Academy Schools, he entered competitions in which juvenile

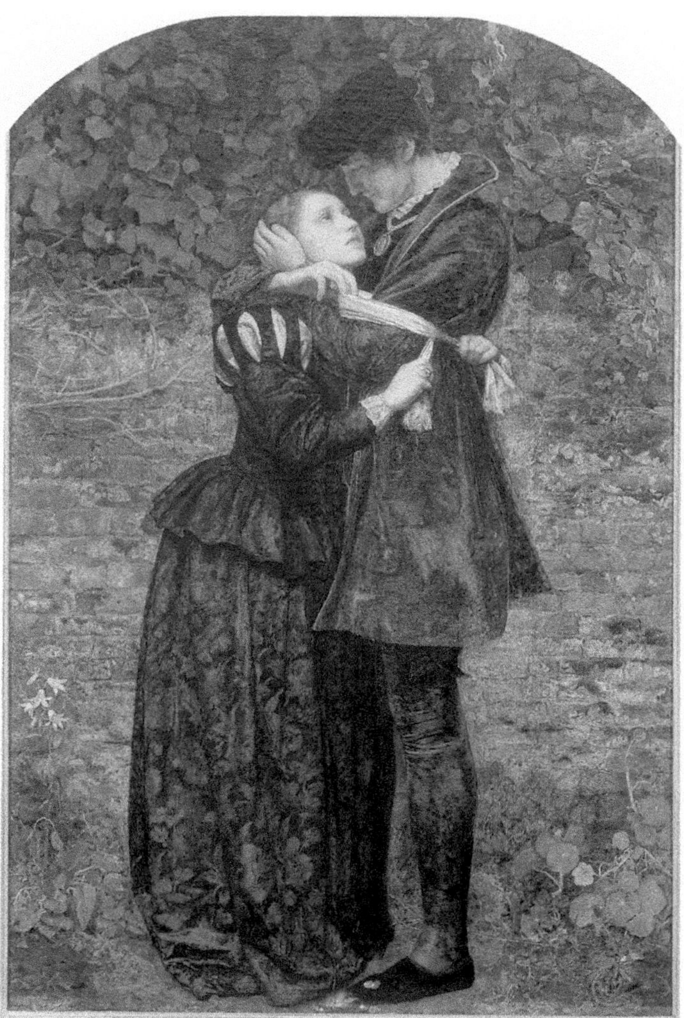

10.1
John Everett Millais,
A Huguenot, 1851–52.
Exhibited: Royal
Academy, 1852. Oil on
canvas, arched top, 92.7
× 62.2 cm.

artists could win both cash and prestige, painted small genre subjects for a minor dealer, worked on commission for patrons who took an avuncular interest in him, exhibited large history-pictures at the Academy, and began to attract well-known collectors. He sold his first Pre-Raphaelite paintings to dealers, although after the biting critical attacks on *Christ in the Carpenter's Shop* (Tate, London), he took refuge in the kindly and hospitable patronage offered by Thomas Combe, Superintendent of the Clarendon Press in Oxford. In 1852 he won popularity in the public arena with *Ophelia* (Tate, London) and *A Huguenot* (figure 10.1), a scene of star-crossed lovers embracing before the massacre of St. Bartholomew's Day. Both went to prominent London dealers. Henry Farrer bought *Ophelia* for 300 guineas (£315) and David Thomas White bought *A Huguenot* for £250.[4] Farrer and White sold the paintings to the same man, Benjamin Godfrey Windus, a retired coachbuilder and pill manufacturer who had been an important patron and collector of J.M.W. Turner. Windus was Millais's most avid collector of the 1850s. He bought not only these pictures of 1852 but also the earlier *Isabella* (National Museums Liverpool, Walker Art Gallery) and *Mariana* (Tate, London), all from dealers rather than directly from the artist.

The £350 that Millais earned for the portrait of John Ruskin (private collection) that occupied so much of his time in 1853–54 seemed hardly to cover the amount of work, discomfort, and emotional distress the commission had entailed.[5] It was his last involvement with the kind of patronage in which he played the protégé, and his further successes at the Royal Academy exhibitions of 1855 and 1856 made him more confident still of his potential in the open market. His principal painting of 1855 was *The Rescue* (National Gallery of Victoria, Melbourne), his first major venture in painting modern life, which showed a fireman carrying children out of a fire and into the arms of their mother. He sold the work to Joseph Arden, a London barrister, for £580.[6] It was a modern-life pendant to *The Order of Release, 1746* (Tate, London), a scene of a Jacobite rebel being returned to his family, which he had shown to acclaim at the Academy exhibition of 1853. Since Arden already owned that earlier work, for which he had paid £400, he was a natural buyer – possibly even targeted as such – for the new one. Millais was well versed in the marketing advantages of the follow-up painting, and throughout his career would take the basic narrative and compositional formula of a successful work and play a series of variations on the same theme.

The year 1856 was Millais's most lucrative of the decade. At the Academy exhibition he showed *The Blind Girl* (Birmingham Museums and Art Gallery) and *Autumn Leaves* (Manchester City Galleries). *Autumn Leaves* was an experiment in a poetic, melancholy type of 'mood-picture', without definite narrative content. He painted it in response to a commission, perhaps specifically for a work on a seasonal theme, from James Eden, a Lancashire bleachworks owner, who paid him 700 guineas (£735).[7] The dealer Gambart bought *The Blind Girl* for 400 guineas (£420). But what made 1856 an outstanding year for Millais from the financial point of view was the sale of another, less familiar exhibition picture, *Peace Concluded, 1856* (Minneapolis Institute of Arts), a scene of an army officer at home with his family after being wounded in the Crimean War. This he sold to another Lancashire industrialist, the cotton manufacturer Thomas Miller, for the impressive sum of 900 guineas (£945).[8] At first he intended to ask Miller for £1,000 but brought the price down on the advice of the painter Augustus Egg. 'Egg is more my friend than Mr. Miller's', he wrote to his wife, Effie Millais, who clearly felt the matter was none of Egg's business, 'and only gave it as his opinion that Mr. Miller would be surprised at the *suddenness* of my increase of charge from preceding years. It is all very well to do this, but it must be done gradually.'[9] Millais and Effie were living in Perth, Scotland, but around the time of the opening of the Academy exhibition Millais would stay in London for a while, writing many letters home.

Millais sold all three of his principal paintings at the 1856 Academy without copyrights, hoping to sell these for a further £1,000. He was especially ambitious about the copyright of *Peace Concluded, 1856*, which he believed Henry Graves, the pre-eminent British print publisher, would buy for at least £500. He wrote to his wife on 8 May that this was 'an understood thing', but the deal must have fallen through.[10] Indeed, despite his success in selling paintings in this year, he had no success in selling copyrights. His expectations were high, not only because his pictures sold but also because he was making his debut in the print market with engravings after his earlier successes *The Order of Release, 1746*, published by Graves on 1 May 1856, and *A Huguenot*, published by Graves and D.T. White on 30 June. For the engraving of *The Order of Release, 1746* he received 300 guineas (£315) and for that of *A Huguenot* only a courtesy payment of £50 since he had not reserved the copyright for himself when he sold the painting to White, a mistake he would not make again.[11] Both proved popular, and the next of Millais's paintings to be engraved were follow-ups to *A Huguenot* – *The Proscribed Royalist, 1651* (Lloyd-Webber Collection) and *The Black Brunswicker* (see figure 10.7), published in 1858 and 1863 respectively.[12]

Full of confidence after his successes of 1856, Millais undertook another variation on the theme of *A Huguenot* and a large composition similar in feeling to *Autumn Leaves*. These were *The Escape of a Heretic, 1559* and *A Dream of the Past: Sir Isumbras at the Ford* (figures 10.2 and 10.3). As a historical lovers subject, *The Escape of a Heretic, 1559* served as a safety measure, offsetting the considerable risk involved in *Sir Isumbras at the Ford*, and Millais undoubtedly hoped to sell its copyright for an engraving to match that of *A Huguenot*. The painting was bought by William Agnew for Agnew's, who were still based in Manchester at this point. Millais wrote to Effie on 9 April 1857: 'Agnew saw his picture & is *enraptured*. He gave me a bank note for 500 which I have for safety put into Coutts.'[13] This was apparently the first instalment on a payment of £1,000 for the painting and its copyright.

According to a gossipy letter of 16 February 1858 from the sculptor Thomas Woolner to Pauline Trevelyan, however, Millais's important relationship with Agnew's was to suffer a setback:

Millais has drifted or rather sneaked into a dreadful mess with Agnew – a keeper of a print and curiosity shop. Agnew paid £500, half the sum, for

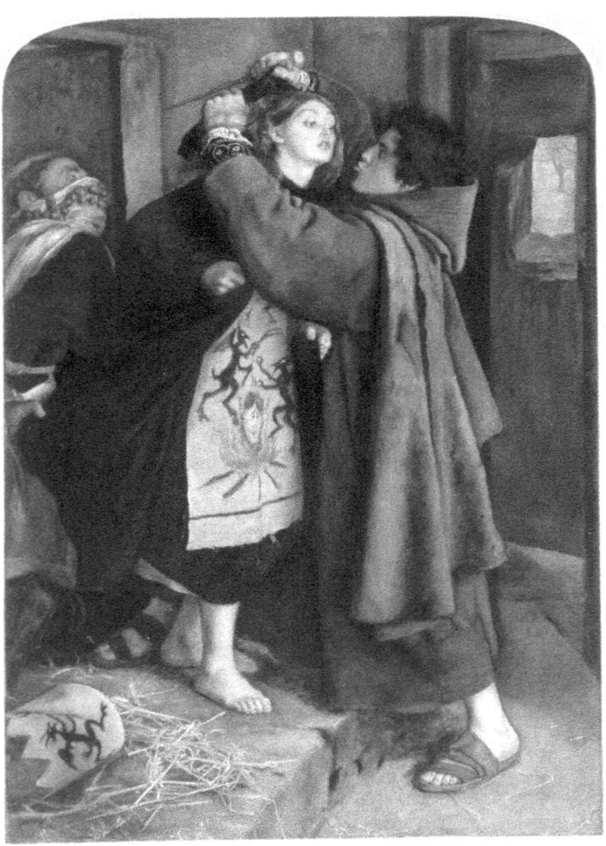

10.2
John Everett Millais, *The Escape of a Heretic, 1559*, 1856–57. Exhibited: Royal Academy, 1857. Oil on canvas, arched top, 106.2 × 76.2 cm.

10.3
John Everett Millais, *A Dream of the Past: Sir Isumbras at the Ford*, 1856–57. Exhibited: Royal Academy, 1857. Oil on canvas, 125.5 × 171.5 cm.

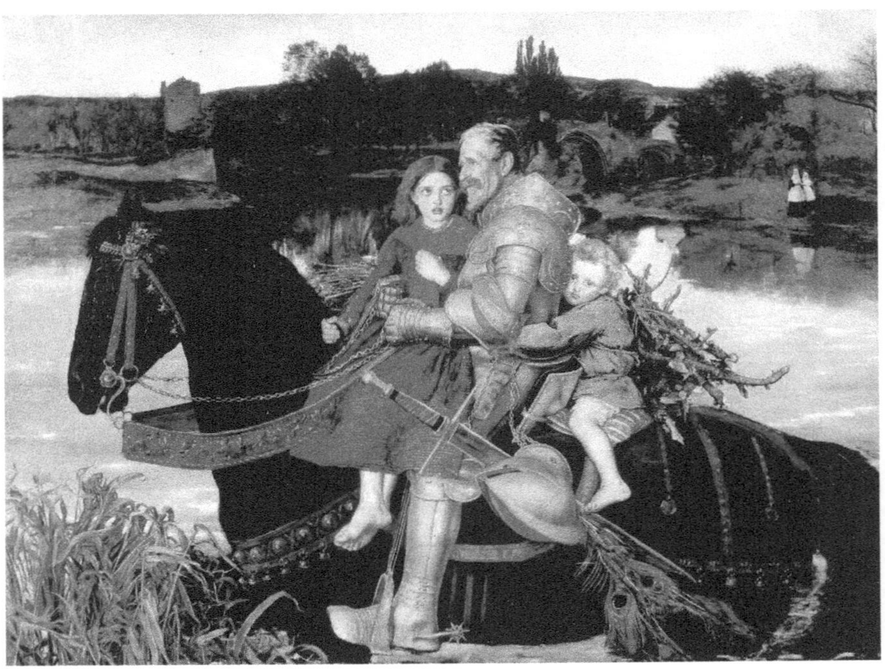

the 'Heretic' but as it was so slovenly executed it was sent to Millais to touch up in certain parts: instead of doing so, Millais painted a copy and sold it to Gambart, a picture-dealer, altho the copyright had been sold to Agnew: the consequence is that Agnew says Millais has broken the treaty and must refund the £500, instead of receiving another £500, and may take back his 'Heretic'.[14]

Since the Agnew's stock books show that in December 1858 the firm sold the original painting for 750 guineas (£787 10s), they clearly did not make Millais take it back for good. Furthermore, although Millais did make a smaller version in oil on panel (private collection), he sold it to Agnew's themselves – in July 1859 – and not to Gambart.[15] It may be that Agnew's refused to pay the second instalment because £500 of the agreed-upon £1,000 was for a copyright that Millais breached when he made his copy, and then insisted that he sell the copy to them instead of Gambart. Certainly they never used the copyright to publish the work as an engraving.

From a financial point of view, *The Escape of a Heretic, 1559* was no great success. Millais must have expected more than £500. But this was a mild disappointment compared to that of *Sir Isumbras at the Ford*. Like *Autumn Leaves*, *Sir Isumbras at the Ford* was more about conjuring a mood, a gentle wistfulness and sense of transience, than telling a story. On the other hand, the touch of anecdote and the historical setting do suggest that Millais was attempting something a little more accessible this time – understandably, since *Autumn Leaves* was commissioned and *Sir Isumbras at the Ford* was not. According to the artist's wife, Gambart offered £800 for the picture while it was still under way in Perth, which Millais refused; the dealer also said that the horse was too small, at which Millais repainted it too large.[16] On 9 April 1857, while the finished work was on display in London at Langham Chambers – in the second of the exhibitions Millais and some of his friends held in their studios before sending works to the Academy – both Gambart and Farrer were showing an interest. But neither was prepared to come up to Millais's ambitious asking price of £1,200. 'How stupid these dealers are', he wrote to Effie. 'Really I am surprised to think that I know so much more about their business than they.'[17] The painting remained unsold not only at Langham Chambers but also at the Academy, the first of the artist's works to suffer this indignity since *The Woodman's Daughter* (Guildhall Art Gallery) in 1851. After the close of the Academy exhibition in August, and another repainting, Millais sent it to the annual exhibition at the Liverpool Academy, where it again remained unsold. Finally it found a buyer in the shape of Charles Reade, the novelist, some time in 1858.[18] Millais and Reade agreed on a price of £300 or £400 on condition that the artist should make further alterations.[19] In the end this troublesome picture, twice the size of *Peace Concluded, 1856*, earned him less than half as much money. Probably realizing he had sold the work too hastily for too little, he tried to buy it back from Reade two years later, offering him £500, but Reade refused.[20]

Millais blamed the failure of *Sir Isumbras at the Ford* partly on unfavourable reviews from *The Times* and Ruskin.[21] But normally he sold major works such as this some time before the critics even had a chance to see them. The problem with *Sir Isumbras at the Ford* was its size, and Millais admitted as much: 'I find all men dislike the great size of the Knight picture – Farrer, Gambart, White, all. They say it is too large for a room, and almost all of the purchasers are without galleries.'[22] In a letter of 15 May 1857, he wrote of a visit from Thomas Combe: 'He wants me to paint him a picture about the size of the "Heretic" (*anything larger than that size is objected to*). There is no encouragement for anything but *cabinet pictures*. I should never have a small picture on my hands for ten minutes, which is a great temptation to do nothing else.'[23] The demand for small, readily saleable works, especially from dealers, was a symptom of the crisis that hit the art market in 1857 and would last throughout the 1850s. It was a hard time for both artists and dealers, and a number of dealers went bankrupt, including Richard Colls and William Wethered, who had been in the consortium that bought *Isabella* and sold it to B.G. Windus. 'I have proved it impossible to sell at the moment', Wethered wrote in 1858, 'unless at ruinous prices'.[24]

When he mentioned cabinet pictures, Millais was thinking of two main types that he would paint over the next few years as a hedge against the risk involved in large, uncommissioned exhibition pictures. One was the reduced version of an exhibition picture – such as the version of *The Escape of a Heretic, 1559* that landed him in trouble with Agnew's. It was a common enough practice for Victorian artists to make the most of a successful composition by painting copies and versions. Millais's other safe bet was the painting of simple oil sketches of girls' heads, several of which he had made in 1854. In 1857 he painted sketches of Effie's two sisters, Sophie and Alice, and sold them to the artist George Price Boyce and his sister Joanna for 60 guineas (£63) each.[25] In 1858 he made two similar sketches from an unknown model, one of which was by the following year in the Windus collection.[26]

Millais was an ambitious artist, however, and placed a premium on painting serious, substantial pictures for the Academy exhibitions, regarding any other kind of work as more or less marginal. The thought of making a modest income from small works like Rossetti was anathema to him. So too was the idea of closing ranks with his less commercially successful Pre-Raphaelite colleagues. He sent only minor works to the Pre-Raphaelite exhibition at Russell Place in 1857; he contributed nothing to the touring exhibition of British art that William Michael Rossetti organized in America in 1857–58, and in April 1858 declined membership in the Hogarth Club.[27] 'One great reason why I think withdrawing ourselves from the body of Artists a *great mistake*', he wrote to Holman Hunt on 16 May 1858, 'is that they gain by *avoiding the comparison*, & we would lose by simply battling against each other'.[28] By 'body of Artists' he meant those who showed their work at the Academy exhibition. Yet in 1858, perhaps suffering a crisis of confidence after *Sir Isumbras at the Ford*, he himself failed to submit anything to the Academy. He worked on a major composition through the winter of 1857–58, *The Return of the Crusader*, but never brought the work to completion. It was to have been a variation on *The Order of Release, 1746*, using the winning formula of lovers separated by historical circumstances or (as in this case) being reunited. He abandoned the canvas until 1862, when he cut a fragment from the right side and worked it up as *The Departure of the Crusaders* (Oldham Art Gallery).[29]

Whatever the reason the Crusader subject proved abortive, the frustration it engendered may have predisposed Millais toward further ventures in his far more interesting and original line of non-narrative mood-pictures. With the Academy of 1859 in mind, he began work in earnest on *Spring* and *The Vale of Rest* (figures 10.4 and 10.5). After the failure of *Sir Isumbras at the Ford*, it is certainly surprising to find him risking pictures such as these, which were almost as large and even more challenging to conventional taste, without the support of a commission. It is

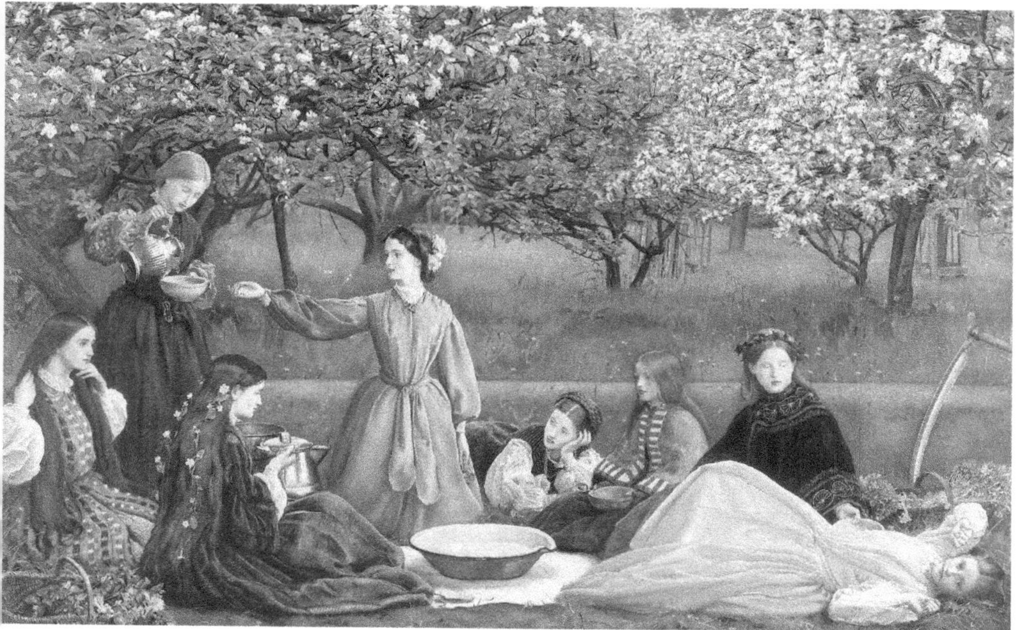

10.4 John Everett Millais, *Spring*, 1857–9. Exhibited: Royal Academy, 1859. Oil on canvas, 113 × 176.3 cm

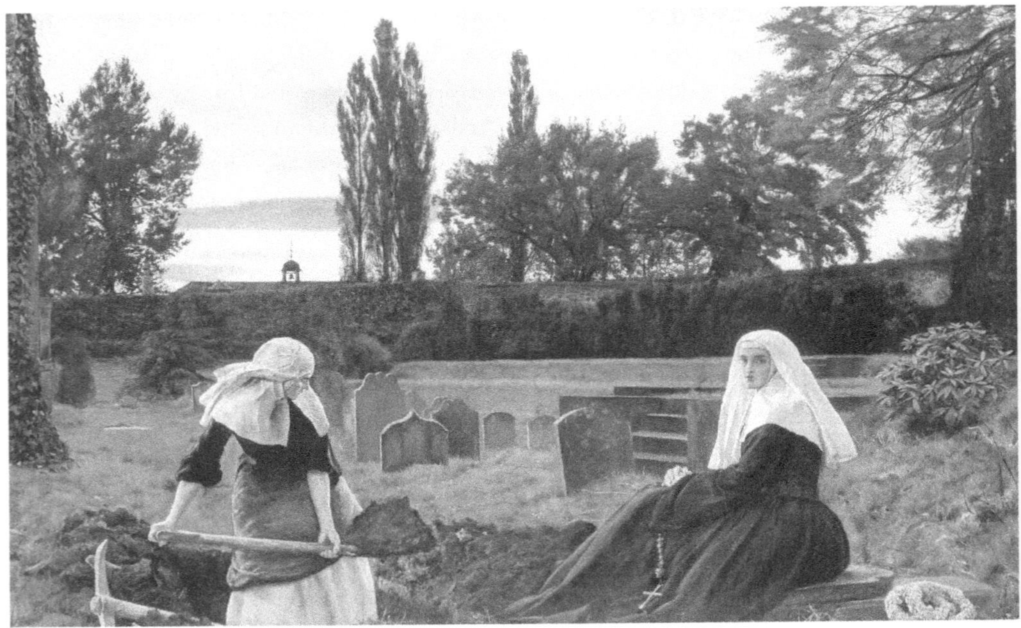

10.5 John Everett Millais, *The Vale of Rest*, 1858. Exhibited: Royal Academy, 1859. Oil on canvas, 102.9 × 172.7 cm.

almost as if, wondering whether he could ever move forward artistically and still prosper, he was deliberately setting up 1859 as a make-or-break year. The idea of painting a picture featuring apple blossoms had occurred to him in 1856 as a springtime follow-up to *Autumn Leaves*.[30] Initially he envisaged a chivalrous subject like *Sir Isumbras at the Ford* and entitled 'Faint Heart Never Won Fair Ladye', but this he abandoned in the following year in favour of a study of a group of girls like those in *Autumn Leaves*.[31] With *Spring* under way, he conceived *The Vale of Rest*, which is similarly symbolic rather than narrative in emphasis, as a darker pendant. His third picture for the 1859 Academy, *The Love of James the First of Scotland* (figure 10.6), was smaller, more conventional in its historical subject, and, featuring a pretty young woman, an altogether safer bet for a sale than the others.

In the event, selling any pictures that year was to be an ordeal. For *Spring* and *The Vale of Rest* Millais's father-in-law George Gray, a lawyer in Perth, advised him to ask 1,500 guineas (£1,575) each, without copyright. They were both large pictures and Millais's first for two years, so he was naturally tempted to try his luck with high prices. He felt that 1,500 guineas was a little too ambitious, however, and at the Langham Chambers exhibition offered them at 1,000 guineas (£1,050). The dealers were decidedly unenthusiastic. 'Called on

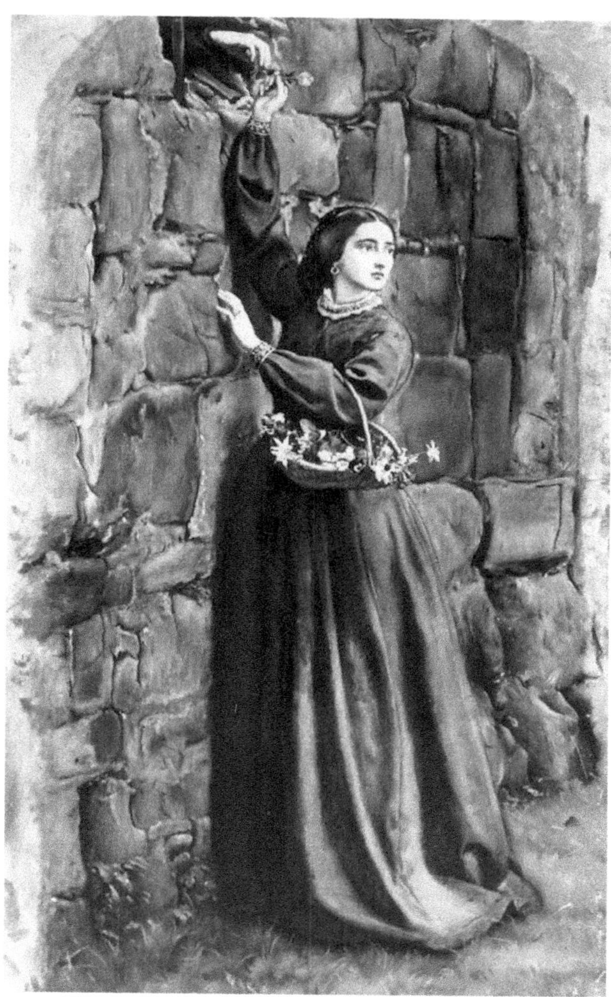

10.6
John Everett Millais,
*The Love of James the First
of Scotland*, 1858–59.
Exhibited: Royal
Academy, 1859. Oil
on canvas, arched top,
105.4 × 53.3 cm.

Farrer who scarcely mentioned my pictures although he saw them', he wrote to
Effie on 7 April. 'White too is very silent … & Gambart was quite impudent'.[32]
As Millais realized, buying large, expensive pictures was a greater gamble than
most dealers would willingly take at a time of continuing uncertainty in the art
market. His hope was that collectors might this year trust his reputation enough
to buy directly from him. He was momentarily encouraged by the news that his
old patron Thomas Combe, always attracted by religious subjects, was thinking
of buying *The Vale of Rest*. He wrote offering it to him – but Combe was also
interested in Holman Hunt's *The Finding of the Saviour in the Temple* (Birmingham
Museums and Art Gallery) and decided that 'his purse would not admit of his
having both'.[33] In the end he bought neither. There were collectors with much

deeper pockets than Combe's, but they seemed unlikely to buy pictures without the 'hallmark' that the involvement of an established dealer conferred, especially when the pictures in question were not only expensive but also idiosyncratic and not easy to like.[34] 'My pictures are not vulgar enough for the City merchants, who seem to be the only men who give these great prices', he wrote bitterly to Effie on 13 April.[35] As ever, the art market was an index of the national mood – at this point there was much fear of a war with France – and Millais was keenly conscious of the fact. 'If War comes on', he wrote with unintended bathos, 'I certainly shall not get 1000 apiece.'[36]

On 25 April, no further collectors having shown any interest, Augustus Egg advised Millais to drop the prices of his principal pictures to 800 guineas (£840) each and that of *The Love of James the First of Scotland*, which had probably been 500 guineas (£525), to 400 guineas (£420).[37] This he did, but to no avail, and by 30 April he was becoming desperate. 'The truth is', he wrote to Effie:

> I am knocked in the head if I don't sell any of these pictures & we must *economize as much as possible*. If I don't sell them I must go over to America, New York, and see what I can do there with them as selling off my small stock during this state of affairs would be *dreadful*. I confess I am completely staggered with the way things go. I have put as I told you 800 on each of the large ones & I could not well take less. The Private View is always about the best day for selling, and now this is over with no result I am quite at a loss what to think. You know how little faith I have always had in the profession and now you will see my reasons & that my anxiety about it is not unfounded. It is by no means unlikely that they will remain on my hands which is of course a very great trial after my work. Between ourselves I feel very downhearted in the matter.[38]

At the Academy dinner on 2 May, Millais spoke about his problems to Edwin Landseer, who had a calming influence. Though still regarding himself as 'a man who has carried everything before him & is suffering from a reaction of patronage', he was given heart by Landseer's renewal of a promise he had made a week earlier, half in jest, to try to help him sell his pictures.[39] The recommendation of the most highly respected British painter of the day ought, after all, to count for just as much with collectors as that of a dealer. For a time it even seemed that Landseer might buy a painting himself. Millais wrote on 3 May: 'The purchasers seem to be quite staggered & uncertain, and are mostly so dependent upon the judgment of the Dealers that they hang back. Directly some more enlightened man possesses one of the pictures the others will follow. I believe that *Landseer will himself*, from what he said, purchase one of them if they remain unsold any time, as his opinion is most gratifying.'[40] On 4 May, Landseer asked Millais for his address in case he found a purchaser for him.[41] Valuable though his support may have been for Millais's self-confidence, however, he neither bought nor induced anyone else to buy a picture.

No buyers had come forward by 13 May and Millais began to worry, probably quite rightly, that the longer they remained unsold, the less confidence an investment-conscious collector would have in them, making them even harder to sell by the day. He began to give up hope of selling directly to collectors altogether. 'There is no chance of my selling my pictures to *gentlemen* – the dealers are too strong', he wrote to his wife. The dealers could offer not only the security of the hallmark but also a greater flexibility about terms, a willingness to exchange or part-exchange one picture for another: 'Picture-buyers can barter with them when they cannot with the artist.'[42] Indeed it was a dealer who made the longed-for breakthrough with Millais's 1859 pictures. Though unwilling to buy on a speculative basis, D.T. White managed to line up a collector for *The Vale of Rest* and on 17 May offered £700, which the artist accepted.[43] For once, Millais seems not to have been irritated by the fact that the collector in question, B.G. Windus, should again be buying through a dealer when he could easily have bought directly from him. Any sale was to be jumped at, even though it was at a reduced price and apparently on condition that he prettify the face of the nun after the close of the Academy exhibition.

Hoping to recoup some of the £140 by which he had reduced the price of *The Vale of Rest* for White, and believing that the sale of that work increased the saleability of its pendant, Millais marked the price of *Spring* back up from 800 to 900 guineas (£945).[44] By 25 May, Gambart had bought *The Love of James the First of Scotland* for 200 guineas (£210) and Henry Graves had bought its copyright for a further 100 guineas (£105) – although no engraving of it was ever published.[45] Gambart seems also to have made an undertaking to buy *The Bridesmaid* (private collection), a smaller study of a girl in costume on a terrace; he paid 100 guineas for it when it was finished in July.[46] But *Spring* remained unsold and Millais remained depressed. He can hardly have been cheered by the sight of his earlier exhibition picture *The Woodman's Daughter*, now owned by his half-brother Henry Hodgkinson, put up for sale at Christie's on 13 June to be bought in at a mere 210 guineas (£220 10s). After the Royal Academy exhibition, he sent *Spring* to the Liverpool Academy with a similar lack of success. D.T. White seems to have been looking for prospective buyers as he had for *The Vale of Rest*. Though assuring Millais on 16 November that it was 'certain to sell this winter', however, he seems not to have found any.[47]

It was Gambart who eventually bought *Spring*, probably in the spring of 1860, about the same time he bought Millais's next major work, *The Black Brunswicker* (see figure 10.7).[48] From the dealer's point of view, buying *Spring* was probably more for the good of his relationship with the artist than the prospect of commercial gain. In spite of extensive repainting, he failed to interest any client in buying it and put it up for auction at Christie's on 3 May 1861. It sold for 460 guineas (£483). Gambart is unlikely to have paid Millais more than that sum for the work and may well have paid him less.

Having such difficulty selling his work and being forced to reduce prices so drastically made Millais yearn again for a securer way of making a living. '*Another year*', he wrote to his wife on 17 May 1859, 'I will do *commissions* & know beforehand what I shall get.'[49] He received a commission that summer from D.T. White for a reduced version of *Sir Isumbras at the Ford* (Lloyd-Webber Collection).[50] What most encouraged him to think in terms of commissioned works, however, was the pleading of Gambart for small-scale, saleable pictures. 'He overwhelms me with small commissions', he wrote, 'which after all pay mightily well'.[51] During the summer and autumn of 1859 he painted more studies of girls in the same line as the ones he had painted in 1857 and 1858. Gambart commissioned two, one of which he exhibited at his French Gallery in November.[52] Also for Gambart, who already had a buyer in the shape of Thomas Plint, he finished the reduced version of *A Huguenot* that he had had in mind since 1856 (Lloyd-Webber Collection).[53] He probably charged £100. As owner of the original large oil, B.G. Windus had earlier refused to allow him to copy from it. He therefore worked from the engraving and, although Windus had no legal grounds for objection, told Gambart that it might be a good idea not to mention it to him.[54]

Another kind of commissioned work was illustration, which Millais had been doing regularly over the past four years but stepped up considerably following the disappointments of 1859. He had been working on *The Parables* since the previous year and these continued to form a steady part of his output as an illustrator until 1863. He did usually three or four per year and was paid £20 for each.[55] What enabled him to boost his income from such 'black-and-white' work was the rise of the illustrated magazines. On 6 May 1859, his pictures still unsold at the Academy, he met with the editor of the soon-to-be-launched *Once a Week*, Samuel Lucas, who invited him to contribute. 'The pay [is] to be *first rate*', Millais wrote to his wife that day, 'so you see there are some prospects of making money'.[56] That year he did eight illustrations for *Once a Week* and in 1860 twelve, apparently for eight guineas (£8 8s) each.[57] Later in 1859 or early in 1860, his friend William Makepeace Thackeray invited him to contribute to the more expensive *Cornhill Magazine*, a monthly, of which he was editor. During 1860 Millais sent in six illustrations for the *Cornhill*, four of them for Trollope's serialized *Framley Parsonage*; the payment he received is unknown, but the *Cornhill* probably paid higher than *Once a Week*. In 1858 his income from illustrations had been about £100, the same kind of return as for one of the 'small commissions' Gambart was always offering him. In 1859 it rose to about £150 and in 1860 to about £350, the price he would normally expect for a second-string exhibition picture such as *The Love of James the First of Scotland*.

At thirty, Millais could look back on some remarkable successes but remained anxious about his professional future. The highest price he realized for any single picture in the 1850s was the 900 guineas (£945, without copyright) that Thomas Miller paid him for *Peace Concluded, 1856*. This put him in prestigious company. As he reported with delight to his wife, it was second only to the price for which Landseer sold his principal work at the same Academy exhibition, *Saved* (private collection).[58] In 1858 William Powell Frith made a great deal more for his blockbuster hit *The Derby Day* (Tate, London) — a total of £3,000, half from the collector Jacob Bell for the painting and half from Gambart for the copyright.[59] Given that *The Derby Day* was twice the size and much more elaborate than *Peace Concluded, 1856*, however, Millais's return on his picture was actually commensurate with Frith's — the important difference being that Frith sold the copyright and Millais did not. Millais's prices in the 1850s were those of an up-and-coming artist who could occasionally vie with older professionals of the top flight but was not enough of a name to command a consistently high return or expect to sell copyrights on a regular basis.

Certainly he was closer commercially to Landseer and Frith than to most painters his own age. D.G. Rossetti, for instance, was far more original in his attitude to matters of patronage, but his income was a mere fraction of that of his more conventionally minded Pre-Raphaelite comrade. Between 1849 and 1854, Rossetti's average income from his art was about £50 per annum; it rose to about £300 when Ruskin took him up in 1855 and further to about £600 in the early 1860s, first breaking the £1,000 barrier in 1864. Millais's income was around £300 as early as 1847 and rose steadily to about £1,000 in 1853 and about £2,750 in his *annus mirabilis* of 1856. There then followed a relative slump to an average of about £1,000 per annum for the rest of the 1850s, rising again in the early 1860s and reaching about £3,700 in 1863.[60] The sums involved were far greater than with Rossetti and so were the fluctuations between good years and relatively bad ones. To Rossetti, Millais's income during his bad years would still have seemed princely. But Millais had much greater expectations.

When we consider Millais's early career from the financial standpoint, his Pre-Raphaelite phase (roughly the early 1850s) emerges in an unexpected light. It was plain sailing, a story of ever-increasing success and saleability that was quite remarkable for such a young artist. The commonly held view of Millais that has him suffering hardships for his Pre-Raphaelite principles then weakening and betraying them for Mammon is simply not true. In fact, the period in which he experienced the greatest insecurity and anxiety over money came after his abandonment of rigorously Pre-Raphaelite painting. It was the slump years of 1857–59, following his marriage and the arrival of his first children, when he was living in Perth and painting mood-pictures that turned out to be so hard to sell.

The mood-pictures, from *Autumn Leaves* to *The Vale of Rest*, which constitute a distinct 'post-Pre-Raphaelite' phase in Millais's development, arguably rank alongside or above his earlier works. Certainly the artist thought so. Later in life he spoke of *The Vale of Rest* as his favourite picture, 'that by which, he said, he set most store'.[61] The problem was that, lacking strong narrative content, the mood-pictures were by their nature less saleable than most of Millais's work of the 1850s. Perhaps Millais would have done better with them in better times, but never in his life had the art market been in such a depressed state. They were not only an acquired taste but also large, and the demand was for safe, small works. Millais needed to earn more money than ever before to support his family, and, feeling at the height of his powers and that he was painting more important pictures than ever, was bewildered and embittered by the lack of enthusiasm with which they were received. His misfortune was a coincidence, that of coming to full maturity as a serious, demanding painter just as married life placed new responsibilities on his shoulders and economic circumstances made it more difficult than ever to meet them.

In a sense the failure of the mood-pictures was a failure to circumvent the dealers. Millais's early patronage follows a fairly predictable pattern. As a youth he strove for fame, entering competitions and exhibitions not so much in the hope of financial gain as in that of making his name. His patrons were largely relatives, family friends, and amateurs of art who took a friendly interest in his career. In his early twenties he enjoyed arguably the most beneficial kind of patronage from the artistic point of view, intimate and stimulating, from Thomas Combe, his other Oxford friend James Wyatt, and Ruskin. He continued to benefit to some degree from connections – Thackeray introduced him to Joseph Arden, for example. But in time his increasing financial expectations led him to reach beyond family, friends, and friends-of-friends to a wider circle of collectors with whom he did not necessarily have any personal contact.

The paintings the young Millais produced in response to commissions could be as radical and difficult as *The Return of the Dove to the Ark* – painted for Combe and now at the Ashmolean Musuem, Oxford – the Ruskin portrait, or *Autumn Leaves*. By contrast, the works that he made for the open market and which appealed most to the dealers were pictures of a straightforwardly touching narrative content – the engrave-able pictures, the prototype of which was *A Huguenot*. The demand for this kind of work was almost limitless. Perhaps partly for snobbish reasons, however, Millais resisted the temptation to become entirely a dealers' artist. As he knew perfectly well, the mood-pictures were not the kind of work the dealers wanted from him. He would never have turned them away, of course, but what he set his heart upon was selling directly from the studio or exhibition to collectors sympathetic to his work and brave enough to buy large, expensive pictures without the dealer's hallmark. This turned out to be a miscalculation.

By 1875, the dealers had become more firmly established, respectable, and numerous than they were in the 1850s and Millais was full of gratitude toward them:

> I am inclined to think we are chiefly indebted to the much abused dealer for the great advance in the prices paid for modern art. It is he who has awakened the Spirit of Competition. Where the Artist knows of only one purchaser, the dealer knows many, and has no scruples of delicacy in accommodating what is choice and admirable. If he has not forgotten himself he has on the whole been the Artist's best friend and scores of times has bought on the easel what the connoisseur has from timidity refused. An Artist cannot grumble if such a man obtains cent per cent for his purchase. He has been paid what was asked and after considerable experience I do not remember much unpleasantness or haggling between seller and buyer in such negotiations ... Another good deed must be placed to their account. They have created the taste of encouraging Art amongst the wealthy manufacturing classes and in so doing have produced a market value which is likely to be sustained as in the case of property.[62]

In short, the dealer exposed pictures to many competing collectors so they sold for the best possible prices; because of his experience he bought from the easel more confidently than the private collector; he encouraged the rich to buy art, and promoted the idea of art as a good investment.

But the dealers not only bought and sold. In their dealings with both artists and collectors they exercised influence, and it was this side of their business that the Millais of the late 1850s found oppressive. For obvious reasons, they did not welcome idiosyncratic works of art that spoke volumes to one person in a thousand. They wanted tried and tested subjects, pictures that everyone would like and any collector might buy, engravings of which would have mass appeal. Once an artist had come up with such a picture, the dealer's tendency was to encourage them to paint variations on the same theme, to become as reliable as a good brand name. Hence the constant demand from Gambart for repetitions of the engraved *A Huguenot*, and the fact that Millais followed his failures of 1859 with a succession of pictures based on old ideas.

'I have striven in the hope that in time people would understand me and estimate my best productions at their true worth', he supposedly said to Holman Hunt, 'but they (the public and private patrons) go like a flock of sheep after any silly bell-wether who chinks before them. I have up to now generally painted in the hope of converting them to something better, but I see they won't be taught, and as I must live, they shall have what they want, instead of what I know would be best for them.'[63] Suspiciously Holman-Hunt-like though this may sound, it probably reflects something Millais really said to Hunt, either at the time or later, and does capture the mood of bitter resignation that came over him after the reception of *Spring* and *The Vale of Rest*. What everyone wanted was not something new and original but more of the pathetic scenes of love in adversity that he had begun painting in the early 1850s, the most popular of which was the engraved *A Huguenot*. 'Whatever I do, no matter how successful, it will always be the same story', he wrote to Effie on 17 May 1859, '"Why don't you give us the Huguenot again?"'[64]

The dealer who most strongly urged Millais to repeat his Huguenot painting, and whose urgings prompted the artist's frustrated complaint to his wife, was Gambart. At the time, Gambart was suggesting he should paint Petrarch and Laura, but this came to nothing.[65] For the next Academy exhibition he painted instead a scene that was even more like *A Huguenot* than the Petrarch and Laura composition would have been – *The Black Brunswicker* (figure 10.7), which shows a soldier and his love in a farewell embrace on the eve of the Battle of Waterloo. He began his new painting just as he was finishing his copy of *A Huguenot* for Gambart, and one of the preparatory sketches (Ashmolean Museum, Oxford) shows him working out the composition alongside a sketch of that earlier work, clearly conceiving it as a pendant. *The Black Brunswicker* is slightly larger, but size mattered less than proportion; it was not the paintings themselves that had to work together but the engravings after them. Not surprisingly, it was Gambart who bought *The Black Brunswicker* – he may even have commissioned it – and he paid Millais 1,000 guineas (£1,050).[66] This presumably included the copyright, which, by the time the engraving was published in 1863 – the artist's first for five years – had passed to Graves and Moore, McQueen & Co. Millais had managed to sell a work considerably less than half the size of *The Vale of Rest* for one-and-a-half times the price, which must have been a great relief, both financially and emotionally. It must also have brought home to him, if he did not fully realize it already, how easy it could be to make a good living by playing safe and taking the dealers' advice.

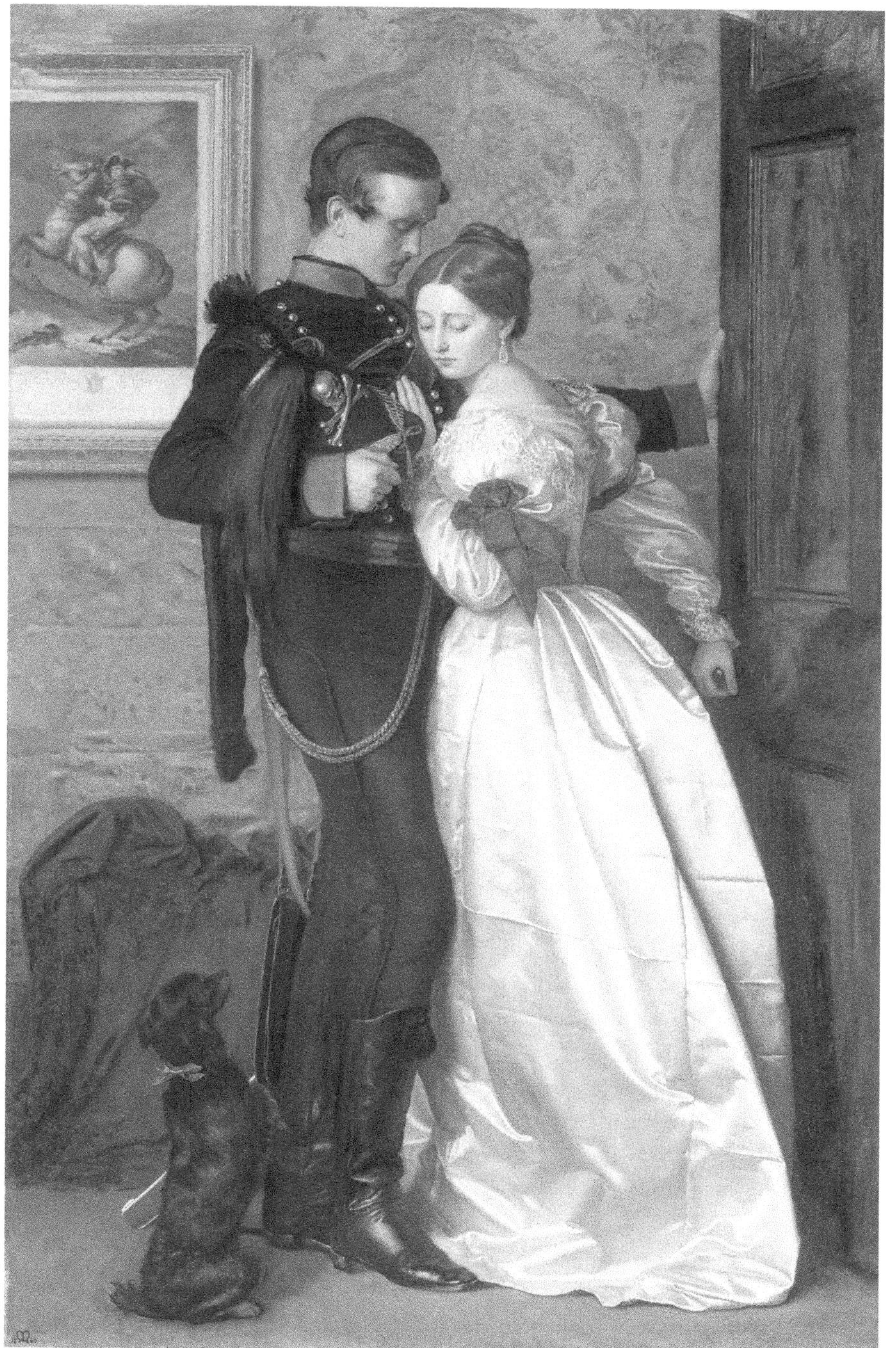

10.7 John Everett Millais, *The Black Brunswicker*, 1859–60. Exhibited: Royal Academy, 1860. Oil on canvas, arched top, 104 × 68.5 cm.

Notes

The abbreviations 'BP' and 'MP' refer to the Bowerswell Papers and the Millais Papers in the Department of Literary and Historical Manuscripts, Pierpont Morgan Library, New York (respectively MA 1338 and MA 1485). 'JEM' and 'EM' are the artist and his wife, Effie Millais.

1 This article is adapted from the discussion of Millais and his patronage in the author's doctoral thesis (see bibliography).
2 Millais, *John Everett Millais*, I, p. 335.
3 Eastlake, 'Memoir of Sir Charles Eastlake', p. 147.
4 Millais, I, pp. 147, 151, 162. In September 1852, the *Art Journal* (p. 290) lamented the fact that dealers had bought both of Millais's paintings and urged collectors to have the courage to buy directly from the easel.
5 Ruskin's father paid Millais on 4 December 1854. See Lutyens, *Millais and the Ruskins*, p. 249.
6 Millais, I, p. 357.
7 For a fuller discussion of the origins and significance of *Autumn Leaves*, see Warner, 'Millais's "Autumn Leaves"'.
8 Millais mentioned the prices of *Autumn Leaves*, *The Blind Girl*, and *Peace Concluded, 1856* in letters to his wife, Effie Millais, on 10 and 12 April 1856 (MP).
9 JEM to EM, 12 April 1856 (MP).
10 JEM to EM, 8 May 1856 (MP).
11 A copy of the contract between Millais and Graves for the engraving of *The Order of Release, 1746*, dated 21 June 1853, is at the British Library (Add. Ms. 46140, f0l. 230). On the copyright and engraving of *A Huguenot*, see Millais, I, p. 147.
12 On Millais and the print market, see Warner, 'Millais in Reproduction', pp. 222–8.
13 JEM to EM, 9 April 1857 (MP). Millais banked at Coutts & Co., whose archives are an invaluable source of information about his commercial fortunes.
14 Trevelyan Papers, Newcastle University Library, Newcastle-upon-Tyne.
15 Information about transactions involving Agnew's comes from stock books still in the firm's archives.
16 From Effie Millais's journal, in Millais, I, p. 309.
17 JEM to EM, 9 April 1857 (MP).
18 Millais, I, pp. 313–14.
19 Walter Armstrong recorded the price as £300 and Holman Hunt as £400. See Armstrong, *Millais*, p. 14, and Hunt, *Pre-Raphaelitism*, II, p. 153.
20 Elwin, *Charles Reade*, p. 119.
21 JEM to EM, 18 May 1857 (MP). For the reviews, see *The Times*, 13 May 1857, p. 9, and Ruskin's *Academy Notes*, issued 16 May 1857, in Cook and Wedderburn, eds. *Ruskin*, XIV, pp. 106–10.
22 JEM to EM, 'Monday Morning', datable to May 1857 (MP).
23 JEM to EM, 15 May 1857, in Millais, I, p. 323.

24 Maas, *Gambart*, p. 98.

25 Surtees, ed. *Diaries of George Price Boyce*, pp. 19, 80.

26 The sketches of Sophie and Alice and one of the sketches from an unknown model are in private collections; the sketch from an unknown model that belonged to Windus, which shows her cutting off a lock of her hair, is in Manchester City Galleries.

27 Cherry, 'Hogarth Club', p. 238.

28 Huntington Library, San Marino (Hunt Collection, HH402).

29 On *The Return of the Crusader*, see Effie Millais's journal in Millais, I, p. 328. Sketches for the composition are at Birmingham Museums and Art Gallery (639'06–645'06).

30 JEM to EM, 29 April 1856, in Millais, I, p. 296.

31 Effie Millais's journal, in Millais, I, pp. 323–4.

32 Millais mentioned his father-in-law's advice, the prices of his paintings, and the response of the dealers in a letter to his wife, 7 April 1859 (MP).

33 JEM to EM, 12 April 1859 (MP).

34 On the dealer's 'hallmark', see Frith, *Autobiography*, I, p. 100.

35 Millais, I, p. 340.

36 JEM to EM, 17 April 1859 (MP).

37 JEM to EM, 25 April 1859 (MP).

38 JEM to EM, 30 April 1859 (MP).

39 JEM to EM, 26 April 1859, in Millais, I, p. 342; and 2 May 1859 (BP).

40 JEM to (?) his father, 3 May 1859 (MP).

41 JEM to EM, 5 May 1859, in Millais, I, p. 344.

42 JEM to EM, 13 May 1859, in Millais, I, p. 346.

43 JEM to EM, 17 May 1859 (MP).

44 Ibid.

45 JEM to his mother-in-law, Sophia Gray, 25 May 1859 (BP).

46 Millais wrote to Effie on 17 May 1859, that Gambart 'will doubtless buy the terrace scene' and on 21 July that he had done so (MP).

47 JEM to EM, 17 November 1859, in Millais, I, p. 349.

48 Millais wrote to his wife on 6 May 1860, that he was intending to get Gambart to pay for *Spring* immediately (MP).

49 JEM to EM, 17 May 1859 (MP).

50 Effie Millais wrote to her mother on 7 June 1859, that White was going to buy 'the little copy of the Knight' (BP). Millais wrote to Effie on 20 July that he was about to deliver it; see Millais, I, p. 348.

51 JEM to EM, 17 May 1859 (MP).

52 The head of a girl that Gambart showed at the French Gallery (as *Meditation*) is now at King's College, Cambridge; the other head he commissioned in 1859 is at the Baroda Museum and Picture Gallery in India. A possible third work in the same group – most likely painted in 1859 and perhaps another Gambart commission – is in a private collection (formerly Sir Colin Anderson).

53 Millais wrote to Effie of his intention to make a small version on 1 May 1856 (Huntington Library, HM 35510).

54 From references in Ford Madox Brown's diary, in Surtees, ed. *Diary of Ford Madox Brown*, p. 125; and a letter from Millais to Gambart, 6 November 1859 (Museum of Fine Arts, Boston).

55 From a list of the artist's works of 1862–64, with prices, made by his wife in a bank account book (Pierpont Morgan Library, MA 4987).

56 JEM to EM, 6 May 1859 (MP).

57 Millais mentioned the price of eight guineas in a letter datable to August 1860 to Bradbury & Evans, publishers of *Once a Week* (draft in his wife's hand, MP).

58 JEM to EM, 29 April 1856 (Huntington Library, HM 35509, in Millais, I, p. 296) and probably 3 May (Huntington Library, HM 35512). *Saved* and its copyright were bought by Henry Graves, who published an engraving after the work in 1859. The price paid to Landseer is unknown, but Graves sold the painting to the collector John Naylor for £1,653. Graves, *Landseer*, p. 32.

59 Frith, I, p. 273.

60 These rough estimates of annual income for Millais and Rossetti are derived from sources too numerous to mention individually.

61 Spielmann, *Millais*, p. 74.

62 From the apparently unpublished manuscript of an essay, 'On Rewards' (MP).

63 Hunt, II, p. 179.

64 Millais, I, p. 348.

65 JEM to EM, 16 May 1859, ibid.

66 Millais, I, p. 354.

11

Branding the vision:
William Holman Hunt
and the Victorian art market

Brenda Rix

When William Holman Hunt's ashes were buried at St. Paul's Cathedral, London on 12 September 1910, *The Times* noted that the 'thousands who assembled in St. Paul's Cathedral yesterday, and the crowds in the churchyard outside, were the representatives of many millions who had never seen Holman Hunt in the flesh but to whom he was far more than a name: for his pictures had carried him a revered and familiar friend into homes without number all over the world'.[1] As this tribute suggests, by the end of a six-decade-long career, Hunt had become a household name. 'Millions' of people in Britain and around the globe who had never seen Hunt, or one of his actual paintings, 'revered' the man and his art. Long before the marketing term 'branding' had been invented, William Holman Hunt was a 'product with a unique, positive and recognizable identity'.[2]

Hunt's celebrity has been rightly attributed to the distribution of black-and-white engravings made after his paintings, but the significance to him of the print trade should be viewed within the larger framework of England's rapidly developing art market of the 1850s and 1860s. While holding fast to his personal vision of art, Hunt aligned himself with a key group of critics, dealers, patrons, arts organizations, printmakers, and publishers. A look into his navigation of the complex system of the commercial gallery, the art press, and the print publishing industry, sheds light on Hunt's rise to fame and illuminates the internal workings of the Victorian art world.

Hunt displayed a pioneering spirit at an early age. The son of a manager of a textile warehouse, Hunt secured a job as a clerk at a muslin and calico printing works at the age of fourteen. Never daunted by technical challenges, he learned the tools of the trade and designed patterns for printed fabric.[3] Despite parental opposition, he studied drawing on the side, finally gaining admittance to the Royal Academy Schools in 1844. These humble origins are often contrasted with the privileged upbringing of his Pre-Raphaelite 'brothers' John Everett Millais and Dante Gabriel Rossetti, but Hunt's early environment surely instilled a strong work ethic and encouraged his innate aptitude for business. He later designed furniture, decorative arts, and costumes, mostly for studio props, and after 1854 conceived and occasionally constructed the remarkable frames on his oil paintings and watercolours.[4]

In August 1849 the members of the fledgling Pre-Raphaelite Brotherhood determined to share their artistic vision through the publication of the first issue of *The Germ: Thoughts Towards Nature in Poetry, Literature and Art*. This serial magazine was intended to appear monthly with one etching and several writings by PRB members.[5] Although a novice etcher Hunt volunteered to contribute the first image, *My Beautiful Lady and Of My Lady in Death*. He supervised the printing and changed the plate at least three times, each version being a 'striking improvement' over the last.[6] His 'hands-on' oversight, his desire to disseminate his images, and his commitment to a quality product, would become lifelong characteristics of Hunt's approach to the print world and to the art market.

Over his career, Hunt produced a small number of major oil paintings which were typically large scale, full of realistic and symbolic detail, rendered in vivid colour, and presented in elaborate frames designed by the artist.[7] His public image was based on perceptions about his bohemian lifestyle, his treks to the exotic Middle East, and his strongly held religious beliefs, and his paintings were admired 'because the making of them has been so laborious' and because of their morally uplifting themes.[8] The popularity of key works such as *The Light of the World*, *The Finding of the Saviour in the Temple*, and *The Shadow of Death* was guaranteed by their link to the print market. His most ambitious and financially successful painting, *The Finding of the Saviour in the Temple* (1860, Birmingham Museums and Art Gallery; figure 11.1) provides a case study, revealing Hunt's artistic goals, working methods, and marketing savvy.

Hunt began work on *The Finding of the Saviour in the Temple* upon his arrival in Jerusalem on his first trip to the Middle East in March 1854. Progress on the painting stalled because of the lack of willing models so he concentrated instead on other projects such as *The Lantern-Maker's Courtship*, *The Afterglow in Egypt*, and *The Scapegoat*. He also contemplated a variety of printmaking projects and busied himself writing letters to friends and colleagues back in London.[9] He was, for example, in a 'long and tortuous correspondence' with his patron, Thomas Combe, the owner of *The Light of the World*, and with the art dealer, Ernest

Gambart, who was keen to buy the copyright for the engraving of this painting.[10] Subsequent negotiations between artist, dealer, and patron illustrate one of Hunt's early forays into the art market.

Thomas Combe was a High Churchman and the head of the Clarendon Press at Oxford. In 1852 he purchased the painting from Hunt for £400 and became the artist's supporter and mentor. Hunt retained the copyright, refusing an offer of £300 from two engravers who he believed could not 'do full justice to his picture'.[11] That the best professional engravers were all otherwise engaged is a testament to the bustling state of the mid-century London print industry. Hunt was willing to be patient to achieve 'a real triumph' that would generate long-term sales locally and in European markets.[12] When Gambart recruited the engraver William Henry Simmons, a master of new tonal processes, Hunt agreed to sell the dealer the copyright for £200. Gambart then persuaded Combe to relinquish the painting to the engraver for two years in exchange for six 'proofs before letters' and a payment of £180.[13]

Gambart took a calculated but relatively small risk given *The Light of the World*'s endorsement in the press by the influential art critic John Ruskin.[14] In fact, sales

11.1 William Holman Hunt (British, 1827–1910), *The Finding of the Saviour in the Temple*, 1854–60. Oil on canvas, 85.7 × 141 cm. In original frame designed by the artist.

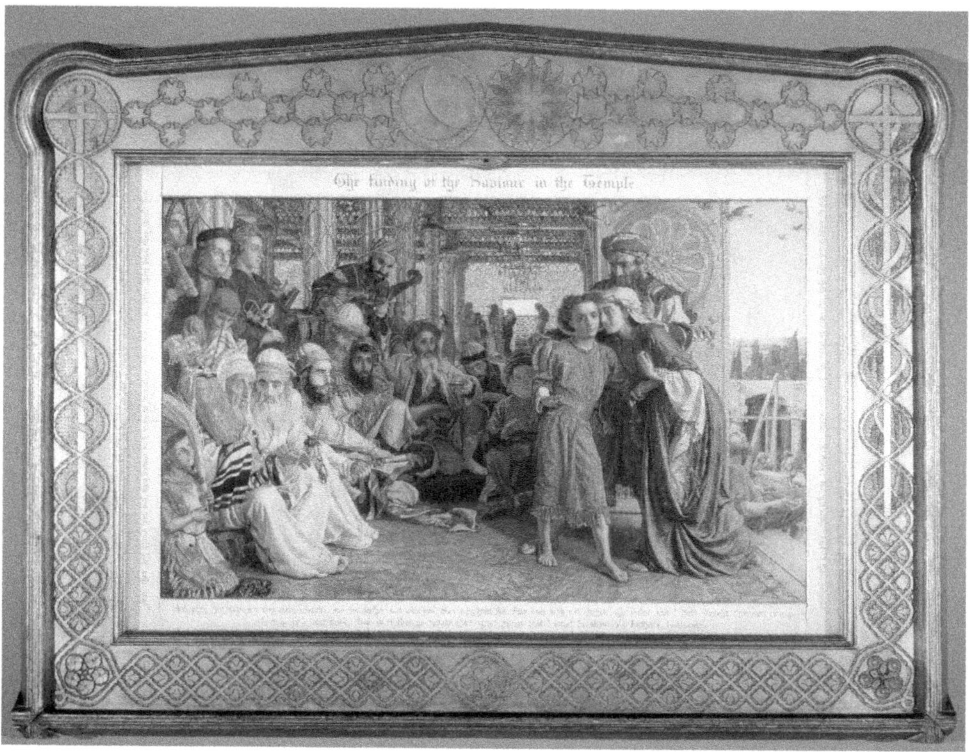

from the engraving would provide the dealer with an annual income of £1,000 for the rest of his life.[15] Simmons's engraving, finally published in 1860, became the first reproductive print after one of Hunt's paintings, inaugurating a long line of printed translations of this famous Protestant image (figure 11.2).[16] Subscription lists for impressions of the engraving grew as the painting travelled to major centres across England beginning in May 1860.[17] This success coincided with the unveiling in April 1860 of Hunt's great *tour de force*, *The Finding of the Saviour in the Temple*.

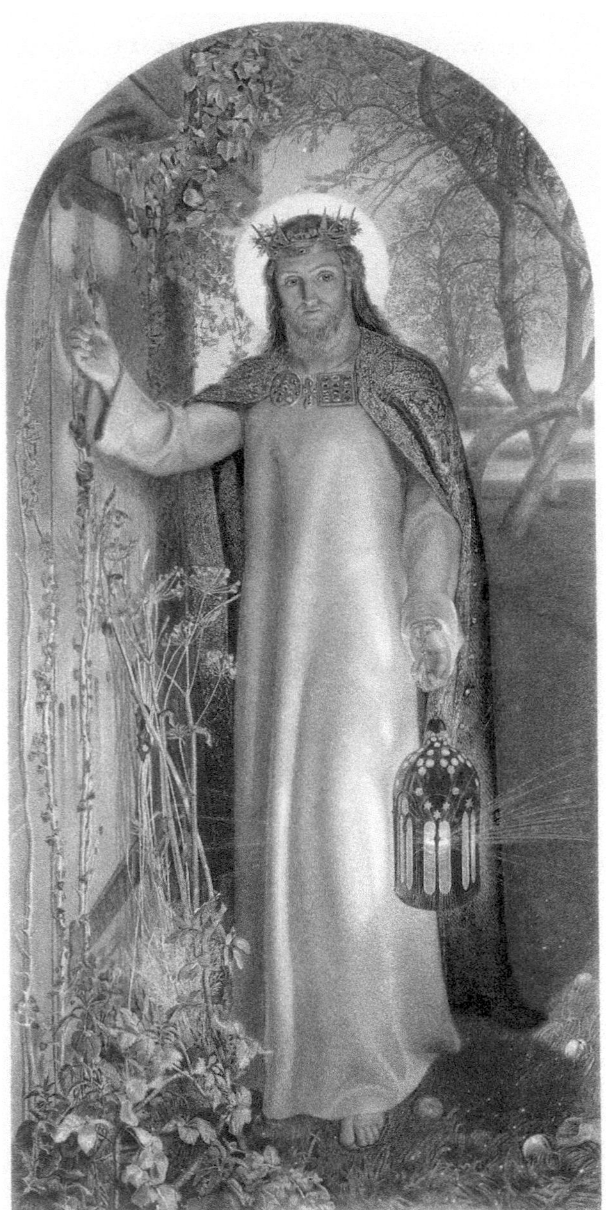

11.2
William Henry Simmons (British, 1811–82) after William Holman Hunt (British, 1827–1910), *The Light of the World*, 1860. Engraving and stipple engraving on chine collé, 74.3 × 42.5 cm.

Hunt explained the significance of this painting to John Ruskin in a letter dated 28 December 1857, in which he stated, 'to me my 'Finding' is as important [as] Da Vinci's *Last Supper* was to him'.[18] Clearly, Hunt saw his representation of Christ's exchange with Jewish teachers in the temple, as the culmination of his artistic practice, his 'chef d'oeuvre'.[19] To Hunt, this large-scale, multi-figured canvas brought together all his efforts to achieve ethnographic realism, biblical accuracy, and a new kind of religious symbolism, rendered in painstaking detail and vivid colour.

Hunt's struggles to complete *The Finding of the Saviour in the Temple* were chronicled in his letters and in the press.[20] This commentary of sacrifice and labour helped to generate publicity for the much-anticipated and costly oil painting. Diligence and fortitude were virtues valued by his Victorian audience; the product of hard work and hard times, Hunt's painting would generate both fiscal and moral rewards. The completion of his major canvases was typically accompanied by this kind of anticipatory build up, with the most extreme cases being *The Shadow of Death* and *The Triumph of the Innocents*.[21] In letters to Thomas Combe, Hunt described his near 'life and death' struggles to complete his paintings and boasted of his obsessive work ethic.[22]

Work on the painting was also delayed when Hunt had to 'turn the Temple picture to the wall to pay the bills'. He then produced small-scale replicas of paintings such as *The Eve of St. Agnes* and *The Light of the World*, and took up book illustration, designing wood engravings, and preparing plates for the Etching Club.[23] Over his career, Hunt's personal forays into printmaking were intermittent and resulted in a small output of five etchings and twenty-five wood engravings and in a modest income.[24] Eventually, his sale of the copyright for the painting *Claudio and Isabella* to Gambart gave him some breathing space, and then Combe advanced him £300 to finish *The Finding of the Saviour in the Temple* so that he would not be 'forced to set to some other pot-boiler'.[25]

As the painting progressed, Hunt considered his options for its exhibition and sale, and reports by those who caught a glimpse of the unfinished canvas in his studio increased the suspense.[26] The Royal Academy remained the premier annual exhibition venue for contemporary artists. Hunt had a chequered relationship with the RA, having applied three times before achieving entrance into the RA Schools. Following the exhibition of *The Scapegoat* and three of his Middle Eastern watercolours at the RA in May 1856, he learned that he had received only one vote at elections for associate membership. This rejection was a 'devastating blow' which 'turned him into a lifelong enemy of the Academy'.[27] So when the President Sir Charles Eastlake entreated him to send the *Finding* to the Royal Academy, offering to install it in a prominent place, Hunt refused. He determined instead to 'look to the special exhibition of it as one chance of remuneration' and he received overtures from prominent commercial gallery owners including Thomas Agnew and Ernest Gambart.[28]

By mid-century Ernest Gambart's gallery was one of the first London galleries devoted to the sale of contemporary art. Hunt clearly desired to unveil his major new painting in a prestigious and fashionable venue. He needed compensation for his time and devotion to this work and was acutely aware that he was bargaining with several separate and valuable commodities, which included the painting, the exhibition rights, and the copyright for the engraving.[29]

According to Hunt's autobiography, a fortuitous meeting with the author Charles Dickens gave him confidence to pursue a hard bargain with Gambart. Hunt told Dickens that he intended to ask the dealer for £5,500, the highest price ever paid for a painting by a living artist. He provided Dickens with a tally of the dealer's expenses and revenues. Along with the purchase of the painting and the copyright, costs to the dealer included the rent on his gallery, and the salaries of the toll-keeper (who sold admission tickets), the canvasser (who took names of people subscribing to the engraving), and the engraver (of '£800 or so'), as well as the cost of printing and distribution of the engraving. On the revenue side, the dealer had exhibition rights at his gallery (admission revenue at 'a shilling a head' for a total of £20–30 a day), engraving rights (at £3, £5, and £8 for various levels of proofs), and the eventual resale of the painting.[30] Dickens supported the enormous price Hunt was asking and, drawing on his own experience in the publishing industry, suggested Hunt allow the dealer to pay in instalments of £1,500 down, £1,000 in six months, and the other sums 'at periods extending over two and a half or three years'.[31] Although Gambart was incredulous at the price he became convinced of the potential value of the transaction. Shortly after the painting went on view in April 1860 the final contract was drawn up by their respective lawyers.[32]

The build-up to the public unveiling continued with viewings in Hunt's studio from 9 to 11 April, followed by a private viewing in the rented space known as the German Gallery at 168 New Bond St. on 17 April. Surprisingly, Hunt later remembered a poor turnout on the grand opening day apparently because of the lack of advertising.[33] This oversight was quickly remedied, and Bond Street was soon 'choked up' with carriages.[34] On 17 May 1860, Hunt's friend, the artist Thomas Woolner wrote to Emily Tennyson, 'You must have heard about the prodigious success of Hunt's picture in a popular sense, nothing like it in modern times ... it is so unusual that a fashionable public goes mad about anything more dignified than a Crystal Palace, crinoline, or a Railway King'.[35] The crowds were so large that when Prince Albert could not get close to the picture Gambart arranged (without Hunt's knowledge) for the painting to be sent to Buckingham Palace for the day on 11 May.[36] By 28 July receipts at the door were up to £40 per day. And by October Gambart had apparently 'cleared more than the princely-money paid to Mr. Hunt' on the gate receipts alone.[37]

The painting was 'arranged with all due artistic effect of darkened room, rich sombre draperies, and concentrated light'.[38] It was surrounded in a '*cassetta* frame with gabled top, reminiscent of a temple-like structure' designed by Hunt.[39] The symbolic detail includes stars, the moon, and the sun along the top flanked by a serpent on a pole on one side and a cross with a briar on the other. Such details provide Old Testament foreshadowing of Christ's earthly mission which is depicted in the painting. Hunt reinforces that a new order (represented by the youthful Christ and the New Testament) has displaced the old dispensation (represented by the rabbis and the Old Testament). The biblical inscription on the ivory slip quotes Christ's prophetic words to his earthly parents from the gospel of Luke, 'Wist ye not that I must be about my Father's business?'[40] Together, the painting and frame created a unified decorative ensemble which the artist wanted to be appreciated for its artistic merit. Millais called the painting a 'jewel in a gorgeous setting'.[41]

Reviews for the painting poured in and Hunt became the 'plebeian lion of the season'.[42] One critic proclaimed, 'No picture of such extraordinary elaboration has been seen in our day.'[43] On 21 April 1860, within a few days of the opening, Hunt's friend, the art critic Frederic G. Stephens, wrote a long article in the *Athenaeum* proclaiming:

After eighteen months spent in Jerusalem, and nearly five years of study, Mr. Hunt places his work before the public ... No one will deny that the result is, in all respects, a grand one, and almost unequalled, in our time, for power of design or splendour of execution ... Mr. Holman Hunt is essentially an English painter, and has taken a thoroughly national idea of his work.[44]

For those shocked by the vivid colours and overwhelming accumulation of 'oriental' (foreign and exotic) detail, Stephens (and, by extension, Hunt) declares the whole concept to be thoroughly 'English and Protestant', a new, authentic reconstruction of the biblical subject.

Hunt was keenly aware that the 'extraordinary elaboration' of the painting could be 'read' on different levels. At face value it was a depiction of a biblical and historical event, but multiple entry points into the content were provided by the inscription on the slip inside the frame, and the symbolism in the painting and on the frame. By November, a booklet, written by Stephens, described the details in the painting and compiled many congratulatory reviews.[45] Although intended to attract potential subscribers for the engraving, this publication suggests that comprehension of the arcane symbolism required literary supplementation.[46]

In November 1860 the painting (minus copyright) was purchased by Thomas Plint, a Leeds stockbroker and, over the next few months, more excitement was generated when it came perilously close to being destroyed as the curtains around the painting caught fire. The flames were extinguished by a visitor's valuable Indian shawl and the picture needed only minor repairs.[47] The painting remained on view at the German Gallery for approximately two years. In 1861, *Claudio and Isabella* along with five of Hunt's Middle Eastern watercolours were added to the installation to attract new audiences.

Before the painting went on tour in 1863, Hunt began a half-size replica which was mounted in a similar frame. A few variations were introduced to distinguish the copy from the original and thereby 'comply with copyright requirements by Gambart'.[48] This version (now in Sudley House, National Museums Liverpool) was completed in 1865 and sold through Gambart to a 'rich purchaser', probably the Mancunian cotton and shipping magnate, Sam Mendel.[49] Replicas offered another opportunity to generate revenue and to diffuse the image. Over the course of his career, Hunt painted reduced-size versions of most of his major paintings.[50]

In January 1863 the original painting began its travels across England and Ireland – a circuit that continued for five and a half years and gathered subscribers for the engraving along the way. Gambart developed an elaborate business plan in which he offered the print seller George Pennell a half-share in the receipts from the engraving for 10,000 guineas. This appealing offer was taken up by the businessman and collector, Joseph Gillot. Gambart noted that further revenue could be generated through future gate receipts, the subscription sales of the engraving, and by travelling the painting 'possibly to America and other Parts'.[51] Nine years after the opening at the German Gallery, Gambart was still entertaining the prospect of touring the painting outside the British Isles. In April 1869 the *Athenaeum* announced an exclusive opportunity to see the painting in King Street 'for a limited period' before it went to the United States.[52] Finally, Gambart abandoned the American tour because of the high travel costs.[53]

Ultimately, nothing contributed more to the financial rewards of *The Finding of the Saviour in the Temple* than the eventual publication of the related reproductive engraving (figure 11.3). Exhibitions alone would not sustain new commercial art galleries and their success rested on the established foundation of the print trade.[54] Gambart expected a high return on his investment in the copyright and had masterminded Stephens's booklet largely to promote the subscription sales of the engraving. As the text promised, 'a national service is rendered by the publication of really noble transcripts from noble pictures like these. Where the pictures cannot go, the engravings penetrate.'[55]

The engraving after Hunt's painting was first announced at the time of the exhibition in 1860. Gambart officially registered the print with the regulatory body, the Printsellers' Association, in June 1863, and the print was finally published and for sale by 1 August 1867. An interval of two to four years to engrave a large metal plate was not unusual; the process – transferring the image, engraving the large metal plate, and printing the edition – relied on time-consuming manual labour. Hunt played an integral role in this production and in 1861 devoted early-morning hours before Gambart's gallery opened to the public to preparing a tracing of the painting. The painting was removed from the gallery for a period in August 1861 and Hunt's tracing was in turn worked up into an elaborate 'to scale' chalk drawing by Signor Morelli[56] for use by the illustrious French engraver, Auguste Blanchard.[57]

Blanchard's traditional technique of line-engraving was sympathetic to the elaborate detail of Hunt's painting. In keeping with his usual practice Hunt was on hand to vet and touch up proofs, in this case travelling to France to visit the engraver in his home.[58] Blanchard apparently received 2,000 guineas for his

11.3 Auguste Blanchard (French, 1819–98) after William Holman Hunt (British, 1827–1910), *The Finding of the Saviour in the Temple*, 1867. Line-engraving on chine collé, 39 × 65 cm. In original frame designed by F.G. Stephens.

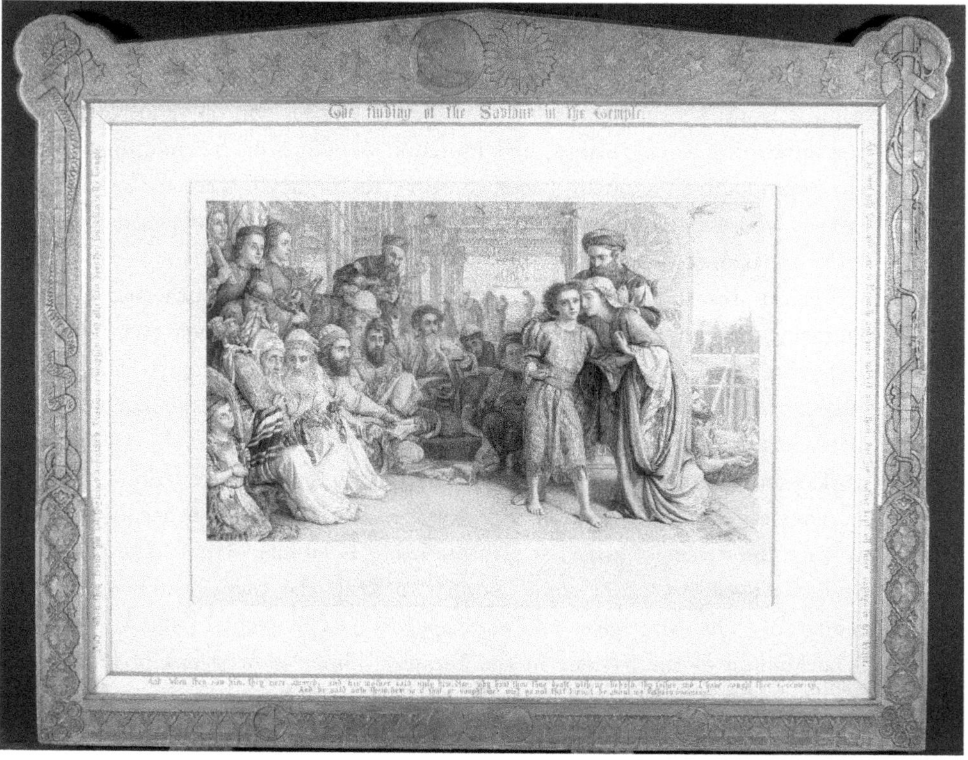

work.[59] A vast edition of over 3,000 'proofs' and up to 10,000 regular prints garnered £10,000 in 1867, the first year of publication. Gambart nevertheless lamented that the exceptionally long wait of seven years had 'marred the success very considerably'.[60]

A select number of proofs were available in frames designed by Stephens which were modelled after the frame on the painting (see figure 11.3). Hunt originally preferred a simple frame for the engraving, fearing that the 'very elaborate one' might look too heavy but later deciding that it 'really looks well much beyond my expectations'.[61] An additional 'key plate', identifying the individuals and other details, was also available at the time of the engraving's publication in 1867.

The *Art Journal* praised the engraving, yet cautioned that the line-engraving technique resulted in a 'certain hardness' that contrasted with the 'mellow richness' found in more popular mixed-method engravings. Nevertheless, the 'character of the picture is well preserved; the masterly touches of the painter have been rendered by the engraver. The print … will be universally accepted as an acquisition of rare value, destined to occupy the place of honour in tens of thousands of homes where Art is loved, and the Christian faith venerated'. The presumed accessibility of the content is reiterated by the comment that the 'story is written in the language that all can read and understand'.[62]

Reproductions such as this were accepted as substitutes for originals; they reflected Victorian morals and expanded knowledge about art to an ever growing audience.[63] Along with painted copies of popular canvases, reproductive prints were luxury items, objects of fine art, and, as noted in the *Art Journal* in 1853, a 'numerous body of the community not possessing the means to purchase the original works of our painters … are able to acquire, and do acquire, the next best substitutes – engravings, and imitation drawings or chromolithographs'.[64] The reproductive engraving provided entry to the art market for middle-class patrons who wanted framed works for their walls, and who possessed a patriotic desire to support British contemporary art.

The art press fuelled this process, offering regular reviews of the arrival of new engravings. Commentaries discussed prints as works of art in their own right or, as in the case of Blanchard's *The Finding of the Saviour in the Temple* (figure 11.3), praised the engraver on the close approximation of the reproduction to the painted surface of the original. Reproductive prints functioned on several levels: as affordable works of art, commercial commodities, and marketing tools for painters.

A review in the *Standard* on 28 November 1873 noted: 'It is hardly necessary to trace the career of an artist so remarkable as Holman Hunt. The print-shop windows usually contain some picture to keep the public interested in the painter of "The After-glow", "The Scapegoat", "The Light of the World", and "The Finding of the Saviour in the Temple".' Since impressions of Blanchard's

The Finding of the Saviour in the Temple, for example, ranged from eight to over fifteen guineas for proofs, members of the working class settled for viewing revolving displays of such engravings in dealers' shop windows or buying cheap printed renditions – including pirated photographs of the engravings.[65] Other opportunities to acquire reasonably priced engravings were provided by the art unions or art lotteries, such as the Art Union of London founded in 1837 which had a subscription list of nearly 14,000 people in 1844. For a modest sum members of the public could purchase a ticket to receive an impression of a reproductive engraving of a painting and possibly win an original work of art commissioned annually by the Art Union.[66]

William Ivins has noted that more prints were produced in the nineteenth century than in all previous centuries combined.[67] The trade was divided into specialized roles including publishers, engravers, printers, and print sellers.[68] From illustrations in books, periodicals, and newspapers, to expensive single sheet engravings and original etchings and lithographs, the printed image proliferated during the reign of Queen Victoria. In William Hogarth's London of the 1730s there were only twelve print sellers; by 1839 there were seventy-two and by 1892 the Printsellers' Association listed an impressive total of two hundred members.[69] By mid-century a flourishing trade had created a hierarchy ranging from street hawkers with 'penny plain, tuppence coloured' prints pinned to umbrellas, to large, glossy, elaborate engravings hanging in a descending order of value in the shop windows of family businesses such as Thomas McLean or Rudolph Ackermann.

Many factors played a role in the rapid expansion of the print trade, from advances in technology at the production end, to improvements in communication and transportation which improved advertising and distribution locally, nationally, and internationally.[70] Reforms in tax and copyright laws resulted in benefits such as the retraction of import duties on glass in 1845, which made possible the glazing of oversized prints.[71] Similarly, the repeals of duties on paper and on stamps for newspapers in 1861 had a positive effect on the market.

Within the printing industry sophisticated iron rolling presses replaced older wooden presses, and metal printing plates underwent a succession of improvements.[72] In the 1820s new steel plates permitted runs of thousands of prints, instead of hundreds, from a single plate or matrix. By the 1830s stereotypes allowed for the duplication of the printing matrix and the 1850s saw the introduction of steelfacing wherein a thin layer of hard steel could be applied to softer engraved copper plates.[73] New 'mixed-method' engraving using combinations of etching, mezzotint, aquatint, and stippling, along with devices such as 'ruling-machines' allowed large areas of the plate to be engraved quickly, and led to increasingly more mimetic reproductions.[74]

A flourishing print trade meant high commercial gain and the possibility of corruption. The Printsellers' Association attempted to regulate print production through a set of intricate guidelines and by requiring all proofs to be declared and stamped by the PSA.[75] Nevertheless, a bewildering array of 'proof' states were accepted, including artist's proofs, unlettered and lettered proofs, and India paper proofs, as well as vast editions of regular 'plain' prints.[76]

This method of sorting an edition anticipates today's 'limited edition' signed proofs, but 'rarity' was only an illusion given the enormous number of virtually identical impressions.[77] For *The Finding of the Saviour in the Temple* Gambart registered 1,000 'artist's proofs', 1,000 'before letters', and 1,000 'after letters' proofs. Similarly, for *The Shadow of Death* (published in 1877), the dealer Thomas Agnew registered a staggering 1,485 'artist's proofs', 600 signed and unsigned 'before letters' proofs, and 2,000 'lettered' proofs.[78] Agnew made over £20,000 from sales of the proofs alone.[79] In addition, dealers were not required to list the number of (potentially unlimited) plain impressions.

The art press regularly debated topics related to the print market, such as the role and effectiveness of the PSA, or the related controversial issue of copyright.[80] In 1736, the artist William Hogarth had been instrumental in establishing the first copyright law in the sphere of visual art which determined the legal rights of the individual artist. According to the 'Hogarth Act', an artist's prints were protected from piracy for fourteen years. Following the institution of this act, authorship rights, such as the recognition of the artist's relationship to his/her work and the reproduction of artwork were codified in numerous laws and conventions pertaining to intellectual property. A significant amendment by Act of Parliament on 29 July 1862 resulted in the Fine Art Copyright Law, which gave the author/artist copyright for life and seven years after his/her death if the work was registered. However, if the artist sold the copyright he/she no longer had the right to reproduce the work without consent of the copyright holder.[81] When the law was under review in 1879, Hunt argued that the artist should continue to retain control of this valuable commodity. As someone who owed much of his artistic success to the sale of reproductive engravings, Hunt maintained that the artist deserved to own and sell the copyright as recompense for his labours and as an incentive to produce higher quality work.[82]

In 1863 Ernest Gambart published a pamphlet *On Piracy of Artistic Copyright* in which he lamented the laxity of penalties for piracies: 'How defective the law is will appear when I state that I have appealed to it for protection, against pirates of artistic copyright, in nearly every Court, and, to my cost, found that none could help me.' He was particularly exercised since he had 'works as yet in the hands of the engravers, which require protection, amongst these are Mr. Holman Hunt's 'Finding of the Saviour in the Temple' ... How deeply I am interested in this question will be understood, when I state that for this ... picture I paid £5,500, the largest sum ever paid for a modern picture'.[83]

The problem was primarily with 'cheap photographic piracies' which seemed to proliferate particularly in smaller English towns.[84] Gambart launched twenty lawsuits related to *The Light of the World* alone, the most frequently pirated of his prints. Hunt appreciated Gambart's dilemma – if the engraving was not popular the dealer would lose money, but if the engraving was popular a photographer could pirate it; legal proceedings would cost the dealer £70 with the only penalty to the perpetrator being the loss of his camera.[85]

Closely related to this debate was the one related to the merits of photography versus engraving for the reproduction of paintings. Those who claimed engravers were translators or interpreters, and not mere 'ingenious mechanics', held that photography left no room for the master's hand, and sacrificed 'all the poetry of the original in a dead statement of facts'.[86] Hunt had an uneasy relationship with photography and was never keen to have small-scale photographic reproductions of his paintings published in books because he felt the integrity of his work would be compromised.[87] In 1857 Hunt explained that he did not want the publisher P. & D. Colnaghi to photograph his paintings for a volume of plates. He had 'a secret intention to etch [engrave]' his pictures and his 'chance of repayment for this expensive but more truthful and artistic means of representation' would be 'very much interfered with by the previous appearance of these photographs'.[88]

Nevertheless, by the 1870s processes such as photogravure were assuming the role previously held by engraving for reproductive printmaking. The demands of the market led to the ascendance of the process that was faster, cheaper and, in theory, resulted in more 'exact' copies. In the late 1880s and 1890s the Berlin Photographic Company and the Autotype Company published photogravures after Hunt's paintings. The artist was generally pleased but did not always find the results met his standards for accuracy. He occasionally found the image to be lacking in contrasting light and shade, and displaying characteristic perfectionism, he touched up hundreds of proofs by hand with black chalk 'to make the general effect true'.[89]

Such efforts indicate Hunt's recognition that the reproductive print market was inextricably tied to the paintings' market. Painters' reputations were made or broken by their successful navigation of this twinned structure, and fortunes were made by a select group of fashionable painters such as Hunt, William Frith, Edwin Landseer, and John Everett Millais, who were supported by prominent art dealers.[90]

In Hunt's case, a few dismal failures, including the engravings after *The Scapegoat, Claudio and Isabella*, and *Isabella and the Pot of Basil*, were overshadowed by the extraordinary success of the prints after *The Light of the World, The Finding of the Saviour in the Temple*, and *The Shadow of Death*.[91] While the laborious detail of his paintings generally translated well into reproductive engravings, the esoteric themes of some of his works puzzled and even repelled segments of the market. Other subjects clearly struck a chord, especially among the vast ranks of middle-class, Protestant Victorians who responded to both the 'sound workmanship' and the inspirational message.[92]

Hunt was not willing to modify his paintings to meet market expectations and, as the century progressed, he held fast to his increasingly out-of-fashion artistic ideals. His 'brand' did not essentially change over time although he continued to seek new marketing strategies to influence public and critical reception as well as financial outcomes. In 1873 Hunt contemplated donating his painting *The Shadow of Death*, product of his second trip to Jerusalem from 1869 to 1872, to a public museum. While 'gifting it to the nation' was certainly a generous philanthropic gesture, this was also a good marketing ploy which could only enhance his public image and increase sales of the related prints.[93] Instead, a deal was struck for *The Shadow of Death* with Thomas Agnew and Sons for the enormous price tag of £10,500. The package included the cost of the painting plus a quarter-size replica of the painting, exhibition rights, copyright to the engraving, and the artist's promise to supervise the engraving process and sign nearly 1,500 artist's proofs.

Near the end of his life, Hunt reached a new plateau in his quest to promote his artwork when he and his sponsor Charles Booth created one of the first travelling 'blockbuster' exhibitions. From 1905 to 1906 the large version of *The Light of the World* (St. Paul's Cathedral) was showcased in venues across Canada, South Africa, Australia, and New Zealand where it was promoted as a symbol of peace. The painting was seen by close to seven million people and was called 'the greatest religious allegory in English painting'.[94] This grand gesture marks the closing chapter in the narrative that had peaked with the artist's early success with *The Finding of the Saviour in the Temple*. It also underscores that Hunt never stopped looking for new and ingenious ways to promote his artistic vision.

Notes

I would like to thank the following people: in particular, Martha Tedeschi, Carol Jacobi, and Milijana Mladjan for reading drafts of the essay, and Paul Gilbert, Debbie Johnsen, Katharine Lochnan, Nicholas Tromans, and Ryan Whyte for advice and assistance.

1 *The Times*, 13 September 1910, p. 11; quoted in Bronkhurst, *Holman Hunt*, I, p. 3.
2 For an overview of the world of 'branding' see: Keller, *Strategic Brand Management*.

3 Richard Cobden & Co. Muslin and Calico Printers at 40 Cateaton Street, Aldermanbury. See Parry, 'Textile Background', pp. 57–9.

4 For Hunt's forays into a variety of media, see Bronkhurst, 'Holman Hunt's Picture Frames', p. 231; Bronkhurst, II, pp. 295–8; Parry, p. 71.

5 Fredeman, ed., *The P.R.B. Journal*, 13 August 1849, p. 10.

6 Fredeman, ed., *The P.R.B. Journal*, 24 December 1849, pp. 36, 118. Hunt became the 'go to' person for fellow PRB artists on technical matters related to etching. See also Hunt, *Pre-Raphaelitism*, I, p. 193; Fredeman, ed., *The P.R.B. Journal*, 22 January 1850, p. 45.

7 Bronkhurst lists a total of 161 paintings which includes a large number of minor works, copies of major paintings or incomplete studies. Bronkhurst, I.

8 See, for example, a review of a retrospective exhibition in 1906 in which the reviewer summarized the long-term appeal of Hunt's work while adding that 'beauty itself, the great essential, evaded him in his pursuit of unnecessary fact and irrelevant detail'. *Nation*, 25 October 1906; quoted in Bronkhurst, I, p. 35.

9 Letter from Hunt to Millais, 16 March 1854; quoted in Hunt, I, p. 381. See also: Bronkhurst, I, p. 174. For a discussion of the other printmaking ventures Hunt was contemplating while in the Middle East see, Rix, 'Prints', pp. 177, 179.

10 Maas, *Gambart*, p. 67.

11 Hunt to Thomas Combe, 10 July 1854; quoted ibid.

12 Hunt wanted the engraving to be 'extremely good, for a good engraving might get abroad to France and Germany, where they are very impudent about British art'. Hunt to Thomas Combe, 10 July 1854; quoted ibid.

13 Simmons used line and stipple engraving and was one of the finest Victorian engravers in the new 'mixed-method' techniques. The two year period was needed to engrave the plate.

14 John Ruskin's endorsement of the PRB appeared in two long letters to *The Times* in May 1851. In 1854 Ruskin wrote an influential article describing *The Light of the World* painting as 'one of the very noblest works of sacred art in this or any other age'. *The Times*, 5 May 1854, p. 9; Bronkhurst, I, pp. 11–12.

15 Maas, *Gambart*, p. 160.

16 Mane-Wheoki, 'The Light of the World', pp. 128–32. See also Maas, *Holman Hunt and the Light of the World*, pp. 73ff.

17 Bronkhurst, I, p. 44.

18 Hunt to Ruskin, 28 December 1857; quoted in Landow, '"Your Good Influence on Me"', p. 121.

19 Stephens, *William Holman Hunt and His Works*, p. 8.

20 A review in the *Art Journal*, June 1860 p. 182, for example, notes that the painting was the 'result of his prolonged seclusion'. F.G. Stephens writing in the *Athenaeum*, 25 February 1860, p. 274, notes that the 'long expected work … is on the very eve of completion'.

21 Jacobi describes Hunt's long, agonizing struggles to complete his paintings. Jacobi, *Holman Hunt*, pp. 228–59.

22 Hunt, I, p. 344; II, p. 187. Codell quotes his letters to Combe on various dates from 1853 to 1872. Codell, *Victorian Artist*, pp. 46, 49–50. The letters are in the Bodleian Library, University of Oxford. Codell also discusses the various personas Hunt developed in his memoirs which revolved around his conflicting presentations of himself as a suffering genius, the saviour of British nationalism, and a successful entrepreneur (pp. 138–41).

23 Hunt, II, pp. 136, 148, 169.

24 By comparison, Millais made twelve etchings and designed over 270 wood engravings. See Rix, 'Prints', pp. 171–88. Etching and wood engraving catered to specialized 'elite' audiences and ultimately Hunt was more interested in reaching the 'many' through reproductive engraving as opposed to the 'few' that could be reached through the medium of etching. See Tedeschi, 'The New Language of Etching', pp. 26–7.

25 Hunt, II, p. 184.

26 By March 1856, Ford Madox Brown, D.G. Rossetti, W.M. Rossetti, and Ernest Gambart had seen and admired the half-finished painting in Hunt's studio. Bronkhurst, I, p. 175. Hunt, II, p. 191 lists his visitors including the President of the Royal Academy, Charles Eastlake, and his wife.

27 Bronkhurst, I, p. 14. The election was held in November 1856.

28 Hunt, II, p. 191.

29 See Bayer, 'Marketing of Genius', pp. 51–2, and Bayer, 'Money as Muse', pp. 107–8.

30 Hunt, II, pp. 187–91. Macleod, *Art and the Victorian Middle Class*, p. 210, p. 255 fn. 10, suggests a method of computation to determine the amount in 1990s currency. £5,500 would equal approximately 1 million US dollars.

31 Hunt, II, p. 190.

32 Maas, *Gambart*, pp. 117–18.

33 Hunt, II, p. 193.

34 Hunt, II, pp. 188–90, 197. Hunt's 'business adviser' Charles Dickens chided him, 'You have caused my hatter to be madder than ever. He declares that you have choked up Bond Street with the carriages for your exhibition, so that none of his established customers can get to his shop.'

35 Amy Woolner, *Thomas Woolner, R.A. Sculptor and Poet. His Life in Letters* (London: Chapman and Hall, 1917), p. 193; quoted in Bronkhurst, I, p. 3.

36 Bronkhurst, I, p. 44; Hunt, II, p. 193.

37 Maas, *Gambart*, p. 128 and *Illustrated London News*, 13 October 1860, p. 337.

38 *Daily News*, 1 December 1873, describes how the *Shadow of Death* was displayed. The writer indicates that this was the usual presentation method for Hunt's works and lists previous paintings which had been shown this way including *The Finding of the Saviour in the Temple*, *The Afterglow in Egypt*, and *Isabella and the Pot of Basil*.

39 Bronkhurst, II, p. 314.

40 Luke 2:49.

41 Millais; quoted in Hunt, II, p. 193.

42 Letter from Hunt to Stephens, 25 May 1860, Bodleian Library; quoted in Bronkhurst, I, p. 173; see also p. 176.

43 *Manchester Guardian*, 24 April 1863. Quoted in Bennett, *Pre-Raphaelite Circle*, p. 80.

44 *Athenaeum*, 21 April 1860. The review is reproduced in Stephens, *William Holman Hunt and His Works*, pp. 85–8.

45 Stephens, *William Holman Hunt and His Works*. Gambart paid Stephens £30 to write the booklet. Hunt, II, p. 198.

46 Bronkhurst, I, pp. 6–8. However, from 1860 to 1873, the pamphlets issued with his paintings were largely descriptive rather than interpretive suggesting that interested viewers would still need to de-code the content on their own and that more than one interpretation was possible.

47 Hunt, II, p. 219.

48 Bennett, *Holman Hunt*, p. 79.

49 Bronkhurst, I, p. 196.

50 Hunt used a studio assistant, Albert Heywood, to help him with this version. Bronkhurst, I, p. 195. For a discussion of the proliferation and purposes of copies and replicas in the Victorian period, see Macleod, *Art and the Victorian Middle Class*, pp. 68–74.

51 Maas, *Gambart*, pp. 131–2. The original business proposition appears to have been drafted in November 1860.

52 Advertisement in the *Athenaeum*, 10 April 1869.

53 Maas, *Gambart*, p. 221.

54 Bayer, 'Money as Muse', pp. 147–83.

55 Stephens, *William Holman Hunt and His Works*, p. 79.

56 Noted in the *Athenaeum*, 24 August 1861, p. 256. This is probably the same Signor Morelli who made monochrome crayon copies of paintings in the National Gallery; photographs of these drawings were then sold as reproductions. Drawings also played an intermediary role in reproductive engraving where they were used to assist in transferring the image to the plate. *Fine Arts Quarterly Review* (n.s.), 2 (1867), pp. 391–7; cited in Fawcett, 'Graphic versus Photographic', p. 210, fn. 61.

57 French engravers had a reputation for doing fine work, especially in line-engraving. Gambart was criticized in the press for giving preference to French engravers over English ones. 'Line-engraving is at a low ebb in this country when preference is given to a foreigner.' *Art Journal*, November 1864, p. 347.

58 Stephens, *William Holman Hunt and His Works*, p. 79. Hunt visited Blanchard's studio and home outside Paris in 1867 and inspected the plate for *The Finding of the Saviour*. See Holman-Hunt, *My Grandfather*, pp. 257–8. Hunt was usually involved in 'superintending the engraving' and in the contract signed by Hunt and Gambart, Hunt agreed that the 'engraving will be made entirely from the said drawing, which, being made with the assistance of Hunt, will be in every way satisfactory to engrave from'. For the *Shadow of Death* he wrote to William Agnew to say 'It seems scarcely necessary to add that I should be glad to give

you my help as usual in such cases to superintend the engraving.' In addition to providing the copy, Hunt agreed to give the engraver all 'necessary instructions', to 'inspect and touch upon' artists' proofs and sign all the artists' proofs'. Contract with Agnew's; quoted in Engen, *Pre-Raphaelite Prints*, p. 51.

59   Engen, p. 49. In November 1860 Gambart projected that the printing costs for the engraving would be 3,000 guineas. Bayer, 'Money as Muse', p. 164, fn. 361.

60   Maas, *Gambart*, p. 229.

61   Hunt to John Tupper, 19 December 1867; quoted in Coombs, ed. *A Pre-Raphaelite Friendship*, no. 54, p. 81.

62   *Art Journal*, May 1868, p. 100.

63   For a fuller discussion see: Tedeschi, 'How Prints Work', pp. 82–9, and Tedeschi, '"Where the Picture Cannot Go"', pp. 8–19.

64   *Art Journal*, November 1853, p. 308; quoted in Tedeschi, 'How Prints Work', p. 14, fn. 1.

65   When *The Shadow of Death* painting travelled to the north of England members of the working class were able to purchase impressions of the engraving on an instalment plan.

66   For a fuller description of the practices of the Art Union see Tedeschi, 'How Prints Work', pp. 60ff., and King, *The Industrialization of Taste*. Two paintings by Hunt were chosen as Art Union prizes: *Dr. Rochecliffe Performing Divine Service in the Cottage of Joceline Joliffe, at Woodstock* (1847) and *The Flight of Madeline and Porphyro (The Eve of St. Agnes)* (1858). His etchings of *The Abundance of Egypt* and *The Desolation of Egypt* were published by the Art Union as part of a series submitted by the Etching Club in 1857.

67   Ivins, *Prints and Visual Communication*, p. 93.

68   Well-known printers included Dixon & Ross, McQueen, Lemercier, Cadart, and Brugman. Printers rarely worked exclusively for the fine art trade, often printing book illustrations, maps, stamps, and banknotes. For an in-depth look at the business side of the print trade see, Dyson, *Pictures to Print*; Beck, *Victorian Engravings*; and Verhoogt, *Art in Reproduction*. There was a significant increase in the number of printers from twenty-one in 1822–23 to fifty-two by 1852. Tedeschi, 'How Prints Work', p. 51.

69   Rix, *Pictures for the Parlour*, p. 60. Pigot's *Directory* of 1839 lists seventy-two printsellers and print publishers. Maas, *Gambart*, p. 122.

70   By mid-century American dealers were coming to Europe to buy prints.

71   Wax, *Mezzotint*, p. 117.

72   Dyson, *Pictures to Print*, pp. 105–11.

73   'A Process of Hardening Engraved Copper Plates', *Art Journal*, December 1858, p. 356 lists four 'Art-Auxilliaries': lithography, hardening of steel plates, photography, and the steel facing of copper plates.

74   A change in shoe styles led to a proliferation of available stipple engravers who were no longer needed as 'buckle-punchers'. Tedeschi, '"Where the Picture Cannot Go"', p. 89, fn. 25; Beck, p. 20.

75 *Alphabetical List of Engravings.* For example, p. 18, Rule 16 states: 'No Member or Members shall publish impressions in any state of the plate bearing the autograph either of the painter or engraver, other than Artists' proofs.' And p. 16, First schedule: they were to be stamped as follows: 'Artists' proofs at the left hand corner, all other classes of proofs at the right hand corner.'

76 Sharper impressions were possible using India paper which was smoother and more pliant than the standard wove paper. Wax, p. 103.

77 Lambert, *The Image Multiplied*, pp. 32–3.

78 Declared by Thomas Agnew and Sons, 13 July 1877.

79 Plomer, 'Agnew's', p. 65.

80 *Art Journal*, April 1860, p. 126. The writer suggested that the copyright debate was a matter of 'extreme delicacy' and hoped that 'while the good was obtained, the evil will be avoided'. The debate revolved, in part, around whether artists should be allowed to retain copyright on their paintings and whether copyright should be a saleable commodity.

81 See, Verhoogt, pp. 158–88; Sherman and Bently, *Making of Modern Intellectual Property Law*; Bently and Kretschmer, eds. *Primary Sources on Copyright*; and Plowman and Hamilton, *Copyright*.

82 William Holman Hunt, 'Artistic Copyright', *Nineteenth Century*, March 1879, pp. 418–24. Hunt implies that if the artist was allowed to own and sell the copyright, he would have sufficient income to devote his efforts toward the production of high quality artwork. Bayer, 'Money as Muse', p. 238, notes that in 1897 copyrights of paintings ceased to be a property independent of the original work and that the owner of a work of art also owned its copyright.

83 Gambart, *On Piracy*, p. 3.

84 Gambart, p. 13. According to Gambart photographic piracies of *The Light of the World* engraving appeared in a variety of sizes in the town of Brighton; they were produced quickly and cheaply and were all poor quality.

85 Hunt, II, pp. 95–6, and Hunt, 'Artistic Copyright', p. 421. See also: Tedeschi, 'How Prints Work', p. 127; Maas, *Gambart*, pp. 68, 159ff.

86 Ruskin, *The Works of John Ruskin*, XIX, p. 89; quoted in Fawcett, p. 207. Henri Delaborde, article in *Revue des Deux Mondes*, 1856; cited in Fawcett, p. 193.

87 Ray, *Illustrator and the Book*, p. 139. An exception was the group of photogravure illustrations of five of Hunt's best-known paintings in Sir Edwin Arnold's volume, *The Light of the World, or the Great Consummation*, quarto edition, 1893. See: Bronkhurst, II, p. 196, pp. 282–4.

88 2 November 1857; quoted in Ray, p. 139.

89 Hunt, II, pp. 343, 378. This occurred with the proofs of the photogravures of *The Triumph of the Innocents* and *May Morning on Magdalen Tower*.

90 Bayer, 'Money as Muse', p. 166. Bayer cites the important influence wielded by dealers. Some artists appear to have customized their paintings for reproduction. Tedeschi, 'How Prints Work', pp. 25–8; Dyson, 'Landseer and the Engraving Trade'; and the essay on Millais by Malcolm Warner in the present volume.

91 *The Scapegoat* was engraved by Charles Mottram and published by Henry Graves and Co. on 29 November 1861; *Claudio & Isabella* was engraved by W.H. Simmons and published by Gambart on 8 June 1864; and, *Isabella; or, The Pot of Basil* was engraved by Auguste Blanchard and published by Gambart on 29 September 1869. Maas, *Gambart*, p. 219. Maas quotes a letter from Gambart to Hunt, 19 July 1869, 'The Isabella Engraving pleases but few sell, the subject being against it –'.

92 Hunt maintained that the poor always looked for 'sterling purpose and sound workmanship'. Letter to M.H. Spielmann, August 1889, Rylands Library; quoted in Bronkhurst, I, p. 6.

93 Bayer suggests that Hunt recognized that the removal of one of the painting's commercial properties would increase the value of the two remaining – copyright and exhibition rights. Bayer, 'Money as Muse', p. 173, fn. 386.

94 *Toronto World*, 13 June 1905, p. 4; quoted in Mane-Wheoki, p. 128. See also: Maas, *Holman Hunt and the Light of the World*.

12

Negotiating a reputation: J.M. Whistler, D.G. Rossetti, and the art market 1860–1900

Patricia de Montfort

In 1865 Rossetti wrote to his friend Frederic Shields to congratulate him on his election to the Old Watercolour Society. Although he assured Shields that 'competition & due appreciation are among an artist's best privileges', the event also seems to have reminded him of his own isolation from the public exhibition system: 'I hope you do not suspect me', he wrote, 'of any pigheaded or antagonistic notions as to the natural ways of coming before the public. I simply found in youth that the worry of getting ready for exhibitions was unsuited to my disposition.'[1] Rossetti was aged thirty-seven and exhibited only rarely[2] – it had been over five years since he had exhibited privately at the Hogarth Club.[3] His absence from public exhibition remained a matter of public comment – in 1877, he felt compelled to write to *The Times* to explain his absence from the opening exhibition of the Grosvenor Gallery: 'What holds me back', he declared, 'is simply the lifelong feeling of dissatisfaction which I have experienced from the disparity of aim and attainment in what I have all my life produced as best I could'.[4]

Rossetti's self-diagnostic remarks should be seen against a mid-nineteenth-century landscape of burgeoning art institutions and art audiences. Critics were quite clear that the role of art works was to be publicly seen: 'The exhibition', wrote his brother William Michael, 'is the accepted mart of artistic work: public patronage demands it'.[5] The modern exhibition system was about speed and supply: '[it] heaps together productions of all subjects and styles, induces artists to work up to a certain level of effectiveness, which is quite as likely to be detrimental as otherwise, and hurries them on to catch a particular day, whether the work is really completed to the best of their power or not'.[6] Neither of these elements resonated with Rossetti's painstaking and anxiety-ridden artistic practice.

Whistler, too, was self-conscious about his relationship to the art marketplace. He wrote to his lawyer Anderson Rose during his libel case against Ruskin in 1878:

> I am *known* and *always have been known* to hold an independent position in Art and to have had the Academy opposed to me … I don't stand in the position of the popular picture maker with herds of admirers – My Art is quite apart from the usual stuff furnished in the mass … In defending me it would be bad policy to try and make me out a different person than the well-known Whistler … more is to be gained by sticking to that character.[7]

Whistler's instincts were with private enterprise and self-determination: after the initial rejection of his *Arrangement in Grey and Black: Portrait of the Painter's Mother* at the Royal Academy in 1872, he never exhibited there again. Beginning with his first solo exhibition at the Flemish Gallery, No. 48, Pall Mall in 1874,[8] he developed distinctive strategies for the display of his work outside the public exhibition system. These focused upon using smaller-scale private gallery spaces to exhibit his works together in a carefully orchestrated fashion and the creation of a sympathetic decorative scheme.[9]

The successful promotion of Whistler's artistic wares was dependent upon the ever increasing presence of the modern media. In 1874, the critic Sidney Colvin was impressed by the simplicity and low-key display, 'pleasantly matted, tinted and arranged' of Whistler's gallery which he contrasted to the 'importunate arrangements of certain well-known galleries in Bond Street'.[10] In 1877, Whistler (in importunate vein himself) angered his most important patron Frederick Leyland by inviting press and public to view his latest decorative scheme, the Peacock Room (which incorporated his oil, *La Princesse du pays de la porcelaine*). He also printed an explanatory pamphlet that was distributed to visitors, thus turning Leyland's private house not only into a palace of art but a *public* palace of art. The following year, Whistler agreed that the Ruskin libel case had been a valuable 'advertisement'[11] for his work upon which he hoped to capitalize.[12] Whilst the conditions of the marketplace changed in the late 1880s and 1890s, opening up more possibilities to work with dealers in his own fashion and to circulate his works abroad, this spirit of independence and enterprise remained a constant in Whistler's relations with the marketplace through the intervening years.[13]

Here, it seems, are two artists at odds with the conventional workings of the mid-nineteenth-century marketplace that depended upon the interaction of the public exhibition system (led by the Royal Academy), the auction room, and the dealer. Each had differing survival instincts, despite moving in similar artistic circles and sharing art patrons. Both countered nineteenth-century notions of linear progress and order through the art principles they espoused – Rossetti via the principles of the early Brotherhood, which rejected the notion of a progressive kind of representationalism in art since the Renaissance, and Whistler through his refusal to equate time and labour with pictorial completeness and monetary value. But, while their selling strategies and other art market activities are documented, notably in their published correspondence,[14] the context for this is less well understood. Nor is their contribution to the emergence of new modes of art market activity towards the end of the nineteenth century. Juxtaposed, they create a vivid and more complete picture of how astute commercial practices and a well-spun artistic persona became crucial elements in the re-invention of the modern artist. While these elements have been accounted for in existing scholarly work, in relation both to art (Andrew Stephenson's essay on Whistler in *English Art 1860–1914*, for example)[15] and literature (Regenia Gagnier's study of Wilde, *Idylls of the Marketplace: Oscar Wilde and the Victorian Public*),[16] I argue that investigation of the tactics of individual artists demands a comparative approach that, given wider application, may prove richly rewarding.

Rossetti

Rossetti's reluctance to place himself in the public spotlight created an air of romantic mysticism around him.[17] But, at the beginning at least, ambition and social convention led Rossetti (along with Whistler)[18] towards the Royal Academy and the public judgement of their peers. In Rossetti's case, artistic education was a family affair: in the summer of 1843, he wrote in a letter to his mother Frances: 'You wish me to inform you of my progress in drawing, and of the time at which I hope to become a student of the Academy.' Rossetti goes on to explain his progress towards admission to the Academy Schools but this is coupled with anxiety about his knowledge of anatomy and a deep-rooted fear of rejection: 'very few have the courage to venture on a second trial after the disgrace of a rejection'.[19] This concern about institutional structures and politics permeates Rossetti's view of the marketplace.[20] It may well have influenced also his attendance at the Royal Academy Schools, which amounted only to a year from 1846 to 1847.

In his letter to Shields, Rossetti wrote of his youthful 'misplaced pride' that led him to hold himself aloof from the Royal Academy, 'which I considered (not quite untruly) unfair in its practices'. As well as temperamental disinclination, Rossetti declared his mistrust of its selection policies, reflecting a commonly held view of the Academy. This youthful fear and mistrust metamorphosed into a self-professed philosophy: 'in after life I have adhered to my plan of non-exhibition because I think it is well to adopt early a plan of life & not lose time afterwards in giving second thoughts to it'.[21] Rossetti here creates a positive narrative around the reluctance to exhibit (and potential failure associated with it) that he felt compelled to reiterate.[22] While it is unclear whether Rossetti made a conscious decision[23] to withdraw from the exhibition scene (writing in retrospect in 1865, it was convenient to take this position) his self-imposed situation made it necessary to acquire a circle of supportive patrons.

Who were they? William Michael Rossetti listed his principal buyers from the 1860s and 1870s as follows: 'James Leathart, … George Rae, Frederick R. Leyland, William Graham, and Leonard R. Valpy, and in a minor degree James Anderson Rose, George Clabburn, and Lord Mount-Temple … Messrs Clarence Fry, Constantine Ionides, and William A. Turner'.[24] It was impressive array of patrons, many of whom knew each other. This generated a competitive atmosphere among them in which Rossetti could offer first option on whichever work he judged might appeal to a particular patron. Their loyalty insulated him to a significant degree from the fluctuating fortunes of the art market.[25] Indeed, Rossetti claimed the year 1866, a 'panic year', dominated by a banking crisis and a cholera epidemic, to be commercially 'much my best as yet'.[26]

Leathart and Leyland formed two of the most important collections. Introduced to Rossetti by William Bell Scott, Leathart shared the poetical tastes of his artists and proved a reliable patron. When Leathart bought *Christ and Peter*[27] in August 1859, Rossetti wrote triumphantly that the sale showed 'a steadiness in him viewed as a victim of Art in the future'.[28] Leyland was a stiff, aloof figure who harried Rossetti for his pictures and was forthright in his opinions. But he was straightforward in his business dealings and, almost without exception, he paid prices Rossetti asked, often advancing him loans as well. On occasion, Leyland and Leathart assisted Rossetti with his efforts to control the market value of his works, a matter over which he kept a watchful eye. In c.1874, for example, he enlisted Leyland's help to dispose of a *Lucrezia* drawing at Christie's sale-room: 'Would you mind sending in as yours that little Lucrezia …? If so, I could forward it in your name to the Auctioneers, putting a reserved price of £100. An early — very early — & very quaint thing of mine, painted at 21, was bought by Agnew the other day at Christie's for nearly 400£ … so it might perhaps answer to send this little drawing'.[29] Here, attaching Leyland's name to the work aids in its resale and creates the possibility of inflating its value.

That these patrons were drawn from provincial cities outside London distanced Rossetti from the need to engage with the Royal Academy and other London-based institutions.[30] A further consequence of their patronage was that they helped his works to remain publicly visible. While he was fearful of his patrons lending works to exhibitions without his consent,[31] he did agree, through the intercession of an old and trusted patron John Miller,[32] to allow an oil, *Fazio's Mistress (Aurelia)* (1863–73), to be sent to the Liverpool Academy in 1864. Rossetti's works were otherwise rarely exhibited publicly until posthumous shows of his works took place in 1883 (notably at the Royal Academy). However, the exhibition history of such works as *Aurelia* indicates that his patrons did a good deal to increase the visibility of his work after his death. George Rae, for instance, lent *Aurelia* to the Royal Academy in 1883; the Walker Art Gallery, Liverpool, in 1886; and the Guildhall, London, in 1892.[33]

As his collectors' interest in contemporary avant-garde art grew, Rossetti recommended numerous artists to Leathart: Elizabeth Siddal and J.W. Inchbold in June 1857; Edward Burne-Jones in c.1859; Whistler in February 1863, and Alphonse Legros in December 1863.[34] Rossetti, in effect, became an adept amateur dealer from the private world of the studio, matching artist to the taste of collector. But Rossetti also felt the age-old tension between artistic producer and consumer and at times displayed a contempt for his 'cotton-spinner' clients, telling his mother in 1866 of his relief that the oil *Beata Beatrix* (1864), 'a poetic work', was to go to William Cowper, a senior civil servant with aristocratic connections, 'where it will be seen by cultivated folks'.[35]

Indeed it was the complicated nature of his relationship with a patron and its ultimate end in July 1861 that hastened Rossetti's acquaintance with the world of the high-stake dealer:[36] the Leeds stockbroker and collector Thomas Plint died suddenly. Plint had been in the habit of paying for works in random instalments.[37] The situation left Rossetti, Burne-Jones, and others in the position of having to supply a number of works outstanding to the Plint estate.[38] The Belgian dealer Ernest Gambart was chief among Plint's creditors and an executor of the estate.

Rossetti's acquaintance with Gambart seems to date from 1859 (or possibly earlier),[39] but the relationship failed to flourish, perhaps due to Gambart's reputed ability to drive a hard bargain and the presence of established patrons like Plint and Leathart. But Plint's death (and recent troubles with another patron, the surgeon John Marshall) altered the situation – Rossetti owed three pictures to Plint, a total of £714, according to Rossetti.[40] While the situation with the Plint estate caused Rossetti considerable grief – Gambart seems to have become impatient and begun pressing him for repayment of the advances[41] – it did bring him closer acquaintance with Gambart's business transactions.[42] By 1865, Rossetti's pictures were fetching high prices and Gambart was recast in a letter as 'the great dealer' who had just sold *The Blue Bower* (1865) privately to a Manchester collector for 1,500 guineas.[43] As with his private circle of patrons, Rossetti took an interventionist approach to the process of selling his work through dealers: 'It is of course my interest to help him in getting the highest prices he can for my works, and not express the least discontent at his being the first to profit to such extent by the market he creates for them.'[44] What is important to Rossetti is less the price fetched by the resale of a single picture[45] and more the impact of that sale upon the market. Thus Gambart's role is to facilitate Rossetti's behind the scenes attempts to manipulate the overall market for his works.[46] This brought tensions as William Michael's diary entry, dated 22 May 1872, suggests:

> Gambart wants to engrave Gabriel's large picture of *The Death of Beatrice*: he would entrust the work to Blanchard. What he proposes is that Gabriel should paint a smaller replica of the picture, which Gambart would buy for 1000 guineas, and get engraved, retaining all ensuing interest in the copyright[.] he says he would have to pay £1600 to Blanchard. Gabriel would not accept the proposed £1000, but would probably take £1500, subject to making proper enquiry to ascertain whether the terms demanded by Blanchard are really such as to preclude Gambart from leaving to Gabriel any interest in the copyright. He is to some extent disinclined to close with the offer, having lately come to a strong resolve to do no more duplicates of any kind from his pictures.[47]

While Gambart's art market activity here was little different than that undertaken for artists like Holman Hunt, Rossetti's aversion to being controlled by the machinations of an individual dealer is discernible. For Rossetti, the business of shaping the market for his works was as much about his private correspondence with patrons like Leyland and George Rae as about Christie's sale-room or his dealings with Gambart.

By the 1870s, Rossetti's success with dealers seems to have mellowed his attitude towards the public display of his work. Early in 1873, unsure of what to do with *Dante's Dream at the Time of the Death of Beatrice* (1856), then still in the studio, Rossetti seems to have considered exhibiting it, possibly with Gambart or Agnew.[48] In addition, Rossetti had long recognized the value of reproductions in the sale of his work, devising a scheme to publish 'my works in photography' in quarterly parts, 'the best thing just now I can do for publicity as a non-exhibiting painter'.[49] If he shrank, then, from the public exhibition system, he did seek exposure for his work through smaller, more controllable channels.

Nor did Rossetti ignore another modern-day pillar of the art market – the art press. From 1860, critics ensured that Rossetti remained visible in the press through regular references to his work, notably F.G. Stephens, in his 'Fine Art Gossip' column in the *Athenaeum*.[50] That this visibility was largely mediated textually by the press (led by Stephens and his brother), helped to reinforce a degree of otherworldliness about Rossetti in the public mind. Swinburne, too, another intimate and sometime resident of Rossetti's house at Cheyne

Walk, promoted this view in his eulogy to Rossetti in *Notes to the Royal Academy Exhibition* (1868): 'It is well known that the painter of whom I now propose to speak has never suffered exclusion of acceptance at the hand of any academy. To such acceptance or such rejection all other men of any note have been and may be liable.'[51] Rossetti, the astute dealer-artist, who earned substantial sums for his pictures in his lifetime and concerned himself greatly with what was written about him, became represented in the press as a kind of artist-ascetic, aloof from the institutional politics of the academy.[52]

These comments should be viewed against the background of a nineteenth-century world which, whilst representing a growth point for the global dissemination of images, had limited contexts for viewing works of art (in both original and reproductive form). The viewing of art works involved a visit to a gallery (largely concentrated in major commercial centres) or the purchase of a magazine or engraved reproduction. Advertising was still dominated by text, though this situation changed rapidly as the century progressed. As Rossetti well knew, audiences experienced art works through literary description at least as often as through direct experience in an art gallery. The lack of physical visibility of Rossetti's art works and the regular trickle of press reportage about them thus served to intensify focus on the figure of the artist himself as a kind of romantic genius. As William Fredeman has memorably put it, Rossetti gained 'a reputation incommensurate with his public exposure'.[53] In the end, Rossetti's commercial success (notably with his poetical subjects of the 1860s) became enmeshed with an increasing public mythology around his personality.

Whistler

'I will not have myself *presented* by anyone – or excused – or explained.'[54] So wrote Whistler to his dealer David Croal Thomson in April 1892, as his landmark retrospective exhibition, *Nocturnes, Marines & Chevalet Pieces*, confirmed his reputation in the public eye as a modern master. At this moment his works were entering public collections – beginning with his portrait of Thomas Carlyle,[55] acquired by the City of Glasgow in 1891. In the autumn of 1891, aided by Thomson, *Arrangement in Grey and Black: Portrait of the Painter's Mother* (1871) was exhibited at Goupil's Paris, as Helmreich describes in this volume, and this led to its sale to the Musée du Luxembourg for 4,000 francs – the first Whistler to enter a French national collection. The London press reacted to the sale of the *Mother* by anticipating a rise in the value of his works and, to the Whistlers' amusement, lamenting the loss of the picture from England.[56] Thomson also attempted to secure a work for the British public collections, writing to Whistler not long before the retrospective exhibition opened: 'We want to get some M.

P. to ask the Government if they propose to buy a "Whistler" for the National Gallery. It will advertise the show & we want to make an effort to have one of your works there.'[57] The exhibition was not just about commercial success but became an agent in the passage of Whistler's works to public collections and in the consolidation of his long-term critical reputation.

These were crucial moments in the resurgence of Whistler's critical and fiscal fortunes: the financial and professional consequences of his clash with Ruskin years earlier, in 1878, had been profound, leaving him bankrupt with few prospects of commissions. The memory of the trial lingered, despite the growing clamour of partisan critics in the press such as R.A.M. Stevenson, Malcolm Salaman, and the Pennells. London and the Goupil Gallery seemed good places to kick-start one's fortunes; the city was firmly integrated in a globalizing network of dealers in which the Goupil firm was a leading player (as Helmreich describes here). Sensing a momentum building, Thomson urged Whistler during the winter of 1891–92: 'Let us now gather together your paintings and make a very big splash.'[58] The exhibition of 44 works took place in late January and February 1892 for three weeks only – as Whistler put it, 'much

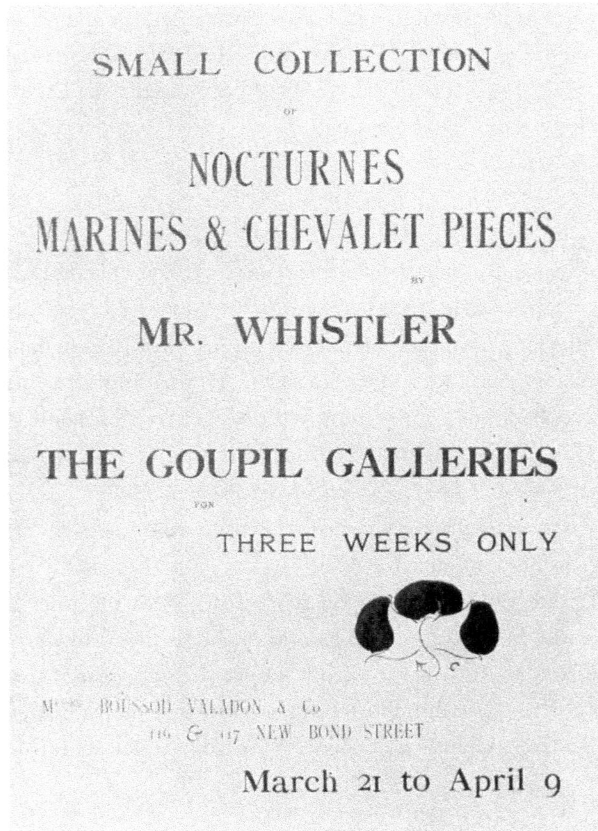

12.1
Poster for Whistler's exhibition 'Nocturnes, Marines & Chevalet Pieces', held at the Goupil Gallery in 1892. Reproduced in J. and E.R. Pennell, *The Whistler Journal* (Philadelphia: J.P. Lippincott Co., 1921, facing p. 10).

more smart and select – and rare' (figure 12.1).[59] Although the exhibition was a resounding success critically, business was difficult to accomplish in the crowded conditions of the gallery and Thomson sounded a warning: 'we must hope that the recompense of the lucre will not be wanting'.[60] The Americans, upon whom Whistler had been relying increasingly, were not buying in London.[61] As Thomson reported gloomily a few months later: 'We have a good many "looking around" & we give them every attention, but they don't buy.'[62]

As Thomson also noted, business was further dampened by political uncertainty around the forthcoming elections in which the Liberal MP William Ewart Gladstone was elected to his fourth and final term as Prime Minister, succeeding the Marquess of Salisbury.[63] Of three possible commissions from aristocratic patrons[64] that summer, only one materialized, a portrait of Sir William Eden. Nor did matters improve in the autumn: 'There is no business of any kind in London', he told Whistler.[65] The paucity of business also owed something to the wider picture. Agricultural depression in the 1890s prompted the disposal by aristocratic families of a steady trickle of masterpieces through the salerooms. Prices slowed, as did the market for art. More crucially for contemporary art, the gallery scene during the early 1890s was interrupted by a catastrophic financial scandal involving Baring's bank, one of the leading and oldest established banking houses in Europe. The Argentine government defaulted on substantial loans overseen by the bank that had depended greatly on English private capital.

Thomson wrote in March 1893:

Things are *very bad* in London & they will not be better for some time yet until this Baring business altogether disappears. So far as I know none of your pictures have recently changed hands, but we are trying to sell one for the owner – I have promised him not to give his name at the present. But in *confidence* I will tell you it is the Lange Leizen & we ask £800 only for it. I feel as if I am putting my head in the lions mouth in telling you, but there is nothing to be upset about I assure you for the owner is simply 'hard up'.[66]

Thomson's hope that the Government might purchase a Whistler for the National Gallery seemed also to have faded.

Hence, whilst Whistler's pursuit of galleries and collectors abroad during the 1890s owes a good deal to his uneasy relationship with the London critical and artistic establishment, there were sound reasons to focus attention on other centres of artistic commerce – Paris, Munich, Berlin, New York, Chicago, and Boston. Aided by contacts such as the British diplomat James Rennell Rodd in Germany, and the dealer Wunderlich in New York, he made a concerted effort to show comprehensive selections of his work in thriving centres of artistic activity and patronage. In 1892, he sent four nocturnes, a seascape, and his portrait, *Harmony in Pink and Grey: Portrait of Lady Meux* (1881–82) to the Société Nationale des Beaux-Arts in Paris, a breakaway group from the Société des artistes français with an intended constituency of well-heeled bourgeois collectors. Between 1891 and 1901 he exhibited twice in Berlin and three times in Munich.[67] Rodd urged him to focus on Munich: 'Munich is much more important artistically than Berlin, in fact whereas Berlin is a city of politics and finance, Munich is entirely consecrated to the Muses ... and there are lots of gold medals going about'.[68] Whistler would later send a comprehensive selection of his work to the 6th Munich Internationale Kunst-Austellung, 1892.

But whilst these international exhibitions offered encouraging signs, they did not result in the flood of public acquisitions that Whistler might have hoped for. Indeed, the Goupil exhibition was barely over before a number of Whistler's patrons, many of whom had owned his works since the early days of his career, saw an opportunity to sell. In June 1892, John Cavafy sold five works, including *The Last of Old Westminster* (1862) and *Battersea Reach* (c.1863), to the New York dealer E.G. Kennedy for £650.[69] A year later, John Gerald Potter sold *Symphony in White No. 2: The Little White Girl* (1864) for a large profit,[70] followed by *Blue and Silver: Blue Wave, Biarritz* (1862) in about September 1894 for £1,000.[71]

Whistler was shaken by this and embittered by what he saw as their profiteering: whilst, like Rossetti, he accepted that dealers could make vast profits on the sale of his works since it inflated the overall value of his work, he resented what he called the 'amateur tradesmen',[72] that is, patrons, carrying out backroom deals. Abroad, preferably France, was the best place for his works, he thought: 'I do want them to be got out of England!'[73] In Paris, his friendships with Monet, Duret, and the Symbolist poet Stephane Mallarmé absorbed him into the circle of Mirbeau and Huysmans, Henri de Régnier, and André Gide. The poet and aesthete Robert de Montesquiou introduced him to upper echelons of Parisian society and to his cousin Elizabeth, Comtesse Greffulhe, patron of artists. De Montesquiou commissioned a portrait, *Arrangement in Black and Gold: Comte Robert de Montesquiou-Fezensac*, in 1891. But despite Whistler's belief that he would be appreciated in Paris, the New York dealer E.G. Kennedy attempted to persuade him that America offered better material success: 'I notice that most the painters in Paris depend on the foreign markets, the disliked English or the derided American being especially desirable ... This French "appreciation" has rather a wearying effect after a while. Appreciation in the form of dollars and cents is more practical.'[74]

In fact, Whistler was already beginning to realize this, telling the Scottish dealer Alexander Reid in June 1892 that *La Princesse du pays de la porcelaine* (1864) should be exhibited at the World's Columbian Exposition in Chicago the following year, as he believed that it offered commercial opportunities. 'There', he wrote, 'is where all the thousands will come to you for these pictures of mine.'[75] And Americans *were* buying enthusiastically by the mid-1890s. Chief among them was the railroad-man Charles Lang Freer, a Whistler patron since 1890. In Freer Whistler found a compliant patron of advanced aesthetic taste and ultimately a gallery in Washington DC for his works to go on public display for perpetuity. Having sold *Rose and Brown: La Cigale* (1899?), and *Rose and Gold: The Little Lady Sophie of Soho* (1898/99) to Freer, he wrote: 'I think I may tell you without the least chance of being misunderstood, that I wish you to have a fine collection of Whistlers!! – perhaps *The* collection.'[76] Over the next few years, Whistler alerted Freer whenever important works came on the market as well as supplying works directly from the studio. He recognized that encouraging the preservation and large-scale accumulation of his work in one place was crucial for the long-term survival of his reputation.

The Chicago Exposition was also successful in another sense: it led to the display of Whistler's works in Philadelphia and the eventual purchase (in 1895) of his *Arrangement in Black: La Dame au brodequin jaune – Portrait of Lady Archibald Campbell* (1882) for the Philadelphia Museum of Art. It was the first Whistler art work to enter an American museum. The purchase was aided by a new American patron, John Graver Johnson, a lawyer and serious art collector, who had recently purchased *Purple and Rose: The Lange Leizen of the Six Marks* (1864). Artist admirers, too, rallied to encourage the sale of Whistler's works to other museums – William Merritt Chase and Julian Alden Weir campaigned to have the *White Girl* purchased by the Metropolitan Museum of Art in New York.[77] The Museum of Fine Art in Boston considered purchasing the *Fur Jacket* before choosing *The Little Rose of Lyme Regis* (1895); *The Master Smith of Lyme Regis* (1895–96) instead.

Hence, by the mid-1890s, Whistler was becoming an ever more intensely international artist with an international network of patrons. Throughout this time, he followed closely the labyrinthine movement of his works around the world. This is vividly illustrated by a letter to his Scottish dealer Alexander Reid which documents the progress of *Arrangement in Black and Brown: The Fur Jacket* (1876) over a period of months from the Munich International Exhibition in 1892, to Reid in Glasgow, to Kennedy in New York, and finally to the World's Columbian Exposition at Chicago.[78]

By the late 1890s, then, Whistler's works became a shifting commodity moving between different countries and capitals. Exhibition societies as well as dealer networks enabled him to maintain momentum: societies in art centres across Europe– the Secessionists in Vienna and Berlin, the Société Nationale des Beaux-Arts, and the Société Internationale de Peinture et de Sculpture in Paris encouraged the participation of honorary artist members, as did international exhibitions of fine art in Venice and Munich and of art and industry like the Chicago Exposition of 1893 and the Paris Exposition Universelle 1900. Amidst all this activity, Whistler began to be claimed as a distinguished artistic son of Britain, France, and America[79] – his career and varied artistic heritage seemed to fit not only with romantic notions of the outsider genius but also a turn-of-the-century desire for a universal kind of artistic narrative.

It is clear, then, that Rossetti and Whistler proved that loyalty to the traditions of the academic system was not a prerequisite for commercial and critical success. Both attempted to negotiate the art market on their own terms, therein creating innovation in the presentation and sale of art. They also exploited capitalistically their contacts in the modern day press. Through temperamental inclination and necessity, Rossetti masterminded his own system of patronage and commercial transaction, one that enabled him to exert control over the market for his art from his studio, having rejected the exhibition conventions of the day. Whistler, by contrast, made the public exhibition gallery his focus – from his earliest solo exhibition in 1874 to the Goupil exhibition of 1892, he attempted to control its space via décor, guests, and press reports. His letters to the press and spats with artists and critics amplified his witty, brittle public persona. Whilst it is unlikely that Whistler had a defined exhibition policy during the 1890s, I suggest that a number of circumstances coincided to enable him to strategize the exhibition of his work and secure a place for his works in public collections.

Taken together, the approaches of the two artists contribute strongly towards new models for the modern day commercial transaction of art: in Rossetti's case, he is brought to attention by a leading critic (Ruskin), supported by a small private circle of patrons among whom he sets out to create a competitive internal market; Whistler ensures that his work becomes known through a variety of channels and demonstrates a well-learned knowledge of market segmentation (notably through his marketing of his prints). Over time, he intensifies his focus on the international stage and his works travel the world in a dense, shifting pattern of exhibition activity. The work of both artists becomes packaged and fetishized in its presentation (in such matters as titles of art works, framing, display, and photographic reproduction). Purchasers are encouraged to buy into the mindset of the artists.[80]

While their desire to carve out a secure marketplace for their works might be regarded as normative behaviour when compared with other artists covered in this volume, I would argue that the two men possessed strongly individualistic character traits that led them to cultivate outsider status – both, after all, shared an immigrant background involving revolution and dislocation. They also possessed hyper-awareness of how persona could help situate their art within a globalized cultural map that went beyond the narrow boundaries of day to day commercial transaction.

The activities of both artists developed at a crucial juncture for the late nineteenth-century art market, when commercial galleries had already begun an inexorable march on the Academy. Their reputations and artistic personas were not shaped by conventional rules governing peer recognition and commercial success, but happened in a more haphazard way that chimed with modern capitalism and modern press culture, with its sensationalizing and heroizing tendencies. Their attitudes brought about a change in perception regarding the artist's place in the modern day cycle of artistic production and consumption; Rossetti and Whistler disrupted conventional routes to artistic legitimation and value – the public exhibition system and the Academy – and nineteenth-century ideas about the artist as male, (usually) middle-class professional who could be classed with doctors and engineers and other newly emerged professionals (a discourse described by Codell in this volume). They shifted what Lisa Tickner calls the 'agency' of a picture's patrons, critics, and 'conversational community'.[81]

Moreover, Rossetti and Whistler engaged with the art market in a period in which the idea of a religion of art was being widely promoted, to varying effect. In Whistler's *Symphony in White No. 2: The Little White Girl* (1864) – the most visibly Pre-Raphaelite of all Whistler's pictures – Kathleen Pyne observes a promotion of 'the religion of art as a ritual that promises beneficent effects'[82] that appealed to his patron Charles L. Freer (who tried to buy it in 1905). Although their art was known personally to a limited audience of art connoisseurs and their attitudes considered eccentric, both men, as Pyne suggests of Whistler, seem to arrive 'at a visual trope that concretized the idea of the religion of art'.[83] This religiosity is echoed in the tone of Leighton's tribute in 1882: Rossetti's art and poetry, he declared to his fellow Royal Academicians, was 'filled with a peculiar fascination and fervour, which attracted to him from those who enjoyed his intimacy a rare degree of admiring devotion'.[84]

Whilst the aestheticism practised by Rossetti and Whistler (via differing routes) distanced them from art products driven by a democratizing or moralizing impulse (and indeed, a belief in their alleged beneficent effects) and, for Whistler, religiosity was less about spiritual intensity and more about so-called 'ancient and "universal" aesthetic principles',[85] both men were obliged to share the same art marketplace. In doing so, they created a new kind of religion of the marketplace that was more about individual sensation than universal approbation.

Notes

1 D.G. Rossetti to Frederic Shields, 19 February 1865, Fredeman, ed. *Correspondence of Rossetti*, III, Letter 65.31, p. 258.

2 Rossetti exhibited twice only at the Free Exhibition, later the National Institution, in 1849 and 1850.

3 Rossetti exhibited at No. 4 Russell Place, Fitzroy Square in July 1857 and at the Hogarth Club in February 1860.

4 D.G. Rossetti, letter to *The Times*, 26 March 1877, p. 6.

5 William Michael Rossetti, 'The Royal Academy Exhibition', *Fraser's Magazine*, June 1865, p. 737.

6 William Michael Rossetti, 'The London Exhibitions of 1861', *Fraser's Magazine*, November 1861, pp. 583–4.

7 Whistler to Anderson Rose, [21 November 1878], Glasgow University Library (hereafter GUL), MS Whistler R128, GUW 05230. GUW numbers refer hereon to record numbers from MacDonald et al., *Correspondence of Whistler*. For more on the libel case Whistler v. Ruskin see Merrill, *A Pot of Paint*.

8 For an in-depth examination of this exhibition, see Spencer, 'Whistler's First One Man Exhibition'.

9 Whistler's approach to exhibition design and promotion is examined in more detail in Spencer, and elsewhere, e.g., Curry, 'Total Control: Whistler'; Bendix, *Diabolical Designs*.

10 Sidney Colvin, 'Exhibition of Mr Whistler's Pictures', *Academy*, 13 June 1874, p. 673.

11 Whistler to Anderson Rose, [6 December 1878], Library of Congress, Pennell-Whistler Collection, PWC 4/27, GUW 08751.

12 All these events were covered in the press and, as Whistler's press-cuttings books attest, syndicated widely. The press-cuttings books are now in the Whistler Archive, Department of Special Collections, GUL.

13 Indeed, Whistler put his entrepreneurial skills into practice once again in 1897, when he acquired the lease of a shop at Manchester Square and installed a manager to display and sell his etchings, lithographs, and drawings. The venture was unsuccessful and ended in 1901. For a detailed account, see Hopkinson, 'Whistler's "Company of the Butterfly"'.

14 See ibid.; Fredeman, ed. *Correspondence of Rossetti*; and MacDonald et al., *Correspondence of Whistler*.

15 Stephenson, 'Modern Masculinity'.

16 Gagnier, *Idylls of the Marketplace*.

17 This mysticism was acknowledged by Rossetti's contemporaries as well as later critics: Leighton spoke in his Royal Academy presidential address of Rossetti's 'jealous seclusion as far as the general world was concerned', which wielded him 'considerable influence in the world of Art and Poetry' and called him 'a mystic by temperament and right of birth'. See anon., 'The Royal Academy Banquet',

The Times, 1 May 1882, p. 7.

18 Whistler first exhibited at the Academy summer exhibition in 1859 when he showed two etchings.

19 D.G. Rossetti to Frances M.L. Rossetti, 7 July 1843, Fredeman, ed. *Correspondence of Rossetti*, I, Letter 43.3, p. 25.

20 And probably contributed towards his decision to exhibit with the Free Exhibition. Later, when it appeared that he might be elected an Academician, he seemed, above all else, to fear the administrative and teaching duties that it would involve (see Bornand, ed. *Diary of W. M. Rossetti*, p. 122, entry dated 1 November 1871).

21 Fredeman, ed. *Correspondence of Rossetti*, III, Letter 65.31, p. 258.

22 For example in 1877, when Rossetti wrote to the London *Times* explaining his absence from the first Grosvenor Gallery exhibition. 'The Grosvenor Gallery', *The Times*, 27 March 1877, p. 6.

23 That the previous year Rossetti had told a family member that he hoped to borrow the recently completed *Seed of David* triptych for 'exhibition in London … as I mean to do at some date, I hope not very distant' rather undermines his assertion to Shields. See D.G. Rossetti to Charlotte Lydia Polidori, 25 June 1864, Fredeman, ed. *Correspondence of Rossetti*, III, Letter 64.84, p. 162.

24 Rossetti, *Some Reminiscences*, II, pp. 340–1.

25 Rossetti was perhaps fortunate in this respect although his income, estimated by Francis Fennell as having reached an average of £1,000 per year by the 1860s, was modest by Millais's standards at the height of his financial success (as Malcolm Warner notes in his essay). Whilst the death of Thomas Plint, an earlier patron, in 1861 left him in professional distress, key patrons of the 1860s like Leyland and Leathart remained. For biographies of these patrons, see Macleod, *Art and the Victorian Middle Class*. Discussion of Rossetti's income at this time is found in a number of sources including Fennell, ed. *Rossetti-Leyland*, p. xii; Rossetti, *Dante Gabriel Rossetti*, I, pp. 248–9.

26 D.G. Rossetti to Frances Mary Lavinia Rossetti, 24 August 1866, Fredeman, ed. *Correspondence of Rossetti*, III, Letter 66.144, p. 463.

27 Possibly *The Sermon on the Mount*.

28 D.G. Rossetti to Ford Madox Brown, Fredeman, ed. *Correspondence of Rossetti*, II, Letter 59.34, [23 August 1859], p. 269.

29 D.G. Rossetti to F. Leyland, 31 May [1874], Fennell, ed. *Rossetti-Leyland*, Letter 79, p. 64. According to Surtees, the Lucrezia watercolour had been acquired by Leyland in c.1868 but by November 1873 he had returned it to Rossetti by way of exchange for another picture. Surtees, *Paintings and Drawings of Dante Gabriel Rossetti*, cat. 124.

30 The importance of provincial exhibitions (especially Liverpool) for Pre-Raphaelite artists is well documented. See, for instance, Macleod, *Art and the Victorian Middle Class*; Bennett, 'Pre-Raphaelite Pictures'.

31 'I have lately made the stipulation, when parting with my works, that they are

not to be exhibited without my consent.' See D.G. Rossetti to Ellen Heaton, 9 January 1868, Fredeman, ed. *Correspondence of Rossetti*, IV, Letter 68.4, p. 11.

32 D.G. Rossetti to Ford Madox Brown, [3 September 1864], Fredeman, ed. *Correspondence of Rossetti*, III, Letter 64.135, p. 188.

33 Surtees, cat. 164.

34 Macleod, 'Avant garde Patronage', p. 36, n. 43.

35 D.G. Rossetti to Frances Rossetti, 24 August [1866], Fredeman, ed. *Correspondence of Rossetti*, III, Letter 66.144, p. 463.

36 Albeit so too did a downturn in the market that affected artists like Rossetti selling directly from the studio and may have made a relationship with a dealer seem more appealing. Rossetti's situation is reflected in a letter to Ellen Heaton (Fredeman, ed. *Correspondence of Rossetti*, II, Letter 61.105, 26 December 1861, pp. 429–30) offering her *St George and the Princess Sabra* (1862) at a reduced price 'which I am induced to do by the comparative difficulty, which all artists are experiencing just now … I speak of *artists*. The *dealers* seem able to make profit enough on one's works certainly.' As Rossetti notes elsewhere, Gambart and another dealer, David Thomas White had just profited handsomely on the sale of his *The Farmer's Daughter* (1860). See also Fredeman, ed. *Correspondence of Rossetti*, II, Letter 62.24, p. 463.

37 Burne-Jones, *Burne Jones*, I, p. 174.

38 There were three by Rossetti, which according to Surtees, included *Burd Alane* (1861) and *My Lady Greensleeves* (1863) but there remains a good deal of confusion about the identity of the three pictures. Surtees, cat. 144. Two Plint estate sales took place at Christie's, the first on 7 March 1862 and the second on 17 June 1865.

39 References to Gambart begin in a letter to W.M. Rossetti, dated 14 May 1854 (Fredeman, ed. *Correspondence of Rossetti*, I, Letter 54.45, p. 348) but a later letter to Gambart himself in February 1859 suggests their meeting was recent (Fredeman, ed. *Correspondence of Rossetti*, II, Letter 59.6, pp. 245–6).

40 'I am in debt to the estate for 3 pictures to the amount of 680 guineas.' D.G. Rossetti to W.M. Rossetti, Fredeman, ed. *Correspondence of Rossetti*, II, Letter 61.61, p. 393.

41 As Fredeman records, Rossetti eventually settled the debt through a combination of pictures and cash payments (Fredeman, ed. *Correspondence of Rossetti*, II, Letter 61.61, n. 2, p. 394).

42 As his letter to Ellen Heaton suggests (see n. 36).

43 D.G. Rossetti to Henry Francis Polydore, 15 November 1865, Fredeman, ed. *Correspondence of Rossetti*, III, Letter 65.163, p. 347.

44 Ibid.

45 Virginia Surtees states the sum quoted by Rossetti for the *Blue Bower*, 1,500 guineas, was incorrect, the figure being much lower at £500. Nevertheless this was considerably higher than the price of £120 paid by Gambart when the picture was first sold. See Surtees, cat. 178.

46   In a letter to George Rae, Rossetti makes much of the sale of the *Blue Bower* and uses its 'fabulous price' to induce him to purchase *Sibylla Palmifera* (1866–70), then in progress. D.G. Rossetti to George Rae, 7 December 1865, Fredeman, ed. *Correspondence of Rossetti*, III, Letter 65.172, p. 355.

47   Bornand, ed. *Diary of W. M. Rossetti*, p. 202. Rossetti painted two replicas of the picture for the collector William Graham, the first having been already completed. (see Surtees, cat. 81.R.1, R.2). Auguste Blanchard was a Paris engraver used by Gambart.

48   D.G. Rossetti to W.M. Rossetti, 7 January 1873, Fredeman, ed. *Correspondence of Rossetti*, VI, Letter 73.15, p. 28. Rossetti is referring to the first version in watercolour. No exhibition appears to have taken place, although *Beatrice* may well have been included in winter displays of British art routinely advertised by Gambart's French Gallery.

49   D.G. Rossetti to William Bell Scott, 5 October [1860], Fredeman, ed. *Correspondence of Rossetti*, II, Letter 60.40, p. 319. Rossetti had previously used photography to record his work – Fredeman notes that he had a daguerreotype made of *The Girlhood of Mary Virgin* before it was sent to its purchaser the Marchioness of Bath. See Fredeman, ed. *Correspondence of Rossetti*, I, Letter 49.12, n. 4, p. 97.

50   Also documented in Rossetti's correspondence with Stephens and W.M. Rossetti: see D.G. Rossetti to W.M. Rossetti, 7 January 1873, Fredeman, ed. *Correspondence of Rossetti*, VI, Letter 73.15, p. 28.

51   Quoted from transcribed text, available online via the Rossetti Archive, www.rossettiarchive.org/docs/n5054.r47.rad.html. Accessed 8 October 2007.

52   Anon., 'Mr Rossetti's Pictures', *Musical World*, 22 July 1882, p. 452.

53   Fredeman, ed. *Correspondence of Rossetti*, I, p. xxv.

54   Whistler to D.C. Thomson, [2 April 1892], Library of Congress, Pennell-Whistler Collection PWC 3, GUW 08339.

55   *Arrangement in Grey and Black No. 2: Portrait of Thomas Carlyle* (1872–73; Glasgow Museums).

56   Beatrix Whistler to C.L. Freer, [19 March 1892], Freer Gallery of Art Archives, FGA Whistler 274, GUW 11670.

57   D.C. Thomson to Whistler, 4 March 1892, GUL, MS Whistler T40, GUW 05695.

58   J. and E.R. Pennell, *Whistler*, II, p. 120.

59   Whistler to D.C. Thomson, [20 February 1892] Library of Congress, Pennell-Whistler Collection, Box 3, GUW 08219.

60   D.C. Thomson to Whistler, 19 March 1892, GUL, MS Whistler T50, GUW 05705.

61   Although Whistler did secure the sale of an oil from the exhibition, *Grey and Silver: Battersea Reach* (1863) to Mrs Potter Palmer in Chicago for £450 (see Young et al., *Whistler*, cat. 46).

62   D.C. Thomson to Whistler, 18 June 1892, GUL, MS Whistler T95, GUW 05750.

63 Ibid.

64 The Earl of Plymouth, the Duke of Marlborough and Sir William Eden, D.C. Thomson to Whistler, 23 July 1892, GUL, MS Whistler T99, GUW 05754.

65 D.C. Thomson to Whistler, 12 September 1892, GUL, MS Whistler T100, GUW 05755.

66 D.C. Thomson to Whistler, 21 March 1893, GUL, MS Whistler T116, GUW 05771. Thomson is referring here to *Purple and Rose: The Lange Leizen of the Six Marks* (1864).

67 Exhibited in Munich and Berlin in 1891, Munich in 1892 and 1901, and Berlin in 1900.

68 J.R. Rodd to Whistler, 12 January 1888, GUL, MS Whistler R107, GUW 05207.

69 Cavafy made a substantial profit: *The Last of Old Westminster* and *Battersea Reach*, for example, were purchased by Cavafy's father from Whistler in 1863 for 30 guineas and £30 respectively (see Young et al., cat. nos. 39, 45).

70 Whistler to J.G. Potter, [21 February 1894?], GUL, MS Whistler P650, GUW05010.

71 Potter had purchased it in 1862/63 for £50 (Young et al., cat. 41).

72 'If you – or Goupil – or Kennedy buy a picture of mine for £5 – and sell it for £5000, up goes my price in the market – and most legitimate is your transaction and all to the good – But when these sneaking amateur tradesmen, under the cloak of Art Patronage, acquire a work for eighteen pence and sell it for thousands, it is quite a different matter!' Whistler to A. Reid, 14 February 1894, Freer Gallery of Art Archives, FGA Whistler 235, GUW 13374.

73 Whistler to A. Reid, 26 June 1892, Freer Gallery of Art Archives, FGA Whistler 199, GUW 03206.

74 E.G. Kennedy to Whistler, 14 December 1894, GUL, MS Whistler, W1232, GUW 07244.

75 Whistler to A. Reid, 26 June 1892, Freer Gallery of Art Archives, FGA Whistler 199, GUW 03206.

76 Whistler to C.L. Freer [29 July 1899], Freer Gallery of Art Archives, FGA Whistler 40, GUW 03196.

77 It went to the National Gallery of Art in Washington DC instead.

78 Whistler to A. Reid, [1/2 November 1892], Freer Gallery of Art Archives, FGA Whistler 207, GUW 03235. The picture had just been exhibited at the 6th Internationale Kunst-Austellung, Munich, 1892.

79 The *Moniteur des Arts* reported: 'M. Whistler, incompris au début, est reconnu aujourd'hui comme un maître anglais, et il a fallu que ce soit la France, suprême arbitre en matière artistique, qui consacre définitivement la gloire du peintre. Mais M. Whistler n'est pas Anglais, il est Américain, ou plutôt il est Français; les Anglais le reclament à présent, ils ont raison. Mais il n'en demeure pas moins Français.' *Le Moniteur des Arts*, 1 April 1892.

80 Rossetti's renown as a poet flourished alongside his reputation as an artist and

while the relationship between the literary and artistic marketplaces for his work is too complex a subject to consider here, it does seem reasonable to acknowledge its place in this mindset.

81 Tickner, 'English Modernism in the Cultural Field', p. 24.

82 Pyne, 'Charles Lang Freer', p. 83.

83 Pyne, p. 84.

84 *The Times*, 1 May 1882, p. 7.

85 Pyne, p. 93.

13

Home from home:
some Australasian artists
in London, 1900–14

Pamela Gerrish Nunn

At the beginning of the twentieth century, London was the many-spoked hub of a cultural network with political and social connections that sprawled across the globe. In this larger British world, the capital's commercial potential as well as its cultural influence appeared unparalleled. This essay considers the efforts of individuals who were the habitual outsiders in this world – women and colonials – to establish a professional presence in London in the first decade or so of the twentieth century. The London experience demanded talent, craft, and luck, but promised a ticket to success.

The identities they sought in London were various: the qualifiers 'woman', 'lady', and 'colonial' added to the base term 'artist' were to be negotiated and bargained over with differing degrees of vigour by different individuals. Women going Home, as it was termed, from either Australia or New Zealand to the city which was simultaneously the capital of England and the heart of British Empire were not country cousins coming to gawp at the urban phenomenon: they came, for instance, from states or countries which had already granted female suffrage and had seen female graduates benefit from progressive education provision. Even so, as Angela Woollacott and Ros Pesman have both pointed out, the colonial metropolis London, being a distant, enormous, and heterogeneous community, might accommodate personal development which would have been beyond the pale in their home towns.[1] However, the evidence tends to show that colonial women, even when white, were hardly likely to be able to enter into the Bohemia that Peter Brooker has described as the crucible of British modernism,[2] and the combination of outsiderness they exhibited saddled them with a mix of novelty and handicap which would not be entirely cancelled out even by that classic mechanism of incorporation – alliance with a male member of the in-crowd. The cases of New Zealander Frances Hodgkins (1869–1947) and Australian Thea Proctor (1879–1966) will be presented here to emphasize what a conflicted opportunity the London art world presented to such incomers, far from their homes and families in this place perversely called Home. This essay's aim, in presenting these two instances as case studies, is to examine what moves or shifts transformed an outsider into one who belonged – one who became, so to speak, at home at Home, whether for the long term or merely until they repatriated. It will be seen that there was a general consensus among this population of what constituted success, formed as much by opinion at Home as by the artists' own aims, but that women were differently placed from men in its conception and its achievement.

Documentary evidence from primary sources such as letters home lays out the fundamentals in both Hodgkins' and Proctor's cases, providing a running commentary on these artists' experiences, and such evidence will be relied upon extensively here.[3] This is not to naively endow the artist's own testimony with Biblical authority but, firstly, to allow the outsider to speak for herself and, secondly, to recognize that this London experience belonged also to the people left behind. Contemporary press comment, similarly, fed those left behind with reports that the artists abroad were expected, as part of their obligation to the community, to supply. Throughout this written discourse of the experience, the investment of the artists and their compatriots in the capital city of their universe is vividly conveyed.

On one occasion, when she was asked by fellow Australasians to account for herself, Frances Hodgkins gave the following reason for leaving New Zealand for England: 'Perhaps I ought to have been content with what was a very interesting life, but I felt I was only grasping; that I had not realised myself; that I wanted to see the masterpieces of all time; learn what was being done in my chosen medium; and measure myself with the moderns.'[4] Hodgkins was born in New Zealand in 1869, the second daughter of an amateur artist father. Hodgkins senior was an English immigrant whose crucial role in establishing the artistic culture of his adopted city Dunedin is unargued.[5] Frances began exhibiting her own work in the South Island centres of Dunedin and Christchurch in 1890, and, by 1896, she had set herself up as an art teacher, a common-sense step for a single woman in turn-of-the-century New Zealand.

It was assumed that any artist would want at some stage to go Home, as England was termed, to profit from the wider world that it was in itself but also gave on to, and she departed for London in 1901, as her first biographer

E.H. McCormick wrote, 'not on a European career, it must be emphasised – but on a trip of one year's duration which would add to her equipment as teacher and painter in a remote colonial centre'.[6] Hodgkins arrived in England just before her thirty-second birthday in April 1901, equipped with £100. En route, via Sydney, she met 'a host of sister brushes, they all seem a poverty-stricken lot and would hardly believe I had made enough by my brush to go Home'.[7] The aim was to make an impact in that larger arena and return home to establish a trans-Tasman practice given credibility by success in London, Paris, Munich, and so on. Thus wrote Hodgkins to her friend Kate Rattray after four months away, 'I have vowed not to return [to New Zealand] till I have written the name of Frances Hodgkins in capital letters across – is it the scroll of fame, or what, that we are all so anxious to sign.'[8] There were two courts of judgment: London and one's home town.

Most new arrivals equipped themselves with letters of introduction, and Hodgkins was no exception. They had plans based on their assiduous reading of *Royal Academy Pictures* and the *Studio*, whose influence on the colonial art-lover is indicated by Ysanne Holt's essay elsewhere in this volume; on the recommendations of compatriots who had already been to London; and on examples of British work they had seen in the exhibitions originating in London that circulated in the colonies in the closing decades of the nineteenth century. They knew they needed to penetrate the nexus of dealers, patrons, critics, and viewers which was so much larger and denser than in their home countries. London, as a cosmopolitan centre far larger than any city they had experienced, promised to transcend such narrowness of outlook while presenting a daunting complexity.

On arrival Hodgkins was put up by New Zealand acquaintances. But, as she wrote home after only two weeks:

> It is simply impossible to live economically in London. You can't move without spending money – and the sooner I am out of it the better for my purse. It has been pay, pay, pay ever since I arrived [...] train fares and busses [sic] which are nothing in themselves, but when you multiply them by six they soon mount up [...] Mr Spence took me to the Bank of NSW where I deposited my draft and opened an account. I am not going to get any clothes but am going to make my NZ things do so do not be surprised if I arrive home again in the same coat and skirt I set out in [...] It's a wonderful world this London but a cruel place for those who can't afford it.[9]

This was perhaps the discourse of housewives – she is writing here to her mother – but money was the most persistent leitmotiv of Hodgkins' correspondence, personal and professional. Artists of both sexes coming from the southern hemisphere had to have saved hard to accumulate a lump sum, or to rely on an allowance that could make them hostage to familial authority. Immediately prior to their departure they had usually held an 'art union' to augment these funds.

Further training and gallery-going as well as commercial success were the usual aims of people in Hodgkins' situation. While women had not necessarily suffered an inferior art education in their home country – as would have been the case had they been already living anywhere in Britain apart from London itself – a colonial instinct of deference to the mother country tended to generate the assumption that they still had much to learn. As an unidentified Australian woman wrote for the *Sydney Morning Herald* in 1907, 'It is a liberal education to see the old masters and the galleries -Rembrandt, Titian, Franz Hals, Velazquez, Reynolds, Gainsborough, Romney – one knows not which to appreciate most. It is necessary to know what is the world's record, so to speak, in art, to know what the standard is, and how far below it we are.'[10] Accordingly, when Hodgkins had been in London for a month, she reported home, 'I have decided to take advantage of the cheap classes at the Polytechnic and draw from the nude for the next month ... [then] I am joining Norman Garstin's sketching class, they are going to Caudebec in Brittany and probably I shall go on to Paris in the autumn'.[11] Established artists such as Garstin could be useful not just as teachers, but as mentors and 'fixers': thus shortly after joining his class in Brittany, Hodgkins wrote: '[Mr. Garstin] wants me to work here for a while and then go down to Spain for the winter, get plenty of material there then go back to Penzance and take a studio there for a while and get all my sketches in order and then have a show in London in the Spring – he has promised to write me up in the *Studio*, he writes a lot for that paper and has influence'. Though Hodgkins had launched a career of her own in New Zealand, she took it for granted that it took an insider's knowledge of the London market to devise a credible action-plan at this juncture, and Garstin evidently commanded Hodgkins' sympathy and confidence from the beginning.

The web of contacts anchored in London spread out around the country and into western Europe, and the colonial artist trying to establish herself in the London art market could make headway in it even while she was in Cornwall, Brittany, Italy, or Spain. The building of a reputation began to gather momentum once the incomer had found her way into some set or another, and it was Garstin's circle that started Hodgkins on her way. Thus his Brittany class yielded her buyers, potential students, and promises of commissions from their friends when they all should return to England. In particular a widespread sorority of upper-class women, usually single and so in command of their own time and resources, interested in art and keen to support artists of their own sex, provided Hodgkins with companionship, patronage, and moral support, in varying combinations. In October 1901, on this first trip to France and Italy, Hodgkins could report to her mother:

Next week a friend of Miss R's, a Miss Astley, is coming from England to join us for a few weeks. She is an invalide [sic] and has a villa in San Remo. She wants to take lessons from me before going on there so will break her journey for that purpose. I have also a commission to paint a £10 picture from a cousin of Miss R's so my little artistic pot is kept boiling gently, is it not?[12]

These factors were huge determinants in the artist's larger project as well as in her immediate plans, and their influence can be seen in the emergence of the purposeful tone in Hodgkins' letters to her mother over the following month: 'I am quite ready to go back to NZ after I have had a show in London but certainly not before.'[13]

Having fixed on this goal, she had to prioritize producing a body of work for that purpose, though this conflicted with other aims: 'I had hoped to afford a trip to Florence from here', she wrote to her mother from France in December 1901, 'but I am afraid it cannot be managed, tho it seems such a great pity to miss such a chance of seeing it when I am so near, but if I am to have a Show in London I must have enough money to keep me going while there'.[14] Experience, funds, and focus were all needed to construct – and project – a professional identity, a higher aim than that assumed by the numberless female amateurs rattling around the sketching grounds, art schools, and galleries, who fuelled the persistence of the reactionary image of the female artist as unserious and inconsequential. Hence another value that the Miss R referred to above had for Hodgkins: 'I have had an ideal time with Miss Dorothy Richmond who is as much in earnest as I am [...] With the exception of Miss Richmond and a very few others I have never met anyone who is really serious about their work.'[15] One of these few others was compatriot and fellow watercolourist Margaret Stoddart,[16] who had been in England since 1898 and whom Hodgkins was discouraged to find at that time living on just £1 a week: did this venture have to exact such a high price?

It was not only the need to prove to her loyal family that she was making good use of her time that prompted Hodgkins' constant monitoring of the field of opportunity but also the sense that coming into the London art world was something like going to the circus, where a good seat must be secured in the Big Top if one was to keep abreast of all that was going on and catch hold of whatever goodies might be thrown out: if this seat was vacated for but a moment it could be that it would be taken by another, equally driven and in pursuit of the same ends – and this, anyway, was just the preface to securing a performing role. The artist felt as though the opportunities London offered were on the one hand multifarious and endless, but on the other also finite, and precisely the right choices had to be made to yield the desired result: 'I am getting impatient to get back to England and see about my exhibition. Mr Garstin writes urging me to go at once as he thinks I am leaving it too late and will find a difficulty in getting a gallery ... He is sanguine that if I can but get them to look at my work I will have a success but who knows!', she wrote in February 1902.[17]

The dependence upon a trusted insider alternates hectically with the artist's confidence in herself as an autonomous agent. It is telling that in the second stage of her London career (from 1905), Hodgkins retained H.W. Taylor of Bayswater as what she termed her 'framer-agent-man'.[18] As it was, Hodgkins' effort to penetrate Bond Street on her own account provoked a deeply felt letter home which renders vividly the complexity of the situation facing the outsider, and of the London art market at that precise moment:

> The first morning I met Miss Richmond a foggy dirty morning, everything looking like a big inkpot, and we proceeded to Dowdeswells with a portfolio of sketches under my arm. I now found out I made a grave mistake not mounting and framing a few before I showed them to the dealers ... We swam into Dowdeswells heads high – crimson pile carpet and damask hangings costing at least £10 a foot – Dowdeswell Senior received us, a benevolent looking old man – and he liked my things so much that I was deceived into thinking he meant business – however he said he would like to show them to his son – who was then out and would we leave them and then return in an hour. We did so – but alas when we returned the benevolent old man had disappeared and in his place was a dreadful person with a brutal jaw and a shark like expression – cad, cad, cadissimo! He said my work was *very nice* but not what *his* clientele wanted – now if I had brought flower gardens for instance it would have been quite another matter. The general public *must* have flower gardens just now at any cost and he didn't think there was any demand for my kind of work. Early Italian work was also very popular and if I could show them any decorative sketches a la Botticelli he thought they would stand a better chance. By this time I began to grasp that until I had made some kind of a name I could hope to get no dealer to run a show for me – they won't take the risk until they are assured of a success – and they accordingly make all sorts of excuses to get rid of you. We next went on the Fine Arts – I had two letters to the proprietor Mr Huish, one from Mr Garstin and another from his Mr H's brother in law whom I met in Dunedin before I left. Mr Huish however was ill and we could not see him – I was sorry for I heard he was a gentleman and a very artistic man. His gallery is considered even better than Mr Dowdeswell's but oh! the rubbish I saw on his walls – it made me sad and ever so many sold – they were nearly all flower gardens – there is a horticultural wave

passing over the art world just now … Our next visit was to the Editor of the *Studio* Mr Holme, he is a busy man but I had a letter from Mr Garstin which proved an open sesame. Mr Holme was delightful and soothed my ruffled feelings with judicially administered praise … and he told us much concerning wicked hardhearted dealers and their little ways – he advised me strongly to exhibit at the different galleries before trying to have a show and he offered me any letters I wanted to enable me to do so … Next day we tramped round some more galleries – Graves and Clifford's in the Haymarket, this time without my sketches, merely enquiring their terms, which in most cases was about the same – 25% on the profits and in some cases a deposit.[19]

It was something of a vicious circle that needed to be penetrated: dealers looked for artists who had been successful in exhibition to attract the buying public, and exhibiting societies looked for members with proven standing to add lustre to their shows. Hodgkins' targets were shaped both by what was respected in New Zealand and by her own preferences, the artists she arrived in Britain admiring being Garstin, Elizabeth Forbes, Eleanor Fortescue Brickdale, Byam Shaw, John Singer Sargent, and Frank Brangwyn.[20] These affinities put her on moderate ground in 1902 Britain. That her aims were driven by no aesthetic doctrine can be seen in her simultaneous attempts that year to show in the Royal Academy, the Royal Society of Watercolourists, and the New English Art Club. Just as in her assault on the commercial sector, this programme of penetration into the artist-run sector was eclectic if not indiscriminate. As Pamela Fletcher shows elsewhere in this volume, the diversification of the London art world may have been considerable and ongoing but that did not mean that no points of distinction could be drawn between the various outlets for contemporary art. Hodgkins' attempted entry into any forum that had a record of endorsing work like her own, which evoked the English watercolour tradition, the plein-airism of Newlyn, and the well-established taste for touristic sights of foreign people and places. As it was, Hodgkins' work was rejected by both the RA and the NEAC that year although it was praised outside London, at the Newlyn exhibition which previewed the work which members of that colony planned to send to the London exhibitions. That Hodgkins had already described the NEAC as 'a queer Slade School clique who pride themselves on their chucking out propensities and slay unmercifully even their own members'[21] suggests her dependence on and faith in opinion borrowed from the sector she had aligned herself with (she eventually showed with the NEAC in 1912), and the self-conscious factionalism of the English art world.

All this played out alongside her sending work back to her sister and mother to handle for local exhibition. At this date, each of the four major New Zealand cities had an art society which held annual exhibitions of contemporary art in a chronological cycle enabling work to be circulated around the country in search of buyers; patronage was largely reliant on private individuals since only Hodgkins' home town of Dunedin and the largest of the cities, Auckland, had public art galleries. Her Caudebec works had been sent straight back to her home town to feature in the Otago Art Society show in November 1901, and a further sixteen watercolours from her Continental trips appeared in the Society's next show, after a solo show of thirty-seven watercolours arranged at a Wellington dealer gallery for the preceding August.[22] The aim in maintaining a presence in her home country was twofold: she was afraid of losing ground in the market to which she would presumably return sooner or later, and she needed to finance the prolongation of her stay abroad, a combination of aims which highlights the vexed questions of identity and location. Was it as a New Zealand artist she wished to make her name or as an adopted Briton? And in her home land, where she had a pedigree, or at Home, where she was a minnow in an ocean? The contribution her brother Willie made to the question at this point illuminates this vortex by its vocabulary: he urged their sister Isabel to 'endeavour to persuade Fanny not to come out [i.e. back to New Zealand] while she can possibly stay at home [i.e. in England] for she is now so much in her congenial atmosphere of art that I think it would be a great pity to even suggest such a thing as leaving Europe for the drudgery of teaching here'.[23] The vacillation this ambivalence led to was never-ending: shortly after the incident described above Hodgkins wrote, 'I must abandon all idea of having a show in London, it can't be done without money, and also it is difficult to get enough work together. New Zealand exhausts my supply and I can't feed two markets',[24] while just two months later she had resolved to 'keep my best work by me [and] send to some London galleries when the next watercolour shows come on in the spring'.[25] In both markets, an annual calendar determined the cycle of artists' activities, although the London timetable was becoming more and more rich with possibilities (see Fletcher, chapter 2), which was probably why Hodgkins could not entirely withdraw from its lure.[26]

Indeed, at this point Hodgkins was preparing work for a group show in the Baillie Gallery, Bayswater. John Baillie was an expatriate New Zealander, but Hodgkins was ambivalent about using the New Zealand connection, and Bayswater was far from the commercial 'nerve-centre' of the Bond Street area. When the show came on in October 1902, it was entitled 'Colonial Art Exhibition', about which she was also ambivalent. This identification or positioning – what would nowadays be called branding – featured too in a proposition to share a show at the New Bond Street Doré Gallery, where she would be billed as 'the well known New Zealand painter'. The proposer, Miss March Phillips, whom Hodgkins had met as a pupil, would pay for the rooms and Hodgkins' only cost would be 15 per cent commission on sales. The temptation to believe that this would be the tipping point was great but, though fraught with ambition to achieve her aims before giving in to maternal pressure to return home, Hodgkins was only too aware of the relational or associative aspect of success: 'The only crumple in the rose leaf', she wrote, 'is the extreme badness of [Miss Phillips'] work, or rather it is not so bad as banal and commonplace and I do not quite relish the idea of hanging cheek by jowl with so many inartistic and frightening daubs'.[27] An exhibition was all very well, but if no work was bought one had not so much a career as an expensive hobby. The vexing fact for Hodgkins was that, as can be seen in this instance, female amateurs did get shows in certain commercial venues, either through personal influence or through self-financing, leaving the question of professionalism to be decided by the simple conviction of the work. In the event, Hodgkins showed ten watercolours in the November 1902 show, reporting to her friend D.K. Richmond: 'It has *not* made the commotion in art circles I thought it would in fact so far has been entirely overlooked by the Press. Business was bad – Miss March P sold 3 the first day (2 aunts and a friend were the purchasers) … and I nil … the rooms were packed with people and Bond Street with carriages but they were not a buying lot'.[28]

While Hodgkins then went on a trip to Morocco which would produce exotic subject-matter for her repertoire, she had Richmond submit work on her behalf to the Academy. This time her two submissions were accepted and, although only one was hung, it was on the line, an achievement in the eyes of New Zealand opinion unmarred by the waning prestige of the Academy in Britain. It was difficult for that distant audience to appreciate the stale fruit that the Academy yielded by that time, especially when further success seemed to flow from this event, with early offers of purchase for the exhibited work, and the Fine Art Society that Hodgkins had courted in vain twelve months previously offering an almost immediate appearance.[29] In addition, an invitation came to submit to the Liverpool Autumn Exhibition, and Hodgkins found herself hung at the Academy in the following two years (1904, 1905), to all intents and purposes an English artist. All this could be attributed to the Academy appearance which, though signalling the conservatism of Hodgkins' art, to New Zealanders signalled successful assimilation into British art.

Though this was a conventional achievement, then, it persuaded Hodgkins to leave Britain at the end of that year. The spur can be surmised to have been not only the sense of having slaked her ambition but a salutary meeting in early June with the aforementioned Margaret Stoddart, who was considering a teaching post in South Africa simply because it promised a salary of £300 a year — a prospect that appalled Hodgkins. Submitting to the nagging guilt towards the family that had financially supported her for the past three years in the absolute assumption that she would return home eventually and vindicate their investment, Hodgkins arrived back in her home country in time for Christmas 1903.

As Hodgkins sailed from the UK to the southern hemisphere, Australian Thea Proctor set out in the reverse direction. Again, the artist's experiences are reflected – or rather, it should be said, refracted – through an extensive correspondence and complementary commentary in the local press. Ten years younger than Hodgkins, Proctor began her art career in Sydney in 1896. A typical opinion in her homeland, expressed in 1899, was that 'There can be no question that in Australia an artist however gifted has little to look forward to; in the old world the rewards are necessarily greater.' [30] Proctor's mother was, it has been said, 'desperate' for her daughter to get a chance at those rewards, and in 1903 the two women sailed to London, where Proctor enrolled at St. John's Wood art school,[31] whose advertisements specified 'All classes open to ladies'. This move was meant by Proctor to be a preparation for learning painting at the Royal Academy Schools; a letter home rich with the contradictions of the newly arrived outsider outlined her plan:

> Did you hear that I thought of trying to get into the RA Schools? … Nearly everyone tells me to go to Slade School – even old RA students – but when one tries to think of good people who have come out of the Slade – one can't think of anyone – and heaps of clever people have come out of the Royal Academy – I'm afraid it would be my only chance of learning to paint as the Academy Schools are free and the others so expensive.[32]

While aesthetic choices seem to be indicated here, in fact, once again money lies at the heart of the matter.

One of the other foundational tasks was to make oneself known to useful people by doing the rounds of contacts. Hodgkins, as has been seen, was a single woman alone in London, and accordingly was always on the lookout for companions even though she was in her thirties and possessed of a typical New Zealand self-sufficiency. Proctor, an unmarried woman in her early twenties, initially had an automatic chaperone in her mother. Proctor was introduced to Eleanor Fortescue Brickdale, whose work she admired 'more than any other woman's', and through her the painter Gerald Moira.[33] Then through former art school colleague George Lambert, who had settled in London in 1901 on a state scholarship, Proctor met the three Halford sisters, one of whom was married to the collector Edmund Davis, and at one of their studios Proctor met the artists Charles Ricketts, Charles Shannon, and Charles Conder. This was the chain of acquaintance by which the outsider hoped to become known and helped into a milieu. Lambert must also have assisted his friend's attempt to establish visibility by exhibiting a named portrait of her at the 1904 Royal Academy. 'I have met heaps of artistic people but I don't feel it does me much good', Proctor wrote home somewhat naively; 'it only makes me dreadfully discontented',[34] perhaps because Lambert had made a viable place for himself in London so rapidly.

Typically, Proctor's progress in London was being closely monitored – or rather judged – in Australia: 'Miss Thea Proctor', reported a column in the *Sydney Morning Herald* in late 1904, 'has recently removed from St John's Wood School, and is now located at South Kensington. She has won two competitions, but her decision to give up decorative work altogether in favour of figure painting is regarded by many of her friends as an unwise step.'[35] There was further comment on women who had gone to Europe not so much to make their names as to spend their family's money in finding out they had no talent.[36] In the event, Proctor seems to have abandoned formal study, instead learning from Lambert and trying to get illustration work and portrait commissions. Like many in her position she was offered copying and fell into modelling for other artists, since both activities paid in cash if not in glory.[37] The demarcation between roles that firmly divided the executive artist from the artist's model was no longer necessarily fatal to a woman's standing, and enlarged Proctor's earning capacity at a time when her eventual success as an artist was by no means assured.

In mid-1905, family finances and responsibilities obliged Proctor's mother to return to Australia, leaving her daughter with a parting gift of £25. Proctor said later, 'I decided I would stay on in London. I would have faced anything rather than return',[38] and the genuine risk in such a decision is indicated by friends using the terms poverty and penury to describe the next few years she spent in the British capital; the £25 lasted a mere four months. Most historians believe that although she was ostensibly living on her own after her mother's departure, in effect Proctor functioned as a member of the much better off George Lambert's household, which consisted of him, his wife, and their two sons, playing the various roles of colleague, best mate, baby-sitter, model, and aunt.[39]

Proctor did not make the breakthrough to public notice that could ease this hand-to-mouth existence until 1907, when she debuted at the RA (reappearing there over the next three years). A month or so later she had three pieces on show at a new London event, the exhibition of Australasian women's work, at which she won a prize (Hodgkins, who had returned to Britain in 1906, won first prize for watercolour);[40] and, to cap the *annus mirabilis*, that November she was included with five drawings in the Goupil Gallery salon, a show of the grab-bag kind which commercial galleries used to try out potential sellers for their stables (see Helmreich, chapter 3). The work she was showing was all in the secondary media of pen and ink, pencil, and watercolour, often on silk in the form of fans, provoking English reviewers to connect her with Conder,[41] whose first fans and designs on silk had been shown in London in 1899.[42] This connection did not necessarily profit her: for instance, she secured no appearances at the modish Carfax Gallery which hosted the Conder circle as well as a range of up-and-coming men such as Roger Fry, Augustus John, and William Orpen; and the artist herself was later said to 'deplore the decorative influence of Conder' on her development,[43] declaring in a retrospectively modernist voice, 'It would have been better if I had gone to France and come under the influence of Cézanne.'[44] She could not afford to, of course, and neither had she learnt oil painting, which was as much the definitive medium of avant-gardism as it was of the academic tradition. Though her Australian training had taught Proctor to disregard the traditional hierarchy of media, the London art market did differentiate between the various kinds of commodity that artists might offer up, and a decorative artist was still a less consequential figure than an oil painter. Proctor's comment also exposes how in the crucible of the century's first decade there were differing trends in play, commanding unequal credibility in the long term, with the perpetuation of decadence which she espoused at the time becoming thoroughly eclipsed by modernism.

As Hodgkins had found, the colonial identification could bring its own opportunities, and Proctor appeared in the Australian women's section of the Franco-British exhibition in July 1908 (where she shared an award once more with Frances Hodgkins). She was also simultaneously represented at the inaugural exhibition of the huge, universalizing London Salon or Allied Artists Association where identity was nothing, though name might be all, so vast was the crowd of exhibitors. At the beginning of 1909 she had a fan in the International Society exhibition,[45] and in the autumn three pieces at the Grafton Galleries' *Exhibition of chosen Pictures*. These shows presented her not only in diverse company but in an up-to-date British cohort, where her work was seen alongside that of Roger Fry, William Orpen, Samuel Peploe, Ethel Walker, and Harold and Laura Knight. The Goupil Gallery's so-called salon, for instance, was characterized in 1908 by *The Times* as containing 'a strong element of the New English Art Club, with a dash of the International. That is to say, it is typically modern, and much of it is, according to the standards of taste now widely accepted, very good.'[46] In such settings Proctor's work would have been at the cheaper end of the scale, and thus amongst the more affordable items even if not the most widely praised. But how well any one exhibitor was noticed on these occasions is moot: in the former of the 1909 exhibitions, for instance, Proctor's exhibit was one among 447, in the latter hers were three among 305: a far cry from the solo show which was any artist's supreme target. Even so, the quality of the company could be valuable, not just because of its associative value but also because it allowed the artist to learn from and measure herself against more successful contemporaries, and influences from painters such as Orpen, Laura Knight, and Philip Wilson Steer surfaced in Proctor's work as she spread her exhibition net wider.[47]

In 1909 and 1910 Proctor may have visited Paris (her artist cousin John Peter Russell lived nearby) and Rome, but continued to position herself on the London scene. Her identity shifted when the New English Art Club accepted her in 1910, and she 'dropped the Academy',[48] appearing at the NEAC for three years running. However, her modernization may have been checked rather than boosted by attending the first Post-Impressionist exhibition in the Grafton Galleries at the end of 1910 and performances of the Ballets Russes in the following year for, though Proctor was exactly the same age as Vanessa Bell, whose alliance was with the avant-garde Bloomsbury Group identified with the Post-Impressionist show (see Gruetzner Robins, chapter 4), her response to the Ballets Russes, *Souvenir des Ballets Russes: le Carnaval*, is conspicuous for its preference for Rococo ornament over formal experimentation.[49] It can be compared rather with the aesthetics of Laura Knight, Ethel Walker, Ethel Gabain, or the Zinkeisen sisters – popular, fashionable, and up-to-date but not modernist.

This refusal of modernism may, of course, have had everything to do with commercial needs, since avant-gardism was endorsed by only a small section of the critical community and the buying public, and other signs of Proctor's likely pragmatism included her continuing willingness to undertake child portraiture and her diligent re-exhibition of pieces which didn't sell on first appearance. Despite such across-the-board efforts, when Proctor secured her first substantial appearance on the London scene in the spring of 1911 – a share in a group show at the Goupil Gallery with six other Australian artists – sales were few though she exhibited by far the largest number of works, thirty-seven items of some variety.[50]

Another of the Australian painters who made this obligatory foray into the international art world was Arthur Streeton, twelve years Proctor's senior, who, at the end of 1906, had just returned to his homeland from ten years in Britain, and was interviewed by the *Sydney Morning Herald*: 'Every man has to undergo an apprenticeship in London', he is reported as saying, 'I don't care who he is.' 'They have to fight their way', paraphrases the reporter; 'and a fight of that kind, against discouragement, poverty, and the feeling of strangeness and solitude in a great city is more disheartening for a woman than for a man … Hard work and hard study are the conditions of success, and the young Australian who goes to London to win high fame without these finds that he had better have stayed at home.'[51] The achievements of Streeton's London sojourn were listed thus: 'he has been represented at various times at all the big exhibitions in the United Kingdom, while of the only two pictures he sent to the [Paris] salon both were accepted, and one earned the distinction "*mention honorable*". Last year alone his pictures were shown in the Royal Academy; the New Gallery, to which he now sends annually by invitation; the New English Art Club, whose reputation as the most exclusive affair of its kind in England has travelled this far; and the Irish Exhibition at Limerick.'[52]

Proctor had spent over a decade trying to achieve this kind of portfolio, moving on from the Academy to the NEAC and taking the commercial sector in her stride, with an alleged appearance at the International Exposition in Berlin in 1909, and a documented appearance representing Britain at the Venice Biennale in 1912,[53] but the constant struggle was beginning to tell on her. Though her name appeared consistently here and there, she seems to have made no major sales to big-name buyers and the trajectory of her career, though perhaps proceeding upward, was doing so on a very shallow incline. The trials named by the reporter – discouragement, poverty, the feeling of strangeness and solitude, disheartenment – had figured largely in her experience, though later in life she said, 'I have no regrets about having stayed in London with no money. There are things one simply *has* to do in life. To stay in Australia would have been the finish for me. And I had to learn to draw – and I got away from Sydney suburbia ... When after seven years I couldn't stand it any longer I came back to Australia.'[54] A probable impetus for her departure from Britain for her homeland in August 1912 was that a number of works that had failed to sell from the Goupil show in spring 1911 found a very favourable reception at the Sydney Society of Women Painters' annual shows in the July and October, displayed in a room of their own as in effect a one-woman show.

Though Proctor indeed had some additional success when she reached Sydney,[55] it was not enough to persuade her to stay in her native land: 'Nothing would have induced me', she later said.[56] And so she and Frances Hodgkins, who had criss-crossed the hemispheres once again meanwhile, both arrived back in London in 1914. Although Hodgkins had publicly declared only a few months previously, 'If I had known what was before me, I should never had had the courage to begin',[57] an irresistible magnetism drew them to the city which ultimately did make both their names. Hodgkins and Proctor came to the city's challenges at a time when it was arguably even more in flux than when those other outsiders discussed in this book, Dante Gabriel Rossetti and James McNeill Whistler, were attempting to forge a career. Gender and geography complicated these two women's experiences further. Their engagement with the London art market of the early twentieth century shows vividly how the outsiders of Greater Britain brought with them an idiosyncratic map of that vibrant, promising but mercurial place, both enabling them to recognize its very varied possibilities but also hampering them in claiming its greatest rewards. Its position was unique and its lure remained irresistible but its fascination came at a cost.

Notes

1 Woollacott, 'White Colonialism'; Pesman, *Duty Free*.

2 Brooker, *Bohemia in London*.

3 The chief source of Hodgkins' letters in the public domain is Gill, ed. *Letters of Frances Hodgkins*; and of Proctor's, Morgan, 'Thea Proctor the Artist'.

4 A.G. Stephens, 'Frances Hodgkins', Supplement to the *Bookfellow* (Sydney), 1 May 1913, pp. ix–x. See also: anon., 'An Artist of the Moderns', *Everylady's Journal*, 6 January 1913, p. 12.

5 See: Entwisle, *William Matthew Hodgkins and his Circle*. See: Auckland City Art Gallery's *Frances Hodgkins and her Circle* for a more rounded but also more cursory context for Hodgkins' artistic development.

6 McCormick, *The Expatriate*, p. 49; his comment is based on a report in the *Otago Witness*, 13 February 1901, p. 63.

7 Gill, ed., letter 62, p. 72.

8 FH to KR, 27 August 1901. qMS-0965. Alexander Turnbull Library. National Library of New Zealand/Te Puna Matauranga o Aotearoa.

9 Gill, ed., letter 69, pp. 82–4; letter 72, pp. 89–90.

10 Anon, 'An English Portrait Class', *Sydney Morning Herald*, 23 January 1907, p. 5.

11 Gill, ed., letter 70., pp. 84–7. Norman Garstin, an artist of the Newlyn School, was often referred to and advertised as a teacher in the *Studio* from the late 1880s, and was a favourite of Hodgkins' friend Dorothy Kate Richmond.

12 Gill, ed., letter 78, pp. 100–2.

13 Gill, ed., letter 75, pp. 94–7.

14 Gill, ed., letter 81, pp. 106–9.

15 Gill, ed., letter 90, pp. 129–30; letter 93, pp. 133–4.

16 A few years Hodgkins' senior and also from the South Island of New Zealand, see: King, *Margaret Stoddart*.

17 Gill, ed., letter 84, pp. 113–14.

18 Gill, ed., letter 122, p. 184.

19 Gill, ed., letter 86, pp. 119–24. The Dowdeswells' gallery (father Charles and son Walter) was in the heart of dealer-gallery territory, at the south end of New Bond Street, and would have been known to Hodgkins for hosting solo shows of Fortescue Brickdale's work; Marcus Huish edited *The Year's Art* as well as being managing director of the Fine Art Society, whose premises were situated on New Bond Street, among whose best known artists were Helen Allingham and Kate Greenaway; Charles Holme 1848–1923, founded the *Studio*. For more on the *Studio*, see the essay by Ysanne Holt in this volume.

20 See Gill, ed., letter 64, p. 75; letter 86, pp. 119–24; and others.

21 Gill, ed., letter 86, pp. 119–24.

22 For details of these showings, see: Collins and Buchanan, *Frances Hodgkins*, pp. 12, 33.

23 Quoted by McCormick, p. 67.

24 Gill, ed., letter 93, pp. 133–4.

25 Gill, ed., letter 95, pp. 136–7.

26 For a thoughtful essay on these questions see: Barton, *Expatriates*.

27 Gill, ed., letter 96, pp. 137–40.

28 Gill, ed., letter 100, pp. 144–5.

29 In the July, of nine Moroccan pictures in a mixed watercolour show: it could well have been occasioned by the need to fill a gap in the gallery's schedule, of course, a possibility supported by the fact that Hodgkins never showed there again. In the 'complete list of exhibitions' published by the FAS on its centenary (*One Hundred Years of Exhibitions* (London: The Fine Art Society, 1976)) this show is mistakenly listed for July/August 1904.

30 A.J. Daplyn, *Australasian Art Review*, 1 May 1899, p. 14; quoted by Morgan, 'Thea Proctor the Artist', p. 30.

31 Roland Wakelin, quoted in Butler et al., *Thea Proctor: The Prints*, p. 7; it was allegedly on the advice of painter Tom Roberts, who had emigrated from England to Australia, but lived in the land of his birth from 1903 to 1923.

32 Letter to Mrs. Irvine, 20 November 1903. National Gallery of Australia Research Library. She later revised this view.

33 Letter from TP to Mrs. Irvine, 20 November 1903; quoted by Morgan, 'Thea Proctor the Artist', p. 31.

34 Quoted by Sarah Engledow in Humphries et al., *The World of Thea Proctor*, p. 29.

35 Mrs. E.L. Paul, 'Australian Artists Abroad: A Sydney Lady's Impressions', *Sydney Morning Herald*, 11 October 1904, p. 3. One of the competitions referred to was the Gilbert Garrett competition that she had entered as a student of St. John's Wood school, the other is unidentified.

36 Topliss, *Modernism and Feminism*, p. 37.

37 Sweetapple, 'Thea Proctor'.

38 Quoted from Thea Waddell in Morgan, 'Thea Proctor the Artist', p. 34.

39 See: Gray, *George Lambert 1873–1930*; Gray, *George W. Lambert Retrospective*.

40 See: Anon., 'Australians in England', *Sydney Morning Herald*, 14 August 1907, p. 5.

41 See, for instance: 'The Goupil Gallery', *The Times*, 22 March 1911, p. 7.

42 See Daw, 'The Ill-fated Pierrot', pp. 80–3; and Gerrish Nunn, 'Fine Art and the Fan'. For Proctor's subject-matter see, Morgan, 'Thea Proctor in London'.

43 Sweetapple, p. 183.

44 Though the example of Hilda Rix Nicholas, five years Proctor's junior, proves that time spent in France did not necessarily modernize an artist: see Pigot, *Hilda Rix Nicholas*.

45 She appeared there again in 1912.

46 Anon., 'Art Exhibitions', *The Times*, 17 November 1908, p. 4.

47 Pyms Gallery, *Orpen and the Edwardian Era* (London: Pym's Gallery London, 1987).

48 Letter to Isabel Craig, June 1963; quoted by Sarah Engledow in Humphries et al., p. 34.

49 See Proctor, 'Russian Ballet', p. 25, which shows similar preferences.

50 The other exhibitors were Patrick Adam, J.C.W. Cossar, Arthur Friedenson, R. Givelo Goodman, Alexander Jamieson, and Douglas Wells.

51 Anon., 'Our Artists Abroad', *Sydney Morning Herald*, 31 December 1906, p. 6.

52 Anon., 'Our Artists Abroad', *Sydney Morning Herald*, 31 December 1906, p. 7.

53 In the black-and-white section; also at Ghent in 1913, in unidentified fora in Rouen, Dusseldorf, Rome, and Paris. Morgan, 'Thea Proctor the Artist', p. 51, fn. 144.

54 Letter to Thea Bryant, c.1966; quoted by Engledow in Humphries et al., p. 36.

55 A substantial selection of works was included in the New South Wales Society of Artists' show in Sydney, November 1912, from which the Art Gallery of New South Wales bought a piece; a solo exhibition in Melbourne, September 1913, yielded two purchases by the National Gallery of Victoria; a solo exhibition in Sydney, May 1914 attracted considerable attention and was followed by a solo show in Adelaide (July).

56 Wakelin, *Thea Proctor*, unpaginated. Morgan contends that the trip was not intended to be a repatriation: Morgan, 'Thea Proctor the Artist', p. 52.

57 Stephens, 'Frances Hodgkins', p. ix.

Selected galleries, dealers, and exhibition spaces in London, 1850–1939

Pamela Fletcher and Anne Helmreich

Note: this glossary focuses on significant commercial spaces for the sale of fine art. Dates and addresses given are based on exhibition catalogues, press coverage, and directories, but these data can be incomplete or inconsistent. Starting and ending dates may thus reflect the limits of the evidence rather the actual opening or closing of a gallery space. In the absence of data about a gallery's closing date, we tracked the gallery until the volume's chronological limit of 1939.

R. Ackermann and Co.
7 Little Russell Street, Covent Garden (1794)
96 Strand (1795–97)
101 Strand (1797–1827)
96 Strand (1827–57)
R. Ackermann typifies the commercial art dealer whose trafficking in prints emerged from supplying artists' materials and various sundries. Rudolph Ackermann (1764–1834) became best known for his shop, the Repository of Arts, and publishing prints and illustrated journals, including the *Repository of Arts,* begun in 1809. His business was formulated through a variety of partnerships. The business closed in 1855 and the stock sold off through auctions from 1855 to 1857. Various members of the family continued as prominent art dealers located in London. Bibliography: *British Artists' Suppliers*, Rudolph Ackermann: www.npg.org.uk/research/programmes/directory-of-suppliers/a.php. Accessed 28 February 2010; Ford, *Ackermann, 1783–1983*.

Agnew and Sons
5 Waterloo Place (1860–77)
39 (later 43) Old Bond Street (1877–2008)
35 Albermarle Street (2010–present)
Thomas Agnew began his business in Manchester, and remained an important presence in that city throughout the Victorian period. In 1860, the firm opened a branch in London at 5 Waterloo Place, and the business was soon taken over by Agnew's sons, Thomas, Jr. and William. The gallery handled the work of contemporary artists, including Dante Gabriel Rossetti, William Powell Frith, and Fred Walker, as well as eighteenth-century British masters (including Reynolds, Gainsborough, and Hogarth) and Old Masters. In 1867, the gallery hosted its first annual exhibition of watercolours, a practice they continued into the 1960s. In 1877, the firm moved to larger premises at 39 (later 43) Old Bond Street. Microform copies of various stock books from 1853–1939 are available at National Art Library, London and the Getty Research Library, Los Angeles. Bibliography: Agnew, *Agnew's 1817–1967*.

Allied Artists' Association
The Allied Artists' Association was an artists' exhibiting society, founded by Frank Rutter in 1908, following the example of the French Société dés Independants. The international group had no jury; artists paid an annual fee and in exchange could exhibit five (later three) works of art at the annual London Salon. The display was organized by a Hanging Committee, the membership of which rotated among the members in alphabetical order. The first exhibition, in July 1908, included over 3,000 works of art. The first six exhibitions (1908–13) were held at the Royal Albert Hall; the seventh exhibition (1914) was hosted by the Holland Park Hall. No exhibition was held in 1915 because of the debts carried by the organization. In the eighth year (1916), the London Salon moved to the Grafton Galleries where the annual exhibitions were held until 1920. It then transferred to Messrs. Heal's Mansard Gallery before it ceased existence. Bibliography: Bullen, ed. *Post-Impressionists in England*; Rutter, *Since I was Twenty-Five*; Spalding, 'Allied Artists' Association'.

Arts and Crafts Bureau
34 Bloomsbury Street (1928–29)
This organization, governed by a council composed of such designers as Gordon Russell, Edward McKnight Kauffer, William Aumonier, Bernard Leach, and Claude Flight, began in May 1928 under the auspices of the magazine *Arts and Crafts*. The space (a former hotel, three floors and eight galleries) permitted the permanent display of suites of furniture and decorative arts. Bibliography: Harrod, *Crafts in Britain*.

Art Union of London (also sometimes known as The London Art Union)
112 Strand (1880–1912)
The organization was established in 1837, at the recommendation of the Select

Committee on the State of Arts and Manufactures in England, as a subscription society dedicated to the 'advancement of fine arts'. Payment of annual fees (originally one guinea) entitled subscribers to prizes in the forms of oil paintings, watercolours, sculptures, or prints. In 1838, the union expanded its activities to include commissioning graphic reproductions of paintings. In 1844, the Art Union was temporarily shut down; two years later, art unions were legalized and placed under the auspices of the Board of Trade and in that same year the Art Union of London received a Royal Charter that permitted incorporation. This led to reorganization of the group, including formation of a committee to select prize works of art. Exhibitions of prize-winning art were held annually; the first, in October 1839, was organized at Rainy's Gallery. In 1840, exhibitions moved to the rooms of the Society of British Artists at Suffolk Street; from 1867 to 1879 exhibitions were held at the spaces of the Institute of Painters in Water Colours. In 1880, the Art Union of London acquired its own building in the Strand and held its exhibitions there. The gradually declining income of the organization led to the decision, in 1892, to rent its spaces for other exhibitions. In 1912, with declining subscriptions, the organization voted to disband. Bibliography: King, *The Industrialization of Taste*.

Baillie Gallery
1 Princes Terrace, Hereford Road Bayswater (by 1902–5)
54 Baker Street (1905–8)
13 Bruton Street (1908–at least 1916)

In its early years it seems to have been an informal exhibition space in the dealer John Baillie's home: *The Times* described the space as 'a private house, where from time to time small and interesting shows are held' (*The Times*, 14 March 1904, p. 3). Despite its out-of-the-way location, it quickly acquired a good reputation, and a critic in the *Academy* hoped that Baillie's 'fresh discriminating view' might soon be seen closer to Piccadilly. ('Art Notes', *Academy*, 20 February 1904, p. 202). In 1905, Baillie moved his gallery space to 54 Baker Street, where he held a memorial exhibition of the work of Simeon Solomon from December 1905 to January 1906. In mid-1908, the gallery moved again to 13 Bruton Street. Exhibitions ranged from annual exhibitions of flower paintings, to the works of J.D. Fergusson, Glyn Philpot, and Aubrey Beardsley. The last exhibition catalogues from the Baillie Gallery in the National Art Library are dated to 1914, while the latest advertisement we have found appeared in *The Year's Art 1916*.

Beaux Arts Gallery
1 Burton Place, Burton Street (1923–65)

Established in 1923 and ceasing operations in 1965, the gallery was the responsibility of painter Frederick Lessore; his wife Helen Lessore took over the operations upon his death in 1951. The firm often showed the work of graduates of the Slade School of Art, where Helen Lessore had trained. Her book, *A Partial Testament*, focuses on artists exhibited at the Beaux Arts Gallery, including Craigie Aitchison, Michael Andrews, Frank Auerbach, Francis Bacon, Leon Kossoff, Evert Lundquist, Raymond Mason, and

Euan Uglow. The gallery also showed the work of Winifred Nicholson, Ben Nicholson, and Christopher Wood as well as potters W. Staite Murray and Reginald Wells. In addition, it hosted artists' groups, including the Seven and Five Society and the British Independent Society. Bibliography: Lessore, *A Partial Testament*; Bohm-Duchen, 'Lessore, Helen'.

Belgian Gallery
28 Old Bond Street (1875–77)
112 New Bond Street (1877–at least 1880)
In 1875, W.M. Rossetti greeted the opening of the Belgian Gallery at 28 Old Bond Street with considerable scepticism. An offshoot of the International Exhibitions at Albert Hall and under the management of Mr. J.H. Gammon, the exhibition was filled, in Rossetti's view, with 'slight, rough, and even rubbishy performances', primarily by Belgian artists (*Academy*, 24 April 1875, p. 434). In 1877, Gammon and his partner E.J. Vaughan moved to new premises at 112 New Bond Street, and the exhibitions they held there received more positive attention from the *Art Journal* and other periodicals. The gallery was not listed in *The Year's Art* and we have found no mention of it after 1880.

British Institution
52 Pall Mall (former Boydell Shakespeare Gallery) (1805–67)
Founded in 1805 as an exhibiting society for the work of living and dead artists and intended 'to encourage the talents of Artists of the United Kingdom; so as to improve and extend our manufactures, by that degree of taste and excellence which are to be exclusively derived from the cultivation of the Fine Arts; and thereby to increase the general prosperity and resources of the Empire' (Pullen, p. 277). It was distinguished from the Royal Academy by its subscription base of collectors and connoisseurs rather than artists, and was run by a governing Committee of Directors and Visitors. In 1805, the Directors of the British Institution purchased the lease of Boydell's Shakespeare Gallery for £4,500. The English Heritage Survey of London provides a useful description of the simple, 'monumental' facade and the exhibition rooms, which created 'over four thousand square feet' for hanging pictures. In 1806 the organization initiated a regular cycle of exhibitions devoted to the works of living artists; in 1815 and 1816 they added an additional exhibition devoted to past masters (loaned for this purpose). At the exhibitions, annual premiums were offered. Revenues were generated from entrance fees to its exhibitions. It ceased operations in 1867 and sold the building to the Marlborough Club. Bibliography: Ann Pullan, 'Public Goods or Private Interests: The British Institution in the Early Nineteenth Century', in *Art in Bourgeois Society*, eds. Hemingway and Vaughan, pp. 27-44; Tromans, 'Museum or Market?'; Pomeroy, 'Creating a National Collection'; 'Pall Mall, North Side, Past Buildings', *Survey of London: Volumes 29 and 30: St James Westminster, Part 1* (1960), pp. 325–38. URL: www.british-history.ac.uk/report.aspx?compid=40580&strquery= Boydell gallery. Accessed 22 February 2010.

Burlington Gallery
27 Old Bond Street (1883–at least 1907)

Multiple entities, at a variety of addresses, used the name the 'Burlington Gallery' in the nineteenth and twentieth centuries. Richard Altick notes an exhibition of an embalmed woman at the 'Burlington Gallery' at 191 Piccadilly in 1862, and advertisements for exhibitions at that address continue into the 1870s. (Altick, *Shows of London*, p. 267.) A Burlington Gallery at 27 Old Bond Street is listed in *The Year's Art* from 1882 to 1902, and we have found mention of the gallery at that address as late as 1907. During the years of their operation, they mounted various 'Colonial Exhibitions', as well as the work of Charles Sainton and Henry Riviere. In 1919, an exhibition catalogue at the National Art Library announces what seems to be a new 'Burlington Gallery' at 15 Green Street, Leicester Square, which 'aims at becoming the centre for the display of the best modern painting'. An item in the *International Studio* in 1918 reports that the space had previously been devoted to colour reproductions, but has recently inaugurated an exhibition of modern original art, including the work of J.D. Fergusson. (*International Studio*, 1918, p. 28). In the 1930s, the Goupil firm conducted business with the 'New Burlington Gallery', located at 3/5 Burlington Gardens.

Carfax Gallery
17 Ryder Street (1899–1905)
24 Bury Street (1905–at least 1920)

The Carfax Gallery, first located at 17 Ryder Street and then 24 Bury Street, was begun in 1899. Its physical situation at Bury Street was markedly different from nearby Bond Street galleries in that its rooms were small and the basement gallery presumably lacked the top lighting of most galleries. Solicitor Arthur Clifton managed the business affairs of the Carfax. John Fothergill appears to have approached William Rothenstein, who functioned as artistic adviser, with the idea of a 'shop' in 1898. Around 1901, Rothenstein left the firm, stymied with the difficulty of negotiating with his artist colleagues such as Charles Conder. Art critic Robert Ross then took over management of the firm, with the assistance of More Adey as well as Arthur Clifton. When Ross became the official critic of the *Morning Post* in 1908 he gave up his position with Carfax.

Carfax's stock and rotating exhibitions were a mix of contemporary British artists, such as Conder, Rothenstein, Augustus and Gwen John, Philip Wilson Steer, Max Beerbohm, William Orpen, and Paul Nash, and Old Masters and antiquities as well as deceased British masters such as William Blake. The firm also brokered the commission of a version of Auguste Rodin's *The Kiss* for antiquities collector E.P. Warren who may also have helped to finance the gallery. In 1911 and 1912, the gallery hosted the three Camden Town exhibitions. Bibliography: Ross, ed. *Robbie Ross*; Samuel Shaw, 'The Carfax Gallery and the Camden Town Group', *Camden Town Group Online Research Project*, www.tate.org.uk

Chenil Gallery
183a King's Road, Chelsea (1905–27)
The gallery, directed by Jack Knewstub (brother-in-law of William Orpen and William Rothenstein), opened in 1905 in a Georgian house. Artists' supplies and picture framing were also sold at the premises under the name 'Charles Chenil and Co.' Exhibitions were held in two upstairs rooms, the former site of the Arts Club dining and billiard rooms. On the lower level was a studio space with a printing press, often used by Augustus John. John was a frequent exhibitor as were Orpen, Ambrose McEvoy, and James Pryde; the firm particularly supported the younger generation of British modernists of the early twentieth century, such as David Bomberg, Eric Gill, and J.D. Innes. By the post-war period, the firm's reputation for bohemianism with a focus on individual personalities was no longer an effective marketing tool and Knewstub remodelled and expanded the premises to function more as an art and entertainment centre with funds derived from taking the business public and offering shares. The design, executed by George Kennedy, allowed for six galleries and included space for artists' studios, an art school, theatre, chamber orchestra, dance hall, and restaurant. The first exhibition, June 1925, was selected by the Chelsea Arts Club and included over 250 pictures. This was followed, in December of 1925, by an 'Exhibition of Tri-National Art' (British, French, and American) and in 1926 the 'Multi-national exhibition of works', both organized by Mrs. E.W. Harriman. One-person shows included Gwen John, Harry Fidler, Wilfred de Glehn, Martin Hardie, and Lucien Pissarro. But the firm was not financially successful and closed in 1927. Bibliography: *British Artists' Suppliers*, Chenil, www.npg.org.uk/research/programmes /directory-of-suppliers/c.php. Accessed 22 February 2010; Helmreich and Holt, 'Marketing Bohemia'.

Clifford Gallery
21 Haymarket (by 1895–at least 1910)
12 Bury Street, St. James's (1911–13)
3 Regent Street (1914–22)
8 Albany Street (1923–at least 1931)
This gallery was operated by the dealer C.E. Clifford, with William Batley added to the list of proprietors by 1906. Exhibitions included the work of Louise Jopling, and Albert Ludovici, and a wide range of topographical exhibitions.

Colnaghi
13/14 Pall Mall East (c.1821–1911)
144/6 New Bond Street (c.1911–40)
15 Old Bond Street (c.1940–at least 2011)
In 1780, Anthony Torre, whose father had run a shop that included print publishing and selling, liquidated the business. One of the creditors was the Italian-born Paul Colnaghi who joined forces with Torre in opening a shop in Market Lane, and then subsequently 132 Pall Mall, focusing on print selling. In 1788, Colnaghi assumed full

ownership of the business (although was briefly partnered with Anthony Molteno). In 1799 the firm moved to 23 Cockspur Street. In 1821, the firm passed to the two sons, Dominic and Martin, and after a law suit Paul Colnaghi regained ownership of the firm and he and Dominic reorganized the business at 13/14 Pall Mall East. While the firm's initial reputation was as a print seller, it branched out into the sale of contemporary art and Old Masters. In 1865, Dominic Colnaghi retired and his cousin Andrew McKay took over the business of the firm. The business passed to Andrew's son William McKay, who, in 1894, entered into partnership with E.F. Deprez and Otto Gutekunst (who had a close working relationship with Bernard Berenson), who helped the firm move into the American market. In 1907 Deprez retired followed by McKay in 1911. That same year, Gustavus Meyer joined Gutekunst and the firm conducted business under the name Messrs. P. & D. Colnaghi & Obach (for three years), taking up new premises at 144–6 New Bond Street (designed by Lanchester and Rickards). In 1937, Colnaghi became a limited company, directed by O. Gutekunst. In 1940, in partnership with Knoedler's, with whom they had had a long working relationship, they relocated to 15 Old Bond Street where the firm remains today. Bibliography: Garstang, ed. *Art, Commerce, Scholarship*; Jeremy Howard, ed. *Colnaghi, Established 1760: the History* (London: Colnaghi, 2010).

Continental Gallery
157 New Bond Street (by 1885–at least 1904)
Managed by Arthur William Binstead, the Continental Gallery specialized in, as the name suggests, paintings from Europe. Annual exhibitions advertised pictures by a variety of French, German, Italian, and Norwegian artists. The gallery regularly highlighted pictures from the Paris Salon, including an exhibition in 1896 of *Startling Pictures from the Paris Salons*, which included work by Jan van Beers, Jean Delville, and Jean Veber.

Crystal Palace Picture Gallery
Sydenham (1856–c.1900)
The Crystal Palace – built to house the Great Exhibition of 1851 – was relocated to Sydenham after the Exhibition closed, and a Picture Gallery was opened in 1856 as one of many attractions in the entertainment complex. The Picture Gallery was managed by Charles Wentworth Wass, and exhibited paintings by both British and foreign artists.

Doré Gallery
35 New Bond Street (1868–1914)
Established in 1868 by Messrs. James Fairless and George Lord Beeforth to showcase the work of French artist Gustave Doré, who had previously exhibited in London at the Egyptian Hall (1867) and the German Gallery (1868). They commissioned the *Fall of Paganism* (now known as *Triumph of Christianity over Paganism*) (1867–68), the success of which led to the establishment of the gallery at 35 New Bond Street, as well as an ongoing project in which Doré annually produced a major work of religious art to

be sent to London for display at the gallery (perhaps after having been shown at the Salon), with smaller replicas and prints after the painting to be sold at the gallery as well as drawings. The London gallery also arranged for the works to tour in New York. Around the turn of the century, Joseph Fishburn took over the management of the firm, expanded the space to approximately six large galleries, and organized a series of rotating exhibitions. This eclectic mix included the work of Walter Crane (1902), battle pictures by Henri Dupray (1902), and exhibitions of coloured etchings and engravings organized by the Parisian Galleries' Georges Petit (1907, 1914). In 1913 and 1914, the venue hosted several important modernist exhibitions including the *Post-Impressionist Poster Exhibition* and *Post-Impressionist and Futurist Exhibition*, both organized by Frank Rutter, as well as pictures by John Duncan Fergusson and works of the Italian Futurist painters and sculptors, both in 1914. The firm ceased operation in 1914. Bibliography: 'Sotheby's and the Doré Gallery', *The Times*, 7 November 1913; Zafran et al. *Fantasy and Faith*.

Dowdeswells
36 Chancery Lane (by 1865)
133 New Bond Street (by 1880–86)
160 New Bond Street (1887–1916)

Charles William Dowdeswell operated a frame and print shop on Chancery Lane in the 1860s and by 1880 had opened a fine art gallery on New Bond Street. The gallery is best known for handling the work of James McNeill Whistler, and publishing prints by Whistler, Seymour Hayden, and Charles Meyron, but they also held exhibitions of the work of Birket Foster, Sutton Palmer, and a wide variety of British watercolour artists. Dowdeswell died on 11 May 1915. Exhibitions continued through 1916, but by 1917 the business was liquidated. Bibliography: 'Dowdeswell, William (C).' In *Grove Art Online. Oxford Art Online*.

Dudley Gallery (see Egyptian Hall)

Dutch Gallery (E.J. van Wisselingh)
14 Brook Street (by 1894–1904)
14 Grafton Street (1905)
14 Grafton Street (as E.J. van Wisselingh's Gallery) (1906–at least 1914)

This firm of fine art dealers was founded in Amsterdam in 1838 by Henrik Jan van Wisselingh, who sold a variety of materials, including artists' materials and prints. By the mid-century, the firm developed a reputation for handling Barbizon School work as well as the work of Antoine Vollon and Gustave Courbet. In the 1860s, the firm began to sell the Hague School.

A London branch was initiated in 1892, under the name The Dutch Gallery, capitalizing on the growing taste for Barbizon and Hague school painters fostered by such collectors as James Staat Forbes. The firm also handled the work of contemporary British artists including William Rothenstein, Charles Ricketts, Charles Shannon, and

Charles Conder. Bibliography: Heijbroek and Wouthuysen, *Portret van een kunsthandel*; Hopkinson, 'Review of *Portret van een kunsthandel*'.

Duveen Brothers
21 Old Bond-Street (c.1892–1914)
4 Grafton Street (1920–41)
14 Albermarle Street (1941–at least 1947)
Duveen Brothers was an international art, furniture, and decorative arts firm with locations in New York, London, and Paris. Here we discuss the London branch. Joseph Joel Duveen first immigrated from Holland to operate an import–export business in Hull with Barney Barnett; this partnership ended in 1876. The first London gallery associated with Joel Duveen, located at 357 Oxford Street, is thought to be associated with the Hull business. Around 1879 Joel Duveen purchased the lease at 181 Oxford Street for the sale of decorative objects. In 1893, according to Secrest, Joel Duveen moved to 21 Old Bond Street, organizing rotating exhibitions in a ground floor gallery and displaying goods, including porcelains, tapestries, and pictures (pp. 35–6). Joel's well-known son Joseph Duveen helped to expand the business into Old Master paintings, as well as sculpture, and cultivated relationships with important collectors, such as Henry Clay Frick, Henry Huntington, Samuel H. Kress, and Andrew Mellon, and connoisseurs, including Bernard Berenson and Wilhelm von Bode. By the 1890s, the firm was known as the Duveen Brothers in recognition of a partnership with Henry Duveen and Joel Duveen. In 1914, before the outbreak of the war, the firm decided to leave its London premises to concentrate the business in Paris and New York. For the duration of the war they made the Old Bond Street premises available to charities, and in 1920 opened a new space at 4 Grafton Street. The London branch, by 1941, functioned, according to *The Year's Art*, as 'correspondents' for Duveen Brothers, New York, indicating that the focus of business had shifted to that city. The firm passed to Armand Lowengard and Edward Fowles upon Joseph Duveen's death on 25 May 1939 and closed in 1964 with Fowles's death. The majority of the Duveen Archive (1876–1981) is presently owned by the Getty Research Institute, which has made it more widely accessible through microfilm. The Clark Library owns the library and any related business records. Bibliography: Getty Research Institute Finding Aid: http://archives.getty.edu:8082/cgi/f/findaid/findaid-idx?c=utf8a;idno=US::CMalG::960015. Accessed 26 February 2010; Duveen, *The Rise of the House of Duveen*; Secrest, *Duveen*. With special thanks to Charlotte Vignon for her advice.

Egyptian Hall (Dudley Gallery)
Demolished, now 170–1 Piccadilly
In 1812, William Bullock arranged for the construction of a purpose-built space, designed by Peter Frederick Robinson, to house his natural history collections. Robinson's building featured an Egyptian inspired facade and two large exhibition galleries. The space was shared with Bullock's brother, George, a furniture designer and seller, who sold his wares from the Egyptian Hall. By 1816, Bullock was advertising

a 'sales area', also denoted the Roman Gallery, within the Hall, 'for the reception, exhibition, and sale, by commission, of every article connected with the fine arts, antiquity, and natural history' (Pearce, p. 21), probably designed by J.B. Papworth. This space also contained pictures and this was most likely where Benjamin Haydon and Théodore Géricault displayed their major works to the public in 1820. Bullock went on to organize a number of ethnographic displays. In 1825 Bullock relinquished his lease to George Lackington, a bookseller, who continued to use the Hall for exhibitions and then, in 1831, as a bazaar. In the 1830s and 1840s, the space was occasionally let for panoramic displays, including the Battle of Waterloo (1838, 1845). Lord Dudley, in 1850, used the Egyptian Hall to display his personal collection; the Survey of London reasons that this was the 'western wing at the rear of the main building'. This space became known as the Dudley Gallery and was hired for a number of rotating exhibitions, including those of watercolour artists as well as the New English Art Club. The lease, as of the 1870s, was managed by J.M. Maskelyne, who provided 'magical entertainments' in the first floor room. The lease expired in 1905 and the Egyptian Hall and neighbouring properties were demolished and redeveloped. Bibliography: Pearce, 'William Bullock'; 'Piccadilly, South Side', *Survey of London: Volumes 29 and 30: St James Westminster, Part 1* (1960), pp. 251–70. URL: www.british-history.ac.uk/report.aspx?compid=40571&strquery=Egyptian Hall. Accessed 22 February 2010.

Fine Art Society
148 New Bond St (1876–at least 2010)

The Fine Art Society was founded in 1876. The firm published reproductive engravings and exhibited and sold paintings and drawings, primarily by British artists. Managed by Marcus Bourne Huish, the gallery exhibited the work of a wide range of Victorian artists, including John Everett Millais, Frederic Leighton, Elizabeth Thompson, Helen Allingham, and James MacNeill Whistler. Bibliography: Faberman, '"Best Shop in London"'.

Flatou, Louis (1820–67)

Louis Flatou (sometimes spelled Flatow) was a major dealer in contemporary art in the 1850s and 1860s. He began his career by dealing in 'Old Masters' and seems to have worked for a period of time as a chiropodist, before moving back into art dealing at mid-century. He was reputed to be illiterate and many contemporary accounts of Flatou are shaped by stereotypical, even anti-Semitic, views about art dealers. He worked with many of the leading artists of the period, including Henry O'Neil, Frederick Goodall, and George Elgar Hicks. His most famous collaboration was with William Powell Frith, whom he paid £4,500 for the painting, sketches, and engraving rights of *The Railway Station*. Bibliography: Maas, *Gambart*; Frith, *Autobiography*.

The French Gallery
120 and 121 Pall Mall (by 1854–1929)
158 New Bond Street (1930–31)
11 Berkeley Square (c.1932–at least 1937)
35 Old Bond Street (by 1937–at least 1939)
The French Gallery was founded by the picture dealer and print publisher Ernest Gambart by 1854. The gallery held annual spring exhibitions of the French School from 1854 until at least 1896, and annual winter exhibitions of the British School. During Gambart's tenure, the gallery exhibited work by many of the most prominent artists of the period, including John Everett Millais, William Holman Hunt, Ford Madox Brown, Barbara Leigh Smith Bodichon, and Rosa Bonheur. In 1867, Gambart sold the lease of the gallery to the dealer Henry Wallis (who had been managing the space since 1861). Wallis's son Thomas took over the business, and the French Gallery continued to mount regular exhibitions well into the early twentieth century. Around 1932, the firm moved to 11 Berkeley Square where it incorporated the bankrupt Goupil Gallery. The exact nature of the merger is unclear, but Goupil continued to be a recognizable brand. Listings in *The Year's Art* between 1933 and 1937 note that the Goupil Gallery 'is now embodied with the French Gallery', and the annual Goupil Gallery Salon retained its title, though catalogues were published by the French Gallery. The French Gallery continued to have an autonomous listing, and moved to 35 Old Bond Street by 1937. Bibliography: Maas, *Gambart*; Fletcher, 'Creating the French Gallery'.

Gambart, Ernest (1814–1902)
See also: French Gallery, Lefevre Gallery
Belgian-born Ernest Gambart arrived in London in 1840, as an agent of the French print publisher Goupil. He quickly struck out on his own, operating a print export, import, and publishing business at 25 Berners Street. In 1854, he began mounting annual 'French Exhibitions' at 120 and 121 Pall Mall, a space that would soon become known as the French Gallery. One of the most successful galleries of the 1850s and 1860s, it was known for its annual exhibitions of French art and Winter exhibitions of British art, as well as for showing the work of artists such as Rosa Bonheur, John Everett Millais, and Lawrence Alma-Tadema. In 1867, he sold the lease of the gallery to Henry Wallis, and moved his business temporarily to 22 Albemarle Street, near Burlington House, the new home of the Royal Academy. He soon opened a new gallery space at 1A King Street with his nephew Léon Lefèvre and F.J. Pilgeram. In 1870, he retired to his lavish home in Nice, France, where he died in 1902. Bibliography: Maas, *Gambart*.

'German Gallery'
168 New Bond Street
A wide variety of exhibitions were held at the 'German Gallery' from the late 1830s on. While the space was regularly identified in the press as the 'German Gallery', it was not exclusively identified with a single dealer or firm. The name seems to have come from a series of exhibitions of contemporary German art that were held in the

space beginning in the spring of 1853. In a review, the *Art Journal* indicates that it is to be an annual event organized by a dealer. (*Art Journal*, June 1853, p. 161) Between the 1850s and the 1870s, many prominent dealers and artists held exhibitions in the space, including Gambart's exhibition of Rosa Bonheur's paintings (1858); the photographs of Julia Margaret Cameron (1868); the work of Gustave Doré (1868); and the exhibitions the French dealer Paul Durand-Ruel organized under the name of the 'Society of French Artists' (1871–75), which included work by Edouard Manet and Claude Monet.

Goupil Gallery
17 Southampton Street (1857–75)
25 Bedford Street (1875–c.1883)
116 and 117 New Bond Street (c.1883–92)
5 Regent Street (c.1893–1931)
11 Berkeley Square (c.1933–c.1937)
3/5 Burlington Gardens (c.1937–41)
In the early 1850s, the Paris firm Adolph Goupil & Co. opened a branch in London. In 1857, the firm's name appears in London Post Office directories as booksellers located at 17 Southampton Street, the Strand. By 1865, Post Office directories designate the firm as printsellers and print publishers and Henry Gutekunst as the firm's agent. In 1868, Post Office directories indicate that Charles Obach was the branch manager. The firm took up new premises in 25 Bedford Street, Strand in 1875; Post Office directories list the firm as picture dealers and importers as well as printsellers and print publishers. The firm relocated its shop to 116 and 117 New Bond Street c.1883 and was managed by David Croal Thomson. Because of the restructuring of the Paris main house, the London firm was also known at this time as Boussod, Valadon & Co. By 1893, the firm moved to 5 Regent Street. In 1898 William Marchant became the London branch manager. Post Office directories indicate that the Paris main house re-opened the branch at 25 Bedford Street at this time, focusing its business on printselling and publishing. In 1901, William Marchant became the owner of the Goupil Gallery and, in 1907, successfully brought suit against the Paris main house to retain use of the name Goupil Gallery. Around 1906 he began the practice of the annual Goupil Salon. In 1925, upon William Marchant's death, his wife Cicely Marchant, began managing the firm. In order to raise cash, she formed the company the Goupil Gallery Ltd. In 1933, following bankruptcy of the firm, the Goupil Gallery Ltd. was liquidated. Mrs. Marchant then moved her business to 11 Berkeley Square, home of the French Gallery, and sometimes adopted that name but continued to host the Goupil seasonal Salons. In c.1937, the firm moved again to 3/5 Burlington Gardens, readopting the name The Goupil Gallery but also using The New Burlington Galleries for the premises. In 1941, the gallery was bombed. Bibliography: Bailey, *Van Gogh in England*; Helmreich, 'Art Dealer and Taste'; Eric Gill Archive, Clark Library, UCLA; Tate Archives, Finding Aid: http://archive.tate.org.uk/DServe/dserve.exe?dsqServer=tb-calm&dsqIni=Dserve. ini&dsqApp=Archive&dsqCmd=Show.tcl&dsqDb=Catalog&dsqPos=11&dsqSearch=% 28%28text%29=%27Marchant%27%29. Accessed 27 February 2010.

Grafton Galleries
8 Grafton Street (1891–at least 1920)
The Grafton Galleries were incorporated in June 1891 as the Grafton Galleries Limited for the purpose of establishing galleries for the display of art, as well as rooms for public entertainments, such as music and dancing, and refreshment. The company was also given the power to establish a Club on the premises. The initial directors included Viscount Baring, MP, Alfred Farquhar, Esq., the Marquis of Granby, MP, the Rt. Hon. Lord Hothfield, W.G. Rathbone, Esq., Emanual Maguire Underdown Esq., QC, and the Rt. Hon. The Earl of Wharncliffe, each of whom owned at least 100 shares. *The Year's Art* reported that the structure was built in 1893; designed by Messrs. Wimperis and Arber. According to Frank Rutter, by 1915, the Grafton Galleries were owned by the Yorkshire Penny Bank at Leeds (p. 197). Roger Fry was appointed the artistic adviser to the Grafton Galleries around 1905 and organized there the two important Post-Impressionist exhibitions. The Grafton Galleries also hosted the Allied Artists' Association exhibitions, 1916–20. Bibliography: Memorandum and Articles of Association of the Grafton Galleries Limited, Incorporated the 17th of June, 1891, Tate Gallery Archives TGA 73–7/1; Fry, Roger to William Rothenstein, 4 August 1905; Roger Fry to William Rothenstein, 28 March 1911, Sir William Rothenstein Correspondence and Other Papers (MS Eng 1148), Houghton Library, Harvard University; Rutter, *Since I was Twenty-Five*.

Henry Graves and Co.
6 Pall Mall (by 1890–1919)
60 and 61 Old Bond Street (1920–at least 1922)
182 Sloane Street (by 1928–at least 1936)
38 Bury Street (1940–41)
Henry Graves was a London-based art dealer instrumental in founding the *Art Journal*. His firm, founded in 1844, initially focused on print publishing, but expanded into the fine arts. In 1920, the firm moved to 60 and 61 Old Bond Street in an amalgamation with the firm of Gooden and Fox, but by 1923 was trading under the name Henry Graves & Co. Bibliography: Chapel, 'The Papers of Joseph Gillott'.

Grosvenor Gallery
135–7 New Bond Street (1877–90)
The Grosvenor Gallery, founded by Sir Coutts Lindsay (1824–1913) and Blanche, Lady Lindsay (1844–1912), was dubbed a 'palace of art' by the London press because of its grand scale and spectacle. Built by William Thomas Sams, the facade was executed in a 'Neo-Renaissance' manner. The interiors, in addition to galleries, also allowed for entertaining. In 1877, the owners instituted a membership policy whereby members (limited to 500) could purchase a season ticket for admission at any time. The Grosvenor featured a summer exhibition of contemporary art and winter exhibitions that included Old Masters, as well as one-person shows of contemporary artists such as George F. Watts and John Everett Millais. The Grosvenor Gallery gained a

reputation for Aestheticism for its predilection for showing the works of such painters as Whistler and Edward Burne-Jones. The Lindsays earned income for the gallery by charging admission (one shilling; season tickets for five shillings), selling catalogues, and taking a 5 per cent commission on sales. The Grosvenor sought to suppress its commercial status by mimicking the spaces of private aristocratic homes. In 1883 Sir Coutts Lindsay instituted electricity for lighting the galleries and, based on demand from neighbours, created a generating station at the gallery under the auspices of the newly formed Sir Coutts Lindsay and Company. This led to the establishment, in 1887, of the London Electric Supply Corporation Limited and the generating station was moved to Deptford. In 1890, Coutts could no longer financially support the Grosvenor Gallery and its galleries were taken over by the Grosvenor Club. Bibliography: 'Bourdon Street and Grosvenor Hill Area', *Survey of London: Volume 40: The Grosvenor Estate in Mayfair, Part 2 (The Buildings)* (1980), pp. 57–63. URL: www.british-history.ac.uk/ report.aspx?compid=42105&strquery=New Gallery regent. Accessed 28 February 2010; Casteras and Denney, eds. *Grosvenor Gallery*; Denney, *Temple of Art*; Newall, *The Grosvenor Gallery Exhibitions*.

Heal's Mansard Gallery
196 Tottenham Court Road (1917–70s)

Heal's is a well-known London department store, begun by John Harris Heal in 1810. In 1840, the business located to Tottenham Court Road and in 1854 a purpose-built space was constructed to house the department store. In 1916–17, the store, then under the management of designer Ambrose Heal, was redesigned by Cecil Brewer. At this time, space on the top floor was created for an art gallery, which existed until the 1970s. Roger Fry was responsible for curating the first exhibition; interior designer Prudence Maufe ran the gallery from 1917. The gallery hosted a number of important group exhibitions, such as that of the London Group and Group X; favoured the work of graduates of the Slade School of Art; and included designs, crafts, and fine art. Bibliography: www.heals.co.uk. Accessed 28 February 2010; Goodden, *At the Sign of the Four Poster*.

Japanese Gallery (Renaissance Gallery; Larkin Gallery)
14 Grafton Street (1881–84)
7 King Street, St. James's (1884–88)
28 New Bond Street (1889–at least 1900)
104 New Bond Street (by 1906 (as Renaissance Gallery) –at least 1919)

The Japanese Gallery was run by Thomas Joseph Larkin, a dealer and member of the Japanese Fine Art Association. Larkin had learned about Japanese art and ceramics during his time as a civil engineer for the Japanese government and established his business in London in 1881. The Japanese Gallery exhibited ancient and modern Japanese art and ceramics, as well as paintings done by British artists in Japan. They also held an annual exhibition of British watercolours, and occasional exhibitions of other topographical or historical works. After 1900, the gallery also did business as the

Renaissance Gallery and the Larkin Gallery. Larkin died in 1915, leaving the business under the management of his son, Frederick J. Larkin. Bibliography: 'Thomas Joseph Larkin', *Burlington Magazine* 26 (March 1915), p. 263; 'The Late Thomas Joseph Larkin', *Connoisseur* 41 (1915), p. 232.

Lefevre Gallery
1A King Street, St. James's (by 1868–1943)
131 New Bond Street (1944–50)
30 Bruton Street (1950–2002)
The firm's origins can be traced to Ernest Gambart and his nephew Léon Lefèvre. After selling the French Gallery to Henry Wallis in 1867, Gambart, Lefèvre and F.J. Pilgeram (both of whom had worked for Gambart at the French Gallery) opened a gallery space at 1A King Street, St. James's. After Gambart's retirement in 1870, Lefèvre and Pilgeram operated the gallery in partnership. In 1915, upon Lefèvre's death, the firm passed to his son Ernest-Albert. In 1923, Glasgow-based dealer Alexander Reid, who had developed a reputation for selling Impressionist and Post-Impressionist French painting, collaborated with the Lefèvre firm on several exhibitions of modern French art and the positive results led to the formation of the firm Messrs. Alex Reid & Lefèvre, whose directors included Reid's son A.J. McNeill Reid and the influential French dealer Etienne Bignou. Bombing in 1943 led to the relocation of the firm to New Bond Street; the Bruton Street locale allowed for larger galleries. The gallery closed in 2002, the victim, managing director and partner Martin Summers explained, of the rise of the New York art market and the impact of new EU taxes. Bibliography: Maas, *Gambart*; *Alex Reid & Lefevre*; Colin Gleadell, 'London out of the picture as gallery closes'. *Daily Telegraph* 12 January 2002, www.telegraph.co.uk/news/uknews/1381188/London-out-of-the-picture-as-gallery-closes.html. Accessed 9 March 2010.

Leicester Galleries
Leicester Square (1903–77)
The Leicester Galleries were established in 1903 by the firm of Ernest Brown & Phillips. Like other galleries at this time specializing in contemporary art, its early exhibitions included topographical subjects as well as the work of better-known artists such as James McNeill Whistler (1903) and John Lavery (1904). It adopted the strategy of using well-known artists, such as George Clausen, and critics, such as Frederick Wedmore, F.G. Stephens, Sidney Colvin, and Laurence Binyon, to author exhibition catalogues as well as the practice of leavening exhibitions of contemporary British and French art with that of the previous generation, and with the occasional Old Master. A full list of the exhibitions organized by the gallery can be found at www.ernestbrownandphillips. ltd.uk/Static/Monographs.html. Accessed 28 February 2010.

Little Gallery
Ellis Street (1928–39)
This firm was initiated in 1928 by two former employees of the Three Shields

Gallery, Muriel Rose and Margaret Turnbull. The gallery interior was designed by Raymond Erith. In addition to displaying contemporary British crafts, the gallery also imported decorative objects from overseas and showed manufactured products such as Wedgwood. Bibliography: Harrod, *Crafts in Britain*.

Mayor Gallery
37 Sackville Street (by 1925–26)
18 Cork Street (1933–36)
19 Cork Street (1936– closed during the war)
14 Brook Street (1946–59)
14 South Molton Street (1959–77)
22A Cork Street (1977–at least 2010)
The Mayor Gallery was founded by Frederick ('Freddy') Mayor (1903–75) in January 1925, and closed in April–May 1926. It re-opened in 1933; *The Times*, in an article of 12 October 1955, attributed it to both Frederick Mayor and the art historian Douglas Cooper. During the gallery's closure, Mayor was involved with the London Artists' Association and in 1928 became director of the Paul Guillaume Gallery in London. In the 1920s, the Mayor Gallery promoted leading younger French artists such as Pablo Picasso, Fernand Léger, Auguste Herbin, and André Lhote and it had connections with the Paris Gallerie de l'Effort moderne run by Léonce Rosenberg. In the inter-war period, the Mayor Gallery was an important site for displays of contemporary British, French, and, in the 1930s, German art. Its exhibitions included the work of Paul Nash, Ivon Hitchens, Matthew Smith, Paul Klee, and Max Ernst. It also hosted exhibitions of Surrealist art (including a Roland Penrose and Ithel Colquhoun exhibition in 1939) as well as the artists' group Unit One (1934, organized by Douglas Cooper), and the Art Now show (organized by Herbert Read in October 1933). The refurbished galleries that opened in April 1933 featured an innovative open plan designed by Brian O'Rorke. The gallery passed to Mayor's son, James Mayor, in 1973. Press cutting albums for the gallery covering the years 1925–26, 1933–35, 1936–37, and 1938–53 are held by Tate Archives, London. (Special thanks to Andrew Stephenson for his advice on this entry.)

McLean's Gallery
7 Haymarket (by 1865–at least 1922)
Thomas McLean was a print dealer and publisher who followed the common practice of exhibiting paintings as publicity for the forthcoming engravings. The *Art Journal* notes that his business is in the Haymarket by 1853, with the street number (7) given in 1865. In the mid-1860s, he began holding annual exhibitions of watercolour drawings and soon expanded his exhibitions to include oil paintings, including works by Frederick Goodall, Vicat Cole, and Lawrence Alma-Tadema. In 1910, *The Year's Art* identified Eugene Cremetti as McLean's 'successor', and the business continued to be listed at 7 Haymarket until at least 1922.

Modern Gallery
175 New Bond Street (by 1897–1904)
61 New Bond Street (1905–at least 1918)
Run by Edward Freeman, the Modern Gallery offered galleries for rent for 'Special' and
'One-Man' exhibitions, and 'At Homes', 'Soirees, Lectures, etc. (*The Year's Art 1905*).
Exhibitions held there included the work of Herbert J. Finn and R. Murdoch Wright.

Curtis Moffat Studio
4 Fitzroy Square (1929–33)
American Curtis Moffat (1877–1949) studied painting and then took up photography in
the early 1920s while living in Paris where he was associated with the circle of Man Ray.
He first opened a photography portrait studio in London in 1925 with Olivia Wyndham
and then, four years later, he initiated an interior design company and showroom,
focusing on modernist furniture and a machine-age aesthetic, and also including
European antiques. He arranged for the architect Frederick Etchells to redesign the
space (originally designed by Robert Adam), producing a quintessential modernist
interior. The firm closed in the wake of the Great Depression. The Victoria and
Albert Museum holds the Moffat archive. Bibliography: www.vam.ac.uk/collections/
photography/features/photo_focus/moffat/index.htn. Accessed 22 February 2010

New Gallery
121 Regent Street (1888–1910)
Founded in 1888 by the former managers of the Grosvenor Gallery, Charles Hallé
and J.W. Comyns Carr, this gallery was located in a purpose-built space designed by
Edward Robert Robson. The luxuriously appointed interior featured several galleries.
The gallery drew upon many of the same artists associated with the Grosvenor Gallery
as indicated by the consulting committee which included L. Alma-Tadema, E. Burne-
Jones, W.B. Richmond, H. Herkomer, A. Gilbert, E. Onslow Ford, W. Holman Hunt,
J.W. North, and A. Parsons. It organized its exhibitions around an annual summer
exhibition of contemporary art and a winter exhibition featuring older work, including
a Stuart Exhibition in 1889, a Tudor Exhibition in 1890, and an exhibition of the works
of the Royal House of Guelph in 1891. It also hosted several exhibitions of the Arts
and Crafts Exhibition Society, the last in 1910 when the gallery closed. It was initially
converted to a restaurant and then a cinema. Bibliography: Blackburn, *New Gallery Notes*.

New Handworkers' Guild Gallery
4 Percy Street (c.1928)
Begun in around 1928 by Philip Mairet, with the assistance of his wife Edith Mairet,
this gallery focused on crafts and also promoted standards and aesthetics in the field
through a series of commissioned pamphlets authored by its exhibitors, including
Romney Green, Bernard Leach, Eric Gill, and Mairet himself. Bibliography: Harrod,
Crafts in Britain.

Gordon Russell Studio
29 Wigmore Street (1929–34)
40 Wigmore Street (1935–40)
Gordon Russell (1892–1980) was raised in Broadway, Worcestershire, where he received early training in furniture repair through his father's business, which also dealt in antiques (he also owned the Lygon Arms inn). After the war, Russell focused on modern furniture design. His first retail showroom was in Broadway but then in 1929 he opened a London showroom, leased from Debenhams, the same year the company was renamed Gordon Russell Ltd. In 1933, facing possible closure because of the financial pressures of the Great Depression, Gordon's brother Dick proposed a new strategy of producing a line of less expensive furniture while simultaneously displaying entire suites of furniture in order to appeal to more high-end buyers. In 1935, in order to accommodate a bigger showroom, a new space was procured at 40 Wigmore Street with an interior designed by Geoffrey Jellicoe. Bibliography: Myerson, *Gordon Russell.*

Salon Parisien
160 New Bond Street (1885–86)
New Bond Street (1887–92)
Operated by Messrs. Cochrane and Mertens, the Salon Parisien had a fairly short existence, and featured the work of Belgian artist Jan Van Beers most prominently among the work of other Continental artists.

Three Shields Gallery
Holland Street (c.1922)
This firm, founded by Dorothy Hutton, mixed the fine arts and crafts and included the work of Frances Richards, Bernard Leach, and John Paul Cooper. Bibliography: Harrod, *Crafts in Britain.*

Arthur Tooth & Sons
Haymarket (1842–1905)
175 New Bond Street (1906–8)
155 New Bond Street (1909–at least 1939)
Established in 1842, Arthur Tooth & Sons opened a new gallery dedicated to fine art at 5 Haymarket in 1867. The new gallery was inaugurated with a 'Winter Exhibition' of watercolours, including work by living and deceased artists including Samuel Prout, J.M.W. Turner, David Cox, and Simeon Solomon. Annual spring and summer exhibitions were added over the course of the nineteenth century. In the post-war years, the gallery continued to exhibit both British and Continental contemporary art as well as Old Master work, including shows devoted to Modigliani (1926), Giorgio de Chirico (1928), Gainsborough (1931), Barbara Hepworth and Ben Nicholson (1932), and Matthew Smith (1932). Various stock books from 1871 to 1941 are held at the Getty Research Library, Los Angeles, as well as some material from the New York branch of

the firm; copyright registers from 1870 to 1924 are held at the Tate Archives, London. Bibliography: Bayer and Page, 'Arthur Tooth'.

Asher Wertheimer
158 New Bond Street (at least 1892–1918)

Asher Wertheimer came to art dealing through his father, Samson, who had emigrated from Germany to Great Britain in 1830 and established a firm in New Bond Street. In 1892 Samson died and the business was divided between his two sons, Charles and Asher, with Asher retaining the galleries. Frank Rutter regarded Asher's firm as comparable to that of Sir Joseph Duveen: 'pictures are not much more than a side-line; they purchase and sell important pictures from time to time, but they also trade in a large variety of other works of art, decorative furniture, tapestries, porcelain and all sorts of *objets d'art*. When they do traffic in paintings it is nearly always in works by Old Masters' (pp. 170–1). In 1898, Wertheimer came to national attention by acquiring the collection of the Hope family, which featured works by early Dutch and Flemish masters. Bibliography: Kleeblatt, *John Singer Sargent*; 'Obituary', *The Times*, 12 August 1918, p. 9; Rutter, *Since I was Twenty-Five*.

Bibliography

Periodicals

Academy

Advertising World

Apollo

Architect and Building News

Artist

Art Journal (Art-Union)

Arts and Crafts: A Monthly Review of Arts and Handicrafts

Arts League of Service Bulletin

Artwork

Athenaeum

Australasian Art Review

Bookman

Building News and Engineering Journal

Burlington Magazine for Connoisseurs

Bystander

Chambers's Edinburgh Journal

Colour

Commercial Art

Connoisseur: an Illustrated Magazine for Collectors

Cork Examiner

Cornhill Magazine

Country Life in South Africa

Daily Express

Daily Mail

Daily Mirror

Daily News

Daily Telegraph

Design for To-day

Drawing and Design

Dublin Express

Everylady's Journal

Fortnightly Review
Fraser's Magazine
Gentleman's Magazine
Harper's Bazaar
Horizon
Illustrated London News
Listener
Magazine of Art
Manchester Guardian
Le Moniteur des Arts
Morning Post
Musical World
Nation and Athenaeum
New Age
New Statesman and Nation
New York Times
Nineteenth Century
Observer
Portfolio
Rhythm
Saturday Review
Scotsman
Star
Studio
Studio Year-Book of Decorative Art
Sunday News
The Sunday Times (London)
Sydney Morning Herald
Tait's Edinburgh Magazine
The Times
Tinsley's Magazine
Truth
Vogue
Weekend Review
Weekly Irish Times
Year-Book
The Year's Art
Yorkshire Evening Post
Yorkshire Telegraph
World

Books, articles, and websites

Agnew, Geoffrey. *Agnew's, 1817–1967*. London: Bradbury Agnew Press, 1967.

Agnew, Julian et al. *Agnew's 1982–1992*. London: Endeavour, [c.1992].

Alex Reid & Lefevre, 1926–1976. London: The Lefevre Gallery, 1976.

Allen, Brian, ed. *Towards a Modern Art World*. London and New Haven: Yale University Press, 1995.

Altick, Richard. *The Shows of London*. Cambridge, Massachusetts and London: The Belknap Press of Harvard University Press, 1978.

An Alphabetical List of Engravings Declared at the Office of the Printsellers' Association, London. London: Printed for the Printsellers' Association, 1892.

Anger, Jenny. *Paul Klee and the Decorative in Modern Art*. Cambridge: Cambridge University Press, 2004.

Appadurai, Arjun, ed. *The Social Life of Things: Commodities in Cultural Perspective*. Cambridge: Cambridge University Press, 1986.

Armstrong, Walter. *Sir John Millais, Royal Academician, His Life and Work*. London: Art Annual, 1885.

Arnold, Matthew. *The Study of Celtic Literature*. 1905; repr. Dallas: Taylor Publishing, 1970.

Arscott, Caroline. *William Morris and Edward Burne-Jones: Interlacings*. New Haven and London: Yale University Press, 2008.

Art, Commerce, Scholarship: A Window onto the Art World: Colnaghi 1760–1984. London: P. & D. Colnaghi, 1984.

Art in Britain 1930–40, Centred Around Axis, Circle, Unit One. London: Marlborough Fine Art, 1965.

Ashwin, Clive, ed. *High Art and Low Life: The Studio and the Arts of the 1890s*. London: Victoria and Albert Museum, 1993.

Athill, Philip. 'The International Society of Sculptors, Painters and Gravers'. *Burlington Magazine* 127 (January 1985), 21–9.

Auther, Elissa.'The Decorative, Abstraction, and the Hierarchy of Art and Craft in the Art Criticism of Clement Greenberg'. *Oxford Art Journal* 27:3 (2004), 339–64.

Aynsley, Jeremy and Kate Forde, eds. *Design and the Modern Magazine*. Manchester: Manchester University Press, 2007.

Baetens, Jan Dirk. 'Vanguard Economics, Rearguard Art: Gustave Coûteaux and the Modernist Myth of the Dealer-Critic System'. *Oxford Art Journal* 33:1 (2010), 25–41.

Bailey, Colin B. *Building the Frick Collection: An Introduction to the House and its Collection*. New York: The Frick Collection in association with Scala Publishers, 2006.

Bailey, Martin. *Van Gogh in England: Portrait of the Artist as a Young Man*. London: Barbican Art Gallery, 1992.

Bailey, Martin. *Van Gogh and Britain: Pioneer Collectors*. Edinburgh: National Galleries of Scotland, 2006.

Bailkin, Jordanna. *The Culture of Property: The Crisis of Liberalism in Modern Britain*. Chicago: University of Chicago Press, 2004.

Bakoš, Ján ed. *Artwork through the Market: The Past and the Present. Bratislava*: VEDA, 2004.

Ball, Michael and David Sunderland. *An Economic History of London, 1800–1914*. London and New York: Routledge, 2001.

Barlow, Paul. 'Fear and Loathing of the Academic, or Just What Is It That Makes the Avant-garde So Different, So Appealing?' In *Art and the Academy in the Nineteenth Century*, eds. Rafael Cardoso Denis and Colin Trodd. New Brunswick: Rutgers University Press, 2000, pp. 15–32.

Barlow, Paul and Colin Trodd, eds. *Governing Cultures: Art Institutions in Victorian London*. Aldershot and Burlington, Vermont: Ashgate, 2000.

Baron, Wendy. *Perfect Moderns: A History of the Camden Town Group*. Aldershot and Burlington, Vermont: Ashgate, 2000.

Barrell, John, ed. *Painting and the Politics of Culture*. Oxford: Oxford University Press, 1992.

Barringer, Tim. *The Pre-Raphaelites: Reading the Image*. London: Weidenfeld and Nicolson, 1998.

Barrington, Emilie. *The Life, Letters and Works of Frederic Leighton*. 2 vols. London: George Allen, 1906.

Barton, Christina. *The Expatriates*. Wellington: Adam Art Gallery/University of Wellington, 2004.

Bätschmann, Oskar. *The Artist in the Modern World: The Conflict between Market and Self-Expression*. Cologne: DuMont Buchverlag, 1997.

Bax, Dirk. 'History of the Building'. In *Michaelis Collection, the Old Town House, Cape Town: Catalogue of the Collection of Paintings and Drawings*, Frans Hansen. Compiled in collaboration with the Netherlands Institute for Art History, The Hague. Incorporating sections of the 1981 catalogue by Dirk Bax and a chapter by Michael Stevenson. Zwolle: Waanders Uitgevers, 1997, pp. 13–26.

Bayer, Thomas. 'Marketing of Genius, Ingenious Marketing: The Role of Engravings in Mid-Nineteenth Century English Art Dealing'. *Athanor* (1992), 50–61.

Bayer, Thomas. 'Money as Muse: The Origin and Development of the Modern Art Market in Victorian England. A Process of Commodification'. Ph.D. dissertation, Tulane University, Louisiana, 2001.

Bayer, Thomas M. and John Page. 'Arthur Tooth: A London Dealer in the Spotlight, 1870–71'. *Nineteenth-Century Art Worldwide* 9:1 (Spring 2010), http:// 19thc-artworldwide.org/index.php/spring10/arthur-tooth. Accessed 26 September 2010.

Beck, Hilary. *Victorian Engravings*. London: Victoria and Albert Museum, 1973.

Beckett, J. 'Circle: The Theory and Patronage of Constructive Art in the Thirties'. In *Circle: Constructive Art in Britain 1934–40*, ed. Jeremy Lewison. Cambridge: Kettle's Yard, 1982, pp. 11–32.

Bendix, Deanna Marohn. *Diabolical Designs*. Washington D.C. and London: Smithsonian Institution, 1995.

Benjamin, Walter. 'The Work of Art in the Age of Mechanical Reproduction' (1936). In *Illuminations*, ed. Hannah Arendt, trans. Harry Zohn. New York: Schocken Books, 1968.

Bennett, Mary. 'A Check List of Pre-Raphaelite Pictures Exhibited at Liverpool 1846–67 and Some of Their Northern Collectors'. *Burlington Magazine* 105 (November 1963), 477, 486–93, 495.

Bennett, Mary. *William Holman Hunt: An Exhibition arranged by the Walker Art Gallery*. Liverpool: Walker Art Gallery, 1969.

Bennett, Mary. *Artists of the Pre-Raphaelite Circle: The First Generation*. London: Lund Humphries, 1988.

Bennett, Tony. *The Birth of the Museum: History, Theory, Politics*. London and New York: Routledge, 1995.

Bently, L. and M. Kretschmer, eds. *Primary Sources on Copyright (1450–1900)*, www.copyrighthistory.org.

Berg, Maxine. *Luxury and Pleasure in Eighteenth-Century Britain*. Oxford: Oxford University Press, 2007.

Berg, Maxine and Helen Clifford, eds. *Consumers and Luxury: Consumer Culture in Europe 1650–1850*. Manchester and New York: Manchester University Press, 1999.

Bionda, Richard. 'The Market for Contemporary Art in the Netherlands'. In *The Age of Van Gogh: Dutch Painting 1880–1895*, eds. Richard Bionda and Carel Blotkamp. Zwolle: Waanders Publishers, 1990, pp. 59–81.

Bionda, Richard and Carel Blotkamp, eds. *The Age of Van Gogh: Dutch Painting 1880–1895*. Zwolle: Waanders Publishers, 1990.

Birchall, Heather. 'An Annex to Trafalgar Square: The Tate Collection 1897–1914'. *Visual Culture in Britain* 6:2 (2005), 21–30.

Blackburn, Henry. *New Gallery Notes*. London: New Gallery, 1888.

Bodkin, Thomas. *Hugh Lane and His Pictures*. Dublin: Stationary Office for the Arts Council, 1956.

Bohm-Duchen, Monica. 'Lessore, Helen'. In *Grove Art Online. Oxford Art Online*, www.oxfordartonline.com/subscriber/article/grove/art/T050618. Accessed 27 February 2010.

Boime, Albert. 'Entrepreneurial Patronage in Nineteenth-Century France'. In *Enterprise and Entrepreneurs in Nineteenth- and Twentieth-Century France*, ed. Edward C. Carter II, Robert Forster, and Joseph N. Moody. Baltimore and London: Johns Hopkins University Press, 1976, pp. 137–207.

Boime, Albert. 'America's Purchasing Power and the Evolution of European Art in the Late Nineteenth Century'. In *Saloni, gallerie, musei e loro influenza sullo sviluppo del'arte dei secoli XIX e XX*, ed. Francis Haskell. Bologna: Cooperativa Libraria Universitaria Editrice Bologna, 1981, pp. 123–39.

Bornand, Odette, ed. *The Diary of W. M. Rossetti 1870–1873*. Oxford: Clarendon Press, 1977.

Bosman, Suzanne. *The National Gallery in Wartime*. London: National Gallery Co., 2008.

Bourdieu, Pierre. *The Field of Cultural Production: Essays on Art and Literature*, ed. Randal Johnson. Cambridge: Polity Press, 1993.

Bowe, Nicola Gordon. 'A Contextual Introduction to Romantic Nationalism and Vernacular Expression in the Irish Arts and Crafts Movement, c. 1886–1925'. In

Art and the National Dream: The Search for Vernacular Expression in Turn-of-the-Century Design, ed. Nicola Gordon Bowe. Dublin: Irish Academic Press, 1993, pp. 181–200.

Bowe, Nicola Gordon. 'The Search for Vernacular Expression: The Arts and Crafts Movements in America and Ireland'. In *The Substance of Style: Perspectives on the American Arts and Crafts Movement*, ed. Bert Denker. Winterthur: Winterthur Museum and University Press of New England, 1996, pp. 5–24.

Bowe, Nicola Gordon, ed. *Art and the National Dream: The Search for Vernacular Expression in Turn-of-the-Century Design*. Dublin: Irish Academic Press, 1993.

Bowness, Alan A. *British Contemporary Art 1910–1990: Eighty Years of Collecting by the Contemporary Art Society*. London: The Herbert Press, 1991.

Boydell, Christine. *The Architect of Floors: Modernism, Art and Marion Dorn Designs*. Coggeshall, Essex: Schoeser Press/RIBA, 1996.

Brake, Laurel. *Subjugated Knowledges*. New York: New York University Press, 1994.

Brake, Laurel and Julie F. Codell, eds. *Encounters in the Victorian Press: Editors, Authors, Readers*. Houndsmills, Basingstoke and New York: Palgrave Macmillan, 2005.

Breward, Christopher. *Fashioning London: Clothing and the Modern Metropolis*. Oxford: Berg, 2004.

Brewer, John and Frank Trentmann. 'Introduction: Space, Time and Value in Consuming Cultures'. In *Consuming Cultures: Global Perspectives, Historical Trajectories, Transnational Exchanges*, eds. John Brewer and Frank Trentmann. Oxford and New York: Berg, 2006, pp. 1–27.

Brewer, John and Roy Porter, eds. *Consumption and the World of Goods*. London and New York: Routledge, 1993.

Briefel, Aviva, *The Deceivers: Art Forgery and Identity in the Nineteenth Century*. Ithaca: Cornell University Press, 2006.

Brigstocke, Hugh. *William Buchanan and the 19th Century Art Trade: 100 Letters to His Agents in London and Italy*. London: published privately by the Paul Mellon Centre for Studies in British Art, 1982.

British Artists' Suppliers, 1650–1950. 2nd edn. London: National Portrait Gallery, May 2008, www.npg.org.uk/research/programmes/directory-of-suppliers/c.php. Accessed 28 February 2010.

Bronkhurst, Judith. 'Holman Hunt's Picture Frames, Sculpture and Applied Art'. In *Re-framing the Pre-Raphaelites: Historical and Theoretical Essays*, ed. Ellen Harding. Burlington, Vermont: Ashgate Publishing, 1996, pp. 231–51.

Bronkhurst, Judith. *William Holman Hunt: A Catalogue Raisonné*. 2 vols. New Haven and London: Yale University Press, 2006.

Brook-Hart, Denys. *Works Exhibited in the Royal Society of British Artists, 1824–93 and the New English Art Club*. Woodbridge: The Antique Collectors' Club, 1975.

Brooker, Peter. *Bohemia in London*. Basingstoke: Palgrave Macmillan, 2007.

Brothers, Ann. *A Studio Portrait: The Marketing of Art and Taste, 1893–1918*. Melbourne: The University of Melbourne, 1993.

Brown, Oliver. *Exhibition: The Memoirs of Oliver Brown*. London: Evelyn, Adams & MacKay, 1968.

Brown University and University of Tulsa. 'Modernist Journals Project', http://dl.brown.edu/mjp/periodicals.html.

Bryan, Michael. *Dictionary of Painters and Engravers* (1816). Revised by George Stanley. London: H. Bohn, 1849.

Buckley, Cheryl. *Designing Modern Britain*. London: Reaktion Books, 2007.

Bullen, J.B., ed. *Post-Impressionists in England: The Critical Reception*. London and New York: Routledge, 1988.

Bulwer-Lytton, Edward. *England and the English*. London: Richard Bentley, 1833.

Burne-Jones, Georgiana. *Memorials of Edward Burne Jones*. 2 vols. London: The Macmillan Company, 1904.

Butler, Roger, Chris Deutscher, and Jan Minchin. *Thea Proctor: The Prints*. Sydney: Resolution Press, 1980.

Byng Hall, Major H. *Adventures of a Bric-a-Brac Hunter*. London: Tinsley Brothers, 1868.

Cameron, Samuel. 'On the Role of the Critics in the Culture Industry'. *Journal of Cultural Economics* 19 (1995), 321–31.

Campbell, Fergus. 'Irish Popular Politics and the Making of the Wyndham Land Act, 1901–1903'. Historical Journal 45:4 (2002), 755–75.

Cannadine, David. *The Decline and Fall of the British Aristocracy*. New Haven and London: Yale University Press, 1990.

Carey, Frances and Antony Griffiths, eds. *Avant-garde British Printmaking 1914–60*. London: British Museum Publications, 1990.

Carman, Jillian. *Uplifting the Colonial Philistine: Florence Phillips and the Making of the Johannesburg Art Gallery*. Johannesburg: Wits University Press, 2006.

Cassis, Yousef. *Capitals of Capital: A History of International Financial Centres, 1780–2005*. Cambridge: Cambridge University Press, 2006.

Cassis, Youssef and Éric Bussière, eds. *London and Paris and International Financial Centres in the Twentieth Century*. Oxford: Oxford University Press, 2005.

Casteras, Susan P. and Colleen Denney, eds. *The Grosvenor Gallery: A Palace of Art in Victorian England*. New Haven and London: Yale University Press, 1996.

Chambers, Emma. *An Indolent and Blundering Art? The Etching Revival and the Redefinition of Etching in England 1838–1892*. Aldershot and Burlington, Vermont: Ashgate, 1999.

Chamot, M., D. Farr, and M. Butlin. *Tate Gallery: The Modern British Paintings, Drawings and Sculptures*. 2 vols. London: Tate Gallery, 1964.

Chapel, Jeannie. 'The Papers of Joseph Gillott (1799–1872)'. *Journal of the History of Collections* 20:1 (2008), 37–84.

Cheetham, Mark. *The Rhetoric of Purity: Essentialist Theory and the Advent of Abstract Painting*. Cambridge: Cambridge University Press, 1991.

Cherry, Deborah. 'The Hogarth Club, 1858–61'. *Burlington Magazine* 122 (April 1980), 237–44.

Chu, Petra. 'The Lu(c)re of London: French Artists and Art Dealers in the British Capital, 1859–1914'. In *Monet's London*. St. Petersburg, Florida: Museum of Fine Arts, 2005, pp. 39–54.

Clark, Kenneth. *Another Part of the Wood: A Self-Portrait*. London: John Murray, 1974.

Clark, Kenneth. *The Other Half: A Self-Portrait*. London: John Murray, 1977.

Clarke, Meaghan. *Women and Art Criticism in Britain 1880–1905*. Aldershot and Burlington, Vermont: Ashgate, 2005.

Codell, Julie. '"The Artist's Cause at Heart": Marion Harry Spielmann and the Late Victorian Art World'. *Bulletin of the John Rylands University Library of Manchester* 71 (1989), 139–63.

Codell, Julie. 'M. H. Spielmann and the Press in the Professionalization of Artists'. *Victorian Periodicals Review* 22 (1989), 7–15.

Codell, Julie. 'Moderate Praise: Art Criticism of The Portfolio'. *Victorian Periodicals Review* 20 (1989), 83–93.

Codell, Julie, 'Artists' Professional Societies: Production, Consumption and Aesthetics'. In *Towards a Modern Art World*, ed. Brian Allen. London: Yale University Press, 1995, pp. 169–87.

Codell, Julie. 'Constructing the Victorian Artist'. *Victorian Periodicals Review* 33 (2000), 283–316.

Codell, Julie. 'Righting the Victorian Artist'. *Oxford Art Journal* 23:2 (2000), 93–118.

Codell, Julie. 'Serialized Artists' Biographies'. *Book History* 3 (2000), 94–124.

Codell, Julie. *The Victorian Artist: Artists' Lifewritings in Britain, ca. 1870–1910*. Cambridge: Cambridge University Press, 2003.

Cohen, Deborah. *Household Gods: The British and their Possessions*. New Haven and London: Yale University Press, 2006.

Collins, Roger and Iain Buchanan. *Frances Hodgkins on Display, Bulletin of New Zealand Art History special series no. 5*. Dunedin: Hocken Library, 2000.

Conekin, Becky and Amy de la Haye. 'Introduction'. *Fashion Theory: The Journal of Dress, Body and Culture* 10:1/2 (March/June 2006), 7–11.

Connelly, Frances S. *The Sleep of Reason: Primitivism in Modern European Art and Aesthetics, 1725–1907*. University Park, Pennsylvania: The Pennsylvania State University Press, 1995.

Cook, E.T. *Highways and Byways in London*. London: Macmillan and Co., 1903.

Cook, E.T. and A. Wedderburn, eds. *The Works of John Ruskin*. 39 vols. London: George Allen, 1903–1912.

Cook, S.B. *Imperial Affinities: Nineteenth Century Analogies and Exchanges Between India and Ireland*. Newbury Park, California: Sage Publications, 1993.

Coombs, James H., Anne M. Scott, George P. Landow, and Arnold A. Sanders, eds. *A Pre-Raphaelite Friendship: The Correspondence of William Holman Hunt and John Lucas Tupper*. Ann Arbor, Michigan: UMI Research Press, 1986.

Copley, Stephen. 'The Fine Arts in Eighteenth-Century Polite Culture'. In *Painting and the Politics of Culture*, ed. John Barrell. Oxford: Oxford University Press, 1992, pp. 13–37.

Corbett, David Peters. *The Modernity of English Art, 1914–1930*. Manchester: Manchester University Press, 1997.

Corbett, David Peters, Ysanne Holt and Fiona Russell, eds. *The Geographies of Englishness:*

Landscape and the National Past, 1880–1940. New Haven and London: Yale University Press, 2002.

Corbett, David Peters and Lara Perry, eds. *English Art 1860–1914: Modern Artists and Identity*. Manchester: Manchester University Press, 2000.

Cowan, Brian. 'Art and Connoisseurship in the Auction Market of Later Seventeenth-Century London'. In *Mapping Markets for Paintings in Europe 1450–1750*, eds. Neil De Marchi and Hans J. van Miegroet. Turnhout, Belgium: Brepols, 2006, pp. 263–82.

Crook, J. Mordaunt. *The Rise of the Nouveaux Riches: Style and Status in Victorian and Edwardian Architecture*. London: John Murray, 1999.

Crouzet, François. *The Victorian Economy*. New York: Columbia University Press, 1982.

Cullen, Fintan. 'The Lane Bequest: Giving Art to Dublin'. *Field Day Review* 4 (2008), 187–201.

Curry, David Park. 'Total Control: Whistler at an Exhibition'. In *James McNeill Whistler: A Reexamination*, ed. Ruth E. Fine. Washington D.C.: National Gallery of Art, 1987, pp. 67–82.

David, Alison Matthews. 'Vogue's New World: American Fashionability and the Politics of Style'. *Fashion Theory: The Journal of Dress, Body and Culture* 10:1/2 (March/June 2006), 13–38.

Daw, Robin. 'The Ill-fated Pierrot'. In *Brought to Light: Australian Art 1850–1965*, eds. Lynne Seear and Julie Ewington. Brisbane: Queensland Art Gallery, 1998, pp. 80–3.

Dawson, Barbara. 'Hugh Lane and the Origins of the Collection'. In *Images and Insight*. Dublin: Hugh Lane Municipal Gallery of Modern Art, 1993.

Dawson, Barbara. 'Hugh Lane's Pictures'. In *Hugh Lane: Founder of a Gallery for Modern Art in Ireland*, ed. Barbara Dawson. London: Scala Books, 2008, pp. 9–14.

De Marchi, Neil and Craufurd D. W. Goodwin, eds. *Economic Engagements with Art*. Durham, North Carolina: Duke University Press, 1999.

De Marchi, Neil and Hans J. van Miegroet. 'Art, Value and Market Practices in the Netherlands in the Seventeenth Century'. *Art Bulletin* 76 (1994), 451–64.

De Marchi, Neil and Hans J. van Miegroet, eds. *Mapping Markets for Paintings in Europe, 1450–1750*. Turnhout, Belgium: Brepols, 2006.

de Montfort, Patricia. '"The fiction of my own biography": Whistler and the Gentle Art of Making Enemies'. Ph.D dissertation, University of St Andrews, 1994.

de Montfort, Patricia. '"Atlas" and the Butterfly: James McNeill Whistler, Edmund Yates and the World'. In *Encounters in the Victorian Press: Editors, Authors, Readers*, eds. Laurel Brake and Julie F. Codell. Houndsmills, Basingstoke and New York: Palgrave Macmillan, 2005, pp. 161–74.

Dearborn, Mary. *Peggy Guggenheim Mistress of Modernism*. London: Virago, 2006.

Deepwell, Katy. 'Women Artists in Britain between the Two World Wars'. Ph.D. dissertation, Birkbeck College, University of London, 1991.

Deepwell, Katy. *Ten Decades: Careers of Ten Women Artists born 1897–1906*. Norwich: Norwich Gallery, 1992.

Dekkers, Dieuwertje. *Josef Israëls 1824–1911*. Zwolle: Wanders Publishers, 1994.

Dekkers, Dieuwertje. 'Goupil en de international verspreiding van Nederlandse eigentidjdse kunst'. *Jong Holland* 11:4 (1995), 22–36, 63–4.

Denis, Rafael Cardoso and Colin Trodd, eds. *Art and the Academy in the Nineteenth Century*. Manchester: Manchester University Press, 2000.

Denney, Colleen. *At the Temple of Art: The Grosvenor Gallery, 1877–1890*. Madison: Fairleigh Dickinson University Press, 2000.

Denvir, Bernard. 'Art Collectors and their Collections: 1 Sir Edward Marsh'. *Studio* (November 1947), 127–33.

Douglas, Mary. *In the Active Voice*. London: Routledge and K. Paul, 1982.

'Dowdeswell, William (C).' In Grove Art Online. Oxford Art Online www.oxford-artonline.com/subscriber/article/grove/art/T023515. Accessed 10 March 2010.

Dreschsler, Maximiliane. *Zwischen Kunst and Kommer: Zur Geschichte des Ausstellungswesens zwischen 1775 and 1905*. Munich and Berlin: Deutscher Kunstverlag, 1996.

Dubow, Saul. 'Colonial Nationalism, the Milner Kindergarten, and the Rise of "South Africanism", 1902–1910'. *History Workshop Journal* 43 (1997), 53–85.

Dubow, Saul. 'Imagining the New South Africa in the Era of Reconstruction'. In *The Impact of the South African War*, eds. D. Omissi and Andrew S. Thompson. London: Palgrave, 2002, pp. 76–98.

Duncan, Carol. *Civilizing Rituals: Inside Public Art Museums*. London and New York: Routledge, 1995.

Duveen, James Henry. *The Rise of the House of Duveen*. New York: Alfred A. Knopf, 1957.

Dyson, Anthony. *Pictures to Print: The Nineteenth-Century Engraving Trade*. London: Farrand Press, 1984.

Dyson, Anthony. 'Edwin Landseer and the Engraving Trade'. *Print Quarterly* 1:1 (1984), 29–43.

Eastlake, Charles Lock. *Hints on Household Taste in Furniture, Upholstery and Other Details*. London: Longman's, 1868.

Eastlake, Lady. 'Memoir of Sir Charles Eastlake'. In *Contributions to the Literature of the Fine Arts*, 2nd series. London: John Murray, 1870, pp. 1–192.

Edwards, Bronwen. '"We Are Fatally Influenced By Goods Bought in Bond Street": London, Shopping and the Fashionable Geographies of 1930s Vogue'. *Fashion Theory: The Journal of Dress, Body and Culture* 10:1/2 (March/June 2006), 73–96.

Edwards, Clive. *Turning Houses into Homes: A History of the Retailing and Consumption of Domestic Furnishings*. Aldershot and Burlington, Vermont: Ashgate, 2005.

Elam, Caroline. 'A More and More Important Work: Roger Fry'. *Burlington Magazine* 145 (March 2003), 142–52.

Elinor, Gillian, Su Richardson, Sue Scott, Angharad Thomas, and Kate Walker, eds. *Women and Craft*. London: Virago, 1987.

Elliott, Philip. *The Sociology of the Professions*. London: Macmillan, 1972.

Elwin, Malcolm. *Charles Reade: A Biography*. London: Jonathan Cape, 1931.

Engen, Rodney. *Pre-Raphaelite Prints: The Graphic Art of Millais, Holman Hunt, Rossetti and their Followers*. London: Lund Humphries Publishers, 1995.

Entwisle, Peter. *William Matthew Hodgkins and his Circle*. Dunedin: Dunedin Public Art Gallery, 1984.

Epstein, Jacob. *Let There Be Sculpture*. London: Michael Joseph, 1940.

Epstein, William. *Recognizing Biography*. Philadelphia: University of Pennsylvania Press, 1987.

Escott, T.H.S. *England: Her People, Polity and Pursuits*. New York: Henry Holt, 1880.

Escritt, Stephen. *Art Nouveau*. London: Phaidon, 2000.

Faberman, Hilarie. '"Best Shop in London": The Fine Art Society and the Victorian Art Scene'. In *The Grosvenor Gallery: A Palace of Art in Victorian England*, eds. Susan P. Casteras and Colleen Denney. New Haven and London: Yale University Press 1996, pp. 147–58, 183–9.

Farrar, F.W. and Alice Meynell. *William Holman Hunt*. London: Art Annual, 1893.

Fawcett, Trevor, 'Graphic versus Photographic in the Nineteenth-Century Reproduction'. *Art History* 9 (June 1986), 185–212.

Fennell, Francis Jr., ed. *The Rossetti-Leyland Letters: The Correspondence of an Artist and His Patron*. Athens: Ohio University Press, 1978.

Fielding, T.H. *The Knowledge and Restoration of Old Paintings: The Modes of Judging Between Copies and Originals*. London: Ackermann, 1847.

The Fine Art Society Story. London: The Fine Art Society, 2001.

Flam, Jack. *Matisse: The Man and his Art*. London: Thames and Hudson, 1986.

Fletcher, Pamela. 'Consuming Modern Art: Metaphors of Gender, Commerce, and Value in Late-Victorian and Edwardian Art Criticism'. *Visual Culture in Britain* 6:2 (2005), 157–70.

Fletcher, Pamela. 'Creating the French Gallery: Ernest Gambart and the Rise of the Commercial Art Gallery in Mid-Victorian London'. *Nineteenth-Century Art Worldwide* 6:1 (Spring 2007), http://19thc-artworldwide.org/index.php/spring07/143-creating-the-french-gallery-ernest-gambart-and-the-rise-of-the-commercial-art-gallery-in-mid-victorian-london. Accessed 1 April 2007.

Fletcher, Pamela. 'The Grand Tour on Bond Street: Cosmopolitanism and the Commercial Art Gallery in Victorian London'. *Visual Culture in Britain*, forthcoming Spring 2011.

Flint, Kate. *Impressionists in England: The Critical Reception*. London: Routledge and Kegan Paul, 1984.

Flint, Kate. 'Moral Judgment and the Language of English Art Criticism, 1870–1910'. *Oxford Art Journal* 6:2 (1985), 59–66.

Flint, Kate. *The Victorians and the Visual Imagination*. Cambridge: University of Cambridge, 2000.

Ford, J. *Ackermann, 1783–1983: The Business of Art*. London: Ackermann, 1983.

Ford, Sheridan. *Art: A Commodity*. New York: [Press of Rogers & Sherwood], 1888.

Forster, Henry C., *The Stowe Catalogue, Priced and Annotated*. London: David Bogue, 1848.

Foss, Brian. *War Paint Art, War, State and Identity in Britain 1939–1945*. London: Yale University Press, 2007.

Foster, Roy. '"A Family Affair": Lane, Gregory, Yeats and Educating the Nation'. In *Hugh Lane: Founder of a Gallery for Modern Art in Ireland*, ed. Barbara Dawson. London: Scala Books, 2008, pp. 29–36.

Fowle, Frances. 'Alexander Reid in Context: Collecting and Dealing in Scotland in the Late Nineteenth and Early Twentieth Centuries'. Ph.D. dissertation, University of Edinburgh, 1993.

Fowle, Frances. 'Vincent's Scottish Twin: The Glasgow Art Dealer Alexander Reid'. *Van Gogh Museum Journal* (2000), 91–9.

Fowle, Frances. 'Following the Vision from Brittany to Edinburgh'. In *Gauguin's Vision*, ed. Belinda Thomson. Edinburgh: National Galleries of Scotland, 2005, pp. 101–9, 140–1.

Fox, Celina, ed. *London: World City 1800–40*. New Haven and London: Yale University Press, 1992.

Frances Hodgkins and her Circle. Auckland: Auckland City Art Gallery, 1954.

Fransen, Hans. *Michaelis Collection, the Old Town House, Cape Town: Catalogue of the Collection of Paintings and Drawings*. Compiled in collaboration with the Netherlands Institute for Art History, The Hague. Incorporating sections of the 1981 catalogue by Dirk Bax and a chapter by Michael Stevenson. Zwolle: Waanders Uitgevers, 1997.

Fraser, M. 'Randlord (act. 1880s–1914)'. *Oxford Dictionary of National Biography*, online edn. Oxford: Oxford University Press, October 2006.

Fredeman, William E., ed. *The P.R.B. Journal: William Michael Rossetti's Diary of the Pre-Raphaelite Brotherhood 1849–1853*. Oxford: Clarendon Press, 1975.

Fredeman, William E., ed. *The Correspondence of Dante Gabriel Rossetti*. 8 vols. Woodbridge, Suffolk and Rochester, New York: D.S. Brewer, 2002–9.

Fredericksen, Andrea. 'The Etching Club of London: A Taste for Painters' Etchings'. *Philadelphia Museum of Art Bulletin* 92 (2002), 2–3, 6–35.

Freedman, Jonathan. *Professions of Taste: Henry James, British Aestheticism, and Commodity Culture*. Stanford: Stanford University Press, 1990.

Frey, B.S. and W.W. Pommerehne. *Muses and Markets: Explorations in the Economics of the Arts*. Oxford: Blackwell, 1989.

The Frick Collection: An Illustrated Catalogue. 9 vols. New York: The Frick Collection distributed by Princeton University Press, 1968.

Friedman, Marilyn F. *Selling Good Design: Promoting the Early Modern Interior*. New York: Rizzoli, 2003.

Frith, William Powell. *My Autobiography and Reminiscences*. 2 vols. New York: Harper & Brothers, 1889.

Funnell, Peter. 'The London Art World and its Institutions'. In *London: World City 1800–1840*, ed. Celina Fox. New Haven and London: Yale University Press, 1992, pp. 155–66.

Fyfe, Gordon. 'Art Exhibitions and Power during the Nineteenth Century'. In *Power, Action and Belief: A New Sociology of Knowledge*, ed. John Law. London and New York: Routledge and Kegan Paul, 1986, pp. 20–45.

Gagnier, Regenia. *Idylls of the Marketplace: Oscar Wilde and the Victorian Public*. Stanford: Stanford University Press, 1986.

Galenson, David W. and Robert Jensen. 'Careers and Canvases: The Rise of the Market for Modern Art in the Nineteenth Century', National Bureau of Economic Research Working Paper No. 9123, September 2002, www.nber.org/papers/w9123. Accessed 2 December 2008.

Galenson, David W. and Robert Jensen, 'Careers and Canvases: The Rise of the Market for Modern Art in Nineteenth-Century Paris'. *Current Issues in 19th-Century Art* (Special Issue: Van Gogh Studies I). Zwolle: Waanders Publishers and Amsterdam: Van Gogh Museum, 2007, pp. 137–66.

Gambart, Ernest. *On Piracy and Artistic Copyright*. London: William Tegg, 1863.

Garstang, Donald, ed. *Art, Commerce, Scholarship: A Window onto the Art World. Colnaghi 1760–1984*. London: P. & D. Colnaghi, 1984.

Gee, Malcolm. *Dealers, Critics, and Collectors of Modern Painting: Aspects of the Paris Art World*. New York: Garland Publishing, 1981.

Gellner, Ernest. *Nations and Nationalism*. Oxford: Basil Blackwell, 1984.

The Germ: The Literary Magazine of the Pre-Raphaelites (1849–50), ed. Andrea Rose. Oxford: Ashmolean Museum, 1992.

Gérôme & Goupil, Art and Enterprise. Paris: Editions de la Réunion des musées nationaux, 2000.

Gerrish Nunn, Pamela. 'Fine Art and the Fan 1860–1930'. *Journal of Design History* 17:3 (2004), 251–66.

Gerstein, Alexandra, ed. *Beyond Bloomsbury: Designs of the Omega Workshops 1913–19*. London: The Courtauld Gallery/Fontanka, 2009.

Gill, Anton. *Peggy Guggenheim: The Life of An Art Addict*. London: Harper Collins, 2002.

Gill, Linda, ed. *Letters of Frances Hodgkins*. Auckland: Auckland University Press, 1993.

Gillett, Paula. *Worlds of Art: Painters in Victorian Society*. New Brunswick: Rutgers University Press, 1990.

Gledhill, John. *Catalogue Raisonné of the Oil Paintings of Matthew Smith With a Critical Introduction to His Work*. Surrey: Lund Humphries, 2009.

Goldin, Marco and Rochelle Keene, eds. *Da Corot a Monet: opera impressioniste e post-impressioniste dalla Johannesburg Art Gallery*. Conegliano, Italy: Linea d'ombra Libri, 2003.

Goodden, Susanna. *At the Sign of the Four Poster: A History of Heal's*. Aldershot and Burlington, Vermont: Ashgate, 1984.

Goodwin, Craufurd D., ed. *Art and the Market: Roger Fry on Commerce in Art*. Ann Arbor: The University of Michigan Press, 1998.

Graves, Algernon. *Catalogue of the Works of the Late Sir Edwin Landseer, R.A.* London: Messrs. Henry Graves & Co., 1875.

Gray, Anne. *George Lambert 1873–1930: Catalogue raisonné*. Perth: Bonamy Press, 1996.

Gray, Anne. *George W. Lambert Retrospective: Heroes and Icons*. Canberra: National Gallery of Australia, 2007.

Green, Nicholas. 'Dealing in Temperaments: Economic Transformation of the Artistic Field in France during the Second Half of the Nineteenth Century'. *Art History* 10 (March 1987), 59–78.

Green, Nicholas. 'Circuits of Production, Circuits of Consumption: The Case of the Mid-Nineteenth-Century French Art Dealing'. *Art Journal* 48:1 (Spring 1989), 29–34.

Gregory, Lady Augusta. *Hugh Lane's Life and Achievement, with Some Account of His Dublin Galleries*. London: John Murray, 1921.

Gronberg, Tag. *Designs on Modernity: Exhibiting the City in 1920s Paris*. Manchester: Manchester University Press, 1998.

Guerzoni, Guido. 'Reflections on Historical Series of Art Prices: Reitlinger's Data Revisisted'. *Journal of Cultural Economics* 19 (1995), 251–60.

Guerzoni, Guido. 'The British Painting Market 1789–1914'. In *Economic History and the Arts*, ed. Michael North. Köln, Weimar, Wien: Böhlau Verlag, 1996, pp. 97–132.

Guggenheim, Peggy. *Out of This Century: Confessions of an Art Addict*. London: André Deutsch, 2005.

Gutsche, Thelma. *No Ordinary Woman: The Life and Times of Florence Phillips*. Cape Town: Howard Timmins, 1966.

Haight, Gordon S., ed. *The George Eliot Letters*, vol. 3. New Haven: Yale University Press, 1954.

Hall, Samuel Carter. *Retrospect of a Long Life: From 1815 to 1883*. New York: D. Appleton, 1883.

Halliday, Francis and John Russell. *Matthew Smith*. London: Allen and Unwin, 1962.

Harding, Ellen, ed. *Re-Framing the Pre-Raphaelites: Historical and Theoretical Essays*. Aldershot and Burlington, Vermont: Ashgate, 1996.

Harrison, Charles. *English Art and Modernism*. London: Allen Lane, 1983.

Harrod, Tanya. *The Crafts in Britain in the Twentieth Century*. London and New Haven: Yale University Press, 1999.

Haskell, Francis. *Rediscoveries in Art: Some Aspects of Taste, Fashion and Collecting in England and France*. London: Phaidon, 1976.

Haskell, Francis. *The Ephemeral Museum: Old Master Paintings and the Rise of the Art Exhibition*. London and New Haven: Yale University Press, 2000.

Haslam, Malcolm, *William Staite Murray*. London: Crafts Council, 1984.

Heijbroek, J. F. and E. L. Wouthuysen, eds. *Portret van een kunsthandel: De firma Van Wisselingh en zijn compagnons 1838–heden*. Zwolle: Waanders Uitgevers and Amsterdam: Rijksmuseum, 1999.

Helmreich, Anne. *The English Garden and National Identity: The Competing Styles of Garden Design, 1870–1914*. Cambridge: Cambridge University Press, 2002.

Helmreich, Anne. 'The Art Dealer and Taste: The Case of David Croal Thomson and the Goupil Gallery, 1885–1897'. *Visual Culture in Britain* 6:2 (2005), 31–49.

Helmreich, Anne. 'The Death of the Victorian Art Periodical'. Festschrift for Helen Roberts, ed. Julie Codell, *Secondhand Art. On Art's Media and Venues: The Art Press and Photography*, special issue of *Visual Resources* 27:2 (December 2010), 242–53.

Helmreich Anne and Ysanne Holt, 'Marketing Bohemia: The Chenil Gallery in Chelsea, 1905–1926'. *Oxford Art Journal* 33:1 (2010), 43–61.

Helsinger, Elizabeth, ed. *The Writings of Modern Life: The Etching Revival in France, Britain, and the U.S., 1850–1940.* Chicago: Smart Museum of Art, University of Chicago, 2008.

Hemingway, Andrew and William Vaughan, eds. *Art in Bourgeois Society, 1790–1850.* Cambridge: Cambridge University Press, 1998.

Hendy, Philip. *Matthew Smith.* London: Penguin, 1944.

Herbert, Robert 'The Decorative and the Natural in Monet's Cathedrals'. In *Aspects of Monet: A Symposium on the Artist's Life and Times*, ed. John Rewald and Frances Weitzenhoffer. New York: Abrams, 1984, pp. 162–9.

Herbert, Robert. *Nature's Workshop: Renoir's Writings on the Decorative Arts.* New Haven: Yale University Press, 2000.

Henry, Nancy and Cannon Schmitt, eds. *Victorian Investments: New Perspectives on Finance and Culture.* Bloomington and Indianapolis: Indiana University Press, 2009.

Hermann, Frank. *The English as Collectors: A Documentary Chrestomathy.* London, Chatto & Windus, 1972.

Hermann, Frank. 'Peel and Solly: Two Nineteenth-Century Art Collectors and Their Sources of Supply'. *Journal of the History of Collections* 3:1 (1991), 89–96.

Hobart, Allen. *Orpen and the Edwardian Era.* London: Pyms Gallery, 1987.

Hobsbawm, Eric J. *Industry and Empire: The Making of Modern English Society, Vol. II 1750 to the Present Day.* New York: Pantheon Books, 1969.

Hochstrasser, Julie. *Still Life and Trade in the Dutch Golden Age.* New Haven: Yale University Press, 2007.

Holman-Hunt, Diana. *My Grandfather: His Wives and Loves.* London: Hamish Hamilton, 1969.

Holroyd, Michael. *Augustus John: The New Biography.* London: Chatto & Windus, 1996.

Holt, Ysanne. *British Artists and the Modernist Landscape.* Aldershot and Burlington, Vermont: Ashgate, 2003.

Holt, Ysanne. 'Eddie Marsh: A Picture-Collector's "Lust for Possession"', *Visual Culture in Britain* 6:2 (2005), 125–37.

Honeycombe, Gordon. *Selfridges: Seventy-Five Years.* London: Park Lane Press, 1984.

Hopkinson, Martin. 'Whistler's "Company of the Butterfly"'. *Burlington Magazine* 136 (October 1994), 700–4.

Hopkinson, Martin. 'Review of Portret van een kunsthandel: De firma Van Wisselingh en zijn compagnons, 1838–heden', *Burlington Magazine* 142 (November 2000), 712–13.

Horner, Libby and Gillian Naylor, eds. *Frank Brangwyn, 1867–1956.* Leeds: Leeds City Art Gallery, 2006.

Houfe, Simon. *The Birth of The Studio, 1893–1895.* Woodbridge: Antique Collectors' Club, 1990.

House, John, ed. *Impressionism for England: Samuel Courtauld as Patron and Collector.* New Haven and London: Yale University Press for The Courtauld Institute Galleries, 1994.

Humphries, Barry, Andrew Sayers, and Sarah Engledow. *The World of Thea Proctor*. Canberra: National Portrait Gallery/Craftsman House, 2005.

Hunt, William Holman. *Pre-Raphaelitism and the Pre-Raphaelite Brotherhood*. 2 vols. London: Macmillan & Co., 1905.

Hutchinson, John. *The Dynamics of Cultural Nationalism: The Gaelic Revival and the Creation of the Irish Nation State*. London: Allen and Unwin, 1987.

Hutchison, Sidney C. *The History of the Royal Academy 1768–1986*. 2nd edn. London: Robert Royce, 1986.

Ingamells, John, ed. *The Hertford Mawson Letters*. London, Wallace Collection, 1981.

Ivins, William M. *Prints and Visual Communication*. Cambridge, Massachusetts: MIT Press, 1969.

Jackson, Peter. *John Tallis's London Street Views 1838–1840*. London: Nattali & Morris, 1969.

Jacobi, Carol. *William Holman Hunt: Painter, Painting, Paint*. Manchester: Manchester University Press, 2006.

James, Henry. *The Painter's Eye: Notes and Essays on the Pictorial Arts*, ed. John L. Sweeney. Madison: University of Wisconsin Press, 1989.

Jameson, Anna, *A Handbook to the Public Galleries of Art In and Near London*. London: John Murray, 1842.

Jarves, James Jackson. *Old Masters of Italy*. New York: Derby and Jackson, 1861.

Jensen, Robert. *Marketing Modernism in Fin-de-siècle Europe*. Princeton: Princeton University Press, 1993.

Jones, Jeffery. *Studio Pottery in Britain, 1900–50*. London: A and C Black, 2007.

Kahnweiler, Daniel Henry, with Francis Crémieux. *My Galleries and Painters*, trans. Helen Weaver. Boston: MFA Publications, 2003. (Orig. pub. 1961.)

Kantor, Sybil Gordon. *Alfred H. Barr, Jr., and the Intellectual Origins of the Museum of Modern Art*. Cambridge, Massachusetts: MIT Press, 2002.

Kay, Michael. 'Under the Hammer: Is Joint Account Bidding at Auction Legal?' In *Art, Commerce, Scholarship: A Window onto the Art World. Colnaghi 1760–1984*, ed. Donald Garstang. London: P. & D. Colnaghi, 1984, pp. 57–9.

Keene, Alice. *The Two Mr Smiths: The Life and Work of Sir Matthew Smith 1879–1959*. London: Lund Humphries, 1995.

Keene, Ralph. 'Famous Artists No. 33 Matthew Smith'. *Artist* 8:1 (1934), 22–5.

Keller, Kevin Lane. *Strategic Brand Management: Building, Measuring and Managing Brand Equity*. 3rd edn. New Jersey: Prentice Hall, 2008.

King, James. *The Last Modern: A Life of Herbert Read*. London: Weidenfeld and Nicolson, 1990.

King, Julie. *Flowers into Landscape: Margaret Stoddart 1865–1934*. Christchurch: Hazard Press, 1997.

King, Lyndel Saunders. *The Industrialization of Taste: Victorian England and the Art Union of London*. Ann Arbor, Michigan: UMI Research Press, 1985.

Kleeblatt, Norman. *John Singer Sargent: Portraits of the Wertheimer Family*. New York: The Jewish Museum, 1999.

Klonk, Charlotte. *Spaces of Experience: Art Gallery Interiors from 1800–2000*. London and New Haven: Yale University Press, 2009.

Korn, Madeline. 'Collecting Modern Foreign Art Before the Second World War'. Ph.D. dissertation, University of Reading, 2001.

Korn, Madeline. 'Collecting Paintings by Van Gogh in Britain before the Second World War'. *Van Gogh Museum Journal* (2002), 120–37.

Korn, Madeline. 'Collecting Paintings by Matisse and Picasso in Britain before the Second World War'. *Journal of the History of Collections* 16:1 (2004), 111–29.

Korn, Madeline. 'Exhibitions of Modern French Art and Their Influence on Collectors in Britain 1870–1918: The Davies Sisters in Context'. *Journal of the History of Collections* 16:2 (2004), 191–218.

Lafont-Couturier, Hélène. *Gérôme & Goupil, Art and Enterprise*. Paris: Editions de la Réunion des musées nationaux, 2000, pp. 13–29.

Lambert, Susan. *The Image Multiplied: Five Centuries of Printed Reproductions of Paintings and Drawings*. New York: Abaris Books, 1987.

Landow, George. 'There Began to Be a Great Talking About the Fine Arts'. In *The Mind and Art of Victorian England*, ed. Josef P. Altholz. Minneapolis: University of Minnesota Press, 1976, pp. 124–45.

Landow, George P. '"Your Good Influence on Me": The Correspondence of John Ruskin and William Holman Hunt'. *Bulletin of the John Rylands University Library of Manchester* 59 (Autumn 1976), 95–126; (Spring 1977), 376–96.

Landow, George P. *William Holman Hunt and Typological Symbolism*. New Haven: Yale University Press, 1979.

Lane, H. *Catalogue of the Exhibition of Works by Irish Painters*. London: Guildhall, 1904.

Lang, Leonora (Mrs. A.). *Sir F. Leighton, President of the Royal Academy: His Life and Work*. London: Art Annual, 1884.

Lapine, Michelle. 'Mixing Business with Pleasure: Asher Wertheimer as Art Dealer and Patron'. In *John Singer Sargent: Portraits of the Wertheimer Family*, ed. Norman Kleeblatt. New York: The Jewish Museum, 1999, pp. 43–53.

Larmour, Paul. *The Arts and Crafts Movement in Ireland*. Belfast: Friar's Bush Press, 1992.

Larson, Magali S. *The Rise of Professionalism*. Berkeley: University of California Press, 1977.

Leahy, Helen Rees. 'Desiring Holbein'. *Journal of the History of Collections* 19:1 (2007), 57–87.

Lennon, Joseph. *Irish Orientalism: A Literary and Intellectual History*. Syracuse: Syracuse University Press, 2004.

Leonard, Anne. 'Internationalist in Spite of Themselves: Britain and Belgium at the Fin de Siècle'. In *Internationalism and the Arts in Britain and Europe at the Fin de Siècle*, ed. Grace Brockington. Oxford, Bern, Berlin, Brussells, Frankfurt-on-Main, New York, Vienna: Peter Lang, 2009, pp. 225–46.

Lessore, Helen. *A Partial Testament: Essays on Some Moderns in the Great Tradition*. London: Tate Gallery Publications, 1986.

Levine, S. 'Décor/Decorative/Decoration in Claude Monet's Art'. *Arts Magazine* 51 (February 1977), 136–9.

Levy, Amy. *The Romance of a Shop*, ed. Susan David Bernstein. London: T. Fisher Unwin, 1888; repr. Orchard Park, New York: Broadview Press, 2006.

Lewison, Jeremy, ed. *Ben Nicholson: The Years of Experiment 1919–39*. Cambridge: Kettle's Yard, 1983.

Lippincott, Louise. *Selling Art in Georgian London: The Rise of Arthur Pond*. New Haven and London: Yale University Press for the Paul Mellon Centre for Studies in British Art, 1983.

Little, James Stanley. *The Life and Work of William Q. Orchardson, R.A.* London: Art Annual, 1897.

Lochnan, Katharine and Carol Jacobi, eds. *Holman Hunt and the Pre-Raphaelite Vision*. Toronto: Art Gallery of Ontario, 2008.

Low, Sampson. *The Charities of London*. London: Sampson Low, 1850.

Lowe, Rosalind. *Sir Samuel Rush Meyrick and Goodrich Court*. Logaston, Herefordshire: Logaston Press, 2003.

Lowry, Donal. *The South African War Re-Appraised*. Manchester: Manchester University Press, 2000.

Lutyens, Mary. *Millais and the Ruskins*. London: John Murray, 1967.

Lutyens, Mary, ed. 'Letters from Sir John Everett Millais, Bart, P.R.A. (1829–1896) and William Holman Hunt, O.M. (1827–1910) in the Henry E. Huntingdon Library'. *Walpole Society* 44 (1972–74), 1–93.

Lyons, Francis Stewart Leland. *Ireland Since the Famine*. London: Weidenfeld and Nicolson, 1973.

Maas, Jeremy. *Gambart: Prince of the Victorian Art World*. London: Barrie & Jenkins, 1975.

Maas, Jeremy. *Holman Hunt and The Light of the World*. London and Berkeley, California: Scolar Press, 1984.

MacCartney, D. 'MacNeill and Irish Ireland'. In *The Scholar Revolutionary: Eoin MacNeill, 1867–1945, and the Making of the New Ireland*, eds. Francis X. Martin and F.J. Byrne. Shannon: Irish University Press, 1973, pp. 75–98.

MacDonald, Margaret, ed. *Whistler's Mother: An American Icon*. Aldershot and Burlington, Vermont: Lund Humphries, 2003.

MacDonald, Margaret F., Patricia de Montfort, and Nigel Thorp, eds. *The Correspondence of James McNeill Whistler, 1855–1903*. University of Glasgow, 2003–4. Online edn. www.whistler.arts.gla.ac.uk/correspondence.

MacGregor, Arthur. 'Collectors, Connoisseurs and Curators in the Victorian Age'. In, *A.W. Franks, Nineteenth-Century Collecting and the British Museum*, eds. Marjorie Caygill and John Cherry. London, British Museum Press, 1997.

Macleod, Dianne Sachko. 'Avant garde Patronage in the North-east'. In *PreRaphaelites: Painters and Patrons in the North East*, ed. Jane Vickers. Newcastle upon Tyne: Laing Art Gallery, 1989, pp. 6–33.

Macleod, Dianne Sachko. *Art and the Victorian Middle Class: Money and the Making of Cultural Identity*. Cambridge: Cambridge University Press, 1996.

Magidson, Phyllis. 'Fashion Showdown: New York versus Paris 1914–41'. In *Paris–New York: Design Fashion Culture 1925–1940*, ed. Donald Albrecht. New York: Monacelli Press, 2008, pp. 102–8.

Mainardi, Patricia. *Art and Politics of the Second Empire: The Universal Exhibitions of 1855 and 1867*. London and New Haven: Yale University Press, 1987.

Malvern, Sue. *Modern Art, Britain and the Great War*. London and New Haven: Yale University Press, 2004.

Mandler, Peter. *The Fall and Rise of the Stately Home*. London and New Haven: Yale University Press, 1997.

Mane-Wheoki, Jonathan. 'The Light of the World: Mission and Message'. In *Holman Hunt and the Pre-Raphaelite Vision*, eds. Katharine Lochnan and Carol Jacobi. Toronto: Art Gallery of Ontario, 2008, pp. 113–33.

Marchand, Roland. *Advertising the American Dream: Making Way for Modernity 1920–1940*. Berkeley and Los Angeles: University of California Press, 1985.

Marks, Shula and Stanley Trapido. 'Lord Milner and the South African State'. *History Workshop Journal* 8 (1979), 52–80.

Matthew Smith. London: Barbican Art Gallery, 1983.

McCormick, E.H. *The Expatriate*. Wellington: New Zealand University Press, 1954.

McDiarmid, Lucy. *The Irish Art of Controversy*. Ithaca: Cornell University Press, 2005.

McEvansoneya, Philip. 'Lane's Choices: Degas, Monet, Pissarro and Puvis de Chavannes'. In *Hugh Lane: Founder of a Gallery for Modern Art in Ireland*, ed. Barbara Dawson. London: Scala Books, 2008, pp. 37–44.

McIntosh, DeCourcy. 'The Origins of the Maison Goupil in the Age of Romanticism'. *British Art Journal* 5:1 (Spring/Summer 2004), 64–76.

Mellor, David, ed. *Germany: The New Photography 1927–33*. London: Arts Council of Great Britain, 1978.

Merrill, Linda. *A Pot of Paint: Aesthetics on Trial in Whistler v. Ruskin*. Washington D.C. and London: Smithsonian Institution, 1992.

Meynell, Wilfred, *The Life and Work of Lady Butler (Miss Elizabeth Thompson)*. London: Art Annual, 1898.

Michie, Ranald C. 'The City of London as a Global Financial Center, 1880–1939: Finance, Foreign Exchange, and the First World War'. In *Centres and Peripheries in Banking: The Historical Development of Financial Markets*, eds. Philip L. Cottrell, Even Lange, and Ulf Olsson, co-edited by Iain L. Fraser and Monika Pohle Fraser. Aldershot and Burlington, Vermont: Ashgate, 2007, pp. 41–79.

Miegroet, Hans J. van. 'Recent Publications on Painting and the Market'. *Art Bulletin* 82 (2000), 582–5.

Millais, John Guille. *The Life and Letters of Sir John Everett Millais, P.R.A.* 2 vols. London: Methuen & Co., 1899.

Miller, Andrew. *Novels Behind Glass: Commodity Culture and Victorian Narrative*. Cambridge, Cambridge University Press, 1995.

Minihan, Janet. *The Nationalization of Culture: The Development of State Subsidies to the Arts in Great Britain*. New York: New York University Press, 1977.

Monod-Fontaine, Isabelle, ed. *Daniel-Henry Kahnweiler*. Paris: Centre Georges Pompidou, 1984.

Montagu, George Earl of Sandwich. 'Reminiscences'. Unpublished manuscript, 1961.

Montias, J. Michael. 'Cost and Value in Seventeenth-Century Dutch Art'. *Art History* 10 (March 1987), 455–66.

Montias, J. Michael. 'Socio-Economic Aspects of Netherlandish Art from the Fifteenth to the Seventeenth Century: A Survey'. *Art Bulletin* 72 (1990), 358–73.

Moore, George. *Hail and Farewell!* 3 vols. London: W. Heinnemann, 1911–14.

Morgan, Helen, 'Thea Proctor the Artist: Career before 1921 and the Question of Aesthetic Reputation'. Master's thesis, University of Melbourne, 1994.

Morgan, Helen. 'Thea Proctor in London 1910–11'. *Art Bulletin of Victoria* 36 (1995), 27–36.

Morris, Edward. *French Art in Nineteenth-Century Britain*. London and New Haven: Yale University Press, 2005.

Morrison, Kathryn A. *English Shops and Shopping: An Architectural History*. London and New Haven: Yale University Press, 2003.

Myerson, Jeremy. *Gordon Russell, Designer of Furniture, 1892–1992*. London: The Design Council, 1992.

Myrone, Martin and Lucy Peltz, eds. *Producing the Past: Aspects of Antiquarian Culture and Practice, 1700–1850*. Aldershot and Brookfield, Vermont: Ashgate, 1999.

Nadel, Ira. *Biography: Fiction, Fact and Form*. New York: St. Martin's Press, 1984.

Nagai, Kaori. *Empire of Analogies: Kipling, India, and Ireland*. Cork: Cork University Press, 2006.

Nash, Paul. *Room and Book*. London: Soncino Press, 1932.

National Gallery, *Millbank: A Record of Ten Years 1917–1927*. Glasgow: Robert Maclehose at the University Press, 1927.

Newall, Christopher. *The Grosvenor Gallery Exhibitions: Change and Continuity in the Victorian Art World*. Cambridge and New York: Cambridge University Press, 1995.

Nicholson, Virginia. *Singled Out: How Two Million Women Survived without Men after the First World War*. London: Viking, 2007.

North, Michael. *Art and Commerce in the Dutch Golden Age*, trans. Catherine Hill. New Haven: Yale University Press, 1997.

North, Michael and David Ormrod, eds. *Art Markets in Europe, 1400–1800*. Aldershot and Burlington, Vermont: Ashgate, 1998.

Nowell-Smith, Simon. *The House of Cassell, 1848–1958*. London: Cassell, 1958.

O'Brien, Joseph V. *'Dear Dirty Dublin': A City in Distress, 1899–1916*. Berkeley: University of California Press, 1982.

O'Byrne, Robert. *Hugh Lane, 1875–1915*. Dublin: Lilliput Press, 2000.

Ohashi, Satomi. 'The Auction Duty Act of 1777: The Beginning of Institutionalisation of Auctions in Britain'. In *Auctions, Agents and Dealers: The Mechanisms of the Art Market 1660–1830*, eds. Jeremy Warren and Adriana Turpin. Oxford: Archaeopress, 2007, pp. 21–31.

Orcutt, Kimberly. 'Buy American? The Debate over the Art Tariff'. *American Art* 16:3 (Autumn 2002), 82–91.

Overy, Paul. *Light, Air and Openness: Modern Architecture Between the Wars*. London: Thames and Hudson, 2007.

Packer, William. *The Art of Vogue Covers 1909–1940*. London: Octopus, 1981.

Paraskos, Michael, ed. *Re-reading Read: New Views on Herbert Read*. London: Freedom Press, 2007.

Parris, Leslie, ed. *The Pre-Raphaelites*. London: Tate Gallery, 1984.

Parry, Linda, 'Textile Background: Cloth and Costume'. In *Holman Hunt and the Pre-Raphaelite Vision*, eds. Katharine Lochnan and Carol Jacobi. Toronto: Art Gallery of Ontario, 2008, pp. 57–75.

Pearce, Susan. 'William Bullock: Collections and Exhibitions at the Egyptian Hall, London, 1816–25'. *Journal of the History of Collections* 20:1 (2008), 17–35.

Pears, Iain. *The Discovery of Painting: The Growth of Interest in the Arts in England, 1680–1768*. New Haven: Yale University Press, 1988.

Pennell, Elizabeth R. and J. Pennell. *The Life of James McNeill Whistler*. 2 vols. London and Philadelphia: William Heinemann, 1908.

Perkin, Harold. *The Rise of Professional Society*. London: Routledge, 1989.

Pesman, Ros. *Duty Free: Australian Women Abroad*. Oxford: Oxford University Press, 1996.

Peto, James and Donna Loveday, eds. *Modern Britain, 1929–1939*. London: The Design Museum, 1999.

Pickvance, Ronald. 'L'Absinthe in England'. *Apollo* 77:15 (May 1963), 395–8.

Piggott, J.R. *Palace of the People: The Crystal Palace at Sydenham*. Madison: University of Wisconsin Press, 2004.

Pigot, John. *Hilda Rix Nicholas: Her Life and Art*. Melbourne: Melbourne University Press, 2000.

Plomer, William. 'Agnew's as Publishers of Prints and Printsellers'. In *Agnew's, 1817–1967*. London: Bradbury Agnew Press, 1967, pp. 61–7.

Plowman, Edward W. and L. Clark Hamilton. *Copyright: Intellectual Property in the Information Age*. London: Routledge and Kegan Paul, 1980.

Pointon, Marcia, ed. *Pre-Raphaelites Re-Viewed*. Manchester: Manchester University Press, 1989.

Pomeroy, Jordana. 'Creating a National Collection; The National Gallery's Origins in the British Institution'. *Apollo* 148:438 (August 1998), 41–9.

Potter, Simon. 'Webs, Networks, and Systems: Globalization and the Mass Media in the Nineteenth- and Twentieth-Century British Empire'. *Journal of British Studies* 46 (July 2007), 621–46.

Prettejohn, Elizabeth. 'Aesthetic Value and the Professionalization of Victorian Art Criticism 1837–1878'. *Journal of Victorian Culture* 2 (Spring 1997), 71–94.

Prettejohn, Elizabeth. *The Art of the Pre-Raphaelites*. London: Tate Publishing, 2000.

Proctor, Thea. 'The Lesson of the Russian Ballet'. *Art in Australia* 3:16 (June 1926), 25.

Prown, Jules David. *John Singleton Copley*. Cambridge, Massachusetts: Harvard University Press, 1966.

Pyne, Kathleen. 'Portrait of a Collector as an Agnostic: Charles Lang Freer and Connoisseurship'. *Art Bulletin* 78 (1996), 75–97.

Rabinow, Rebecca ed. *Cézanne to Picasso. Ambroise Vollard: Patron of the Avant-Garde*. New York: Metropolitan Museum of Art; New Haven and London: Yale University Press, 2006.

Rappaport, Erika. *Shopping for Pleasure: Women in the Making of London's West End*. Princeton: Princeton University Press, 2000.

Ray, Gordon N. *The Illustrator and the Book in England from 1790–1917*. London: Oxford University Press, 1976.

Read, Benedict and David Thistlewood, eds. *Herbert Read: A British Vision of World Art*. Leeds: Leeds City Art Gallery, 1993.

Read, Herbert. *Art Now*. London: Faber and Faber, 1933.

Read, Herbert. *Art and Industry: the Principles of Industrial Design*. London: Faber and Faber, 1934.

Reader, William J. *Professional Men: The Rise of the Professional Classes in Nineteenth-Century England*. New York: Basic Books, 1966.

Redford, George. *Art Sales: A History of Sales of Pictures and Other Works of Art*. London: Bradbury, Agnew, & Co., 1888.

Reed, Christopher. *Bloomsbury Rooms: Modernism, Sub-culture and Domesticity*. New Haven and London: Yale University Press/Bard Centre for Study of Decorative Arts, 2004.

Reed, Christopher. 'A Vogue That Dare Not Speak Its Name: Sexual Subculture During the Editorship of Dorothy Todd, 1922–26'. *Fashion Theory: The Journal of Dress, Body and Culture* 10:1/2 (March/June 2006), 51–7.

Reed, Christopher, ed. *A Roger Fry Reader*. Chicago and London: The University of Chicago Press, 1996.

Reid, Forrest. *Illustrators of the Eighteen-sixties*. London: Faber and Gwyer, 1928; repr. New York: Dover Publications, 1975.

Reitlinger, Gerald. *The Economics of Taste*. 3 vols. London, Barrie & Rockliffe, 1963–70.

Rendell, Jane. *The Pursuit of Pleasure: Gender, Space and Architecture in Regency London*. London: Athlone, 2002.

Riefstahl, J. Meyer. 'Vincent Van Gogh'. *Burlington Magazine* 18 (December 1910), 154–7, 160–2.

Rix, Brenda D. *Pictures for the Parlour: The English Reproductive Print from 1775 to 1900*. Toronto: Art Gallery of Ontario, 1983.

Rix, Brenda. 'Prints: Spreading the Word'. In *Holman Hunt and the Pre-Raphaelite Vision*, eds. Katharine Lochnan and Carol Jacobi. Toronto, Art Gallery of Ontario, 2008, pp. 171–89.

Roberts, Helene. 'Exhibition and Review: The Periodical Press and the Victorian Art Exhibition System'. In *The Victorian Periodical Press: Samplings and Soundings*, eds. Joanne Shattock and Michael Wolff. Leicester and Toronto: Leicester University Press, 1982, pp. 79–107.

Roberts, William. *Memorials of Christie's: A Record of Art Sales 1766 to 1896*. 2 vols. London, G. Bell, 1897.

Roberts, W. 'Collecting as an Investment'. *The Connoisseur: An Illustrated Magazine for Collectors* 7 (September–December 1903), 44–50.

Roberts, William. *Five Posthumous Essays and Other Writings*. Valencia: 1990.

Robbins, Anne. *Cézanne in Britain*. London: National Gallery Company, 2006.

Robins Anna Gruetzner. *Modern Art in Britain, 1910–1914*. London: Merrell Holbertson in association with Barbican Art Gallery, 1997.

Robins, Anna Gruetzner. 'The Greatest Artist the World Has Ever Known'. In *Degas, Sickert and Toulouse Lautrec: London and Paris, 1870–1910*, eds. Anna Gruetzner Robins and Richard Thomson. London: Tate Publishing, 2005, pp. 51–93, 212–13.

Robins Anna Gruetzner, ed. *Walter Sickert: The Complete Writings on Art*. Oxford and New York: Oxford University Press, 2000.

Rose, June. *Daemons and Angels: A Life of Jacob Epstein*. London: Constable, 2002.

Ross, Cathy, ed. *Twenties London: A City in the Jazz Age*. London: Museum of London/ Phillip Wilson, 2003.

Ross, G. Campbell. *Catalogue of the Municipal Gallery of Modern Art*, Johannesburg. Johannesburg: Argus Company, 1910.

Ross, Margery, ed. *Robbie Ross, Friend of Friends*. London: Jonathan Cape, 1952.

Rossetti, W.M. *Dante Gabriel Rossetti: His Family-Letters with a Memoir*. 2 vols. London: Ellis and Elvey, 1895.

Rossetti, W.M. *Some Reminiscences*. 2 vols. London: Brown Langham, 1906.

Rothenstein, John. *Matthew Smith*. London: Beaverbrook Newspapers, 1962.

Rothenstein, John. *Summer's Lease*. London: Hamish Hamilton, 1965.

Rothenstein, John. *Brave Day Hideous Night: Autobiography Two*. London: Hamish Hamilton, 1966.

Rothenstein, John. *Time's Thievish Progress*. London: Cassell, 1970.

Rumbaugh, Leila Marilynn. 'The Magazine of Art'. Ph.D. dissertation, Northwestern University, 1969.

Ruskin, John. *Modern Painters*. 5 vols. New York: John Wiley, 1878.

Rutherford, Jonathan. *Forever England: Reflections on Race, Masculinity and Empire*. London: Lawrence & Wishart, 1997.

Rutter, Frank. *Evolution in Modern Art: A Study of Modern Painting, 1870–1925*. London: George G. Harrap, 1926.

Rutter, Frank. *Since I was Twenty-Five*. Boston and New York: Houghton Mifflin Company, 1927.

Salmon, Richard. 'Signs of Intimacy: The Literary Celebrity in the "Age of Interviewing"'. *Victorian Literature and Culture* 25:1 (1997), 159–77.

Samuels, Ernest. *Bernard Berenson: The Making of a Connoisseur*. Cambridge and London: The Belknap Press of Harvard University Press, 1979.

Santori, Flaminia Gennari. 'European "Masterpieces" for America: Roger Fry and the Metropolitan Museum of Art'. In *Art Made Modern*, ed. Christopher Green. London:

The Courtauld Gallery, Courtauld Institute of Art in association with Merrell Holberton, 1999, pp. 107–18.

Santori, Flaminia Gennari. *The Melancholy of Masterpieces: Old Master Paintings in America, 1900–1914.* Milan: 5 Continents Editions, 2003.

Schmutzler, Robert. *Art Nouveau.* London: Thames and Hudson, 1978.

Secrest, Meryle. *Kenneth Clark: A Biography.* London: Weidenfeld and Nicolson, 1984.

Secrest, Meryle. *Duveen: A Life in Art.* New York: Alfred A. Knopf, 2005.

Sharp, Neil. 'The Wrong Twigs for an Eagle's Nest? Architecture, Nationalism and Sir Hugh Lane's Scheme for a Gallery of Modern Art, Dublin, 1904–13'. In *The Architecture of the Museum*, ed. Michaela Giebelhausen. London: Palgrave Macmillan, 2003, pp. 32–53.

Shaw, Jennifer. *Dream States: Puvis de Chavannes, Modernism, and the Fantasy of France.* New Haven: Yale University Press, 2002.

Sheehy, Jeanne. *The Rediscovery of Ireland's Past: The Celtic Revival, 1830–1930.* London: Thames and Hudson, 1980.

Sherman, Brad and Lionel Bently. *The Making of Modern Intellectual Property Law: The British Experience 1760–1911.* Cambridge: Cambridge University Press, 1999.

Simon, Jacob. *Directory of British Picture Framemakers 1630–1950*, www.npg.org.uk.

Simpson, Colin. *Artful Partners: Bernard Berenson and Joseph Duveen.* New York: Macmillan Publishing, 1986.

Skaife, Thomas. *Exposé of the Royal Academy of Arts.* London: Piper, Stephenson and Spence, 1854.

Slive, Seymour. 'Review of The Michaelis Collection'. *Burlington Magazine* 140 (March 1998), 210–11.

Smith, Adam. *An Inquiry into the Nature and Causes of the Wealth of Nations.* 2 vols. London: W. Strahan and T. Cadell, 1776.

Smith, Greg. *The Emergence of the Professional Watercolourist.* Aldershot and Burlington, Vermont: Ashgate, 2002.

Smith, John. *A Catalogue Raisonné of the Works of the Most Eminent Dutch, Flemish, and French Painters.* 9 parts. London: John Smith, 1829–42.

Smollett, Tobias. *The Adventures of Ferdinand Count Fathom* (1753), ed. Damian Grant. London: Oxford University Press, 1971.

Solkin, David H. *Painting for Money: The Visual Arts and the Public Sphere in Eighteenth-Century England.* London and New Haven: published for the Paul Mellon Centre for Studies in British Art by Yale University Press, 1992.

Solkin, David H., ed. *Art on the Line: The Royal Academy Exhibitions at Somerset House, 1780–1838.* London and New Haven: Yale University Press, 2001.

Soussloff, Catherine. *The Absolute Artist: The Historiography of a Concept.* Minneapolis: University of Minnesota Press, 1997.

Spalding, Francis. *The Tate: A History.* London: Tate Gallery Publishing, 1998.

Spalding, Frances. 'Allied Artists' Association'. In Grove Art Online. Oxford Art Online, www.oxfordartonline.com/subscriber/article/grove/art/T001911. Accessed 27 February 2010.

Sparke, Penny. *The Modern Interior*. London: Reaktion Books, 2008.

Sparke, Penny, Anne Massey, Trevor Keeble, and B. Martin, eds. *Designing the Modern Interior: From the Victorians to Today*. Oxford: Berg, 2009.

Sparrow, Walter Shaw. *Memories of Life and Art Through Sixty Years*. London: John Lane The Bodley Head, 1925.

Spatt, Hartley S. 'The Aesthetics of Editorship: Creating Taste in the Victorian Art World'. In *Innovators and Preachers: The Role of the Editor in Victorian England*, ed. Joel H. Wiener. Westport, Connecticut and London: Greenwood Press, 1985, pp. 43–60.

Spencer, Robin. 'Whistler's First One Man Exhibition Reconstructed'. In *The Documented Image: Visions in Art History*, eds. Gabriel P. Weisberg and Laurinda Dixon. Syracuse: Syracuse University Press, 1987, pp. 27–49.

Spielmann, Marion Harry. *Millais and His Works*. Edinburgh and London: William Blackwood and Sons, 1898.

Staley, Allen, Martha M. Evans, Pamela M. Fletcher et al. *The Post Pre-Raphaelite Print: Etching, Illustration, Reproductive Engraving, and Photography in England In and Around the 1860s*. New York: Columbia University, 1995.

Steinlight, Emily. 'Anti-Bleak House: Advertising and the Victorian Novel'. *Narrative* 14:2 (2006), 132–62.

Stephens, C.B. 'The Patronage of Kenneth Clark and Neo-Romanticism'. MA thesis, University of Sussex, 1992.

[Stephens, F.G.]. *William Holman Hunt and His Works: A Memoir of the Artist's Life, With Descriptions of His Pictures*. London: Nisbet, 1860.

Stephenson, Andrew. '"Strategies of Situation": British Modernism and the Slump, c. 1929–34'. *Oxford Art Journal* 14:2 (1991), 30–51.

Stephenson, Andrew. '"An Anatomy of Taste": Samuel Courtauld and Debates about Art Patronage and Modernism in Britain in the Inter-War Years'. In *Impressionism for England: Samuel Courtauld as Patron and Collector*, ed. John House. London and New Haven: Yale University Press, 1994, pp. 35–46.

Stephenson, Andrew. 'Leighton and the Shifting Repertoires of "Masculine" Artistic Identity in the Late Victorian Period'. In *Frederic Leighton: Antiquity, Renaissance, Modernity*, eds. Tim Barringer and Elizabeth Prettejohn. New Haven: Yale University Press, 1999, pp. 221–46.

Stephenson, Andrew. 'Refashioning Modern Masculinity: Whistler, Aestheticism and National Identity'. In *English Art 1860–1914: Modern Artists and Identity*, eds. D.P. Corbett and L. Perry. Manchester: Manchester University Press, 2000, pp. 133–49.

Stephenson, Andrew. 'Edwardian Cosmopolitanism, ca. 1901–1912'. In *The Edwardian Sense: Art in Britain, 1901–12*, eds. Michael Hatt and Morna O'Neill. London and New Haven: Yale University Press, 2010, pp. 251–84.

Stephenson, Andrew. 'From Conscription to the Depression: The Market for Modern British Art in London, c. 1914–1930'. In *Art and Commerce in Great Britain: The Eighteenth to the Twentieth Centuries*, eds. Charlotte Gould and Sophie Mesplède. Forthcoming, Ashgate.

Stevenson, Michael. 'History of the Collection'. In *Michaelis Collection, the Old Town House, Cape Town: Catalogue of the Collection of Paintings and Drawings*. Frans Hansen compiled in collaboration with the Netherlands Institute for Art History, The Hague. Incorporating sections of the 1981 catalogue by Dirk Bax and a chapter by Michael Stevenson. Zwolle: Waanders Uitgevers, 1997, pp. 29–43.

Stocking, George W. *Victorian Anthropology*. New York: Free Press, 1987.

Stolwijk, Chris and Richard Thomson, eds. *Theo Van Gogh, Art Dealer, Collector and Brother of Vincent*. Amsterdam: Van Gogh Museum and Zwolle: Waanders Publishers, 1999.

Street, John. 'Fear of Fridges: Some Aspects of the Politics of Consumption'. In *Understanding the Enterprise Culture: Themes in the Work of Mary Douglas*, eds. Shaun Hargreaves Heap and Angus Ross. Edinburgh: Edinburgh University Press, 1992, pp. 145–60.

Suriano, Gregory. *The British Pre-Raphaelite Illustrators: A History of their Published Prints*. London: Oak Knoll Press; The British Library, 2005.

Surtees, Virginia. *The Paintings and Drawings of Dante Gabriel Rossetti (1828–1882): A Catalogue Raisonné*. Oxford: Clarendon Press, 1971.

Surtees, Virginia, ed. *The Diaries of George Price Boyce*. Norwich: Real World, 1980.

Surtees, Virginia, ed. *The Diary of Ford Madox Brown*. New Haven: Yale University Press, 1981.

Sweetapple, Dora. 'Thea Proctor'. *AGNSW Quarterly* 5:2 (January 1964), 180–3.

Taylor, Brandon. *Art For The Nation Exhibitions and the London Public 1747–2001*. Manchester: Manchester University Press, 1999.

Tedeschi, Martha. 'How Prints Work: Reproductions, Originals, and Their Markets in England, 1840–1900'. Ph.D. dissertation, Northwestern University, 1994.

Tedeschi, Martha. '"Where the Picture Cannot Go, the Engravings Penetrate": Prints and the Victorian Art Market'. *Objects of Desire, Victorian Art at the Art Institute of Chicago, special issue of Museum Studies* 31 (2005), 8–19, 89–90.

Tedeschi, Martha. 'The New Language of Etching in Nineteenth-Century England'. In *The Writings of Modern Life: The Etching Revival in France, Britain, and the U.S., 1850–1940*, ed. Elizabeth Helsinger. Chicago: Smart Museum of Art, University of Chicago, 2008, pp. 25–37.

Theiding, K. Olsen. 'Anxieties of Influence: British Responses to Art Nouveau, 1900–04'. *Journal of Design History* 19:3 (2006), 215–31.

Thirlwell, Angela. *William and Lucy: The Other Rossettis*. London and New Haven: Yale University Press, 2003.

Thomson, David Croal. *J. B. C. Corot*. London: The Goupil Gallery, 1889.

Thomson, Ellen Mazur. *The Origin of Graphic Design in America, 1870–1920*. London and New Haven: Yale University Press, 1997.

Thomson, H. Byerley. *The Choice of a Profession*. London: Chapman and Hall, 1857.

Thomson, Richard. 'Theo Van Gogh: An Honest Broker'. In *Theo Van Gogh, Art Dealer, Collector and Brother of Vincent*, eds. Chris Stolwijk and Richard Thomson. Amsterdam: Van Gogh Museum and Zwolle: Waanders Publishers, 1999, pp. 61–152.

Thomson, Richard. 'Trading the Visual: Theo Van Gogh, the Dealer Among the Artists'. *Van Gogh Museum Journal* (2000), 29–37.

Tickner, Lisa. 'English Modernism in the Cultural Field'. In *English Art 1860–1914: Modern Artists and Identity*, eds. David Peters Corbett and Lara Perry. Manchester: Manchester University Press, 2000, pp. 13–30, 214–21.

Tietze, A. 'Classical Casts and Colonial Galleries: The Life and Afterlife of the 1908 Beit Gift to the National Gallery of Cape Town'. *South African Historical Journal* 39 (November 1998), 70–90.

Tillyard, S.K. *The Impact of Modernism 1900–20: Early Modernism and the Arts and Crafts*. London: Routledge Press, 1988.

Todd, Dorothy and Raymond Mortimer, eds. *The New Interior Decoration: An Introduction to the Principles and International Survey of its Methods*. London: B.T. Batsford, 1929.

Topliss, Helen. *Modernism and Feminism: Australian Women Artists 1900–1940*. Roseville East: Craftsman House Sydney, 1996.

Torrance, David. *The Strange Death of Liberal Empire: Lord Selborne in South Africa*. Montreal: McGill-Queen's University Press, 1996.

Trentmann, Frank. 'Materiality in the Future of History: Things, Practices and Politics'. *Journal of British Studies* 48 (April 2009), 283–307.

Trentmann, Frank, ed. *The Making of the Consumer: Knowledge, Power and Identity in the Modern World*. Oxford and New York: Berg, 2006.

Trodd, Colin. 'The Authority of Art: Cultural Criticism and the Idea of the Royal Academy in Mid-Victorian Britain'. *Art History* 20 (March 1997), 3–22.

Trodd, Colin. 'Academic Cultures: The Royal Academy and the Commerce of Discourse in Victorian London'. In *Art and the Academy in the Nineteenth Century*, eds. Rafael Cardoso Denis and Colin Trodd. Manchester: Manchester University Press, 2000, pp. 179–93.

Trodd, Colin. 'Representing the Victorian Royal Academy: The Properties of Culture and the Promotion of Art'. In *Governing Cultures: Art Institutions in Victorian London*, eds. Paul Barlow and Colin Trodd. Aldershot and Burlington, Vermont: Ashgate, 2000, pp. 56–68.

Tromans, Nicholas. 'Museum or Market?: The British Institution'. In *Governing Cultures: Art Institutions in Victorian London*, eds. Paul Barlow and Colin Trodd. Aldershot and Burlington, Vermont: Ashgate, 2000, pp. 44–55.

The United States Tariff of 1861. New York: Merchants' Magazine, 1861.

Urry, James. 'Englishmen, Celts, and Iberians: The Ethnographic Survey of the United Kingdom, 1892–1899'. In *Functionalism Historicized: Essays on British Social Anthropology*, ed. George W. Stocking. Madison: University of Wisconsin Press, 1984, pp. 83–105.

van der Woude, Ad. 'The Volume and Value of Paintings in Holland at the Time of the Dutch Republic'. In *Art in History, History in Art*, eds. David Freedberg and Jan de Vries. Santa Monica: The Getty Center for the History of Art and the Humanities, 1991, pp. 249–329.

Verhoogt, Robert. *Art in Reproduction: Nineteenth-Century Prints after Lawrence Alma-Tadema, Jozef Israëls and Ary Scheffer*. Amsterdam: Amsterdam University Press, 2007.

Waagen, Gustav. *Treasures of Art in Great Britain*. 3 vols. London: J. Murray, 1854.

Waagen, Gustav. *Galleries and Cabinets of Art*. London: John Murray, 1857.

Wainwright, Clive. *The Romantic Interior: The British Collector at Home 1750–1850*. London and New Haven: Yale University Press, 1989.

Wainwright, Clive. 'The Banker, the Prince and the Dealers: Three Renaissance Objects in the Victoria and Albert Museum'. *Apollo* 152:456 (February 2000), 41–6.

Wakelin, Roland. *Thea Proctor Drawings and Prints Exhibition*. Sydney: Society of Artists, 1962.

Walkley, Giles. *Artists' Homes in London, 1764–1914*. Aldershot: Scolar, 1994.

Walsh, Claire. 'The Newness of the Department Store: A View from the Eighteenth Century'. In *Cathedrals of Consumption: The European Department Store, 1850–1939*, eds. Geoffrey Crossick and Serge Jaumain. Aldershot and Burlington, Vermont: Ashgate, 1999, pp. 46–71.

Ward, Martha. 'Impressionist Installations and Private Exhibitions'. *Art Bulletin* 73 (1991), 599–622.

Warner, Malcolm. 'John Everett Millais's "Autumn Leaves": "a picture full of beauty and without subject"'. In *Pre-Raphaelite Papers*, ed. Leslie Parris. London: Tate Gallery, 1984, pp. 126–42.

Warner, Malcolm. 'The Professional Career of John Everett Millais to 1863, With a Catalogue of Works to the Same Date'. Ph.D. dissertation, Courtauld Institute of Art, University of London, 1985.

Warner, Malcolm. 'Millais in Reproduction'. In *Writing the Pre-Raphaelites: Text, Context, Subtext*, eds. Michaela Giebelhausen and Tim Barringer. Farnham and Burlington, Vermont: Ashgate, 2009, pp. 215–36.

Warren, Jeremy and Adriana Turpin, eds. *Auctions, Agents and Dealers: The Mechanisms of the Art Market 1660–1830*. Oxford: The Beazley Archive and Archaeopress in association with the Wallace Collection, 2007.

Waterfield, Giles. *Palaces of Art: Art Galleries in Britain, 1790–1990*. London: Dulwich Picture Gallery, 1991.

Watson, Francis. *Art Lies Bleeding*. London: Chatto & Windus, 1939.

Watson, Janell. *Literature and Material Culture from Balzac to Proust: The Collection and Consumption of Curiosities*. Cambridge, Cambridge University Press, 1999.

Wax, Carol. *The Mezzotint: History and Technique*. New York: Harry N. Abrams, 1990.

Wedd, Kit with Lucy Peltz and Cathy Ross. *Creative Quarters: The Art World in London 1700–2000*. London: Museum of London, 2001.

Weightman, Gavin and Steve Humphries. *The Making of Modern London 1914–39*. London: Sidgwick & Jackson, 1984.

Werner, Marcia. *Pre-Raphaelite Painting and Nineteenth-Century Realism*. Cambridge: Cambridge University Press, 2005.

Westgarth, Mark. *A Biographical Dictionary of Nineteenth Century Antique and Curiosity Dealers*, special issue of *Regional Furniture* 23 (Glasgow, 2009).

White, Harrison C. and Cynthia A. White. *Canvases and Careers: Institutional Change in the French Painting World*. New York: John Wiley and Son, 1965.

White, James. 'Sir Hugh Lane as Collector'. *Apollo* 99:144 (n.s.) (February 1974), 112–125.

Whiteley, Jon. 'Exhibitions of Contemporary Painting in London and Paris, 1760–1860'. In *Saloni, gallerie, musei e loro influenza sullo sviluppo dell'arte dei secoli XIX e XX*, ed. Francis Haskell. Bologna: Cooperativa Libraria Universitaria Editrice Bologna, 1981, pp. 69–87.

Wildenstein, Daniel. *Monet*. 4 vols. Cologne: Taschen, [c.1996].

Wildenstein, Georges and R. Cogniat. *Paul Gauguin 1, Catalogue*. Paris: Editions Les Beaux-Arts, 1964.

Williams, Gareth. 'The Return of the Curve: Rodney Thomas, Architecture and Interior Design'. *Journal of the Decorative Arts Society* 19 (1995), 45–9.

Wilson, Kristina Forsyth. 'Exhibiting Modern Times: American Modernism, Popular Culture and the Art Exhibit, 1925–35'. Ph.D. dissertation, Yale University, 2002.

Wilson, Kristina. *Liveable Modernism: Interior Decorating and Design During the Great Depression*. London and New Haven: Yale University Press with Yale Art Gallery, 2004.

Wood, Christopher. *William Powell Frith*. Stroud: Sutton Publishing, 2006.

Woodham, Jonathan. *A Dictionary of Modern Design*. Oxford: Oxford University Press, 2004.

Woollacott, Angela. 'White Colonialism and Sexual Modernity'. In *Gender, Sexuality and Colonial Modernities*, ed. Antoinette Burton. London: Routledge, 1999, pp. 49–63.

Wrigley, Neil and Michelle Lowe, eds. *Retailing, Consumption and Capital: Towards the New Retail Geography*. Harlow, Essex: Longman Group, 1996.

Yorke, Malcolm. *Matthew Smith, His Life and Reputation*. London: Faber and Faber, 1997.

Young, Andrew McLaren, Margaret MacDonald, Robin Spencer with the assistance of Hamish Miles. *The Paintings of James McNeill Whistler*. London and New Haven: Yale University Press, 1980.

Zablotney, Sara. 'Production and Reproduction: Commerce in Images in Late-Eighteenth-Century London'. In *Economic Engagements with Art*, eds. Neil De Marchi and Craufurd D.W. Goodwin. Durham, North Carolina: Duke University Press, 1999, pp. 413–22.

Zafran, Eric, ed. with Robert Rosenblum and Lisa Small, *Fantasy and Faith: The Art of Gustave Doré*. New York: Dahesh Museum of Art; New York and London: Yale University Press, 2007.

Zeitz, Joshua. *Flapper: A Madcap Story of Sex, Style, Celebrity and the Women Who Made America Modern*. New York: Three Rivers Press, 2006.

Zelizer, Viviana A. *The Social Meaning of Money*. New York: Basic Books, 1994.

Zimmern, Helen. *L. Alma Tadema, Royal Academician: His Life and Work*. London: Art Annual, 1886.

Index